by Harry Harris

First published in 2020

This book is copyright under the Berne Convention. All rights are reserved. Apart from any fair dealing for the purpose of private study, research, criticism or review, as permitted under the Copyright Act, 1956, no part of this publication may be reproduced, stored in a retrieval system, or transmitted, in any form or by any means, electronic, electrical, chemical, mechanical, optical, photocopying, recording or otherwise, without the prior permission of the copyright owner. Enquiries should be sent to the publishers at the undermentioned address:

EMPIRE PUBLICATIONS

1 Newton Street, Manchester M1 1HW

© Harry Harris 2020

ISBN: 9781909360785

CONTENTS

FOREWORD BY JOHN BARNES 5

IT WAS 30 YEARS AGO TODAY... 9

THE WORLD'S GREATEST COACH 18

THE FIRST THREE YEARS 36

KLOPP PLOTS LIVERPOOL'S GREATEST EVER SEASON 53

AUGUST 62

SEPTEMBER 72

OCTOBER 81

NOVEMBER 95

DECEMBER 129

JANUARY 159

FEBRUARY 178

MARCH 215

THE PREMIER LEAGUE SHUTS DOWN 234

PROJECT RESTART 258

JUNE 294

CHAMPIONS AT LAST! 321

FOREWORD BY JOHN BARNES

When we won the last title in April 1990, it was inconceivable that it would be 30 years until the next one. By 1992 I thought we could win the title again, but by 1996, I didn't think the team I was playing in was capable of it and that it wouldn't be capable of doing it for the next two or three years as Manchester United were dominating the scene, but I had no fears that it would take much longer than a few years before Liverpool would rise again and take over as the country's top team.

However, going back just three or four years, I thought it would be 40 years, not 30 years before the next title! When Jurgen Klopp first arrived I thought he would get the team into fourth place, third at best, but I could not see them winning it within two years, even last season I didn't think they would win it, given the level of performance from Manchester City. So, you count down 28 years since the last title and it would be five or even 10 years before the next one.

What made it change? Well, Jurgen found a consistency of performance, and he knew he needed that high level of consistency to stand any chance of overtaking Manchester City. They were even better last season when they won the Champions League and finished just a point behind City, compared to this season, when they are out of the Champions League and have lost more than one game. The reality is that it is going to be tough going forward to improve on the last two seasons and the only way is to continue to perform to the maximum of their potential. To reach this point, though, the owners had to be patient with Jurgen and they were able to do so because the fans have gravitated towards the manager, they are in tune with him, they see a connection with him in much the same way as has happened at other clubs, at Manchester Untied with Sir Alex Ferguson, at Arsenal with Arsene Wenger and at Chelsea and Tottenham with managers such as Jose Mourinho and Mauricio Pochettino.

The Liverpool fans believe in Jurgen Klopp. When he makes a decision, such as he did about Daniel Sturridge for example, the fans accept it. They didn't accept similar decisions by Brendan Rodgers, and if he left, say, Sturridge out of the team, they would let him know their feelings. If the team lost 4-0 at Stoke, the fans would boo the manager. If Klopp loses a game, like 3-0 at Watford, that doesn't happen, the fans have faith in him, but they also have that connection, the sort of connection that goes back to Bill Shankly and the Boot Room philosophy, the fans love Klopp's character, his passion, his commitment to the cause.

In reality, certainty at first, Klopp's record was no better than that of Brendan Rodgers. It might have been very similar but the fans liked the Klopp attitude, his character, they believed in him the way they believed in Bill Shankly. Klopp is a throwback to Shanks in many ways. Alex Ferguson was one of the best in the world when he took over at Old Trafford but United's board gave him three or four years to turn it around and get it right. By and large the fans took to Fergie even in the early days when he wasn't successful, they liked him and could see what he was doing with the youth team, so they got behind him. If fans don't like the manager, then they are not slow in screaming and shouting about it and letting you know how they feel. It was something similar with Pep at City, it was obvious the guy was a winner and would be successful there so there was an instant connection with the fans, and they backed him, rather than turning on him, when they had a mediocre first season. On the other hand, Jose Mourinho won a few things at United but the fans felt no connection to him because of his style of management and the style of football so the board had to act. It was the same with Louis van Gaal.

Getting that support from the fans is vitally important because, subconsciously at least, the players can absolve themselves from responsibility if the fans are against the manager. I know how it works; the players feel it doesn't matter if they lose as the manager will take the flack from the fans. On the other hand, if the fans back the manager 100% then the players believe in the manager to such an extent that when the boss says jump, they jump because the players know the fans back the manager and the board back the manager. The importance of the fans shouldn't be underestimated. Clubs don't want to sack their managers, but if they lose the confidence of the fans and that transmits itself into the dressing room, then the club has little choice. That certainly was the case at Anfield when the fans turned on Brendan Rodgers, who deserved more time in my opinion. He went on to show what a good manager he is when he moved onto Celtic and now Leicester City

Foreword by John Barnes

John Barnes in his pomp

who were in the title hunt briefly this season. I have to say that I liked Brendan as a Liverpool manager, but equally I am glad that he has gone because now we have Jurgen Klopp.

Too often over the past three decades Liverpool could be accused of living in the past, and Brendan Rodgers suffered from being measured against our great managers of the past but along came Jurgen and gave the club a new identity. You're seeing the same at Manchester United now with his successors questioned over every move they make with fans saying 'this isn't how Fergie would have done it'.

I don't like the idea of comparing this Liverpool title winning team to the last one. If we played to the rules back then we would beat them 6-0, but with the refereeing in the modern day game, this team would beat us 6-0. It isn't about which players are the best in comparison to 30 years ago. The Klopp Identity is vastly different, it has a style and a strategy that is totally different, it is about commitment, determination to such an extent that you don't necessarily have to be the greatest player or even a very good player to fit into that style and strategy. You don't need to be a superstar, the way that Manchester City have superstars. It's similar to a style and strategy that Ajax have employed over the years where they don't necessarily need to have the best players compared to the best teams in the world, but their players fit into their style and strategy.

At Liverpool you have three midfielders who have the Klopp identity, they fit into his style but wouldn't necessarily fit into that of Barcelona and Real Madrid. Klopp wants players who fit into the way he wants to play. To be part of this Klopp Identity you need to be extremely hard working, have a great attitude and application, and this is his recipe for success. It is also a structure that means it wouldn't necessarily cost a fortune to replace most of the component parts of the team. Of course he spent a lot on Van Dijk and Allison, but the rest were moderate fees. If he had to replace a midfield player within his structure, he wouldn't need to splash out £100m plus, he could find someone valued at £30m, providing he fits his criteria, who would perform a specific task, but that player wouldn't necessarily be on the radar of a Manchester United, Barcelona or Real Madrid, the clubs who demand special players.

The hardest thing now is to retain the title, or to win it again within a reasonable time scale because I am not sure in the modern game it is possible to start a new dynasty and maintain dominance the way Manchester United did, Arsenal did for five years and the way Liverpool did throughout the 80s. This time there are so many owners who have a lot of money who are willing to spend big on a group of new players if they wish to with the plan of 'we can win the league next year' if we invest at that sort of level. It remains to be seen if this Liverpool team can dominate for the next five to seven years the way Manchester United did, and I am sure Jurgen Klopp will want to work toward that, but equally he knows that there is a group of top clubs out there who can buy the best five players and reduce those chances considerably. I just don't see one team dominating the game for a period of five or six years.

Yes, the top six will fight for the top four places, but others could break into that elite, Newcastle for example if they decide to spend an awful lot of money doing it in a bid to catch up. You have Manchester City who can regain top spot while Manchester United can pay the sort of wages that makes even the best players think twice. There is not one team that will allow one of their rivals to go so far ahead that they cannot be caught.

IT WAS 30 YEARS AGO TODAY...

On April 28, 1990, Liverpool beat Queens Park Rangers 2-1 at Anfield to claim their 18th top-flight championship. This was the team Kenny Dalglish selected that day: Grobbelaar; Burrows, Hysen, Hansen, Venison; Nicol, Molby, McMahon, Barnes; Rush, Rosenthal - subs: Gillespie, Houghton. It was the club's tenth title in fifteen seasons and few could have imagined it would take three decades for number nineteen.

A lot has happened in those 30 years yet debate will rage about which was the better team, the vintage of the late 1980s under Kenny Dalglish or the current team under Jurgen Klopp. An inevitable consequence of having so many great teams, managers, players, that everyone will discuss which was the best. And it's been so long between trophies that the legend of past glories live on to this day.

So no one is better equipped to start the debate rolling then a few of the iconic names from the team that last won the title, and they spoke exclusively for this book

BRUCE GROBBELAAR

While the two teams, in two different eras and under two vastly contrasting conditions and times, one aspect is identical: both teams had fire in their belly, and that is an aspect that will always be there when analysing title-winning Liverpool teams, whether the present one, as they have it, or the last one, as we had it too. The big difference, of course, is that we needed to play all the time. The present team has a rotation system, which enables players to rest and to be on top of their game when they return refreshed. We never had that luxury.

The modern game is now dictated by science in football, that has become very prominent in every aspect of the game, from the coaching courses where managers become acutely aware of the science of the

The last Liverpool team to win the league in April 1990

games; how far a player can run during a game, whether they run enough, the nutritional aspects and how players have to look after themselves. We played week in and week out and knew each other's game and you knew you would be 100 per cent in the side whereas today they do have the benefit of resting at times. However the conclusion is that both teams possessed dynamic players, and they would still be dynamic whichever era they played in.

In our day we ate okay, and we looked after ourselves, to a point! Perhaps we consumed a little too much alcohol in our time than the players do today. Okay, maybe a lot more! But we abstained two days before every game. We had a Tuesday Club but not if we had a Wednesday midweek game, then it was the Sunday club!

We had fun, lots of fun. I'm not so sure the modern player has as much fun. That's not to say they don't love the game, I'm sure they love it every bit as much as we did but with all the science involved, the levels of fitness, and physical condition, I don't think they could have had as much fun as we did.

However, one aspect of modern day life is the finances. And it does worry me how really young players, uneducated boys, can get to grips with the enormous sums of money they are paid even at such an early age. I'm delighted the way that it has happened for players, that through the enormous sums in advertising and sponsorship, but even more so through the colossal sums in TV rights, that players' salaries have escalated beyond recognition. Good luck to them.

But I do see much greater mental health problems associated with players these day, and maybe it is the enormous wealth they have so early that might be one of the factors contributing to it.

In the 60s and through to my day, football was a working man's sport. Certainly in the 60s footballers weren't earning that much more than the average working man. Then the wages doubles, trebled, then came the first £1m footballer and so on, and so on, it just snowballed, a roller coaster of inflated salaries, a snow ball running down hill out of control. It is now a phenomenal amount of money for so many so young and it is hard, in some cases, for them to get to grips with such wealth. That means the clubs need the science of football even more so, that the medical situation is strong enough to cope with the mental health issues and that is only recently becoming to terms with.

Despite all of this, all the changes, if my generation was playing today, I am convinced we would still derive the same enjoyment from the game.

Naturally with a first title after such a long wait, people will reflect on the team that won it 30 years ago and ask for comparison, debate which of the current team would have got into our team. Well, we had some great players in our day, and although not looking directly at the team that last won the league, we had players like Graeme Souness and Kenny Dalglish that would be selected for any team any time anywhere. Souness was simply the finest player I have ever seen and up front Dalglish has never been bettered. Of course you look at today's side and Virgil van Dijk is a player who would merit a place in any time at any time, even though in our heyday we had centre backs as good as Alan Hansen and Mark Lawrenson. As for a goalkeeper, I'm not sure anyone would get into our team! Well, I would say that, but really Alisson would be right up there as a first choice. But when you look back to the late 70s, even before my time, and the Liverpool team that let in just 16 goals in an entire season, only four at home, Ray Clemence was in goal and that is some record and he was some goalkeeper.

We had contrasting styles. In our last title winning side we played to the old 4-4-2 formation but this team are 4-3-3 with no real No 9 or No. 10, they are the modern day false 10. But the bottom line is that it is actually an injustice to compare the two sides because both sides were excellent in their own right. It's an injustice to put one player ahead of another as they are both brilliant teams.

But you have to hand it to this team under Jurgen Klopp. Look at the stats and they are mind boggling, they are so many points ahead, more so than any other team at any time anywhere in world football. It leaves you gasping at their achievements and they deserve the mantel of being considered one of the best, if not 'the' best team of all-time. But to achieve that accolade and to cement their position as the greatest, they will have to continue to do it again and again, they simply have to carry on as they have been doing, winning even more trophies, breaking even more records, to be the best ever.

The big test is to win the title again next season, we always said in our day, that when you won a trophy, it was your duty to protect it, to go out and retain it, win it again.

It is fair to say, though, that they are already one of the greatest teams in history of the league, for sure, but to be the greatest they must go on and win it next year and year after, so it's up to those players to step up to the plate yet again, but even so there is no getting away from the fact this season is one of the greatest achievements in the club's history.

STEVE McMAHON

Yes, Alan Hansen was club captain the day it was actually won, but I was the one who skippered the side against Derby County when the trophy was handed out - and it has been a source of enormous pride in my life that I was the one who lifted the Football League trophy. Alan Hansen didn't play that day, but he did a John Terry, coming onto the pitch in his track suit and then taking it off to be fully kitted out for the trophy parade on the pitch. If you had told me then that it would be 30 years before the next  one, they would have called for the white van and carried me off!

There are people going to Anfield now who have never seen Liverpool lift the title, and that is just astonishing, in fact it's unique. Who would have believed it? 30 years! However, that's not to say that

It Was 30 Years Ago Today...

I didn't sense the wind of change was blowing in Manchester United's direction at the time.

It was a tough season when we last won the title, we had won the FA Cup but lost the league the previous season and of course it was a season of such sadness. Then it was a season of ups and downs, and when we lost to Arsenal the fear was that we wouldn't do it, so it was quite a challenge and we rose to it and it made it all the more pleasurable to have lifted it at the end. But you knew the bubble was going to burst sooner rather than later. Kenny was leaving, Graeme Souness was taking over and now history tells you for sure that the wind of changing was blowing as Manchester United became a dominant force, and it happened very quickly. But a 30 year wait! Really? No one would have believed it. It's actually quite ridiculous when you think about it that it has been 30 years, astonishing to be truthful.

Yes, I can see there is going to be the inevitable comparisons between this team and the last title winning side 30 years ago, but they are totally different. This team under Jurgen Klopp is an all-round team, that relies on the three up top, but they win together. When we played everybody chipped in, goals from midfield, goals from defenders, as well as goals from the strikers like Ian Rush, with some superstars like John Barnes, Rush Hansen, Lawrenson, Nicol. That's not to say they don't have superstars in the current team like Virgil van Dijk, Alisson while Trent Alexander-Arnold has all the potential to be one of the great right backs, but we had Steve Nicol who played right back, left back could play in midfield and score hat-tricks from full back.

It needs some perspective, though. First of all, what the Jurgen Klopp team has achieved in the past 12 months is fantastic, phenomenal, sensational, amazing, magnificent, breathtaking, but this team is not the finished article until it keeps on winning trophies. People are already talking about it as the Greatest Ever Team, but I don't buy it. To reach those heights you need to carry on winning trophies year after year.

It's the same when people say Jurgen Klopp is The Greatest Ever Manager. Well, hang on a minute there too, and look at Shanks, Paisley and Dalglish. I know that even Jurgen himself wouldn't boast of being the best Liverpool manager, as he knows the history of the club.

Liverpool have produced some great teams down the years, the Phil Neal side, with Souey in midfield won the European Cup back to back and might have kept on winning it if the club hadn't been banned for five years because of Heysel. I'm just playing Devil's Advocate, and I think there is some way to go yet for this team to be in the Hall of Fame as the greatest ever team, but that is not to say they won't make it. However for the minute while it's such a wonderful feeling that Liverpool have won the league again after 30 long years, and while it is such an amazing achievement, let's not get a bit ahead of ourselves when talking about the best ever, until this team has stayed together, and some of the big names have been lured away to Real Madrid, and win some more trophies.

BARRY VENISON

It's just ridiculous the amount of time for the next league title. Who would have believed it? There were signs in the early 90s that other clubs like Manchester Untied were accelerating at a much quicker rate, while Liverpool were standing still, in fact going backwards when Kenny left after Heysel and Hillsborough took such a toll on him. Manchester United started to do things differently while Liverpool continued to rely too much on doing things traditionally. You have to give Manchester Untied credit that they did so well. Yet, Liverpool did suffered a bit of turmoil in its managerial changes after Kenny the club became a bit unsettled, as Graeme Souness left and things didn't gel together as they had done for so long.

But looking back to 1990 and when we lifted the league trophy we thought we would win it again in three years let alone 30 years. In fact we believed we would win it the next year, because that's how we thought at Liverpool, not in any sort of arrogant way, but in the sheer belief in our ability.

Of course teams have come close since 1990 but really it has taken this Jurgen Klopp team to remind us all what we had back in 1990 and before that for many years under such great managers. It really does compare with the those of the old Liverpool in so many ways. Jurgen Klopp's team has desire, determination, unity, the togetherness of

It Was 30 Years Ago Today...

a family feeling, and it has all been evoked by the manager, it all stems from Jurgen Klopp, the way he has all the players fighting for each other, combined with some outstanding, fantastic players in every position. All those outstanding players have gelled together for a team full of intelligence, where each individual understands the Klopp philosophy and combines into a powerful team force.

It has all the hallmarks of the old Liverpool teams that would grind out some horrible little 1-0's if they had to, if the going was tough and the opposition stubborn, and Klopp has done precisely that at times, and there is nothing wrong with that, it's how you win titles.

Back then, we had some incredibly gifted and effective players, none more so than Alan Hansen who was not only a leader, he was a smooth, Rolls Royce of a defender, always in control and commanding in such a key position, and around him he forged a formidable back four. The same is true of Virgil van Dijk.

We had a remarkable goalkeeper in Bruce Grobbelaar, he was insane, but brilliant! As a defender it was great to have someone like him behind you, although at times he was in front of you! Similarly Alisson is outstanding, although more stable, actually a lot more stable. Throughout the teams then and now there was quality wherever you looked.

This team certainly has all the attributes to become one of the greatest teams ever but the barometer of a great team is winning consistently, that was always the yardstick in the past and history shows that Liverpool, in particular, had some outstanding yet also hugely consistently successful teams winning European Cups and League titles.

But the real bread and butter has always been seen as the title, whether it was the old Football league or the Premier League as it is now. You were always judged on that. Now this team has to win the league consistently and they certainly have the squad of players to achieve that, but they will have to do it over and over again, not just once in 30 years! The key is the League to being The Greatest.

GARY GILLESPIE

I don't think anybody would have believed it would be 30 years since the last title win. It's impossible to believe it would take that length of time to win the title again.

I had been a regular in the team until that season as the club bought Glen Hysen from Feyenoord and I played a bit part in that last title winning team as I also had some injuries that season. The team was fantastic, so many match winners, so much brilliance with the likes of John Barnes, Peter Beardsley, Ian Rush when he returned from Italy, all backed up by such a strong back four lead by Alan Hansen, and very much the defence fitting in around him. The key was the strength in defence and real talent all over the pitch from the goalkeeper to the strikers, with such talent in midfield from Steve McMahon who was grossly underrated to Ronnie Whelan and even Nigel Spackman at times, we had that winning mentality to go with it in abundance, and I do see similarities in the current side under Jurgen Klopp, particularly up front with Salah and Mane with Firmino, in my book the man who makes things happen, so when he plays well the whole team is on fire.

When you look at Hansen, you have van Dijk, and they are similar in that they are so commanding. Another similarity is that when the team isn't going as well as expected then there were players then as there are now who can nick a goal.

Certainly the current team have achieved such feats this season that they do have the capacity to become the greatest team in Liverpool's history, and one of the greatest teams of all time, but that accolade can only come with a prolonged run of success, it cannot just be a one-off, they have to keep winning the title next season and the season after that.

If they can keep the team together, and there is no reason why they cannot, then they can keep on winning trophies. Back in the 70s and 80s Liverpool ruled supreme, then came Manchester Untied, and they were all consistent winners all the time, and that's what this team needs to do if they want to be the greatest team.

It Was 30 Years Ago Today...

I was eight years at Liverpool and the lowest we ever finished was second! And that was considered a poor season. We had the winning habit, and second was regarded as coming nowhere. Back in those days that was how high our standards were set. The mentality was you simply had to win things, and that's exactly what we did.

But it all suddenly took a very different path when Kenny left us, and it was clear that Heysel and Hillsborough had a big impact on the football club and Kenny in particular. When he resigned it left a massive hole with regards to who took over and the place just wasn't the same again. But he was still such a young man and we all thought he shouldn't be lost to football and that he still had so much to offer, which he proved nine months later when he took charge at Blackburn Rovers.

It is not intended to be a light or pointing a finger at who took over, whether it was Ronnie Moran or Graeme Souness, the whole structure of the football club seemed to change with Kenny's departure, and we lost our way.

THE WORLD'S GREATEST COACH

When Jürgen Klopp was voted the world's greatest coach by FIFA in September 2019, he was naturally proud of his achievement saying, "Wow, it's quite heavy! What can I say? I have to say thank you to a lot of people obviously. I have to start at the beginning with my family sitting at home and probably watching. It's great – nobody would have expected that I stand here 20 years ago, 10 years ago, five years ago, four years ago probably! And how close it can be; Mauricio, we won that game [the Champions League final] – that's why I'm here and not you. That's how football is, but we all know what an incredible job you did, what an incredible job Pep did, what so many coaches out there did.

"Coming back to saying thank you, I have to say thank you to my outstanding club, Liverpool FC – who doesn't love it has no heart! That's not true, you can love other clubs as well."

After the award, Klopp become the first Premier League manager to sign up to the Common Goal movement, donating 1% of his salary to the charity. The initiative, which funds organisations around the world that use football to tackle social issues, was launched by Manchester United and Spain midfielder Juan Mata in 2017. Speaking on stage at the Milan ceremony, Klopp said: "A few people obviously know it – if not, Google it. It's a great thing." Quoted on the Common Goal website, he added: "While it is flattering to receive an individual award today, in football and in life, nothing is possible without teamwork. That is why I would like to celebrate this occasion by sharing that I am joining Common Goal and pledging 1% of my earnings to help change the world through football. Since Common Goal started two years ago, the movement has grown steadily proving it is a simple, effective and safe mechanism for players and managers to give back through football. As a team, even with a minimum pledge of just 1%, together the football industry is capable of transforming the world. Now is the time for those interested to take a step forward."

Common Goal chief executive and co-founder Jürgen Griesbeck said: "We are thrilled to welcome Jürgen Klopp onto the team. At a time when our world is facing social divides, increasing global inequality and

Jurgen wins FIFA World Coach of the Year 2019

political polarisation, his contribution exceeds the financial and will inspire football fans and non-football fans across the planet." It was the kind of act that had endeared Jürgen Klopp to Liverpool's fans since his appointment in October 2015 and chimed with the values of a club reborn under Bill Shankly in the 1960s with a socialist ethos which went on to dominate football for almost 30 years.

Other coaches signed up to the scheme included Manchester United's Casey Stoney and Denmark's Kasper Hjulmand. The Premier League's Bruno Salter, Leon Balogun (Brighton), Charlie Daniels (Bournemouth), Kasper Schmeichel (Leicester) and Isaac Christie-Davie (Liverpool).

In a column for *The Players' Tribune* Klopp related how "honoured" he felt. "But I really don't like to stand on a stage with a trophy all by myself. Everything I have accomplished in this game is only possible because of everyone around me. Not just my players, but my family and my sons and everyone who has been with me since the beginning, when I was a very, very average person."

The German revealed what he said to his players before they reached the Champions League final after overcoming losing 3-0 to Barcelona in their first leg that he desscribed as "the worst result imaginable." Preparing for the second leg, Klopp said: "My team talk was very straightforward. Mostly, I talked about tactics. But I also told them the truth. I said: 'We have to play without two of the best strikers in the world. The world outside is saying it is not possible. And let's be honest, it's probably impossible. But because it's you? Because it's you, we have a chance.' I really believed that. It wasn't about their technical ability as footballers. It was about who they were as human beings, and everything they had overcome in life. The only thing that I added was: 'If we fail, then let's fail in the most beautiful way.' Of course, it is easy for me to say those words. I am just the guy yelling from the touchline. It is much harder for the players to actually do it. But because of those boys, and because of the 54,000 people at Anfield, we did the impossible."

The outcome is etched in the memory but Klopp had to rely on replays to see Alexander-Arnold's cheeky corner that saw Divock Origi nick the winner as he had turned to his assistant to discuss a sub when the right-back sprung the surprise set-piece and had only the noise of the crowd to tell him Liverpool had completed the stunning comeback. Klopp said: "Unfortunately, the most incredible moment in the history of the Champions League... I didn't actually see it. Maybe this is a good metaphor for the life of a football manager, I don't know. But I completely missed Trent Alexander-Arnold's moment of pure genius."

The German admits he channels his inner Rocky Balboa when giving speeches as "football is the only thing more inspiring than cinema". It dates back to his days working in a warehouse - shortly after becoming a young father where they stored movie reels. It gave him the grounding and inspiration for the work he is doing now. "When I was 20, I experienced the moment that completely changed my life. I was still a kid myself, but I had also just become a father. It was not perfect timing, let's be honest. I was playing amateur football and going to university during the day. To pay for school, I was working in a warehouse where they stored movies for the cinema. And for the young people out there, we are not talking about DVDs. This was the late '80s, when everything was still on film. The trucks would come at 6am to pick up the new movies, and we would load and unload those huge metal canisters. They were quite heavy, honestly. You would be praying that they weren't showing something with four reels, like *Ben-Hur* or something. That was going to be a bad day for you."

The early exposure to film stayed with Klopp on his journey

The World's Greatest Coach

The appointment of throw-in coach Thomas Gronnemark was a typically astute acquisition by Klopp.

through management. He used Sylvester Stallone's Italian Stallion as inspiration during his time with Borussia Dortmund. He admired the passion and work ethic taught by the iconic film series. But most of his Dortmund squad were too young to have seen the movies when he showed clips of *Rocky IV* before a crunch game against Bayern Munich. That didn't stop him going full Mickey Goldmill before Liverpool's legendary Champions League comeback against Barcelona last season.

Klopp's planning is notoriously meticulous, he has even appointed a dedicated 'throw-in' coach. Dane Thomas Gronnemark started working on a part-time basis during the club's pre-season training camp to minimise the number of errors from set-plays. He primarily 'coached' full-backs, Robertson, Gomez, Alexander-Arnold, Clyne and Moreno, while Milner, Mané and Wijnaldum were part of the sessions. Gronnemark, who previously worked with Danish team Midtjylland and Bundesliga sides Schalke and Hertha Berlin was approached directly by Klopp to bring the methods of his 'Long Throw Academy' to Anfield. He worked with Denmark's Athletics and Bobsled teams. A dedicated trainer for throw-ins was a first in English football. Klopp estimated Liverpool take or defend around 50 throw-ins per match, and felt his players squandered possession too often from these set plays.

Rather than encouraging a long-throw, Gronnemark advised on the most effective way of using the restart to launch attacks, and how to avoid putting team mates under pressure when in their own half. He travelled to Liverpool for a couple of sessions a month. Gronnemark holds the world record for the longest ever throw-in – over 56 yards. "When I heard about Thomas, it was clear to me I wanted to meet him. When I met him, it was 100% clear I wanted to employ him. You cannot have enough specialists around you. He has already made a difference. I think it's not only important to me, it's important to everybody. To be honest, I'd never heard about a throw-in coach. How it is as a football manager, you know a lot about different things – I played the game, I've been managing since around about 18 years or so – but that doesn't mean I'm a goalkeeper specialist and I'm obviously not a throw-in specialist. I know about different movements, what we always did, but it was not 100 per cent clear – maybe it's my fault – how I can improve the guy with the ball, not only the movements of all the other guys. When I heard about Thomas, it was clear to me I wanted to meet him; when I met him, it was 100 per cent clear I wanted to employ him. Now he is here and we work on that from time to time. We use his information as well during the weeks when he is not here. We use it of course for the Academy as well. It's good. You cannot have enough specialists around you. I must always be the guy who makes the decisions on when we use all these specialists but you cannot have enough. We have the fitness, medical department, we have the nutrition, and now we have somebody for throw-ins. He's a good guy, to be honest. He has already [made a difference]. The boys like it; when you have somebody who knows what he is talking about, it always helps when you want to improve something."

"I know it is totally the weirdest job in the world," Gronnemark told BBC Sport. Former Stoke midfielder Rory Delap is the best known long throw-in expert in the Premier League era but Gronnemark said his brief at Anfield was "not to turn Liverpool into the second Stoke". The Dane, who had been working with teams since 2004, said Klopp contacted him as he was "curious". "If I was a defender I would not want to be on the end of one of Gomez's throw-ins," said Gronnemark. "In general against Liverpool I would not want to put the ball out for a throw-in. I am not saying Liverpool will do a lot of long throw-ins, but you never know when they may do it."

The move highlighted Klopp's inquisitiveness, which has been a hallmark of his coaching style. In another move the Liverpool boss encouraged goalkeeping coach John Achterberg to take out rugby pads to toughen up Alisson, a technique used on Mignolet and Karius. The sessions involved crosses into the area while someone blocks and buffets the keeper with the pads. "It is what the goalkeepers always do," said Klopp, "it is not really rugby; it is goalkeeper training. All the boys did it. Alisson is doing it as well. It makes sense to do it. We have these situations in training constantly when we do set pieces – the box is full with 22 players. Maybe that is a bit much, but 15 certainly. It is busy, we do it often so that the goalkeeper gets used to that. It is all about timing (when to come for crosses). We'll see how that is. We brought him here because of the things that he is already good at. That is what we want him do. It is not that the goalkeeper has to change completely now for this league, we have to help him too in situations. That is how it is always is. There is not just one player responsible for something. We have to have the right formation around set pieces; set pieces can be quite different here. So far, it has been absolutely okay but it is not solely about Alisson (improving the defensive record). It is down to the whole team."

Klopp also brought in nutritionist Mona Nemmer and at the start of the 2019/20 season he recruited sports psychologist Lee Richardson, who had spells with Watford and Blackburn as a player and managed Chesterfield. He spends three days a week at the club's training ground on an ad hoc basis. The 50-year-old was also filling the role of sport psychology consultant for Lancashire County Cricket Club, as well as his own performance management company, AIM-FOR. In addition pro surfer Sebastian Steudtner gave a series of talks to players and coaching staff over the summer. It's all part of a wide-ranging approach from Klopp that has led his era to be dubbed 'the New Anfield Bootroom'.

Richardson's arrival coincided with the exit of former sports psychiatrist Steve Peters, who had been brought in by Brendan Rodgers. Richardson has had an instant influence as Klopp told *The Athletic*: "He was a player, then a manager and then he studied sports psychology. He's working for us which is great. He works very specifically with the boys and I have no idea what they are talking about. I am not interested. It's just a nice add on. It's just for us the next step. It's difficult to find the right people with how I see it in that part of the business. Now we feel pretty good with him on board and that's cool." He arrived on the recommendation of Philipp Jacobsen, who joined Liverpool in 2018 as medical rehabilitation and performance manager.

Jurgen with his mentor Wolfgang Frank who he has described as "the best manager ever played for".

Part of the basis for Jürgen Klopp's philosophy can be explained by his playing career. He recalls his switch from striker to right-back as a player in Germany, and explained how versatility is key for Liverpool. He was asked to take duties as manager midway through the 2000/01 season after Eckhard Krautzun's dismissal at Mainz, steering them clear of relegation after retiring as a player. Prior to that, he had made 340 appearances for Mainz, with 95 coming under Wolfgang Frank, who he credits as his biggest influence as a manager, who switched Klopp from the role of first-choice centre-forward to starting right-back. He was "always a striker" because he "had a good header and was really quick," but "technical-wise I was not too good. From a nowadays point of view, I would say [moving to right-back] makes complete sense: I would have done the same to me. I would have made myself, maybe a centre-half, but I would have put me in the back. Because really quick, good attitude… but not brilliant with the ball."

On the game that changed his career, Klopp allowed him to go from his own "biggest enemy" to having been "just happy to have a game." He added: "We were a lower-league team, but I scored 10 to 12 goals a year. That was okay. But then at one point a new manager came

The World's Greatest Coach

in, he was the best manager I ever had: Wolfgang Frank. He changed the system. It was a friendly game in the pre-season, we had a game against a team from one league lower, they were first in that league, we were last in the [one above]. That's a difficult game to play as friendly, and he said 'OK, we change the system'. He made the line-up and in that line-up I was at right-back. Half-time in that game was 6-0 to us, we played incredibly, we defended like lions, it was really brilliant. Then we changed completely and the second half team played 0-0, so we won 6-0 and from that moment on, the team from the first half played for the next 50 games and I was right-back. That's how it started, and from that moment on I was the right-back. [I was] 100 percent [fine with changing]. For me there was no problem.

"I was my biggest enemy, because I hated my football, I really didn't like it. When I tried to stop a ball, it bounced. I had these inner talks. I was really not a supporter of myself, but only wanted to play. If he had told me 'you look like a decent goalkeeper... give him the gloves', I would have done it. So I was just happy to have a game, and the pressure went off my shoulders as well. Because in a team [like Mainz] and you don't score a lot of goals as the main striker, each chance you miss it's not like there'll be another one. I was not involved any more in that, and I still scored two, three, four goals on average, it was okay."

Asked about the number of versatile players throughout the Bundesliga, he disagreed that it was German-specific, highlighting a host of examples in his Liverpool squad, that it "helps a lot" to have a variety of options for every role, spread out over a smaller core of players. "We have them as well, James Milner can play around 13 positions probably, he probably would be the first choice if all the goalies were out. Fabinho can play at least two, Trent can play a lot, so we have that. We don't have that many specialists. People think sometimes it's a weakness if you're that versatile, because you think 'OK, I don't have a fixed position, he puts me in there, there, there, then I'm out'. It is [a strength]. It helps in building a squad, especially. That helps a lot. Because you don't have a specialist in these positions, you have three, four, five players that can play really different positions, that helps you a lot."

Jürgen Klopp began his managerial career at Second Division Mainz following an unremarkable ten-year playing career at the club. The then 34 year-old won 6 out of 7 games to steer Mainz to safety and within three years he had got them promoted to the German top flight. Despite having the smallest budget in the league, they finished in respectable mid-table for several seasons before they were relegated in 2006 and after failing to gain promotion the following year Klopp resigned at the end of the 2007/08 season.

A call soon came from Bundesliga giants Bayern Munich and Borussia Dortmund and Jürgen chose the latter. During his time at the Westfalenstadion Klopp made his name with a tactic called *Gegenpresse*, where players attack the ball when they give it away rather than falling back into defensive positions. This all-action style made Dortmund exciting to watch and eventually brought trophies to the fanatical supporters of the Ruhr; the Bundesliga title was eventually wrestled away from Bayern in 2011 and 2012, along with several domestic cups and a Champions League final appearance where they lost to Bayern at Wembley. However by 2015 Klopp was getting diminishing returns with Dortmund and there were fall-outs with match officials and frustration that the club had sold many of its best players to rivals Bayern, most notably Polish striker Robert Lewandowski. Klopp left the club at the end of the season and ended up at Liverpool a few months later.

During these two spells in German football, Klopp's style was characterised by all out attacking play or 'Heavy Metal football' as the man himself described it, while he was regarded as a supreme man-manager who was able to create an unbreakable bond with his players. Yet it isn't all squirrels and picnics; according to the man himself, players tend not to confront him because of his imposing stature. Asked in an edition of *France Football* if he has been afraid of anyone, he replied: "No, never. Fear is never a good thing, even when you have to tell a player that you are not renewing his contract. I think I have a natural authority. I have a voice that carries, and I am 6 foot 3. Apart from Virgil van Dijk and perhaps Joel Matip, who are nice men, no-one is bigger than me."

Klopp's determination is to entertain at all costs, as he told the respected French publication, "What is my style of play? Well, you know what? I have been a coach for 18 years and I haven't even thought about this question, despite being asked this a lot. I don't really get what it means. I love the game, it's as simple as that. It intrigues me 95 per cent of the time. When I watch a match, I always see things I like, if not, it would be a waste of time. Entertainment is the most important part of football. There are too many serious problems in the world to make football boring too. I want to see happiness with my players, passion in their eyes and a desire to fight. I want to see them bursting [with energy maybe he means], to surprise me, to look what's on their right, to try and make a pass to their left, that sort of thing."

In October 2019 former Porto coach Vitor Matos joined Liverpool and was immediately named "signing of the season" by assistant manager Pep Ljinders. Matos is Liverpool's "connector" since being brought in as an elite development coach by Klopp over the summer. Matos said: "Working with Jürgen is like having a masterclass! I am very pleased and happy for the opportunity to work with the best. Really, Jürgen is not only about understanding football, a player or a youth player, he is more than that, it is how he understands life and its values. For me, this fascinating way of seeing things is unbelievable, it's really unbelievable.

"Normally we say that the character of the team is the character of the coach and we can see Jürgen's impact on everything in the club. The way he is as a person makes an influence on the training sessions, in the pre-match meetings, on the environment at Melwood. There is a famous doctor in Portugal who says, 'They who only know about medicine, don't know anything about medicine' and I say that a coach who only knows about football doesn't know anything about football. Jürgen is the perfect example of that. The way he fills all the game ideas, all the tactical principles, all the team organisation with passion and with love is amazing because that is what gives you the way of playing. It's been really amazing to work with him."

Matos explained his role. "My biggest goal is to create development. You can create development in different ways but the most important thing is that you understand football as a collective game. It's something that is built on the interactions between the players and these interactions that you have are related to your way of playing, to your identity, so you can see: 'OK, this is Liverpool's way of playing.' Development or individual development is also connected with this: these game ideas and this way of playing will force the individual development of the players. My role is to say: 'OK, we have these Academy players. How can we help them learn the game ideas of the first team, and how can we use those game ideas to continue their individual development?' My first idea when I arrived was that I needed to know every one of the U18 and U23 players and discuss, 'What's the big idea for him?' I needed to know which person I need to speak to and work with to achieve this. It's about knowing the club, knowing what the expectation is for a youth player to come and train here [at Melwood]."

Former chief executive Ian Ayre commented in an interview in *the Sunday People*, "I was back last weekend and the club are going in the right direction, and, for me, Jürgen Klopp is the anchor. Every now and again in life you meet someone or see something in an organisation where someone is just a complete fit. It's like when you meet the girl of your dreams and with Jürgen, he is simply everything a Liverpool manager should be. He ticks every box. He just fits. I grew up in the era of Bill Shankly and he had everyone hanging off every word. People loved him and won't find any Liverpool fans who don't feel that way about Jürgen either. I love his manner, but he's the same with everybody. He just gets the club, the culture. Brendan and Rafa had that too, but in different ways. They may have been great coaches or tacticians but this is different because Jürgen brings everything, that true connection with the city, the fans, the owners."

Of course Klopp has got in hot water on occasions for getting carried away in the heat of the moment, most notably following his unbridled celebrations after an incredible last second Divock Origi winner in the Merseyside derby in December 2018. "No, I don't regret it, in a way — but it should not have happened. I did it. I broke a rule, I pay for it. That's how it is. I'm not sure football is all about a manager running on the pitch. It didn't happen to 500,000 others. I know that I am rather on the jump and on the run when something happens. When I did it at Mainz, it was for a very important goal and after that it didn't happen any more. At Dortmund, I ran down the side-line when we became champions. The only difference is that when I did it at Mainz, I don't think I broke a rule. I was on the pitch and then the referee told me to get off and I went around the side. I passed the ball and I fell over."

Klopp once damaged a hamstring while celebrating, "That was with a jump at Stuttgart. I jumped in front of the opposite dugout but nobody – nobody – thought it was disrespectful. It's a cultural thing. It's not for you to change and me to explain how the rules are. I did it. I broke a rule, I pay for it. I don't think I have had any problems with dugouts apart from a few words but that is normal. A match ban, for me, would have been too much. Paying money – and not because I earn so much money – a fine is there to make you aware and make sure you don't do it again. I will not do it again, as so much as I can avoid it. Now

I know it, I will not do it. There were 14 years between the first one and the last one. It cannot happen any more – for the next 14 years."

Klopp jokingly confessed that he actually has no idea why he does what he does; he only knows how to react to situations. He has earned a reputation as one of the most charismatic, emotional managers around, with a natural affinity for motivation and man-management. As such, his team talks have become the stuff of legend, with many reports over the years detailing the inspirational things he supposedly told his players to motivate various great Liverpool performances. Speaking to *The Athletic*, however, Klopp confessed that rather than planning his speeches and player interactions carefully, he tends to just gets caught up in the moment and lets his emotions take control. "Sorry, I would write a book about the things I do if I knew why I did them," he confessed. "But I could never write a book because I have no clue about how these things work. I just react in situations. My job, my life is 24/7 thinking about what happens here. The meetings are based on our past if you want — what happened after the last game, what happened yesterday, things like this. What can we use? I always react. I don't usually remember what I say. If the boys didn't say things in the press afterwards then I wouldn't even know I'd said it.

"I remember Divock Origi after the Dortmund game (back in 2016). He said: 'The boss told us at half-time that if we turned the game around it would be a story we'd all be able to tell our grandchildren about so it would be really worth giving it a try.' But if it was that easy I'd tell them things like that constantly! We always want stories to tell the grandkids! When we start a team meeting the only thing I really know what I am going to say is the first sentence."

The off-the-cuff strategy has clearly worked for Klopp. The two-time Bundesliga winner has transformed Liverpool into European champions and one of the continent's most in-form sides over the last couple of years. Klopp insisted that his job is all about taking a reactive approach to what is going on around him. "All that happens through the week, it stays in my mind, I don't write anything down," he added. "I just think about what's worth telling the boys. S**t session, very good session, whatever, little things. I know how it sounds and it should not sound like this — like I know always to say the right words. But I do trust myself 100% to find the right words."

Another member of Klopp's Boot Room was actually hired

by Brendan Rodgers. Klopp kept Pepijn "Pep" Lijnders on his staff and Klopp was disappointed when Lijnders left in January 2018 for a managerial role at NEC in the Netherlands. But he soon offered Lijnders the chance to return as his assistant.

"He was convinced we could conquer a lot together," says Lijnders, who accepted Klopp's offer and left NEC after half a season. "Jürgen can touch someone straight to the heart. He knows exactly what he wants and when we were on the phone it felt just right." Lijnders said in a *Guardian* interview: "Jürgen is the leader and face of the team, the one who defines the character and who stimulates everyone. Pete [Peter Krawietz] is responsible for the analysis and prepares everything in regards to videos which are shown to the players. I'm responsible for the training process. Together we decide what kind of aspects we want to develop for the team and then I create the exercises. It's quite simple; it's just about the continuing stimulation of our mentality to conquer the ball as quick and as high up the pitch as possible. That element comes back in every exercise. We as staff always try to find ways so the players can be more spontaneous and more creative."

Training drills help shape Liverpool's identity. "The players first have to understand the importance of counter-pressing to our team. They have to feel it, not with the head, but with the heart. They start the exercise with the idea to keep the ball, but in the event of losing it they have to be directly on top of things. When a team lose the ball in training, you will hear me, Jürgen or Pete screaming: 'Go! Get it back! Don't stop!' It's so loud they'll even hear that in Manchester, haha. They have to understand why it's so important. That power and emotion is our game. Because our identity is intensity. That comes back in every drill. And that's what I like about coaching: that you can stimulate certain common behaviour and create a lot by specific team training. That's what I live for."

Lijnders says the manager and captain reflects the identity of the club. "The heart of the team is the heart of the coach. So the character of the coach will become the character of the team in the long term. That's it. Because there is no stronger weapon than your own example. If I'm a disciplined coach, then I don't need to discipline the players. Our captains Hendo and Milly, together with Virgil, are so disciplined, which means the rest of the group doesn't need to be disciplined. There is a saying from [Theodore] Roosevelt which says: 'People don't care how much you know, until they know how much you care.' Jürgen does really care about the squad and his staff. Players will understand and absorb more of our philosophy when they feel how much we care about them."

Lijnders spotted another Klopp strength: "He is able to give a completely different perception to a situation inside a few minutes." Such as the Barcelona game last season. "We lost 3-0, but afterwards Jürgen said in the dressing room: 'The only team in the world who can overturn this defeat against Barcelona is us.' It gave the squad a boost, also because of the way we had played that night. When the players walked towards the coach there was already a different feeling."

Occasionally they meet at their homes but most of the time they are at Melwood, where a glass cage adjacent to the Melwood building was specially built for Klopp and Lijnders to house a paddle tennis court. "It's a combination of tennis and squash and because of the glass walls the ball can bounce, which keeps it in play," Lijnders says. "The court is actually meant for two v two, so it's not only a battle against each other, but also yourself. It's fantastic. Perhaps we play two to three times a week, sometimes more often. A perfect way to switch off. You can't play without 100% concentration. For us it's great to just think about nothing during those games. And sometimes it is in these moments that we find a brilliant solution for something."

Former England manager Fabio Capello praised Klopp for creating "something magic" at Anfield, comparing his style to Pep Guardiola's. He observed: "Klopp has made something magic for me. The atmosphere of Anfield is fantastic, the team is like the fans. The connection is fantastic between the team, Klopp and fans, it's a unique thing. Guardiola is different. I think he plays the team like a theatre. The show is really good but it's a theatre."

Carlo Ancelotti, now a rival manager on Merseyside but then at Napoli, said of Klopp, "He is a friend, a complicated opponent to face with great experience. He is a great manager." When Klopp was informed of how complimentary the Italian had been been, he reacted: "I like him a lot; an incredible player, a great manager and a fantastic guy. In Germany, we call him a smart fox. All these very positive things about me are nice but it is tactics. Carlo's been in the business for so long. He wants to bring the nice fella out of me! We're ready for a real battle. I don't care too much for what people say about us or how they see our situation. This is a fantastic manager, a fantastic team and an emotional crowd so that will be a real challenge They are a good team in a good moment. Even the last game was not bad against Juventus. They are in good shape, second in the league, impressive results. We played against Sarri and his new team on Saturday and now we play against his old team, so it will be interesting. It's not exactly the same anymore because they changed style and lost Jorginho, but they're very quick up front, have good footballers, a good counter-press, a good counter... it will be interesting."

Klopp was returning to Napoli, the scene of one of his biggest regrets in football in 2013. "Pathetic," was Klopp's assessment of his behaviour which resulted in a two- game European touchline ban. He watched most of the game on a TV in the stadium after being sent off inside half an hour for an angry outburst at the fourth official. The footage of him ranting went viral. Klopp was furious that defender Neven Subotic wasn't allowed back onto the pitch sooner after an injury, allowing Higuain to open the scoring. Napoli won 2-1. "I apologised immediately after the game to my team, the fourth official and the referee as well," Klopp said. "I have to accept the consequences for my actions. I was like a clown out there. That was stupid. My emotions turned a well-run game into a hectic affair. I did not show my prettiest face out there. I told myself I did not want to see such pictures of me again and I thought I could do it. It was absolutely my mistake."

Now he said: "I understand why I was not happy but the reaction was too much and they gave me a ban. I had to watch two games from the stands, one against Arsenal at home. But my behaviour was not too good, especially in the German Bundesliga before that, but nothing has happened any more. Maybe it was my last time when I was a bit too excited. I know it'll not happen again. During the game here, I tried to go into the stand and it was not nice. I was sitting there and getting all the comments from people, so for the second half I had to do something and I watched the game with the groundsman in a little room with a Diego Maradona shirt on the wall. A few things are the same for me since then and a few things have changed in a better way."

Klopp and Guardiola were inducted into the League Managers Association's Hall of Fame, presented with silver salver to commemorate their inductions by LMA president Gareth Southgate and fellow Hall of Famer Sir Alex Ferguson at a gala evening in Manchester. They followed in the footsteps of legends including Brian Clough, Sir Bobby Robson and Arsene Wenger by being added to the LMA's esteemed list of coaches.

"This is really special," Klopp said. "To be a part of this incredible group of managers is big, really big. Tonight my family and coaches are here. I wanted them all to be here because it is very important in our family history. When I first heard about it [the honour] I couldn't believe it. I've now been in England for a bit longer than four years and I've enjoyed each second, to be honest. I saw all the names with the pictures when I came in, it's really impressive. I don't often feel pride but, in this moment, I'm very proud because this is something really, really special."

Guardiola said: "I do not have any words to express my gratitude. To be part of this family. It is an incredible honour to be a part of it, for the rest of my life and for generations, to be in this Hall of Fame in English football. What a privilege. When you come down the corridor and see all the big names, big managers, big personalities being here that would've helped to make football better, football that we have right now. I think all the managers here that have been inducted into the Hall of Fame is because we were in incredible clubs with incredible players. As long as we can help them and try to think on the same side and the same page, that's the only reason we can do what we do as managers. Without the quality of the players we have, the managers cannot have success."

LMA chairman Howard Wilkinson said Klopp and Guardiola had shown "incredible drive, innovation and dedication" in their roles. "Since arriving in England, they have built two of the best teams in Premier League history and have done so with humility and honour," Wilkinson said. Both managers' style of play was praised by Sir Alex Ferguson, who said: "They are teams with courage. They play to win all the time, they play to attack all the time." LMA Chief Executive Richard Bevan added: "Tonight, the LMA honoured two of the greatest managers of this generation. Pep has achieved remarkable success with three of the world's biggest clubs. His incredible haul of major domestic and continental titles across Europe demonstrate how his coaching and leadership has combined tactical inspiration with an insatiable will to win, to enable the highest level of performance from his players and staff. Not only has Jürgen redefined man-management in the modern era, he has established a footballing identity which each of his teams has personified. Through hard-work and exceptional coaching, he has delivered performance levels and consistency rarely seen in European football. The LMA congratulates both managers on their achievements and looks forward to seeing them continue their pursuit of excellence with their respective clubs."

Klopp tries to live 'a normal life' outside of football management, and when asked, in a BBC podcast, what part of the job he likes the least he said: "It's a very intense job, I have done it for 19 years but if I didn't do this job I would do another intense job. The only difference is it's in public. That's the only part I don't like. It pays my bills but being constantly under observation is not too nice. I have a completely normal life. I go home, walk the dog, from time to time I go to the pub, but not very often because people would say 'Ah, he's drinking. Ah, he's smoking!' The public part is not something I enjoy. I accept it but I don't enjoy it. The first sip of a pint and you are live on social media. I have no problem telling people to respect my borders."

Of course he had to keep a lid on his players' egos after winning the Champions League, but he didn't find that too difficult, "the conscious decision we made with the boys was, as Liverpool players, it was not about winning one thing. It is about winning and there is no limit. The moment we did it was important - but it did not give us a feeling it was done. We like to think we would meet up in 20 to 30 years, look back and mix up the years. Was it 2019 or 2020? So far, so good. We try to squeeze everything we can get from our time together. There is no pressure, it is just opportunity."

Klopp considers himself a man of the players, but he has clear defining lines of friendship and respect. "All my former players have my number and we stay in contact. I support them still, apart from the moment we play each other. If we win 5-1 I would prefer my former player scores the one. It is like a family and friends forever. When I was a very young manager [at Mainz] and I knew my players did not earn very much, I had to tell some of my best friends they would not get another contract and I did not know which way it would go for them. Now it is a different level and I do not put the players on the streets, they will find another club. I do not push them in a dark room and leave them there. The future is still bright for them, and sometimes it is not the right place in our team any more. It is being completely honest in these moments, it is not that I enjoy it. Everything has its time and it's the same with a contract as well. I have never kept a player because I like him so much."

Klopp has been surprised by the emergence of some gifted young players, notably Alexander-Arnold. "I have known Trent Alexander-Arnold since he was 17 years old. He was a big talent but we were not sure he could do it physically. Now he is a machine - so he is a big surprise."

Boris Becker is his great idol, He explained: "He is the same age group as me and he is my hero. When he was 17 in 1985 and won his first Wimbledon, it was one of the biggest days in my life too. My wife and his former wife organised a meeting because he was always on my non-existent bucket list. In that moment, I could not speak, which is difficult to believe. I always knew we could be really good friends - and for that evening, we behaved as such."

THE FIRST THREE YEARS

The *Rocky* theme perfectly summed up Liverpool's epic attempt to topple champions Manchester City and their even more expensive squad under another world class manager in Pep Guardiola. Jürgen Klopp came so close to landing a knock out blow in the race for the title, but had to settle for a points defeat - albeit just one point.

However Klopp soon made up for the disappointment, felt more acutely by the fans, when his players got up from the canvas and delivered that knock out blow in the Champions League final beating Spurs. Ironically City's owners coveted the European crown, while the Liverpool faithful wanted the end of the long wait for the title.

Liverpool might have won an impressive 18 titles in their illustrious history, but the last one was an awfully long time ago, and not even a record busting start to the season seemed to be able to topple a team so many regarded the best in Europe, if not the world. In the final media conference prior to the big kick off in August 2018 Klopp was asked what the key will be to closing the 25-point gap on City from their previous title winning season. "We are still Rocky Balboa, not Ivan Drago," he retorted in reference to the fourth film of the iconic boxing epic.

"Thank you, Jürgen," was Pep Guardiola's response. "For nine years I've lived with it, no problem. Every season except the first one when I arrived at Barcelona, when I had people who didn't know I was a manager, since then we have always been the favourites. But thank you, Jürgen. You are so kind."

He set out and used Liverpool's phenomenal season to inspire his own players; he told them throughout the season, if they slip up just the once, Liverpool would be behind them ready to pounce. In *Rocky IV* the all-American hero travels to Siberia where he trains in primitive surroundings before confronting Drago, the seemingly unbeatable opponent, it was the perfect analogy as Liverpool were in City's faces for the entire season.

Klopp had identified weaknesses immediately after losing to Real Madrid in the Champions League Final, not merely in the one game,

Jurgen Klopp takes charge of Liverpool for this first time on 17th October 2015 for a goalless draw at Tottenham.

but over the course of the season, and went about minimising those weaknesses, with a massive spend to provide more punch, as he planned to go the distance, but City had even greater spending power if they needed it.

He laughed about the Rocky analogy — he has seen all the films "many, many times" and the fourth one is his favourite. "I don't want to be the underdog," said Klopp. "I want to win and Rocky won. It's the only difference. So now we have the best tools of all? It's not true. Manchester City had a fantastic team last year and they have now brought in Riyad Mahrez. It doesn't make them weaker. Our potential is good, what we do with it we will see, and that's only the quality we have. I only want from us that we fight, not that we are the underdog. I am not interested in being the underdog. Yes, it has happened a few times but not because I wanted to be, but because it was a fact. I don't see us an underdog, I see us as a team that challenges... the ones who have to do more, who have to run more, who have to jump more. That's all."

Liverpool had finished fourth the previous season, behind not only City but also Jose Mourinho's Manchester United and Mauricio

Pochettino's Spurs but it was the huge 25-point gap that concerned Klopp. Liverpool's emphatic Champions League quarter-final victory over Pep's side, plus a league win over City, suggested they were much closer than the 25 point deficit indicated and that they could mount their biggest challenge once they had recruited key additions. "You all ask me about the gap to City and what we have to do, it has nothing to do with City. City took three points from us, we took three points from them but we lost them in other games. Win all of them and it is good but it is pretty difficult to do because not only the other Big Six, you see how Wolverhampton acts, how Fulham acts and how Everton acts – they are all ambitious. I don't think too much about what we have to do; I thought about it pre-season but now we have to be in this championship mood. It is like you jump in the water and dive and then let's go for it until you don't have enough air any more or oxygen and you have to go up again. That is the plan, that we really go for it."

Brazilian goalkeeper Alisson was a key acquisition, as Klopp broke the world record transfer fee for a goalkeeper (£67m from Roma) until it was swiftly broken with Chelsea's signing of Kepa Arrizabalaga (£72m). Klopp had no worries about the 25-year-old making an instant impact. "Just be a goalkeeper. Be yourself, in this case, because he is very calm and laid back - and that helps," said Klopp ahead of the opening game. "It's about making the right decisions in the right moments. It's all good. He's settled really quick, as if he's been here longer than two weeks. That's all fine."

Following an encouraging season which had seen Liverpool progress to the Champions League final only to lose to Real Madrid, Liverpool were the summer's biggest spenders. Klopp justified it: "My own expectations are always pretty high, we'll have to make the most of it (the pressure after spending a lot). It's always my expectation to reach the highest level but it doesn't work all the time. I think for us it was pretty normal there would be one point where we spend more money. The last few years I've had to sit here and defend our transfer behaviour, we sold more than we brought in. It all makes sense, we had to create a squad which is strong enough and wide enough to cope with the Premier League. People ask me is it the best squad I've ever had? I don't think about that. It's about what we make of it, how often we deliver, how often we bring ourselves in a mood to fight against all these Premier League teams who want to have our points."

The First Three Years

In addition to the need for a new goalkeeper, following the calamitous performance of Karius in the Champions League final where he was responsible for two of the Madrid goals, Klopp knew Emre Can would be leaving, so he brought in Brazilian Fabinho for £44m plus Naby Keita. "We knew early enough that it was pretty likely he would leave and we were able to plan."

After three eventful years as Liverpool boss, the Anfield club were still searching for their first trophy under him after losing in a League Cup, Europa League and Champions League final. Klopp, then in his fourth season, having taken charge in October 2015 after leaving Borussia Dortmund, believed Anfield was the perfect stage for him to deliver success. Klopp spent £176.8m in the summer window in the quest for major honours but the German still clung to his role as underdog: "I don't want the 'best team' in England. If a team is better than yours, then you have to work out how to be at their level, and then how to beat them. I have never wanted to have the best team. I have never wanted to be the best player or the best manager. What interests me is to beat the best. The best team today in England is Manchester City. That means that other teams are not the best. The goal then is to beat City as often as possible."

Klopp said Liverpool were "in a league that brings together six of the world's biggest clubs, who are all fighting for four Champions League places," which made his task "very difficult." He added: "Apart from Manchester City, who were way ahead early on, it was a huge relief for all the others to qualify. Liverpool's history is made up of battles. And when you battle, you never expect it to be easy. Why would it be now? Yes, we're aiming for the stars, but we respect the game. I feel the size of the club and above all the honour given to me to lead the team. Last year, I turned 50 and I invited quite a lot of people to celebrate. I hadn't seen some of them for 20 years. The words that I heard most were: 'Who would have thought it? That you would, one day, be manager of Liverpool?' It's true that when you're born in the Black Forest and you have played in Germany's seventh division, it seems improbable. I didn't even dream of being a professional or having a career in football... so for me, I'm at the club that suits me to achieve every goal."

Nevertheless there were times during his first three fruitless seasons when fans questioned the new manager. One example came just months into his reign when Klopp ushered his entire team before the Kop for a bizarre celebration following a 2-2 draw against lowly West Bromwich Albion which left the club ninth. The 'celebration' brought mirth from opposition fans and bemusement from some ardent Liverpool followers. In hindsight of course it looks like a stroke of genius: Klopp's philosophy demands a connection between players and supporters and the Liverpool crowd had stuck with their team to the bitter end, Divock Origi netting the equaliser in the 95th minute. It was this sense of togetherness the manager wanted to foster and it stood his team in good stead later that season in pulsating home wins over Manchester United and Borussia Dortmund as Liverpool battled through to the Europa League final and has become a hallmark of a team unbeaten at Anfield since 2017.

Klopp never took his eyes off the big picture and made an unlikely move in the transfer market. Shaqiri had endured relegation at Stoke but scored a wonderful goal for Switzerland at the World Cup that found him reprimanded by FIFA for a goal celebration that politicised his Albanian-Kosovan heritage. Nevertheless he was quickly snapped up by Klopp, who said of the signing: "I think the English phrase is a 'no-brainer'." Shaqiri paid tribute to Klopp. "When he arrived here, the club was totally different. You can see the people have a lot of respect for him and his work. The progress of this club, this team is getting higher every year. He is going about it the right way. Nothing is impossible. We can be everything we want to be. We beat City in the league and the Champions League last season, so I think we can win everything in the world. It has to be our ambition, against whoever we play, to dominate the game. I came here to try to win titles. This club needs to have the ambition to win titles, to be one of the best clubs in the world"

Klopp questioned why Liverpool were perceived as City's only challengers, and why only in England can you seemingly "win the title in the transfer market". He said: "I couldn't be less interested in what other people say of us. What people say is sometimes nice, sometimes not so nice, but it is always not important. What is important is that we know what we want to be, and we want to be a challenger. How can we be something different? We didn't win anything in the last few years, that's the truth. And the other teams, I can't see that they've got weaker. So why should we [be the only challengers] because we made a few signings? It's only an English thing, where you can win the league in the transfer window. It's not possible. It's not interesting. We did our business, other teams did theirs last year, two years ago, whatever. We did it this year because we felt it was the right moment to do so, that's all! We enjoy our role, and all the rest is not important to us."

Then Manchester United manager Jose Mourinho had led the Old Trafford to the runners-up spot a huge 19 points behind City but was touchy when asked if he should still be considered a great if he did not win a title at United, "Do you ask that question to the manager that finished third in the Premier League or fourth? Because he never wins anything internationally, for example." A clear reference to Klopp and Spurs boss Mauricio Pochettino. It was a barb that would back fire on the 'Special One' as he was sacked following a 3-1 defeat at Anfield that December bringing a fractious reign at Old Trafford to a premature close.

By contrast Klopp was in good humour discussing a charity game, joking that he wanted to sort out 'the plumbing issue, electricity and the pool' when he comes face to face with his landlord Brendan Rodgers at Parkhead on the touchline for the Match For Cancer. Having taken over from Rodgers in October 2015, Klopp moved into the Formby mansion his predecessor had bought from Steven Gerrard.

In a video message on Celtic's Twitter page, he joked that he was looking forward to seeing Rodgers for the first time since the house was let to him. "It will be fun for sure. Especially because I meet my landlord, I think for the first time since he left Liverpool and I came here. We have a lot of things to talk about. The plumbing issue, electricity, the pool and stuff like that. So Brendan, hope you are in good shape and we can sort a few things that day." He was excited to visit Glasgow and Parkhead for the first time: "It's my first time in your wonderful, famous stadium and probably my first time in Glasgow in general, so a big day for me and hopefully a very nice day for all of you. As a manager it's always difficult to prepare a game, in this specific case it's even more difficult because nobody can blame me for recruitment, or scouting." He then joked: "I have nothing to do with the team, maybe nothing to do with the lineup, because James Milner is in my team and he's a very demanding person. He will tell me probably 'he plays there, he plays there'."

Klopp demanded desire in enormous quantities to get forward and score late goals despite being physically tired. "In these moments the fuel is really low and maybe the players need a bit of help from an angry manager - 'run or I will kill you' - and they did that with a fantastic counter attack."

Klopp responded after Gary Neville suggested Liverpool should ignore the Champions League to focus on the league which he believes they had a realistic chance of winning. Klopp asked for Neville to come and explain to him how that would work and questioned whether he should play the youth team. "How would that work? We don't play Champions League or what?" Klopp asked at his press conference. "Gary should come over and tell me exactly how that works. How do you prepare for a game when you don't focus on it? I don't understand, do we play our kids or what? I don't know what he means with that, to be honest. We have to play football. A lot of people watch our games when we play Champions League and that's our job that we do the best we can do in all these games. That's what we try. I don't know exactly what it means but to focus on one competition can only be if maybe you are already out of the competition nearly. If it's late in the season that you see you have a chance to do that or do this and all that stuff. Last year, for example, we had no chance to focus on one competition because we had to qualify for the Champions League and I don't think that even Gary Neville would have said, 'Quarter-finals of the Champions League, let City win'. I don't want to be too critical as I don't know exactly how he said it, but it's a bit silly, sitting in an office talking about football, it's different to doing the job."

In an interview with *The Times*, Gary Neville thought Liverpool could win the league if they were able to rest their star men week-on-week, something they particularly need due to their high pressing game "The Champions League - if I was Liverpool, I would kick it into touch," Neville suggested. "I know that's very hard to do but if they could go into February, March, April without it, I think they could have a real chance [of winning the league] if they had free weeks."

Klopp's philosophy was to ensure his players felt enthused by what happened to them the previous season in losing the Final against Madrid, and the determination to get back to the Final to put that right, rather than become subdued by the Final defeat. "No damage. No. Absolutely not. It is a different club to the club I joined. We got a lot of respect because of the way we played last season. Everyone who saw the Final saw that we could have won it against a side in a completely different moment. They see the games we played. They saw

City. They saw Rome. They saw Porto. Going to the Final needed 10 or 12 outstanding performances. They saw so many games which we played in a really good way. There was a lot of respect. It is important for the club and the players. The players we spoke to in the summer were different talks to those I had the previous year or before. We are in the place we want to be without being satisfied with anything. We are a challenger again for pretty much everything, especially in each game. I don't think there is any game in the world where you would say beforehand, 'No chance Liverpool', which is good. That doesn't mean we will win. But that means it is clear that we have a chance if we play our best."

He added: "The best way is when you are experienced you use your new knowledge and start again like a virgin. It is a nice experience, it is a nice memory, but at the end we have to start new, using the experience but not relying on it. We are in a really good moment, but we are not a little bit satisfied. There is nothing in us that thinks that's it. It's good but we want it better for the club."

Klopp did not want to be second best to City, comparing Liverpool's battle for supremacy with tennis rivalry between Germans Becker and Michael Stich. Stich won only one major to Becker's six as City's recent trophy haul outstrips Liverpool. "We cannot wait until City are not there any more. We want to fight them. We want to have battles with them, 100 per cent. We still have to be a bit more passionate. I grew up in a time when Boris Becker and Michael Stich were the best tennis players in Germany and maybe for a few years in the world. Michael Stich was an outstanding tennis player, maybe better than Boris Becker, but he was not Boris Becker."

Klopp marked three years at Anfield with an excellent interview with Melissa Reddy, where Klopp echoed Bill Shankly's famous "if you are second you are nothing", saying he knows being a runner-up won't do: "If somebody wants to judge me because of the last three years then I know what people are saying, and it's the truth. I lost the last six finals [three with Liverpool), it's not something that's really enjoyable, but you can see it from two points. Yes we lost, but at the same time we reached them, that's not cool but in most sports second place is okay. If you go to the Olympic Games and you come home with a silver medal, it's still something but in football it's nothing. It's nothing for me as well, so I don't get up in the morning and say 'I'll reach another final' or whatever. It's not like this, I want to win and I know that's the responsibility."

On his arrival, Klopp was "pretty sure" he would win a title within four years. "I really wanted a change after 14 years managing in Germany, where I knew everything, I knew each team. If you would have asked me about a side in the fifth division, I could have told you the names of at least four of their players. Then I came to England and everything is new. Yes, I watched English football before, but I was busy in Germany with my league and with Champions League and stuff. Then, you come here, we play a team - let's say Hull - and you don't know one player. For the preparations you have pretty much three days so you watch their games completely differently because I had completely no idea of what they do. In Germany, meanwhile, I knew inside-out how every team played. The start at Liverpool was really busy because we had to learn a lot of things while also playing in the Europa League, but it was exactly what I wanted - a new challenge for myself. I wanted to get rid of some routines which were normal after spending such a long time in Germany as a manager and have kind of a new start. I really feel it's a big privilege to have the chance to do so, because it's like an energiser it gives you a real boost, which helps.

"I'm a much better manager now than I was three years ago. I tried to prepare myself a little bit language-wise. I downloaded an app, which I have still and it helped me a lot. I felt that I needed to improve my English a bit, because like a lot of people of my generation in Germany, we learnt it in school, but then we don't use it too much. I tried, at least, to think of a few things that I could say in the meetings with the players and had a look what the English word was for that. That was all my preparations pretty much, because I couldn't do a lot. We left a country and our lives there behind, if you want, so we had to organise a few things. It was quite busy these four days, quite busy, and it was not a lot about football."

Klopp's first opportunity to share his outlook was with Liverpool's in-house TV channel; wanting supporters to change from "doubters to believers." He reiterated that during his first press conference, asking for patience to develop the team. "It was obvious something was wrong at Liverpool, so it was clear that we need a new relationship and that's actually the basis for everything - the people. The first day the manager comes in, all are happy I think most of the time. From that moment on, it only can get worse, step-by-step because you cannot reach all the expectation, it's not possible. I don't know exactly what the people thought about what I could do when I came in, probably they thought 'do something similar like what you did at Dortmund.' Even at Dortmund we needed a start. What I was asking for was just to give us time to start new, because if you don't do that and if we have to start the next game and have in our backpack the last 400 games, that doesn't work. It was cool that they brought a new face in and, of course, if you were used to difficulties in the past then you doubt everything, even the positive things.

"I'm pretty sure a lot of people thought as well, 'okay, a new guy in, but will be the same as always? They have a good few games and in the end, they will win nothing.' And actually it happened like that. I have said it a few times: I have no idea when we will win something, but I'm sure this club will win something. I don't know when so let's have the best times of our lives until then. Let's enjoy the world, let's enjoy the football, let's enjoy the journey and it's what we did so far - it was a good time. Nobody wants to look back in 10 or 20 years and say 'so the best time we had without winning anything was when Klopp was here. It was so funny and all that stuff'. That's not really something you want to achieve, we still have time to do something special and we know that to underline the development and progress, we have to do it. Times change, and to be honest, it is much more difficult than it was in the past. If you think about it, we are maybe in the best moment for ages, but a few other clubs are the same and they made the same steps so that makes it really hard.

"It looks like we are really on a good way and the only thing I can guarantee is that we constantly develop. Our little problem is many other clubs develop as well so it's never that you improve 20% and the others get 20% weaker. They try to do the same, to reach the next level, and that's the challenge we all face. It is interesting, but tough as well. As I said in my first press conference here, if anybody thinks that I can perform wonders, then it could become really difficult in the future, because I can't. I'm a pretty hard-working person, I'm pretty well paid, so I should work hard actually. That's what I do, I try to find solutions for different problems or situations and that's how I understand the job. The only thing I can do is to put all I have - my knowledge, passion, heart, experience, everything - I throw it into this club, 100 per cent. I don't keep anything back and it should work actually at one point. You have to bring yourself in the best situation that you are able to and use it - that's what we do. When we win something, this city will explode - I'm sure - in a very positive way."

Back then the new manager couldn't have possibly imagined that he would set a new Liverpool record of the most points after the opening 15 games in the entire history of the club, and yet still be two points behind champions City until their defeat at Stamford Bridge on Saturday, December 8, a few hours after Liverpool won on the south coast, 4-0 at Bournemouth.

★

The highlight of the 2018/19 season proved to be that stunning comeback against Barcelona in the semi-final, overturning a three-goal defeat from the first leg. It was a truly unforgettable night at Anfield that somehow emerged out of sheer adversity; the huge deficit, no away goal, and the quality of the opposition. And without key players Divock Origi and Gini Wijnaldum proved to be the unlikely heroes making up for the loss of Salah and Firmino. Origi played the central role, flanked by Mané and Shaqiri, who had been involved during the first half of the season, but hadn't started a game since January. Trent Alexander-Arnold was back after his omission from the first leg. Having already won La Liga before their weekend date with Celta Vigo, Ernesto Valverde rested his entire starting team. But they were all back, unchanged from the first leg.

Salah wore a black T-shirt with giant lettering and a simple message: 'NEVER GIVE UP'. Liverpool got the perfect start when Sadio Mané anticipated a loose defensive header by Jordi Alba, slipped a pass to Henderson, whose shot was saved but fell to Origi who tapped in the early goal. Fabinho was booked for a tackle on Suarez, having set the tone with a crunching challenge on Messi. Robertson also went down, after a kick backwards from Suarez. He played on until half-time but Klopp withdrew him at the break and Wijnaldum was on. Six minutes in Alexander-Arnold won the ball back from Alba after losing possession and steered a low pass square across the area, Wijnaldum's side-foot finish crept under ter Stegen's arm and in at the Kop end, and 122 seconds later it was 3-0 – Wijnaldum again. Origi overhit a cross from the right but it was picked up by Shaqiri, who exchanged passes with Milner, before swinging in a cross for Wijnaldum to rise above the rooted defence to head it past a stranded ter Stegen.

The most gripping of ties was decided by some incredible quick thinking from Alexander-Arnold. He won a corner then caught the defence fast asleep and looking like it was organised on Hackney Marshes! He placed the ball in the corner, started to walk off as Shaqiri trotted over to take the kick, then quickly turned and fired in a low corner towards Origi, whose first time shot flew past a startled ter Stegen. Off he ran to celebrate with teammates and substitutes in front of a delirious Kop.

The whole Liverpool contingent formed a line to sing You'll Never Walk Alone in front of the Kop. Klopp's side had led at half-time in 26 games in 2018/19 and won every one. Liverpool had now hosted 19 European semi-finals, winning 15, drawing three and losing only one. It was Barcelona's heaviest defeat against an English side.

Wijnaldum commented: "Unbelievable. After the game in Spain we were confident we could score four and win 4-0. People outside doubted us and thought we couldn't do it. But once again we showed everything is possible in football. I was really angry that the manager put me on the bench. I just tried to help my team, I'm happy I could do that with two goals. [The manager] told us [after the first leg that] the tie was totally winnable. He said we should have every belief we could still win."

Despite a stirring run in Europe, the domestic season ended in disappointment. Liverpool ended their Premier League campaign with a 2-0 home win over Wolves with a brace from Mané, but it was Manchester City who retained the title on the final day of the season, pushed every inch of the way by Liverpool. City had to win each of their final 14 league games of the campaign to succeed by a single point and their triumph at Brighton, after being a goal down, capped a remarkable title race.

Sadio Mané shared the Golden Boot with Mo Salah and Pierre-Emerick Aubameyang but ultimately there was huge disappointment at Anfield, yet at the same time remarkable pride at the extraordinary effort. Klopp's team lost only one game, were unbeaten at home, amassed 97 points which would have won every other Premier League except the last two.

Everywhere in the stadium phones were on, some had radio

commentary as they kept praying for more miracles with news from the South Coast. Cheers went up as rumours – at first incorrect – of a Brighton goal. But then there was actually one. Glenn Murray had opened the scoring for the Seagulls. Agüero quickly levelled and City went ahead through Laporte and with both contenders leading at half-time Mahrez made it 3-1, then 4-1 from Gundogan.

A 21st clean sheet of the league campaign gave Alisson the Golden Glove, and Mané nodded home yet another assist from Alexander-Arnold to match Salah on 22 goals, and for the full-back to break the record for defensive assists with 12. Alex Oxlade-Chamberlain came on to another rousing reception.

Players and their families gave a lap of honour. The title had been so, so close; close enough for a replica trophy to be stationed at Anfield in case City faltered but a club-record 97 points was one short.

Salah and van Dijk became the first outfield Liverpool players since Martin Skrtel in 2010/11 to feature in every Premier League game, Alisson was also ever-present in the league. The Reds went unbeaten at home for a second successive league season for the first time since 1979/80.

Liverpool captain Jordan Henderson said afterwards, "No regrets. We have been outstanding all season and left everything out on the pitch. We have lost one game. People might talk about the draws but we tried everything to win those games. We gave everything over the whole season. City are a fantastic side and you take your hat off to them. Next season we give everything to win it."

Ahead of Liverpool's only fixture ever played in June, Klopp gave the players five days off. Following the final league game, the squad took part in light recovery sessions at Melwood, then relaxed with short holidays before warm-weather training in Marbella. The manager took his squad there before the previous season's final against Real and prior to the tie against Bayern. Klopp described it as "two proper weeks as a pre-season".

The three-week gap persuaded Klopp that, in addition to the usual short-sided games in training, something more was required to keep his side in tune. He arranged a practice match behind closed doors against Benfica B, the Portuguese side's reserve team that plays in their home league's second tier. The two teams' coaches collaborated to set up Benfica's team as closely as possible in terms of personnel and tactics to

The First Three Years

that of surprise finalists Tottenham. Spurs had made remarkable progress, scraping through their initial group before relying on last minute goals, one given, one not, against Manchester City and Ajax respectively, to make it to a first Champions League final.

Klopp knew defeat to Real Madrid in the previous season's final in Kiev was a powerful motivational factor. "[The defeat in the final] had a big influence on us," he said. "I remember that situation when we stood in the queue at Kiev in our tracksuits on the way home. Heads down, very frustrated, everyone very disappointed. You weren't allowed to be angry. There were a lot of different emotions. But the plan was: we'll come again. We'll be there again. Now we are.

"Each team who lost a final will think about putting it right. We have the chance to do that. That was the kick-start for the development of this team. This team doesn't compare to the team last year. These boys want to be there. It's not like [we think] 'Oh, it's coming up' and we get scared. We are a completely different team to last year."

The long gap between games wasn't ideal, but that the players' commitment had been exemplary. "The best moment for the final would've been five minutes after we beat Barcelona," Klopp said. "[But] the mood in the team is brilliant. The work rate and attitude. The best piece of character of this team is the constant readiness for development."

Thousands more fans than could possibly be accommodated in the stadium poured into Madrid, and on match day a wave of red gathered in the fanzone at Plaza Salvador Dalí. Fans proudly wore "Never Give Up" T-shirts.

Tottenham's Harry Kane started, 53 days after an injury in the quarter-final against Manchester City, with semi-final hero Lucas Moura dropping to the bench. Milner missed out, but Roberto Firmino – absent since limping out of the first leg against Barcelona – led the line.

After just 22 seconds the defining moment arrived. Van Dijk won a header on halfway, Wiljnaldum touched on to Henderson who released Mané with a first-time ball over the top. As Mané weighed his options on the corner of the box, Moussa Sissoko tracked back and raised his right arm as Mané tried to clip the ball into the centre. It struck Sissoko's chest and outstretched arm. Referee Damir Skomina pointed straight to the penalty spot. VAR confirmed the award. Salah thumped it down

Champions At Last!

the middle as Lloris dived to his left. Salah's opener was the second-fastest goal in a Champions League final (1 min 48 secs), only behind Paolo Maldini (50 secs) for AC Milan versus Liverpool in 2005.

Around the hour mark, Firmino was replaced by Origi and Wijnaldum by Milner, and with four minutes of normal time remaining, the Reds found a vital second goal. Robertson curled in a dangerous pass looking for Salah, which was put behind by Rose off his shoulder. Milner's corner was flicked out by Son to van Dijk, whose shot was blocked by Dier. The ball looped up and Dier tried to head out but another challenge from van Dijk meant it dropped to Matip, who played it short to Origi. With one touch to set, the Belgian swept his finish into the far corner. Origi scored with all three of his shots in the Champions League this season.

"Allez, allez, allez" rang out around the stadium, followed by "You'll Never Walk Alone" before a chorus of whistles urged the end of the match. With just 35.4% possession, Liverpool became the first side to win the Champions League final with less of the ball than the opposition since Jose Mourinho's Inter Milan beat Bayern Munich in 2010. In truth, Spurs had been kept at arm's length for the majority of the game with star man Harry Kane clearly not 100% fit.

At the final whistle Jürgen Klopp rejoiced, as well he might when he said: "I'm so happy for our boys, I'm so happy for all these [fans] and I'm so happy for my family [who] suffer every year when we go to a final in the last game of the season and we lose. So they deserve it more than anyone as they are so supportive. Did you ever see a team like this, fighting with absolutely no fuel in the tank anymore? And then a goalkeeper who makes difficult things look easy. It'll be the best night of my life."

Klopp hugged every player. Steven Gerrard exchanged handshakes with friends in the crowd. Henderson found his father Brian, the pair embracing. "It's just very emotional," said Brian. "The tears come. You start shaking. You grab your wife, you grab your daughter-in-law, you grab anybody that's around you... just so, so happy."

Liverpool legend Ian Rush brought out the trophy, newly engraved and now with a pair of red ribbons. The players accepted their medals from UEFA president Aleksander Čeferin, with Liverpool owner John W Henry looking on from the podium. Henderson raised the trophy, then the players went over to join the fans as Queen's "We Are the

Jordan Henderson lifts Liverpool's sixth European Cup in Madrid

Champions" rang out, the fans singing along.

A group led by Fabinho and Firmino grabbed Klopp and the whole team raised him above their shoulders, giving the manager the bumps to the delight of the supporters. The manager then conducted his own set of cheers.

In the dressing room, the players danced, sang and posed with the trophy, taking selfies with their medals. In the centre of town thousands of jubilant fans celebrated the victory. Back home in Liverpool, fans poured out of the pubs to celebrate in the streets. Reds fans around the world joined the celebrations.

More than 100,000 Liverpool fans made the trip to Madrid, more than five times as many lined the streets of the city for the homecoming trophy parade the following day as a convoy of vehicles – the main team bus at its centre – made its way along Queen's Drive, along Rocky Lane and through West Derby, along Leeds Street and down to the waterfront to finish at The Strand.

Klopp had his legs dangling off the back corner of the main team bus, sipping a beer, smiling and waving to the assembled fans. Some players wore tops with a gold number "6" and "Champions of Europe" on the back.

Klopp gave his final thoughts from the top of the bus, reflecting on how important his and his team's achievement was for the Red half of the city.

"It's so overwhelming what the people are doing," he said. "When you have a direct eye contact and you see how much it means to them that's touching, to be honest. It's brilliant. You see in their eyes how much it means. It's unbelievable. Crazy."

KLOPP PLOTS LIVERPOOL'S GREATEST EVER SEASON

To ensure that the Champions League victory over Spurs was the start not the end of the trophy haul, Jurgen Klopp opted to retain the squad who had come within a point of winning the league back in May. Crucial to any club's long term success is the short term recruitment; some clubs buy ready made players, others look to the future buying prospects and mould them into superstars.

Klopp knew Liverpool were an attractive club for the biggest players in the world, the natural lure was having landed the biggest prize the Champions League, but while their rivals were splashing the cash, the Liverpool manager had no need to follow suit. He had already landed two of his most expensive signings and both now looked to be bargains.

There was no need to join the scramble for the elite in the market, the superstars such as Kylian Mbappé, who were in reality, out of reach of even the richest Premier League clubs. Reports in Spain suggested the 20-year-old as a possible replacement for Mo Salah, with Real Madrid eyeing the Egyptian winger which stoked the fires of social media with Liverpool fans worldwide desperate for the Anfield club to make a move for the French wonderkid, particularly if the reports were right that Salah was on his way to Madrid. Of course, the rumours were wrong, on all accounts. Transfer planning was meticulous and Klopp had all the ingredients he perceived for a season of great fulfilment.

Klopp had actually tried to sign Mbappé before he joined PSG in 2017, but confessed that Liverpool simply couldn't afford him, even if they wanted him. PSG bought him for 180m euros while Real Madrid were willing to pay 280m euros! Mbappé earns 30m euros a year *after* tax! Klopp said: "I don't see any club at the moment who can buy Kylian Mbappé from PSG. And we are one of the clubs that cannot do it, it is as easy as that. Okay, from a sporting point of view, there are not a lot of reasons to not sign him, what a player he is. It is about the money of course. No chance. Absolutely no chance. Sorry for killing that story."

When asked why there aren't any French players in his team, Klopp told Canal+: "There's no reason for it. Kylian plays for PSG. Griezmann has joined Barcelona. Obviously you know how good your team is. We would like a French player but some of them are too expensive for us."

Klopp's prime concern was to stop a talent drain such as happened when Luis Suarez and Raheem Sterling left Anfield. "We want to be a club in the future for sure whose players don't want to leave," he said in 2016. "That's very important. But it will only be possible with success and the atmosphere we create in and around the club." Although forced to sell Philippe Coutinho to Barcelona in January 2018 for £142m, Liverpool had been transformed into a 'go to' destination for the best players, but not if moneybags clubs like PSG and City wanted to compete, then it's not so easy or straightforward. "I don't think we can compare with Man City, I have no idea which players want to go to Man City, but good players obviously have in the last couple of years, there is no doubt about that," Klopp said. "We have reasons, good reasons why players want to join us, that is clear. City had a very successful spell though, in the last 10 years they have been champions a couple of times. So it is different tastes and that leads to different decisions. I don't think we struggle with convincing players. You can feel it, this year, last year, you can see in the eyes of a player, I am not sure if honour is the right word, but it is good that we speak to them. The club is in a really good position, but unfortunately it does not lead to a situation where you win all the football games. It has to be done on the pitch. Image-wise, it maybe [always] was, but now I think it is easier to live the life of a Liverpool supporter and that means automatically being in a situation to sign the players you want to sign."

Klopp successfully created healthy competition for places, and turned some players into world stars worth three or four times what the club had paid for them, "How do we improve? You only have to look at your passport, as long as you are not dead, you can improve, that is how it is. That's how it is for all of us, so I don't have to convince them. And they know if they don't then there is another player who can in the same position, in a different way, maybe, but for sure not sure and that is the pressure the boys have to deal with. It is not massive [pressure] because we don't use that fact because we really see ourselves as a unit and whoever is in the best shape has to play. So it not about your name, it is 'you're in the best shape to play' because the [difference in] quality is that [small]. The boys are really close to each other and there is not a massive difference between them, so that is good. It keeps them on their toes, playing for Liverpool keeps them on their toes.

"We don't have fringe players here, we only have first team players and a few young guns. We now play a lot Tuesday, Wednesday and Saturday, so we will have to see about [changes]. We don't just play a lot of football we travel a lot, but you know that. Every team has to do that, we don't go for excuses. Other teams have difficult situations, as well, it is like that. You want to play Champions League, desperately and then it starts, you don't say 'oh my God, look at all these games' that makes no sense. It is good.'

Klopp knew his players deep desire was to keep on winning, hungry for more trophies. That "mentality monsters" the phrase he coined the previous season, was just as important to the manager as the raw talent he was moulding. "It is just the simple thought about what a career should be keeps them on their toes and the idea of a collection of silverware, not only one. So there is a lot to come and it is not difficult [to keep players focused]. From a character point of view, we fit really well. The team and the staff and I, we have done really well because we are pretty smilier. We don't think too much about the long term targets, the next game is our final and we play a lot of finals in our season."

Teenagers Harvey Elliott and Sepp van den Berg were the only summer transfer window acquisitions, emphasising that Klopp felt his squad was strong enough, although if he did have an addition in mind, it might have been a question of their availability, and price, when he said: "The players we thought about to make this team better were really expensive and we could not spend the money. That is how it is."

Looking again at the Mbappé situation as the perfect example, he added: "To see a player better than him, or with potential to be better or play exactly the same as him, is really difficult. That is what it was. That was the situation. But was not that we were not real, but we did not want to make five or six changes. Not at all. This team is at a wonderful age, there is still space for improvement, completely fine. We want to do something and we could have done a lot, but could not do the right thing and we only wanted to do the right thing. That is the reason we kept this squad, because it is really good and if you wanted to improve it you have to do it with the right players, not just some players to fix whatever. That is not possible."

Wijnaldum gave an insight into the way the manager develops his players. "I've certainly grown as a player during my time here. The expectations are so high at such a big club and that drives you on to become better. I can't speak for every player but I have a good relationship with him. He has helped me a lot. He can be hard, because he's always on your case and saying what he thinks. But he's honest and I like that. It's always in the right way, always for the right reasons. It's not to make you feel bad or anything like that. He's really hard but, on the other side, he keeps your confidence high. He says that mistakes are just part of football. I remember against Leicester I made a mistake and it led to a goal. He wasn't angry about the mistake, he was more angry about my reaction afterwards. He thought I was too busy thinking about it rather than just putting it behind me.

"Before I signed for Liverpool I was playing for Newcastle as a No 10. Basically, I was always attacking, I didn't have to do much defensive work, I didn't play as the No. 6 or the No. 8. Learning to play different roles has made me a more all-round midfielder. It makes it easier for you to play more often and it makes it easier for the manager if he has players who can be used in different positions. I think I've shown I have the defensive discipline to play deep as the No. 6 and start the build ups with my passing. I can also play higher up the pitch and make a difference in the opposition area. Being able to do both has helped me to play so many games."

He almost joined Spurs, but his talk with Klopp swung it Liverpool's way. "I had a really good conversation with Pochettino, but we didn't come to an agreement," Wijnaldum told the PFA. "Not just me – Newcastle also didn't come to an agreement with Tottenham. When I spoke with Jürgen, he made me feel really good. He gave me a lot of confidence because he said he liked my way of playing football. Three days after our meeting they had reached a deal and I didn't think twice. This is one of the biggest clubs in the world. I wanted to make the transfer and I'm happy that I did. "Everyone talks about winning something and we have to make sure we take that next step. We have the confidence that we can do it. You want to be able to look back and feel you were part of Liverpool's great history – win something here and they will always I want to be remembered as a Liverpool player who was part of something special."

Sadio Mané knew instantly that Liverpool was the right club for him when he met Klopp, as he recalled that first meeting when he was signing from Salzberg with Dortmund also chasing him. Klopp was talking, a lot, while Mané was quiet, as he is a quiet type. He thought it was going to be tricky working for such an extrovert. But as he got to know his manager more, he says: "Klopp is a really nice guy. Everybody loves him and that is more important to be honest (than all the talking!). He is a bit of a funny guy but at the same time he is a serious guy. Usually when I am talking to him off the pitch it is about personal things. Things about lifestyle and life, and that is important to me. I think I have somebody I can confide in"

When asked if Mané specifically was Klopp's favourite, the striker replied: "If I can get to the level of Mo and Sadio maybe I will be his favourite one day."

Mané described his relationship with Klopp whom he describes as a 'great' man. Klopp trusts Mané implicitly, comfortable to deploy the no.10 anywhere across the frontline. There was a time when the strike force relied on Mo Salah, but Mané developed into the teams most important attacker under Klopp's guidance. "His secret, I think, is to be the team's dad. Between us, everything clicked straight away. We all love him like a father and we fear him like one too. He takes up a lot of space in my life, and not just in football. He's great as a person. I trust him blindly, like most of the dressing room, I think. There are a lot of good managers in Europe but what I can say is that our manager always has the right words and the right things to manage his team, especially knowing how to deal with his team. I would always trust his influence on the team. He is a winner and I would say he is the best in the world.'

Klopp marked the four-year anniversary of his appointment in October. Lovren is one of only a handful present since the German's arrival. The Croatia international identified off-the-field instructions which help foster a greater team spirit, "We started to believe when he [Klopp] said: 'From doubters to believers'," said Lovren. "He changed things in the club, from small details like saying good morning to everyone, to cleaning your table. I think some part of these details are missing in some clubs. We are, I think, raised at my age that when you see an older person you will say, 'Good morning'. It is about respect. When you have this outside of the pitch you will feel it also on the pitch. It is simple things. It is about the food as well. He brought in people who are the best in these positions [head of nutrition, Mona Nemmer, from Bayern Munich in 2016], and he knows what he is doing."

Alisson provided an insight into the dressing room philosophy, Klopp's messages and why they are not intimidated by the club's glorious history. The Brazilian No. 1 Alisson said: "I think we, as a team, we are making the things special. The boss keeps us together and we try to make the difference not just on the pitch but off the pitch with the supporters. Every time we say, 'We are Liverpool, this means more' maybe it makes no sense for those who are not Liverpool supporters but we really try to make this special for everybody. Not just for us players, but the supporters also who are all around the world following us. We need to give the best on the pitch. They have already the history but we are making history again. Football is like this. Winning for Liverpool is even more special. We try to do our best, we are thinking about always the next game we have in front of us. We have many games to play, we are just halfway through the season so we have a long way to go and we need to keep playing who we are playing."

James Milner compared Klopp to the formidable former Manchester United manager Sir Alex Ferguson.

Sir Alex promised to "knock Liverpool off their ****ing perch", but now Klopp was looking to knock United off their perch! Klopp famously said he needed to win the Premier League or the Champions League by now "or the next job might be in Switzerland". He landed the Champions League just in time!

Milner launched his book *Ask A Footballer* and told talkSPORT his manager uses press conferences the way managers such as Sir Alex Ferguson did to set the tone for a game. He said: "He's the same as some older managers, like Sir Alex as he thinks the battle starts there. He gives 100 per cent every single day and has been fantastic for the club since he's been here."

Klopp makes his players smile, but he is also strict. Milner said: "The manager is pretty much 'what you see is what you get'. He doesn't have a front for the cameras where he's different behind closed doors. He has that jokey side with us but he can also stick the boot in. He demands the best, the highest standards. He has changed a bit since he came in and realised he can relax a bit more. But the characters in the squad and the players he's got aren't going to take the foot off the gas. You see from him bouncing around on the sidelines how much it means to him."

Klopp is friendly, intense, hands-on, in equal measures. During the off-season and international breaks, Klopp expects regular text message updates from his players, even to the extend to informing their club manager how they feel coming off the pitch, others on set fitness programmes must send daily completion messages. Milner sends a short "Session done" and his manager usually replies with a thumbs-up emoji, and more recently Klopp with cowboy hats. Milner is quite sure what the cowboy hat is supposed to mean! Milner once received a picture message.... Klopp sitting in a hot tub, beaming. "He looked like he was enjoying himself," Milner told the *i* newspaper.

Milner said: "He's not been happy a few times when people haven't messaged him. I don't know if people thought it was a joke the first time he asked and nobody texted him. He said, 'Boys make sure you message me otherwise there's going to be fines bandied about.' It's important, that information.

"That's what he's like: he loves his job, he's 100 per cent in it, he's so focused and demands the highest levels, but he enjoys himself while he does it and can have a joke. Can he do anything to help the player? Can they come back for treatment? He'll be thinking about his next team. He wants to have that information."

Milner can't help but love the way Klopp really wore CR7 boxer shorts did when making his final team talk before Liverpool faced Ronaldo's Real Madrid in the 2018 Champions league Final. "He thinks deeply about what he's going to say before a game – and the CR7 thing broke the ice. This was just before we went to the ground for the final and we had our usual 15-minute meeting. He just lifted his top and had Cristiano's boxer shorts on. Everyone started laughing – as you would before a Champions League final against one of the best players in the world and you're manager's wearing his boxer shorts. He just relaxed everyone. That's why he's such a good manager."

Not so funny, though, when Klopp left Milner out of the next Final despite starting virtually every Champions League game On the bench in the final, but no word of explanation from the boss. "He didn't say anything. He only explained his thinking to me after the game. He said he wanted me on the field at the end. If it got nervy he wanted me playing – especially if it went to extra time or penalties. I was obviously disappointed but you win things as a squad. After a day you think: 'What can I do to help us win this trophy?' Anyway I came on after an hour and we won. When you get over the line it's amazing and you remember all the games you've played – like beating Barcelona 4-0 at Anfield. Winning it was incredible."

Sami Hyypia promised Klopp's players a lifetime of adulation if they landed the title. More than a decade after leaving the club, Hyypia was still revered as part of the miracle of Istanbul in 2005. But landing Liverpool's first League title in 30 years would bring immortality. "Everyone remembers you when you win trophies – even 15 or 20 years on," said Hyypia. "When I'm back in Liverpool, everyone mentions that night in Istanbul in 2005 – something like that stays with the fans. No one forgets those achievements. That's why this city will go crazy if they manage to win the title this year. When we won in Istanbul, the club hadn't won the European Cup for 21 years, so there was great emotion. It was a huge release. And it will be the same next May if we win the title – because it's been so long. There will be wild celebrations and also a place in history for the players. It will be special." Hyypia won't miss the party, after heading home to Finland, following Klopp's triumph in Madrid against Spurs. "Last May, I was in Madrid and people were trying to get me to fly back to Liverpool to celebrate, but I couldn't because I had to be in Finland the next day. "I saw the pictures and the footage of the celebrations and I was sad that I couldn't have been there because it was tremendous," said Hyypia, speaking on behalf of Carlsberg, official beer of Liverpool FC. But I promise I won't miss the party if we become champions next year."

If Klopp delivered a title, he would "never have to do anything again in Liverpool", said Chris Kirkland, who told *Sport Witness*, "Amazing. I've always been a Liverpool fan and my first game was when I was seven years old standing in the Kop. As a Liverpool fan, it's brilliant. It's exciting times. I think Jürgen deserves a lot of credit. Three or four years ago, there was a bit of negativity around the club, but he's brought the whole club back together. I go down to Melwood quite a bit and am lucky enough to watch the training. No matter who's down there, whether it's the person taking the bins out, someone cooking the food or washing the kit, he treats everyone exactly the same way. He's got so much time for everybody and has brought that feel-good factor back. The fans know that – they adore him and they won the Champions League last year. If he can get us the league title for the first time in 30 years, he'll never have to do anything again in Liverpool because he'll be a hero. There's a long way to go. Sunday (the win against Man City) was a huge game and nine points is a big gap. But it's Man City you're talking about – they pulled it back last year. But I'm hoping this is the year. It's been bubbling for a couple of years, we won the Champions League last year for the first time since 2005. It's been bubbling since he [Klopp] came to the club and he's transformed it completely. They have some world-class players. If we can keep the big players fit… I think in the next two months they play Saturday-Tuesday-Sunday-Wednesday every week after the international break until Christmas, so that's going to be a challenging period for them to keep everyone fit. But if they do that, I'm definitely backing them to win it."

AUGUST

SUNDAY 4 AUGUST - COMMUNITY SHIELD - WEMBLEY
LIVERPOOL 1
Matip (76)
MAN CITY 1
Sterling (10)
City win 5-4 on penalties

Manchester City won the Community Shield on penalties, edging Liverpool out at Wembley to take the first piece of silverware of the new season but Liverpool looked good enough to challenge champions City for sure, and the Shield went to Pep Guardiola only after Georginio Wijnaldum's penalty was saved by Claudio Bravo, before Gabriel Jesus scored the winning kick.

The first confrontation of the new season between the two outstanding sides in the country did not disappoint. Raheem Sterling scored his first goal against his old club when he turned home David Silva's flick-on from close range. In the second half Sterling struck the post, van Dijk's shot hit the underside of the bar and Salah hit a post, but they finally levelled when Joel Matip headed home Van Dijk's cross. At that stage Liverpool looked the most likely, with Salah having at least three chances – coming closest when his header was incredibly cleared off the line by a Kyle Walker bicycle kick. The showpiece opener of the season went straight to penalties, with City scoring all of theirs. It had been an entertaining start to the season, but both clubs had far bigger fish to fry.

A change to the way City played saw Bravo take short goal-kicks in his box to Nicolas Otamendi, taking advantage of the new laws allowing passing teams like City and Liverpool to take advantage. Liverpool were determined to make sure the domestic season, at least, doesn't end the way it began last year, with City winning the Community Shield, and ending up with a domestic treble.

Before the game, Jürgen Klopp was surprised the Community Shield is not taken more seriously and questioned the point of it all. It was the first of seven competitions Liverpool would take part in this season, with their Premier League opener against Norwich followed by the UEFA Super Cup against Chelsea in Istanbul. Despite his reservations, Klopp named the strongest team he could - including nine who started the Champions League final in June. Mané had yet to return to training after his Africa Cup of Nations final defeat, while Firmino and Salah played less than 90 minutes in pre-season friendlies after summer internationals.

City and Liverpool had produced one of the great title races in 2018/19, with Guardiola's side beating Klopp's 98 points to 97, and judging by this game, it would be a battle between the two again. Before the game there were the usual mind games, Klopp's barbs about spending that Guardiola did not appreciate. Guardiola got so animated at giving instructions during a break in play that he came onto the pitch and was shown a yellow card, another of football's new laws.

KLOPP: "Wow, it was a really good performance, a powerful one in the second half. Both teams had a similar pre-season. I spoke to Kevin de Bruyne after the game and we both said we don't really know where we are yet. The least we deserved was the equaliser, one save decided it and I cannot be disappointed today. The performance was much more important than a win. We know we are still here, we can still play proper football."

PEP GUARDIOLA: "An incredible final from both sides. No team can dominate for 90 minutes. We had real good moments. In the last 15 minutes we were exhausted and they had chances to win the game. It was a good test for both teams. It's nice for the players to realise what they will face this season. At this level the difference is nothing. One penalty, one point. Manchester United will be back, Arsenal, Tottenham, Chelsea... I don't know what will happen."

FRIDAY 9 AUGUST - PREMIER LEAGUE

LIVERPOOL 4
Hanley (og) (5), Salah (17), van Dijk (26), Origi (39)
NORWICH CITY 1
Pukki (62)

Liverpool began their 2019/20 title charge with an emphatic 4-1 thrashing of newly-promoted Norwich at Anfield on Sky's *Friday Night Football*, racing into a four-goal lead at the break with strikes from Salah, van Dijk, Origi and a Hanley own goal. Teemu Pukki gave the travelling fans something to cheer with a consolation on 64 minutes. It took just seven minutes for Liverpool to open their account; Origi's cross from the left cannoned in off the unfortunate Hanley, who got his legs in a tangle. But it wasn't all plain-sailing as Liverpool lost Alisson to a calf injury just before half-time, the only negative for Klopp on a night The Reds issued an early statement of intent at the start of their bid for a first league title in 30 years.

The Canaries were lively early on and ruffled a few Liver bird feathers before Liverpool's fortunate opening goal. Even then their enterprising football was impressive and suggested they might survive in the top flight. On goalkeeper Alisson Klopp said, "It's not good for us. We have to see how serious it is. It's a calf, that's it. He couldn't carry on, that's not a good sign. The scoreline tells the story of the first 60 minutes. We were really sharp from the first whistle, we did what we wanted to do, we scored goals. There's a lot of space for improvement but a lot of things were there today as well. We should have controlled the game more and kept the ball. It is normal when you're not physically at your highest level and you lose a bit of your concentration. The boys were good, and we deserved the three points, which is the most important. I'm very happy with the start, but the Alisson situation is a shadow on that game.'

KLOPP: "For 60 minutes we looked very sharp, then we have to control the game a bit more. Norwich have all my respect - they stayed cheeky, they enjoyed their football. At the start of the second half we could have scored a fifth or sixth goal, then Norwich scored. After that we were never in danger but had to work hard to keep the score what it was. The players had a break (over the summer). For the body it was

August

long enough, nobody asked for longer, so they didn't lose a lot of their physical standards. We have to be a bit smart for the next two games, we have to make a few decisions and try to win both of those games, which will be difficult."

DANIEL FARKE: "We're disappointed. We were greedy, we wanted to be the first team in two-and-a-half years to win here. But I'm totally in love with this team. The mentality to win the second half in front of an excited home crowd, we showed great character. No-one wanted to hear it at half-time, but I told them we had the same possession and had created more chances. Liverpool had scored four though. It was tough to take but I felt we were not too far away from a good result."

OTHER SCORES

SATURDAY 10 AUGUST
West Ham United 0 Manchester City 5
AFC Bournemouth 1 Sheffield United 1
Burnley 3 Southampton 0
Crystal Palace 0 Everton 0
Watford 0 Brighton & Hove Albion 3
Tottenham Hotspur 3 Aston Villa 1

SUNDAY 11 AUGUST
Leicester City 0 Wolverhampton Wanderers 0
Newcastle United 0 Arsenal 1
Manchester United 4 Chelsea 0

WEDNESDAY 14 AUGUST - EUROPEAN SUPER CUP

LIVERPOOL 2
Mané (46, 96)
CHELSEA 2
Giroud (34), Jorginho (pen) (101)
After Extra Time - Liverpool win 5-4 on penalties

Liverpool landed their second big European prize within three months, albeit on penalties but this time, what a story it turned out to be for Klopp's stand in keeper Adrian, who weeks after training with a semi-pro team, saved a penalty to win the European Super Cup. Champions League holders Liverpool and Europa League winners Chelsea finished extra time at 2-2, and in the shoot out Adrian made the crucial save

Jurgen Klopp and his coaching staff celebrate winning the Super Cup

with his legs to deny Tammy Abraham and give his team a 5-4 win on penalties, in his first start for Liverpool after regular goalkeeper Alisson suffered a calf injury last Friday in the Premier League opener.

Klopp couldn't help himself in a typically unusual celebration. "What a story," Klopp said. "Adrian! Like Rocky! He kept his nerves together. He's loud in the dressing room already. I don't think he's won a lot in his life so it's good for him to win it. He made some unbelievable saves, both keepers did, so I'm really happy for him."

Chelsea took the lead in the 36th minute when Christian Pulisic exposed poor positioning by right back Joe Gomez to pass for Olivier Giroud to shoot low past Adrian. Liverpool stormed back after the break, Fabinho's 48th-minute pass opening up the Chelsea defence and leaving Sadio Mané with an easy finish off Mohamed Salah's flick. In extra time, Mané put Liverpool ahead from a Roberto Firmino cross, but Chelsea quickly responded with a penalty from Jorginho. Stephanie Frappart, the first female referee to oversee a major men's European final, had denied Liverpool a penalty after just six minutes when Mané's overhead kick hit Andreas Christensen's arm, which seemed to be out of a strictly "natural" position. There was no full review by the video assistant referee system. Twice Chelsea put the ball into the net through Pulisic and substitute Mason Mount, but Frappart and her assistants ruled both efforts out for offside.

Skipper Jordan Henderson praised Adrian, "I'm delighted for Adrian who's just come into the club and he's the hero. We're delighted to win because we want to win as many trophies as we can, so we'll enjoy it tonight but then focus on recovering for a big game on Saturday."

Adrian said: "Welcome to Liverpool! It's been a crazy week. I'm really happy for the team, I'm happy to play for Liverpool and happy for the fans. It was a long game but in the end a great finish for us."

KLOPP: "It was a very difficult game for both teams. It was all about winning it and we did that in the end. Nobody in the stadium wanted extra time, it was a killer. I'm not sure about the penalty but who cares now. We started well then dropped off... we could talk about football but it's too late now. We had to fight and the boys did tonight."

FRANK LAMPARD: "I've got nothing but pride in the team and the performance, and confidence in what that means. It was a tough game against a good Liverpool team that had extra time to recover after the weekend. But sometimes football comes down to little moments of luck."

SATURDAY 17 AUGUST - PREMIER LEAGUE

SOUTHAMPTON 1
Ings (81)

LIVERPOOL 2
Mané (44), Firmino (69)

After triumphing in the Super Cup Liverpool beat Southampton 2-1 on the south coast to secure an 11th successive top-flight victory, equalling their best-ever Premier League winning run - despite a late blunder by Adrian who cleared against the shin of substitute Danny Ings to gift the Saints striker a goal against his former club. Sadio Mané had put Liverpool ahead at the end of the first-half with a delicious arrowed finish from the edge of the penalty area. Adrian, who was passed fit despite an ankle injury in a collision with a pitch invader following the UEFA Super Cup win over Chelsea, had earlier kept out Yoshida's header. Mané turned provider to set up Firmino to double Liverpool's advantage with a clever finish. Adrian's error could have been even more costly for the Reds because in a dramatic finale Ings wasted a great chance to equalise inside the six-yard area.

KLOPP: "Adrian had a swollen ankle and we played too many balls back to him in that period," said Klopp. "The other players have to then feel more the responsibility for the build-up and cannot give all the balls back to him and hope the pain killers still help or whatever. I don't think the goal was because of that, but a few other balls were. He is completely good with his feet."

OTHER SCORES

SATURDAY 17 AUGUST
Arsenal 2 Burnley 1
Aston Villa 1 AFC Bournemouth 2
Brighton & Hove Albion 1 West Ham United 1
Everton 1 Watford 0
Norwich City 3 Newcastle United 1
Manchester City 2 Tottenham Hotspur 2

SUNDAY 18 AUGUST
Sheffield United 1 Crystal Palace 0
Chelsea 1 Leicester City 1

MONDAY 19 AUGUST
Wolverhampton Wanderers 1 Manchester United 1

SATURDAY 24 AUGUST – PREMIER LEAGUE

LIVERPOOL 3
Matip (39), Salah (Pen) (48), Salah (58)
ARSENAL 1
Torreira (84)

Liverpool and Arsenal had made perfect starts so something had to give at Anfield in the third league game of the season and it was Liverpool that maintained their 100% winning record with a 3-1 win, their third consecutive win of the campaign, as Matip's header and Salah's second-half brace secured the points at Anfield.

Just before half-time, Liverpool took the lead. A superb out-swinging corner from Alexander-Arnold picked out Matip before Salah netted a ten-minute brace, while the Gunners managed only a consolation goal with five minutes left.

Klopp spoke of his side's greater desire, the way they had done the good things from the earlier weeks of the season for longer, but he acknowledged his team need to control games better. "I was really happy with a lot of parts of the game; I think everything we did well in the first four games we did tonight for longer, more precise and better tuned. I loved the desire, the passion, the power and the energy that we put into this game. It made us really uncomfortable to play against, which is what we wanted and so we deserved the first goal."

Reflecting on the goals, Klopp added: "It was a very determined header as well; Joel was there – big Joel – and scored a fantastic goal. In the second half then, there was the clear penalty. We played nice passes and we were there with a lot of good moments, football moments, today – but you need these decisive moments. The penalty was nicely taken and then the third goal is just incredible again – a really, really good goal."

Klopp was keen to point out that his side still had things to work on, admitting his player's game management had been poor at times. "So, pretty much the story of the game; we could have controlled it better, that's probably our real challenge. [When we were 3-0 up] Arsenal didn't really press anymore, they were deep, together, and we passed the ball into their legs and that makes no sense. It was a brilliant game from my side so early in the season. It was outstanding. It was a performance full of power, energy, greed and passion, which I think you need to have against a team like Arsenal. We are still really early in the season and throwing such energy on the pitch is exceptional. The work rate of the whole team was exceptional. Tactical discipline was exceptional apart from maybe 10-15 minutes."

Mo Salah was the decisive figure – turning David Luiz to gain a penalty which he blasted home in the 49th minute and then beating Arsenal's former Chelsea defender out wide before scoring an outstanding solo goal.

KLOPP: "It was a performance full of power, energy, greed and passion, which I think you need against a team like Arsenal. The last 10 minutes I saw the possession - 53 to 47% or something like that - but over 80 minutes it must have been completely different. We were completely in charge of the game. We are not Disneyland, we do not need to excite everyone in every second."

UNAI EMERY: "We were doing some transitions very good and we had some chances but, in the second half, the penalty was very soft. After 2-0 our reaction was good. We needed to attack and take a different moment in the match. We are disappointed we lost 3-1 but watching some players we can be optimistic. We need to improve in possession and countering the pressure but Liverpool is the best team with this. We have to be realistic but we can fight closer to them."

OTHER SCORES

FRIDAY 23 AUGUST
Aston Villa 2 Everton 0

SATURDAY 24 AUGUST
Norwich City 2 Chelsea 3
Brighton & Hove Albion 0 Southampton 2
Manchester United 1 Crystal Palace 2
Sheffield United 1 Leicester City 2
Watford 1 West Ham United 3

SUNDAY 25 AUGUST
AFC Bournemouth 1 Manchester City 3
Tottenham Hotspur 0 Newcastle United 1
Wolverhampton Wanderers 1 Burnley 1

SATURDAY 31 AUGUST – PREMIER LEAGUE

BURNLEY 0

LIVERPOOL 3
Wood (OG) (31), Mané (35), Firmino (80)

There was a moment of controversy in the fourth game of the season when Sadio Mané reacted to being substituted in the 3-0 win over Burnley at Turf Moor. Jürgen Klopp praised his forward line for helping the club achieve a 13-match winning run in the league, a new club record. They were only the second English top-flight side to win 13 in a row while scoring more than once each time (after Tottenham in 1960). But in the 85th minute with the Reds 3-0 up, Mané walked off making a gesture to the bench and continued to be animated as he sat down, frustrated at Salah's decision not to pass to him in the opposition area moments earlier. Klopp laughed off the incident: "But it's good eh? He was upset, it was obvious. Sadio cannot hide his emotions, I like that. But it's all sorted. We spoke about it and everything is fine. We are individuals, we are emotional. It was a situation in a game. What else could have happened? It was not a phone call."

Mané, Roberto Firmino and a fluke own goal helped the Reds maintain their 100% start to their title campaign. The breakthrough came in the 33rd minute when Alexander-Arnold's intended cross to the far post brushed the back of Chris Wood and sailed over the head of the stranded Nick Pope. Soon after the restart skipper Ben Mee inadvertently found Reds forward Firmino with a short pass, who found Mané who fired low past Pope. Finally, Firmino fired in from the edge of the area after he was teed up by Salah. Firmino became the first Brazilian to score 50 Premier League goals; the ninth player to reach the milestone for Liverpool overall - no other club has had more (level with Manchester United).

Klopp was surprised the league leaders had extended their winning streak, because none of his front three had a full pre-season as Mané and Salah played at the African Cup of Nations, while Firmino competed at the Copa America. "If you ask me four weeks ago I wouldn't expect it would happen," said Klopp. "We had a tricky pre-season. No pre-season for the front three but they still deliver. So far, so good."

OTHER SCORES
SATURDAY 31 AUGUST
Southampton 1 Manchester United 1
Chelsea 2 Sheffield United 2
Crystal Palace 1 Aston Villa 0
Leicester City 3 AFC Bournemouth 1
Manchester City 4 Brighton & Hove Albion 0
Newcastle United 1 Watford 1
West Ham United 2 Norwich City 0
SUNDAY 1 SEPTEMBER
Everton 3 Wolverhampton Wanderers 2
Arsenal 2 Tottenham Hotspur 2

SEPTEMBER

SATURDAY 14 SEPTEMBER – PREMIER LEAGUE

LIVERPOOL 3
Mané (26, 38), Salah (72)

NEWCASTLE 1
Willems (5)

Following an international break, Liverpool shrugged off an early scare to sweep past Newcastle and maintain their 100% start with another dominant attacking display and a 3-1 win at Anfield. Mané scored twice in the first half after Jetro Willems' fine first goal for Newcastle gave Steve Bruce's side a surprise early lead, which turned out to be their only shot on target in the entire match! Salah added a third after the break, with the third member of Liverpool's attacking trinity, Firmino, providing two brilliant assists and stealing the show with a superb man-of-the-match performance from the bench. The Reds had now won 14 league games in a row, stretching back to a draw at Everton in March – the joint third-best winning run in English top-flight history – as they went five points clear at the top after second-placed Manchester City surprisingly lost 3-2 at Norwich in the evening game in one of the shocks of the season so far.

The spotlight was on Salah and Mané after their disagreement at Burnley, but whatever the tensions off the field, there was only unison and joy on it. As Firmino had played an hour for Brazil in Los Angeles in midweek in a game that finished at 06:00 BST on Wednesday morning, the plan was to give him some rest as Origi started on the left of the front three. But an injury for the Belgium striker meant the Brazil forward was introduced earlier than anticipated. Mané had already equalised by that point, collecting a pass from Robertson and curling superbly into the top corner. Salah celebrated with a punch of the air, so there was no animosity between the pair for sure.

Firmino then robbed Atsu and slid in Mané with a beautiful pass. The Newcastle keeper Martin Dubravka should have gathered it but pushed it back towards Mané to allow the Liverpool forward to tap-in for his 19th goal in his last 21 Premier League appearances at Anfield. After the break Firmino was even more impressive, laying on chances for both his full-backs before setting up the previously quiet Salah with a wonderful assist. Receiving the ball with his back to goal, the Brazilian dragged the ball back then back-heeled it into the path of Salah, who did the rest.

Manchester City's record of 18 top-flight wins in a row remained within sight as did Chelsea's record of nine victories in a row at the start of a Premier League season.

KLOPP: "I started enjoying it after 35 minutes when we arrived in the game. It was difficult, Newcastle did what they did and did it well. They had the speed to go in behind on the break, it was not easy. We played them onside for the goal unfortunately and that made the game not easy. We had some time to set the rhythm, we had to play much quicker and then we had chances. We scored two wonderful goals. I'm not too pleased about coming from behind. We have to learn from the game. The challenge is always after the international break to find a common rhythm again. The boys have played in different ways for different countries and we have one-and-a-half days to work on it again."

BRUCE: "We were OK in bits. Unfortunately we made a mistake for the second goal and we are disappointed about that. When you come to an arena like this and give the ball away in the middle of the pitch you are in trouble. Our keeper will think he should do better. Jetro will remember that, it's not often you smash into the top corner with your wrong foot. He has been thrown in at the deep end with us but the more he plays in the Premier League, you can see the ability he has got. Liverpool are as good as you get. You can understand why they are European champions and lost once last year. They are an excellent, excellent team with pace and creativity and at the top end of the pitch they damage you. They are going to be there or thereabouts."

OTHER SCORES

SATURDAY 14 SEPTEMBER
Brighton & Hove Albion 1 Burnley 1
Manchester United 1 Leicester City 0
Sheffield United 0 Southampton 1
Tottenham Hotspur 4 Crystal Palace 0

Wolverhampton Wanderers 2 Chelsea 5
Norwich City 3 Manchester City 2

SUNDAY 15 SEPTEMBER

AFC Bournemouth 3 Everton 1
Watford 2 Arsenal 2

MONDAY 16 SEPTEMBER

Aston Villa 0 West Ham United 0

TUESDAY 17 SEPTEMBER – CHAMPIONS LEAGUE

NAPOLI 2

LIVERPOOL 0

Mertens (Pen) 80', Llorente 90'

Jurgen Klopp signalled the start of the defence of the Champions League telling his players they must prove themselves again as they return to the scene of a rare European humbling in Naples. Klopp had a thirst for more, and sensed that his players did too. Before Klopp and his players secured Anfield immortality, they were outplayed and beaten by Napoli in the group stage. Klopp was typically colourful, recalling Carlo Ancelotti's tactical tweaks on that particular evening. "To make it very simple, we played against them in our defending like they had one No.6 but they had two, the cheeky b-------," said Klopp. "We tried to change it in the game and nobody listened and nobody could change and in the end they were lucky they scored but we were lucky it was only 1-0. It was really this kind of day off."

Lorenzo Insigne's 89th-minute winner in the San Paolo stadium that night hardly looked like the prelude to such glory later in the tournament. Liverpool fans might want to banish 30 years of hurt to win the title, but tell Klopp the focus was on domestic matters and you'd get short shrift. Klopp was adamant he and his players were eager to reaffirm their status as Europe's No 1. "I do not know the last time I thought about winning the Champions League without being asked about it," said Klopp. "It must be months ago. I don't wake up and think about this. Nothing has changed for me. I was self-confident before. I have never had an issue with self-confidence. The boys are young and feel they have things to prove. Not to me. To the outside world, to go for the next one. And the competition in this team is really big. You cannot imagine how normal it is to carry on after all the celebrations.

September

It is so easy to carry on as normal if you have the right character. If you go nuts and start taking drugs and drinking and driving and leave your missus at home because you are now a Champions League winner, I cannot help you. But we are not like that. We want to create more stories to remember in the future not just this one.

"This is a really big club with competition between friends. It is not 'I have to kill him to play', it is really for the team. That is what the boys did so far and as long as we have that we will go for everything. Then we have to see what we get because we have really good opponents. That is the problem."

There was a feeling of deja vu as late goals from Dries Mertens and Fernando Llorente earned Napoli a 2-0 victory as Liverpool made a disappointing start to their defence. For the second campaign in a row, Klopp's side were beaten in the group stage in Naples, and more sloppy defending saw the Group E game slip away from them in the final minutes. The Reds defended against some sustained pressure from the home side, but were unlucky to be punished when Jose Callejon skipped inside of Robertson before making the most of minimal contact and, when a VAR review failed to give the visitors a reprieve, Mertens took full advantage to beat Adrian from the spot."

"For me it's clear and obvious, no penalty, because Callejon jumps before he has any contact," Klopp complained after the game. As Liverpool pushed for a late equaliser, Llorente scored during added-on time after a rare van Dijk mistake, profiting when the defender's mis-hit pass ran into his path and he slotted the ball home to spark wild celebrations on the home bench. Llorente had been in the defeated Spurs squad in last season's final. The reigning champions of Europe were beaten in the first game of their defence for the first time since AC Milan in 1994.

Liverpool chief executive Peter Moore tended to a supporter hospitalised in Naples by fan violence as the build-up to the Reds' opening Champions League tie was marred as Merseyside Police confirmed two men were injured in an assault in the Italian city. One was "believed to have passed out at the stadium and was taken to hospital for a check-up... and has since been discharged", according to a statement from the force. Moore tweeted he had been at a hospital in the city with one of those supporters following an appeal on social media. Moore said: "I'm at the hospital with Steven right now. We will not leave him until we are comfortable that he's fine, so can everyone stop worrying for now. Trying to get him seen by a doctor, but there's a distinct lack of urgency here from the police and medical staff." Later he added: "Update to this. The hospital staff and the police have now helped Steven and been very cooperative. He's been seen and will be monitored throughout the night. He asked me to thank everyone for their concern."

SUNDAY 22 SEPTEMBER - PREMIER LEAGUE

CHELSEA 1
Kanté (70)

LIVERPOOL 2
Alexander-Arnold (12), Firmino (28)

After defeat in Naples in the first Champions League game, Liverpool bounced back with goals from Trent Alexander-Arnold and Roberto Firmino to secure their 15th straight win with a 2-1 triumph over Chelsea at Stamford Bridge. Alexander-Arnold's thunderbolt and Firmino's free header, either side of a disallowed Azpilicueta equaliser, saw the league leaders open up a two-goal lead inside half an hour at Stamford Bridge. N'Golo Kante's brilliant solo effort set up a tense final 19 minutes in which substitute Batshuayi and Mount spurned glorious chances to earn the Londoners a point. Manchester City's 8-0 demolition of Watford on the Saturday had underlined the reigning champion's determination not to relinquish their crown without a fight, but another hard fought victory on tricky away territory proved yet again the Reds were more than capable of going toe to toe with their title rivals.

KLOPP: "The first half was hard work. It is about momentum in games like this and I think we got that in the first half. We scored two wonderful goals and we could have scored directly after half time two more. We deserved the three points, it is difficult to win here. We are only here. Chelsea, six matches in. We haven't won anything domestic apart from games so we have to carry on. We have to be ready for each opponent. They are all waiting and want to give us a knock, rightly so, but we have to be ready to do what we have to do."

FRANK LAMPARD: "Performance-wise we were the better team. We had more energy in our game, character and spirit. That's why the crowd applauded at the end. Let's take this forward. We have to get on with it [VAR]. It is a sad thing for the celebration and the moment but if we are looking for correct decisions that is where we are at. It changes the atmosphere in the crowd, on the pitch. We are slightly deflated and they get a boost. We deserved to be level at that point."

OTHER SCORES

FRIDAY 20TH SEPTEMBER
Southampton 1 AFC Bournemouth 3
SATURDAY 21ST SEPTEMBER
Leicester City 2 Tottenham Hotspur 1
Burnley 2 Norwich City 0
Everton 0 Sheffield United 2
Manchester City 8 Watford 0
Newcastle United 0 Brighton & Hove Albion 0
SUNDAY 22ND SEPTEMBER
Crystal Palace 1 Wolverhampton Wanderers 1
West Ham United 2 Manchester United 0
Arsenal 3 Aston Villa 2

WEDNESDAY 25TH SEPTEMBER
CARABAO CUP SECOND ROUND

MK DONS 0
LIVERPOOL 2
Milner (48), Hoever (68)

Klopp named four teenagers in his starting line-up - including 16-year-old Harvey Elliott - but it was 33-year-old jAMES Milner's experience that ensured the Reds won their first game in the competition for almost three years. Milner opened the scoring before providing the cross for 17-year-old Ki-Jana Hoever to score his first senior goal.

"This man is on fire," said Klopp of Milner "He is a real role model for young players. The team had a lack of experience and a lack of rhythm and the player with the most experience and rhythm was the best player."

A howler by keeper Stuart Moore set Klopp's much-changed side on their way against League One MK Dons. Moore appeared to have

Milner's fierce strike covered but the ball bounced off his chest and squirmed into the net in front of a club record 28,521 attendance at Stadium MK. It was Milner's first goal in the competition since the 2010 final for Aston Villa against Manchester United.

MK Dons missed two glorious chances through Conor McGrandles and Sam Nombe, while Jordan Bowery hit the post in the second half before Hoever's powerful header sealed Liverpool's place in the last 16. Elliott, one of three debutants in Liverpool's line-up, hit the bar twice - as well as missing another chance from close range. Aged 16 years and 174 days, former Fulham midfielder Elliott made history as the youngest ever player to start a competitive match for Liverpool.

SATURDAY 28 SEPTEMBER - PREMIER LEAGUE

SHEFF UTD 0
LIVERPOOL 1
Wijnaldum (68)

Liverpool edged a tight game against the Blades who had proved to be the surprise package of the Premier League thus far. It meant that the Anfield club had won their first seven games of a league season for only the second time, (the last time in 1990-91) and had opened up a five-point lead at the top of the table. Earlier in the week the Champions League winners failed in their attempt to copyright the word Liverpool and this performance also lacked their usual trademark!

Yet Klopp's side had now won their last 16 Premier League games, their best ever top-flight winning streak and one bettered only by Manchester City in the Premier League, and a pattern to the season was beginning to emerge.

Klopp said Liverpool "deserved" their victory despite a "lucky" Georginio Wijnaldum goal to continue their perfect start to the Premier League season at a raucous Bramall Lane. The winner was a moment to forget for the otherwise faultless Blades goalkeeper Dean Henderson, who spilled the Dutchman's tame effort before it squirmed agonisingly over the line. His side were far from their best in South Yorkshire. Substitute Leon Clarke, making his Premier League debut at the age of 34, should have levelled it late on, but blazed over.

When the story of the 2019-20 season is told, this will be looked back on as one of Liverpool's most crucial but perhaps fortunate victories. Liverpool's first clear chance came from a long ball over the top from Virgil van Dijk, but Sadio Mané's finish when through on goal was wayward, while the Senegal forward later struck the post.

There was a penalty appeal for Lundstram's challenge on Mané which wasn't given as it seemed that Liverpool may have to settle for a point.

With time running out Klopp withdrew Jordan Henderson for Divock Origi and the move to a 4-2-3-1 formation ultimately paid off when Wijnaldum's goal on 70 minutes was their first shot on target at last season's Championship runners-up. Wijnaldum's was Liverpool's first shot on target of the game, the longest the Reds have had to wait for a shot on target in the Premier League since 6th December 2015, courtesy of Dejan Lovren's effort against Newcastle on 89 minutes.

As far as their quest for that elusive first Premier League title began to take shape, ex-boss Brendan Rodgers and his Leicester City side would provide another stern test in their next league game.

KLOPP: "It's normal you have to work hard for the points," said Klopp. "You have to stay concentrated and do the right things. We did today. It was never a clicking day, it was an average day. We were deserved winners. If it's 0-0 we cannot moan and would not. But if there's one winner it should be us. We worked had for it. Winning in days like this is extremely worthy. We scored a lucky goal, we know that. But the boys worked so hard for it."

WILDER: "I am not bothered about pride, I am bothered about the result. Liverpool had an off day and I think we missed an opportunity. In pressurised situations we need to remain composed. We were delighted with the shape but their chances came from our mistakes. We have had big moments in the game but we did not take them. We had to jump all over it and we didn't. We had enough to get something out of this game but we did not take our opportunities. Points are the most important thing and we did not get the points we deserved today."

OTHER SCORES
SATURDAY 28 SEPTEMBER
Aston Villa 2 Burnley 2
AFC Bournemouth 2 West Ham United 2
Chelsea 2 Brighton & Hove Albion 0

Champions At Last!

Crystal Palace 2 Norwich City 0
Tottenham Hotspur 2 Southampton 1
Wolverhampton Wanderers 2 Watford 0
Everton 1 Manchester City 3

SUNDAY 29 SEPTEMBER

Leicester City 5 Newcastle United 0

MONDAY 30 SEPTEMBER

Manchester United 1 Arsenal 1

OCTOBER

WEDNESDAY 2 OCTOBER - CHAMPIONS LEAGUE

LIVERPOOL 4
Mané (7), Robertson (23), Salah (34), Salah (68);
SALZBURG 3
Hee-Chan (38), Minamino (55), Håland (60)

Jurgen Klopp wasn't too happy with his team's loss of control after taking a commanding lead only to end up scraped through a dramatic clash against Red Bull Salzburg with a critical win as Anfield witnessed the first away goal from a European team since last September as Liverpool - who had led 3-0 - won 4-3. The last team to score three in a Champions league tie fixture at Anfield was Real Madrid in October 2014 but Liverpool created their own tough predicament having led 3-0 at one stage then becoming far too over-confident. Following a 0-0 draw between Napoli and Genk, the other two teams in Group E, Liverpool were firmly in control of their destiny.

"We lost control of the game," said Klopp, whose side were cruising after first half goals from Mane, Robertson and Salah. "The momentum changed completely [when Salzburg scored their first goal] and it was really difficult to get a foot in the game again. I am not angry or anything like that. I saw us playing very well then we took the wrong decisions. Half-time we tried to change but momentum is a really important thing. We didn't get it until the scoresheet was finally equal. Then we got a really important and nice goal (from Salah). We want to win the game, we did that and now it's fine. It is better you learn the lesson in the game and sort it during the game but you have to talk about it after the game. We made it more intense than necessary. The mistake we made was we lost control. We opened the door for Salzburg."

Erling Haaland, the highly-regarded teenager, scored Red Bull's equaliser and a huge shock looked imminent. Coach, Jesse Marsch, felt his team were in awe of Liverpool to start and that ultimately cost them. "At 2-0 we made a formation switch," said Marsch. "The goal before half-time was really big for us. At 3-3, our guys put a lot into it. The energy of the stadium picked up and it is an incredible team we are playing. We had too much respect for them in the first half."

Klopp threatened to walk out of Liverpool if a video of his half-time team talk was released. Marsch defended his club's decision to publish his passionate Anfield half-time team talk. Marsch admitted it was "not so pleasant" for him to watch back but believed fans would appreciate the footage. "We have this documentary. And usually, it will be released maybe four weeks later, and then the emotion is gone for the moment," Marsch said. "It's for people to see what's happening right now. It was not so pleasant for us all. But this is real. This is us. From the beginning, I've heard in Europe, and I've seen that the dressing room is closed and only for the team. Yes, that's also true for me."

Marsch could be heard telling his players to target van Dijk and aired his frustration at his side's first half performance, 3-1 down at the break but came back to level 15 minutes into the second half before Salah's winning goal.

"Realistic situations of life and people are always interesting. And I think at this moment we have an interesting team with many good players and a good history," added the American coach. "Klopp is in a very different situation than Salzburg. The coach is an employee. And so I have to represent this club, and at this moment it's a new story for Salzburg. And I am here to help in this moment. But I'm not the owner; I'm not the sports director, I'm not the manager. I am the coach. My job is to help the club. And I think this documentary is an important moment for our club."

SATURDAY 5 OCTOBER - PREMIER LEAGUE

LIVERPOOL 2
Mané (39), Milner (Pen) (90+5')

LEICESTER 1
Maddison (80)

Liverpool needed James Milner's injury-time penalty to earn a dramatic win over in-form Leicester City to maintained Liverpool's flawless start to the league season. Brendan Rodgers' side looked to be on course for a hard-earned point on his return to Anfield after Maddison's low finish 10 minutes from time equalised Mané's 40th-minute strike but deep

The current Liverpool boss and his predecessor but only one was smiling at full-time.

in stoppage time, a communication breakdown between Schmeichel and substitute Albrighton ended with the latter bringing down Mané, the penalty awarded after consultation with VAR and Klopp celebrated wildly as Rodgers turned away in despair.

This had been the closest Liverpool had come to dropping points, but once again late Anfield drama provided a twist. Mané was not just his usual attacking threat - scoring his 50th top flight goal for the Reds after racing on to Milner's pass and expertly beating Schmeichel in the first half - he also worked tirelessly in his defensive duties to subdue the threat of full-back Ben Chilwell in the first half. The Senegal forward was now regarded as world-class and came to Liverpool's aid once more when it looked like the visitors would repeat their feat of last season and leave Anfield with a draw. Mané, making his 100th league appearance for Liverpool, scored his 50th Premier League goal for the Reds, the 10th player to reach the milestone for the club in the competition, more than any other side.

Liverpool's run of 17 Premier League victories was bettered only by City's sequence of 18 wins between August and December 2017. They were also unbeaten in 44 league games at home - 34 wins and 10 draws - the longest current run in Europe's top five leagues. Milner's penalty was the 34th time Liverpool scored a 90th-minute winning goal in a Premier League match - at least nine more than any other side. Liverpool were the first to win their opening eight matches of an English top-flight season twice, having also done so in the 1990-91 season. Yet Liverpool were not at their fluent best but, like at Sheffield United, they got a break when they needed one.

Leicester City had arrived at Anfield with many tipping them as serious top-four contenders given the crisis at Tottenham and the transitions taking place at Chelsea and Manchester United. A very impressive side, superbly organised by former Reds boss Brendan Rodgers, would, as the season progressed establish their credentials as much more than just a top four contender, so it was imperative to have won this game in the grander scheme of things.

Klopp was livid with Choudhury's tackle on Salah when the game was 1-1 and Salah was racing towards the opposition box when Choudhury scythed the Egyptian down. The referee brandished a yellow, but it merited a red. Salah was eventually forced off and needed a scan. "It was just a challenge which I really don't understand. I don't understand how he can do it, because the ball is far away. The player is in full sprint, to bring him down without the ball around, for me there is only one colour card. I might be the only one who sees it like this, but it is dangerous as hell. How can Mo be okay? Mo limped off the pitch. That's hard. It was done to slow Mo down and that is not OK."

Leicester felt they had done enough to earn a point and their frustrations boiled over at the final whistle, with substitute Ayoze Perez involved in angry exchanges with several Liverpool players - who were celebrating extending their lead over City to eight points. Perez was involved in a scuffle with Robertson, with others trying to break things up.

But was the result lucky? No way, at least according to the manager; Klopp dismissed the notion although Brendan Rodgers felt Liverpool were fortunate. Nevertheless, Klopp was full of praise for Rodgers but warned that they will find it hard to play so well if they qualify for European football next season. "This one [win] alone feels already big enough, to be honest, because of how difficult this league is [and] how difficult the life of an LFC player is. I think Leicester at the end of the season will be in the top four and then they will realise how different it is when you play Wednesday, Saturday, Wednesday, Saturday. The quality they have is already good and we all know Brendan, what a sensational manager he is and what he's doing with them. So it was difficult, but for 60 minutes we were the clear better side. We played really good football, we forced ourselves for a proper performance, to be honest, but with a little problem: we only scored once. If you score in the 95th minute with a penalty everybody would say that's lucky but over the full game we had more chances, we were the better team, so I'm really happy about that.

James Milner added: "This season we have a team that can do it. I think there's a calm around the club, both inside and outside, and people are confident we can get it done. But City are so good they're capable of winning every game. The gap is not that big so we have to just keep pushing, and not worry too much about the title. A couple of bad games can happen, and with the amount of games we're playing there might be a couple of injuries. It could be a couple of poor performances and the lead's gone. That's why it's so special to win the league. It's so difficult and the best team always wins the league, no matter what. Hopefully winning that first trophy, the European Cup, as a squad will give us the experience to win the league."

KLOPP: "It was a super game. We upped the tempo. The football we played was so important. Leicester's goal really stopped us but then we wanted to go forwards. The penalty was obviously a penalty. We knew it would probably happen, we knew we were going to fight for the win - and we did. Without luck, we cannot win the amount of games we have won, but over the 90 minutes we deserved it - we deserved the three points. Milner held his nerve and that was superb."

BRENDAN RODGERS: "It's cruel to concede so late. I am very proud of the team. We're playing against the European champions and we looked like we could get goals. We were always a threat in the game, we had the confidence to pass the ball. We are showing our personality in how we played. We are bitterly disappointed to concede the penalty and it did not look clear and obvious to me. I think Mané made the most of the contact. I don't think if it had not been given by the referee it would have been overturned by VAR. When the referee gives decisions it is hard for them to overrule it."

OTHER SCORES

SATURDAY 5 OCTOBER
Brighton & Hove Albion 3 Tottenham Hotspur 0
Burnley 1 Everton 0
Norwich City 1 Aston Villa 5
Watford 0 Sheffield United 0
West Ham United 1 Crystal Palace 2

SUNDAY 6 OCTOBER
Arsenal 1 AFC Bournemouth 0
Manchester City 0 Wolverhampton Wanderers 2
Southampton 1 Chelsea 4
Newcastle United 1 Manchester United 0

SUNDAY 20 OCTOBER – PREMIER LEAGUE

MANCHESTER UNITED 1
Rashford (35)

LIVERPOOL 1
Lallana (84)

Ole Gunnar Solskjaer won the tactical battle in a Super Sunday clash that exposed Liverpool's weaknesses for the first time in the season. United led through a 36th minute Marcus Rashford goal as Ole's rapid two-pronged attack and 3-5-2 formation ran Liverpool ragged for over an hour. With Welshman Daniel James and the Mancunian Marcus Rashford upfront it was ann uneasy afternoon for the world's greatest defender, Virgil Van Dijk, who was beaten several times by trickery and blistering pace. In truth a youthful United always needed a second to feel secure and a late defensive mistake allowed Adam Lallana to snatch a point for the Reds to spare their blushes.

Jürgen Klopp was understandably unhappy with the outcome and complained that it is "a fact" that United always set up to defend against his side at Old Trafford after the 1-1 draw left him without a win in five visits to United. "This year, last year, the year before, they just defend," he said. "That's how it is. It is okay. It is no criticism. It is just a fact. When you think about Manchester United against Liverpool, you think both teams are trying like this. But it is not. We try." After eight straight wins, the 100 per cent record ended with a draw at Old Trafford. The result ended Liverpool's 17-match winning run in the

Premier League, one short of matching City's record. Still top, their lead was down to six points.

Jose Mourinho, then a Sky pundit, said Klopp's teams "have limitations against teams with low blocks". He explained: "He [Klopp] didn't like the menu - he likes meat and he got fish. United, with the limitations they have at the moment, played with five at the back, were solid and didn't give the chance of transition. Jürgen didn't like the menu. Liverpool missed quality to play against a team with a low block. They can smash opponents that play the way they want to play against. Jürgen clearly has frustrations. It's a fantastic situation for his team but at Old Trafford - which is a special place to win - he never did it."

Liverpool dominated possession, 68% to 32%, had more shots and more shots on target, but had to wait until the 85th minute for Lallana's equaliser after Rashford had given United a first-half lead. Klopp gave Jon Moss, the fourth official, an ear-bashing on the touchline for much of the game following Rashford's opener. Klopp was adamant his side should have been awarded a free-kick by referee Martin Atkinson for a challenge by Victor Lindelof on Divock Origi in the build-up to the goal. "I think most people thought it was a foul. I am sure it was a foul. Mr Atkinson let the game go on because he knew we had VAR. As soon as they scored they checked it but then it was not obvious because with a challenge you cannot always be 100% sure. But without VAR I am 100% sure Atkinson would have blown for a foul. It's great for offside and handball but for these situations we have not got it right yet. I was so confident that it was going to be overturned. It has to change that not many decisions are overturned.

"Look at Manchester City yesterday - it was so clear and obvious that Kevin de Bruyne was pushed [against Crystal Palace] and if I am saying Manchester City should have had a penalty then it must have been a penalty."

OLE GUNNAR SOLSKJAER: "It's important to get results. That's the only way to grow confidence. A win would have been great but a draw is a step in the right direction. As a manager you want results now - you can't lose four, five or six games on the bounce. We're looking to win games as soon as possible. It's maybe a slight touch [the VAR call before Rashford's goal] but it's not a clear and obvious error. It's still a man's game with tackles allowed, and the second one [Sadio Mané's disallowed goal] was a handball. Today we were on the right end of the VAR decisions."

KLOPP: "The result is OK. It's not what we wanted but we have to be happy given how the game developed. The first half I didn't like because we gave United the chance to do what they want to do - to put us under pressure and be aggressive. They were not better than we were but they did what they wanted to do. They scored a goal which shows all the problems with VAR. Mr Atkinson let the game run I'm sure because there is VAR. For me it was a clear foul. It's a general problem. VAR looks and says 'you decided like this'. But it was a foul. Then we scored a goal that was disallowed. Pretty much everything went against us but we still didn't lose so that is OK. We were in charge 100% towards the end. We wanted a different result but to do that you have to play better."

OTHER SCORES

SATURDAY 19 OCTOBER
Everton 2 West Ham United 0
Aston Villa 2 Brighton & Hove Albion 1
AFC Bournemouth 0 Norwich City 0
Chelsea 1 Newcastle United 0
Leicester City 2 Burnley 1
Tottenham Hotspur 1 Watford 1
Wolverhampton Wanderers 1 Southampton 1
Crystal Palace 0 Manchester City 2

MONDAY 21 OCTOBER
Sheffield United 1 Arsenal 0

WEDNESDAY, 23 OCTOBER 2019 - CHAMPIONS LEAGUE

GENK 1
Odey (88)

LIVERPOOL 4
Chamberlain (2, 57), Mané (77), Salah (86)

Liverpool were second in Group E heading to Genk, the first of two back-to-back fixtures against the Belgian side as Klopp demanded improvement in their away form to avoid an early exit. The Reds lost all three away group games on the way to winning the trophy, and lost in Napoli again. "Last year we were lucky with how tight the group was that we could lose three times away and still have a chance to make it through the group," said Klopp. "That will not happen this year. It's completely different. We know it's not historically good what we have done (in the away group games) in the last few years, but in general the Champions League was obviously really good. We did the right things in the right moment but we don't rely on these things. We know we have to improve and we try again and again and again until it works out."

Liverpool had three points from two games after beating Red Bull Salzburg in the group opener at Anfield, while Salah returned after recovering from an ankle problem before the international break and missed Sunday's 1-1 draw against Manchester United. Alexander-Arnold (virus) and Matip (sore knee) remained on Merseyside. Milner rather than Gomez filled in at right-back with Lovren alongside van Dijk in the first meeting between Genk and Liverpool in any competition. Genk's only previous meetings with English opponents in European competition was in the 2011-12 Champions League group stage, drawing 1-1 at home and losing 5-0 at Stamford Bridge. Liverpool won all five of their European Cup/Champions League matches against Belgian teams, keeping five clean sheets; - one of those wins was in the 1978 European Cup final against Bruges (1-0).

In the event it was Alex Oxlade-Chamberlain who stole the show, scoring twice, including a stunning outside-of-the-boot finish, in an emphatic 4-1 win, but still Klopp wasn't satisfied as he demanded that Liverpool must "improve". Oxlade-Chamberlain missed almost all of last season with a knee injury, but the smile was back when he drilled in a low shot in the second minute and brilliantly converted a second with a cool, first-time finish from Firmino's pass. Mane dinked in the third from Salah's through ball and then he rolled home the fourth late on. With Henderson and Wijnaldum left out of the starting lineup, Oxlade-Chamberlain and the industrious Keita highlighted Liverpool's squad depth, as he made more passes (118) than any other player, winning the ball back 12 times and contributing three tackles. Since the start of the 2017-18 season, Firmino had more assists in the Champions League than any other player (11).

Oxlade-Chamberlain said: "We have gained confidence from the whole season, not just this game and the last 20 minutes against

Manchester United. We saw that we have a lot to improve on and it was the same again tonight, but we're getting results, which is good. The manager will tell us we have a lot of points to improve because we've got to get them right if we're to get another good result at the weekend."

Belgian champions Genk responded to falling an early goal behind and were unfortunate not to equalise, Samatta dragged a shot wide and had a towering header ruled out for a tight offside call. Onuachu had a low shot palmed out by Alisson, and the Brazilian goalkeeper was eventually beaten with two minutes left through a Odey consolation. Liverpool were second in the group, a point behind leaders Napoli who came from behind to beat Salzburg. Klopp was concerned his side kept only three clean sheets in 15matches in all competitions this season. Klopp said "There were good moments. The start was brilliant, we were kind of fluent and asked them a lot of questions but then we started – I'm not sure why – to lose patience and some easy balls. But all four goals were brilliant and we had chances to score more. Job done. In the years before we would have drawn it, maybe even lost, but all's OK. We've just had two away games that were both difficult for different reasons. I don't know where we are now but I know where we need to be on Sunday. It's a refreshed Tottenham. Of course the second they meet us they're back on track. But we're a different team to Red Star Belgrade, just like Tottenham are different to Genk. Oxlade-Chamberlain's goals were brilliant, and very important. We're really pleased for him, it was a big step."

Liverpool condemned as "racist" travelling fans who unfurled a graphic banner depicting Origi's head on a naked body, alongside the Champions League trophy. The club said it "acted swiftly to have the banner removed" and said the image "perpetuated a racist stereotype". "This is completely unacceptable," a club statement said. "Liverpool Football Club condemns the offensive banner displayed in our section of the ground, prior to kick-off. We acted swiftly to have the banner removed and we are now working with the local authorities and stadium team in Genk to identify those responsible. Any subsequent action will be taken in keeping with our sanctions process." Origi had spent nine years at Genk in the club's youth set-up before joining Lille in 2010. He came on off the bench in the fixture at the Luminus Arena. Klopp described Origi as a Liverpool legend, after a reporter failed to mention that the Belgian had come through Genk's academy. "Genk is a very famous club for very big players: De Bruyne, Koulibaly and lots of other players - N'Didi," one journalist said at Klopp's media conference, but before he could finish his question, Klopp jumped in to suggest that his striker is a legend too. "Divock Origi - don't forget him. Liverpool legend by the way. He's very famous here," Klopp said with a big smile before the rest of the room laughed.

SUNDAY 27 OCTOBER - PREMIER LEAGUE

LIVERPOOL 2
Henderson (51), Salah (73)
TOTTENHAM 1
Kane (1)

When Harry Kane scored inside the first minute with a stooping header after Son's shot changed direction hitting Lovren's head, it looked like the pressure would grow on the Anfield side but Klopp's team created enough chances to have been 4-1 up by half time. However Son hit the bar early in the second half when Spurs could easily have been 2-0 ahead. Instead Liverpool kept their heads as the skipper equalised with a close range volley that bounced in, to make up for losing possession when Spurs broke for their opening goal. Mané won another late penalty which Salah converted for the winner.

"Our mentality has improved. That's grown over the last few years and the gaffer has changed that so much," Henderson said as Liverpool remained unbeaten at home in 45 league games. "We have faced adversity at times. It's not always going to go your own way. After 48 seconds I was thinking it was my fault because I gave the ball away for their goal. Thankfully I managed to get a goal to make up for it."

Rival fans claimed Klopp only does the celebration when the cameras are on him. So when the Sky cameras closed in waiting for his usual fist pump to his adoring fans, he waved the cameras away! He put his hand out to block the camera following him closely behind, then indicated to the crowd that he couldn't celebrate the way he'd want to because the camera was on him, making fun of the long-running joke.

KLOPP: "I really liked the way we played against really tough opponents. It was a wonderful game of football, it's how you wish games should be. The boys delivered. We had chance after chance and the keeper had sensational save after sensational save. We started well but the way we conceded was a bit unlucky. Tottenham then defended well, their counter-attacks were incredible. But the best thing was that you couldn't see any influence of the goal. We weren't nervous, we just followed the plan, doing everything in the right way. Their goalkeeper made some incredible saves but we stayed calm. It was just how football should look, how you should play against a really strong, good, organised side with the threat constantly in your mind that each ball you lose will possibly end up in front of your own goal. The counter-press was exceptional, it was kind of back. That was the plan today – we wanted to be really strong, especially in that department, because it was clear we probably might be dominant but that means you loose balls. You cannot finish each situation off and then the counter-press must be there. I loved that, that was really, really good.

"At half-time we said this game only had one problem, the score. There were one or two things we could do better and adapt a little bit. I wasn't surprised by Tottenham. They have the quality to cause any team in the world problems. We had 70% possession but that's okay for a team like Tottenham because each ball you lose, they have speed on the counter-attack and Harry Kane is so strong. But we were in control, we pushed them back and dominated apart from the last five minutes when we felt the intensity of the game. It was a super game and I loved it. We won the game and deserved it."

MAURICIO POCHETTINO: "We tried in the last 10 or 15 minutes and had chances but it was impossible! I've got no complaints about the penalty. You can have your own opinion. It was a fair reaction. He [Gazzaniga] made some good saves but for sure he is so frustrated and disappointed because we lost."

OTHER SCORES

FRIDAY 25 OCTOBER
Southampton 0 Leicester City 9

SATURDAY 26 OCTOBER
Manchester City 3 Aston Villa 0
Brighton & Hove Albion 3 Everton 2
Watford 0 AFC Bournemouth 0
West Ham United 1 Sheffield United 1
Burnley 2 Chelsea 4

October

SUNDAY 27 OCTOBER
Newcastle United 1 Wolverhampton Wanderers 1
Arsenal 2 Crystal Palace 2
Norwich City 1 Manchester United 3

WEDNESDAY 30 OCTOBER
CARABAO CUP THIRD ROUND

LIVERPOOL 5
Mustafi (OG) (4), Milner (41), Chamberlain (56), Origi (60 90+2 (pen))
ARSENAL 5
Torreira (18), Martinelli (25, 35), Maitland-Niles (52), Willock (69)
Liverpool win 5-4 on penalties

A thrilling contest saw Arsenal beaten on penalties as Liverpool marched into the quarter-finals of the Carabao Cup. Celebrations broke out in front of the Kop after 20-year-old Liverpool goalkeeper Caoimhin Kelleher saved Dani Ceballos' penalty in the 5-4 shootout win after the teams shared 10 goals in a topsy-turvy game.

Teenager Curtis Jones coolly thumped the final penalty in off the post to make it five from five for the home side. Divock Origi's 94th-minute scissor kick had sent the game to penalties after Liverpool had twice come from behind to draw level.

Arsenal's Joe Willock thought he had given his side a memorable victory with a sensational long-range strike in the second half but there was more to come on an unforgettable night at Anfield.

The Gunners had been minutes away from victory after Willock's stunning long-range effort put them 5-4 up, before Origi struck. Liverpool led just once during normal time - after just five minutes, when Shkodran Mustafi slid in and diverted the ball into his own net. Midfielder Mesut Ozil, given just his third start of the season, then set-up Bukayo Saka, whose shot was rebounded in by Lucas Torreira to make it 1-1.

Teenager Gabriel Martinelli continued his impressive goalscoring form, pouncing on a loose ball at the near post before slotting in from Saka's pass to make it 3-1 to Arsenal but Liverpool cut their lead to one goal on the stroke of half-time through James Milner's penalty after Harvey Elliott - who became the youngest Liverpool player to start at Anfield (16 years, 209 days) - went down in the box under minimal contact from Martinelli.

It took just nine minutes for the goals to start flowing again in the second half, when Milner uncharacteristically gave the ball away in his own area and Ozil teed up Ainsley Maitland-Niles. Alex Oxlade-Chamberlain fired in an excellent long-range effort for Liverpool and Origi's smart turn and powerful finish made it 4-4 - all this before Willock and Origi's late goals left the teams level at 5-5.

KLOPP: "We made some mistakes, we played some average passes. We were too open at times. We can talk about tactics but who cares on a night like this? I hoped for the boys they would have a game to remember. What they did - I lost it really! It's like a dream to play for the first time at Anfield, but things might not be going right and you have to stay on track. All our goals we scored were wonderful. If you don't win nobody remembers it in three years, if it works out the boys will remember it forever. [Curtis] Jones... it was not my decision in the end for him to take the last penalty. When I saw the list, Origi was the taker of the last one and they changed it obviously."

UNAI EMERY: "It was a crazy match. I am very proud of [the players' work], we had a high rhythm in the first 45 minutes. At the end we were winning until the last action. Penalties are 50/50 and we lost. We are sad but our work, we deserve to have more. There are lots of positives to take. Defensively, both teams cannot be happy with that. But for the supporters it was an amazing 90 minutes. The result was always changing. It was spectacular."

NOVEMBER

The Brazilian spine of Allison, Fabinho, Firmino was a source of pride for Jurgen Klopp. He was particularly effusive about the contribution of Fabinho at this stage of the season. After the 2-1 win over Tottenham, the manager hilariously nicknaming him 'Dyson' for his aptitude for hoovering up loose balls. The equaliser against Spurs came after a sumptuous dink from Fabinho put his captain in behind the defence. Fabinho completed more tackles (4) and interceptions (3) than any other player on the field. Klopp commented: "You saw it, both wings were so strong with the triangles we created there: with Sadio, Robbo and Gini on one side, with Hendo, Mo and Trent on the other side, and then 'Dyson' in the centre, who was there for each ball defensively – what a game he played, unbelievable. Connecting with Bobby in the centre. I said to the boys after the game that I didn't expect it that good, to be honest, before the game. I thought we are ready to show up a little bit again after being away [from Anfield] on tour for a little while, after Leicester I think – that feels long ago. But that was exceptionally good, and necessary because Tottenham was here today to get three points. The way they set up, line-up-wise offensively, really offensive, but set-up-wise just compact and organised and the counter-attacks are incredible. I have to say that's really tough to defend and apart from twice we did it really well so I am really happy."

With Fabinho one yellow card from suspension and would miss the vital City clash if booked again. Ox, Milner or Lallana were in line to replce him. Klopp was tempted to go with The Ox, but the manager still need to coax the best out of him after his long lay off as he said: "I'm going through the process again - he has to remind me again when I get in these areas to shoot. When we are defending I need to be there and here and press more aggressively, so I'm going though that process again. But you can see him clapping and applauding when someone has a shot from 20 yards and it has gone into row Z. It's because he likes us to try these things."

When asked in his pre-Aston Villa press conference if he thought the Ox was setting the bar too high in not feeling he played well yet scored a fabulous goal in the midweek League Cup win over Arsenal in that 5-5 thriller his team eventually won 5-4 on penalties, Klopp responded: "No. He's right, but it's no problem. That's exactly how it is. He had a lot of moments where he was really outstanding, but then other moments where he's not really involved and these things, that's our life as a footballer, we always try to reach perfection. There are so many games where he still needs to find rhythm and stuff like this. But like I said it's no problem. That's for us a long-term injury and a long-term project to coming back from it."

Klopp knew better performances would materialise in time. "It's good that a player thinks like that and doesn't think 'I scored two goals so I played world-class' because a game [involves] more jobs to do and he knows that. I'm completely fine with his shape and form he's in, but we both know there is quite some space for improvement. That's good news. In his best shape ever before he got the injury, it's not about being there. That's something which happens when you are in your best shape, then you have these kinds of performances. It's just being more involved, feeling the spaces better. I don't when, I just know there's still more to come and that's for me really good news."

Asked what he would tell Fabinho should he play, Klopp joked: "No challenges at all! Of course "that's not possible against Aston Villa, playing without challenges, especially in that position". He added: "You cannot ask for this. The player knows it, I know it. Is there any game where you think that's a good game to get a fifth yellow card? Maybe other teams are pretty smart in that and take them, I don't know, I never did it. We have to deal with. Maybe he has to deal with it on the pitch or I have to deal with it with the line-up. We didn't make a final decision yet, so we will see.

Despite concerns that Salah's injury was a problem, Klopp described the issue as more annoying for the player, with a bit of fluid on the anjkle, but was sure he would be fine.

November

SATURDAY 2 NOVEMBER - PREMIER LEAGUE

ASTON VILLA 1
Trezeguet (19)

LIVERPOOL 2
Robertson (87), Mané (90+5)

Well, who would have believed it? At half time on the first Saturday in November the title race was in the balance as the top two trailed going into the second halves of their respective games.

City were losing at home 1-0 to the Southampton side who were trailing 5-0 at half time only the week before, eventually going down 9-0 to Leicester. Liverpool were trailing by the same 1-0 scoreline at Villa Park. Both brilliant Brazilian keepers were at fault for the goals!

3:13pm - SOUTHAMPTON TAKE THE LEAD! Ederson spilled a shot, James Ward-Prowse lifted the rebound over the desperate lunge from the keeper to put Southampton in front.

3:21pm - ASTON VILLA TAKE THE LEAD! A goal down as McGinn's delivery into the box was met by Trezeguet, who found himself unmarked, his close range header squirmed under Alisson. The strike was referred to VAR for a potential offside check...the goal was given.

3:29pm - LIVERPOOL 'EQUALISER' RULED OUT! A fantastic ball from Mané set up Firmino to restore parity only for VAR to rule it out. An ARMPIT offside.

So, Southampton lead at half time in a league game for the first time this season and the gap between City and Liverpool remained six points as a result of the surprise half-time permutations; the day could have ended with Liverpools lead cut to three points, or extended to nine!

Jesus on for David Silva for the second half as the home fans sounded frustrated and Guardiola had had enough! Klopp ordered three subs to warm up.

4:27pm - CITY EQUALISE! Aguero, inevitably. Southampton's players claimed that the ball had gone out of play before Walker's delivery. In theory, City reduced the gap to five points.

Klopp threw on The Ox and Orgi, in place of Salah and Wijnaldum. Klopp gambled by leaving out Fabinho with the looming shadow of City, replaced by Lallana, and it clearly didn't work, and the manager called on his substitutes into the second half.

The Ox had three quick shots in succession, all blocked. Liverpool stuffed Aston Villa 6-0 on their last visit to Villa Park in the Premier League. They were minutes away from a first top-flight defeat of the season

4:43pm - CITY TAKE THE LEAD!

City turned the game around with Angelino's cross palmed out by McCarthy into the path of Walker, who steered home to send the Etihad into raptures.

The gap on closed to THREE points. Seven minutes left, City ahead, Liverpool behind.

4:47pm - LIVERPOOL LEVEL! A fabulous curling cross from Mané was perfectly weighted for the onrushing Robertson, unmarked, firmly on target with his header clipping off Heaton into the roof of the net. The gap increased to five points.

4:53pm - CITY'S VICTORY CONFIRMED City fans waited on tenterhooks for the Liverpool score to filter through via the PA system.

4:54pm - LIVERPOOL WINNER! City thought they ended up within touching distance of the summit but Liverpool struck four minutes into five minutes of stoppage time. Alexender-Arnold's free kick deflected for a corner off the wall, he dashed over to take a near post corner where Mané glanced a header just inside the far post to lead for the first time in the 94th minute. Klopp became a specialist in late goals only matched by Sir Alex's heyday at United. But he was scathing about the VAR decision that ruled out Firmino's striker which made it necessary to stage the latest of his teams late recoveries. "When we talk about serious moments, very important moments in football, it's not right to sit here and everyone wants to laugh about it," he said. "It is not to laugh about. It is too serious. Managers get sacked for losing football games. They just have to clarify it. I am not saying anyone is doing it on purpose." Even Villa manager Dean Smith admitted he thought Firmino's goal should have stood. "I thought it was a goal, but we've had gnats-hair goals go against us too and it is factual so you can't moan."

4:56pm - FULL TIME AT VILLA PARK The final whistle climaxed another pulsating chapter between two Premier League titans going for glory. Villa players collapsed to the floor, The Reds celebrated as if they know they were going to win the title with their six point lead in tact.

November

With their 10-month long unbeaten league record seemingly about to end, the Reds dug deep to conjure a stellar finish, Robertson arriving at the back post to head them level, Mané's glancing header from Alexander-Arnold's corner past Tom Heaton into the far corner of the net.

Klopp was on the pitch handing out his customary hugs, a deliriously happy man after his side turned it around. Mané scored the 35th 90th-minute winning goal by Liverpool in the Premier League - at least 10 more than any other side in the competition's history. Mané was booked for diving, Klopp insisted there was contact on Mané: 'He got the yellow card and when you see it back it was not diving, there was contact but it is a decision we have to accept it.'

Klopp also felt his side should have had a penalty when the ball struck Targett's arm. 'We need to sort a few things obviously. Nobody talks about the Targett handball situation as it was not whistled. Was it a penalty?

31 points from 11 games; two clubs with the same tally at this stage of a Premier League season - Chelsea in 2005-06 and City in 2017-18 - both went on to win the title.

KLOPP: "We made it hard for ourselves. Villa was ready to play for a proper fight, a proper battle, defend with all you have, try to find counter-attack opportunities. We conceded a goal and then it is hard to change this wrong path and wrong decisions immediately. It is lucky to score these goals of course, but when you look at the game, if either side deserved to win it is us. We still need to learn and get better. Sometimes you need to get knocks and today we got knocks. For really little mistakes we got really big knocks but at the end we could sort it. We had our good moments during the game but were not clinical enough, especially in the first half. I don't always believe we can win every game but I never give up. So when we scored the equaliser I thought, 'that's what we deserve'. We know we can do better, but on days like this you just need to be ready to fight. When you play in a stadium like Villa Park it's fair you might get a little knock. After the first half we realised we were in the wrong path and we made changes. I didn't like the body language. We made it difficult for ourselves. We started playing football well but not exactly how we should — Aston Villa were ready for a proper fight, a battle and to defend with all you have. They tried to make space for counter-attacks, they had good set-pieces. We were playful, which looked good but I didn't like it. It was good football but you have to finish it off. In the second half we started more aggressive, our counter-press was better and we could shoot from distance, which Oxlade helps with. Oxlade on the left space meant space for Robbo. It is lucky when you score these goals but if one team deserved to win it, it was us. I can imagine how bad Villa feel as with their hard work they deserved something. We had our good moments during the game but were not clinical enough, especially in the first half. I don't always believe we can win every game but I never give up. So when we scored the equaliser I thought, 'that's what we deserve'. We know we can do better, but on days like this you just need to be ready to fight. When you play in a stadium like Villa Park it's fair you might get a little knock. After the first half we realised we were in the wrong path and we made changes."

SMITH: "It's a tough one to take. We created some big chances in the game but two basic mistakes cost us. We were always a threat on the counter-attack. We knew they were always going to have the ball. Their full-backs are very attacking. I think we got away with one with the VAR incident and Lallana missed a big chance as well."

OTHER SCORES

SATURDAY 2 NOVEMBER
AFC Bournemouth 1 Manchester United 0
Arsenal 1 Wolverhampton Wanderers 1
Brighton & Hove Albion 2 Norwich City 0
Manchester City 2 Southampton 1
Sheffield United 3 Burnley 0
West Ham United 2 Newcastle United 3
Watford 1 Chelsea 2

SUNDAY 3 NOVEMBER
Crystal Palace 0 Leicester City 2
Everton 1 Tottenham Hotspur 1

November

TUESDAY 5 NOVEMBER - CHAMPIONS LEAGUE

LIVERPOOL 2
Wijnaldum (12), Chamberlain (53)
GENK 1
Samatta (39)

Klopp wasn't in the mood to talk about City and Guardiola, but had little choice as the media were far more interested in the next fixture than this Champions League tie. But once Klopp was allowed to get back to the next match, he commented: "The story the boys wrote in the last three years was only possible because we are always focused on the next game completely with all we have. We have big ambitions in this competition and it is an open group, pretty much everything possible. We have to make sure that we get these three points, and that only works if we are 100 per cent focused on it, everyone knows that. I would feel a bit embarrassed if I had to tell them 'Don't think about Man City already'. I know them well enough, I don't have to do that."

Klopp planned changes, although needing two more wins to guarantee qualification before the final group game. That would aid Klopp's December's packed schedule. "I don't think we can do it [qualify] Tuesday but we have to make a big step. We are at home and whoever we play we will try everything we can to win it. We have another home game against Napoli and we cannot waste time. It will be tough when we go to Salzburg. It will be tough at home to Napoli. We cannot expect things will always work like they should so we will just make sure we can have as many points as possible. That is all that we will try to think about."

Genk coach Felice Mazzu described Liverpool as the best team in the world. "It is the moment to enjoy but not to be here to take photos. It is to give their life on the pitch. They play a big game against a big team perhaps for once in our life in a place like this. We play against the best team in the world at the moment." Genk had been beaten 4-1 at home by Liverpool a fortnight earlier and had yet to win any of the 15 matches in their Champions League history. Klopp finally opted for six changes; Milner at left-back with Robertson on the bench, Mane and Firmino rested as Origi started, Oxlade-Chamberlain out wide, Gomez replaced Lovren. Fabinho returned in replace of Henderson. Keita started instead of Lallana. Klopp explained: "I wanted to bring

101

in fresh legs, fresh ideas, new skills and trust different ways to play. We don't always know how the other team will play. We can have different rhythm."

A narrow 2-1 victory meant three straight Champions League wins to move Liverpool top of their group as Napoli were held to a 1-1 by Salzburg. Wijnaldum stabbed into the roof of the net from close range after Dewaest made a mess of clearing Milner's low cross to set up a promising 14th-minute lead, but Tanzanian striker Mbwana Samatta powerfully headed in the equaliser at the near post from a corner five minutes before half-time. Having scored twice in Belgium, Oxlade-Chamberlain was the match-winner early in the second half, spinning and converting a low strike into the bottom corner. Klopp's biggest concern was a lack of clean sheets - one in their past nine games in all competitions - given that their defence provided such a solid base last season. "It's not really a worry, to be honest, but it's of course not what we want," Klopp observed." All the goals we conceded were completely different. They were all different, so it's not about defending, it's about being 100 percent spot on in the situations and we were not."

Klopp's team dominated with 72% possession, 28 shots. Klopp added: "We didn't finish our situations in the way we could have done. We had a lot of shots and some really big chances that we usually use. We didn't do that and it kept the game open. That gave them a lot of energy. The players came through but you saw after a while it gets hard to get that rhythm and at the end of the game it was not there. We got a little bit of trouble but not really. It was job done. If we had scored two or three in the first half, nobody would have thought that couldn't have happened. But it went 1-1 and then it got tricky. Now we are all good. 'Job done' is the headline for the game, pretty much, but the group is not decided. It's a tough group. The most important thing; we won and nobody is injured. Apart from that, the result is the result because we didn't finish our situations off like we should and could have done. That keeps the game pretty exciting, and left Genk alive. It was clear that it would be a bit tricky in some departments because the front three never played together in these positions, in a formation like this.' We are first in the table but we want to be first after the last matchday and now we have to play two tough games, and two important ones. In each of them we can decide it with a win, but that sounds easier than it is because both of them will be really tricky.'

November

THE TITLE DECIDER

Klopp on Guardiola **2016:** *"Johan Cruyff started Total Football, but Pep made it perfect. He's an outstanding manager, 100 per cent. He's very influential."*

Guardiola on Klopp **2016:** *"Maybe Klopp is the best manager in the world at creating teams who attack the back four with so many players, from almost anywhere on the pitch. They have an intensity with the ball and without the ball, and it is not easy to do that."*

2019: *"If it's up and down quickly they are much, much better – they are maybe the best team in the world."*

Now: *"It (diving) has happened many times, what Liverpool have done, in the last few years. Mané is a special talent. Sometimes he's diving, sometimes he has this talent to score incredible goals in the last minute."*

Liverpool v Manchester City was a global phenomenon watched by billions. It was a clash of the titans, English Champions against European Champions. It was always going to be billed as the fixture that would define the season. However the suggestion that it was now the ultimate clash in English football, brought a typical response from Jürgen Klopp: "That is obviously bollocks!"

The build up began instantly after the last round of fixtures when Guardiola accused Sadio Mané of diving, and Liverpool of too often crying how unlucky they had been to lose the title to City the previous season by one point. Guardiola said: "We arrived in the locker room and it was 1-1 and after it was 1-2. When we won, Liverpool still didn't win and at the end, again they won. What happened has happened not once, twice, it happened a lot of times - it is because (Mané) is a talent. Sometimes he's diving, sometimes he has this talent to score incredible goals in the last minute. He's a talent. If it's one time, two times, 'we were lucky, we were lucky', but it happened in the last two seasons many, many times they won many games in the last minutes, they have a special character to do that. We look at ourselves, we know which team we face, I think they have won 10 and drawn one. Next week we go to Anfield to try to play them."

Klopp responded by taking a swipe at City's tactical fouling. WI couldn't really believe it. Do I like that he says this about one of my players? I am not sure if Pep spoke in that moment about Sadio or the team — both is not too nice. I am not too sure if I want to put oil on the fire. I am not interested in these kind of things. And I promise not to mention tactical fouls. That is maybe already too much — but that is the only thing I'll say about it. I do not know how he could have known about the incident so quickly after the game."

Klopp, though, wanted to stress that Mané "is not a diver". Klopp explained: "Yes, there was a situation in the Aston Villa game where he felt contact and went down. Maybe it was not a penalty, but there was contact. It's not like he jumped over a leg or something. All the other penalties were penalties because he was there. If something like that had happened for Manchester City, I'm sure they would have wanted a penalty, too."

Klopp's focus was only on the midweek Champions League tie, but the media only wanted to discuss the clash with City. But until that was the next game, Klopp said: "I'm not really in a Man City mood at the moment. Do I get asked as much about Man City? I don't know. When I came into the interview after the Aston Villa game, I had no clue what the other Premier League results were. That is the truth. It was 45 minutes after the game when I heard the results of the other matches. I didn't ask anybody. I had to speak to the players, I had to speak to a lot of people and then I went into interviews. I didn't think for one second about the other games. Then, after the interviews, 'By the way, how did the other teams play?' Someone told me City had won in the 86th minute and all this happened. I don't understand these types of things. My brain is not big enough to think about another team as well. I have enough to do to think about us and deal with all these things.

"We play Genk and that deserves all my attention — and gets it. That is the only way I can do it. After that, we can speak about Manchester City... we have to! We will internally speak a lot about them, then we will prepare the game. Before then, not at all."

Sergio Aguero confessed that Klopp's side were the only team who could 'hurt' them. "It may be the Clasico for television, but for us, the Clasico, it's the match against United," he told *France Football*. 'Liverpool have always been a tough opponent. But when I arrived, the team we were fighting for the title was United. Initially, it was something strange in [Manchester] that City competes against United. Then there was Chelsea. But these last four seasons, Liverpool have become a very strong team and are now fighting with us to win the Premier League. They are the only team in the league that can hurt us. They have been chasing a new league title for years. Last season, they didn't go all the way, so they are very motivated. This year, they are in front of us and will try to go to the end."

Pep added to the intensity by suggesting City didn't have to win at Anfield. Since Boxing Day 1981, City played 31 times at Anfield and won just once – when Kevin Keegan was manager. Despite the injury to the influential David Silva, the City boss was adamant they were going there with the attitude to win, but he added that it wasn't "necessary". He explained: "How long is it since they lost at Anfield? Last season we did not win there and we won the title.'

Klopp felt Guardiola was becoming increasingly obsessed with Liverpool, and the City boss responded: "I didn't listen to what he said so I don't know," Did he listen? Of course he did! He added: "I don't put oil in the fire."

Guardiola later clarified his 'diving' accusations. "My son and my daughter, all the times when Liverpool win in the last minutes, ask me how lucky they are. I said to them at the time it's not lucky, what Liverpool have done last season and this season many, many times is because they've this incredible quality and this incredible talent to fight until the end. Against Leicester, it was a penalty it was 'wow, like this or like that'. That was the intention for my comment. Far away from my intention to say Sadio is this type of player because I admire him a lot. For Jürgen it (the Leicester decision) is a penalty, for the referee it was a penalty, for the VAR it was a penalty. I was the wrong guy - or maybe not, I don't know. So it was a praise for Liverpool, not just about one action. To say it's lucky again? No. It happens many times at Anfield and away (from home) because they push and they push. That's why it's nice to face them and try to compete with them. Hopefully I can clarify everything for Jürgen."

Mané refused to change his style, sarcastically responding: "If it could be a penalty for sure I will 'dive' again." He said: "If the 'dive' will give me a penalty then I will do it! Why not? But what Jürgen said is correct. I do not dive." Mané thought it was a bit "clever" of Guardiola "to get the attention of the referee".

Klopp was asked about the fall out over Mané. He tried to side step it: "I'm in exactly the same situation as him. We constantly get asked questions, and sometimes we say in that second what is on our mind, without thinking of anything else – that we're in public, that there's a camera. He explained it well, saying when he speaks to his kids, it's like this. It could be a penalty or not, and that's a discussion they had at home. I'm completely fine with it, and I couldn't have more respect for Pep Guardiola. I know him for so long, and for me it's still a big thing to be his contender. For me, he's the best manager in the world, and we have the chance to win against his team which is very difficult but possible which is enough for me. From my side, there is nothing but respect. Of course, you can't leave it completely without a comment, but I'm not interested. There's enough to write about before the game. It's not necessary for us to make it bigger by the things we say. If I could do it again I wouldn't have said it [the tactical fouls response]. It's just not necessary, and I know there's a lot of respect there and the rest will be decided on the pitch."

Jamie Carragher wrote in his *Daily Telegraph* column: "I had an immediate thought when I heard Pep Guardiola and Jürgen Klopp exchange barbed comments ahead of Liverpool against Manchester City this week: 'about time'. There was something unnatural about the Premier League's two leading managers competing for the title without an extra edge to their relationship… I do not believe I am exaggerating when I say the hierarchies of Liverpool and City cannot stand each other, resentments which are reflected in the fanbases. City appear to suspect Liverpool of lobbying governing bodies to investigate the legality of their transfer spending, while they make no secret of their belief that the positive coverage of the Klopp era is disproportionate when compared to Guardiola's trophy haul, and City's in general since the Abu Dhabi takeover. Within Liverpool, eyebrows are raised when stories emerge about fears of another attack on City's bus as happened in the Champions League quarter-final in 2018, and there was incredulity at Guardiola's comments about Sadio Mané's diving. As Klopp suggested, it certainly feels like Guardiola talks about Liverpool more than Klopp does Manchester City, and City generally seem preoccupied with how Liverpool are portrayed in the media."

Klopp acknowledged the rivalry was "getting bigger and bigger" following a string of close games. So this was taking the shape of a really big one. "It's a big game, two really good teams facing each other at Anfield, under the floodlights. The last three games we played 0-0 at home, then lost 2-1 at the Etihad where we nearly scored a goal and then the last one was a draw in the Community Shield, before we lost the shootout. It will be a good football game - I'm not sure whether it will be just from a coaches and tactical point of view or a spectacle one for supporters. But everything is on a plate and no one hides anything, we cannot only be offensive but you have to be brave against Manchester City - even for a point. I take enjoyment and fulfilment from how my players have improved and grown together to bring us to the point that we are involved in great occasions like this. I take enjoyment from the fact these players and this team have earned their status as being one of the best football sides in the world in this moment. I take enjoyment from knowing that these players have total belief in themselves. I could not be prouder of what this squad has done and continues to do.

"Liverpool Football Club is so blessed to have this remarkable group of people together in this moment representing and competing for the club. They are so special, each and every one of them. We cannot and should not ever promise an outcome. We can't promise a specific result today or that in May we will achieve anything specific either – that would be foolish. What we can promise, and what they constantly deliver on, is that this team, whichever players feature on the teamsheet today, will give their all. These players don't know any other way – it's all of themselves and nothing less when they compete for Liverpool."

Fully focused on City after winning their Champions League tie with Genk, Klopp brought the biggest game of the season so far into context: "We are at matchday 12 so obviously there are some games to come. We know about the City situation last year where we only lost one game and that was decisive in the end. That's maybe how people see it, but you have to play all the games. There is so much to come, and the most intense period of the year in November, December and January is still coming so we have to be ready for all these games. At the moment we are focused on preparing for this game, but we don't think too much about what influence it might have on the rest of the season. This season is different to last season, and we don't know how it will go. We pushed each other on a really high level. The previous season, there was the real pressure of the 100-point season and I could not have more respect for them that they had 98 points the year after – but for sure we were a reason for that as we pushed them really hard.

In the last couple of years, we both gave a lot of respect for each other. City's performance at Liverpool last season was probably the biggest show of respect one of my teams ever got. That's how it is. They played differently to what they usually do - that's true. But, that's football. We all have to make a plan for one game, and in this specific case against one of the best sides in the world.

"We play at home, and last season we played a game at theirs where we lost by 11 millimetres otherwise the ball was in [John Stones' clearance on the goal line] and it was another draw. I think that would have been deserved, so there are tight games and that's how it is when high-quality teams face each other, so I expect another tight game."

A 'must not lose' game? "Maybe there are people who are smarter than I am and see it like this, but I don't. For me, it's 100 per cent a 'want to win game' - 100 per cent with all I have. I've never understood 'must-win' games because that doesn't change the chances. For us, as a team to prepare a game like this, you have to do the right thing again and again: being brave, playing football, defending for your lives. All the stuff around the game doesn't really affect us. We want to win, and we'll try everything to make that happen - which is difficult enough. The season will not stop after this, but it's a big one, we know that. The whole world will be watching it, 100 per cent. Everyone I know will. I'm really looking forward to it, but the discussions around, I'm not part of."

Ederson came off at half time in City's Champions League midweek win, with Bravo later red carded and full back Kyle Walker ending up in goal, making Ederson a doubt for the big game. Klopp felt Guardiola would risk Ederson: "If he did not play, it would change. Ederson is an important part of their game, 100 per cent. Claudio Bravo can do similar things, but I expect Ederson to play 100 per cent. He's an ever-present player."

Klopp emphasised the magnitude of the game by suggesting even the hot dog seller needed to be on top of his game, let alone his players! He observed: "City in the last three years have been the team in the Premier League and it has always been our plan to get closer. In the last three games we have drawn once and lost twice, but the guys are showing improvement. Everyone has to be in top shape in the stadium on Sunday, even the guy selling the hotdog. Everyone has to be there from the warm-up and be there. That is what I wish for - that before we even know whether we are going to get something that we invest all our emotions for the game and let's play football.

"The best news is that it is at Anfield, under the floodlights. Everything is on a plate nobody hides anything, if you are not brave against Man City you don't have the chance of even a point. You have to create, but your positioning and protection must be perfect. It is a lot. It is an interesting game!

"From a sport's point of view this rivalry is getting bigger and bigger. We live in now and obviously Man City are a pretty good football and thank god there is a rivalry because it means we are a pretty good team as well.

"Raheem Sterling is always a big threat, and he is always improving. He is a fantastic footballer, I can't say anything bad about him, outstanding. He is not the only threat unfortunately. That is the problem we have."

Klopp, though, was bullish about Liverpool's chances. "It depends on what you want to judge, are we capable of beating the best team in the world? Yes, we are. To compare with Pep, it is easy to understand what I say and with my team, I don't want to make us smaller than we are because we are incredible in moments, really incredible, but we still have a lot of space for improvement.

"It is not too important what you are in this moment but what you can be in the future, but you have to use everything. We all ask for that and it is necessary. Keep a performance level and then we make the next step. That is what we do in life and in football. It doesn't make us smaller, we want to beat Man City. We know how difficult it will be but we want to beat them. We have no excuses before the game, it is only what I said, it should not be an excuse."

Liverpool's 34 points from 12 in games included matches with Arsenal, Tottenham, Manchester United and Chelsea, while City's 2-2 draw with Spurs in August was so far their only fixture against the same clubs, as City had yet to play a team in the top six. Klopp was uninterested by the run of games for the Reds' title rivals. "We have never thought about the fixtures of other teams. OK, now we analyse it and I haven't seen many other games [from other teams], it is a very important game but we know that. We always speak about things like this. It could be three [points], six or nine, whatever. None of these facts make [the league] finished at this moment. It is just three, six or nine, bam! But then we play football games and we will have problems that is clear.

"How do we deal with them? It is only for people I imagine who don't play the game. One says things, the other says they have slipped and it is all crazy, that is all clear already what people will say. It is not important for us. We are fully focused on this opponent and then make sure they come back all healthy from the international break and then go to Crystal Palace as it is the most important game of the year, because that what is actually is.

"It is not really that we are creating stories before it happens because that is not important. We want to win it but if we win it, it does not mean we are already champions. If we lose it, do we not have a chance anymore? No. But we don't have to think about that we just try to win the game. Each step we do between now has to lead in the direction to be ready for this game and that is what we try."

Despite all the pre match hype, this is what Klopp had to say about Guardiola. "I could not respect him more, for me he is the best manager in the world. Wherever he is he has an impact on his team and when you take him away you can see the football change. Our relationship is good, it is very respectful."

City, though, didn't look quite as formidable as in the previous two seasons winning back-to-back titles, contending with injuries to key defenders. Klopp was not having it, he was far from sympathetic as City had the far stronger squad to cope with such set backs. 'We all have problems. Last year De Bruyne couldn't play against us, one of the best players in the world, and they still got results. That shows the quality of Man City.

"Do I like talking about Man City all the time? No. I am more than happy with what we did in the last couple of years but getting 100 points, then 98 points, and looking still greedy, that's a really big strength. We all have to deal with setbacks and injuries, and they did pretty well. It's not about comparing the team from last year, it's about how do they deal with the situation and that's quite impressive. I don't think about the City team of the last few years, I think about the City team of the moment, and that's good enough for a proper game."

Klopp spoke about City having to adapt tactics when facing Liverpool. Guardiola didn't deny it, but it is a normal tactic when confronting one of its major rivals, and he did the same when he was at Bayern Munich and they went to Klopp' Dortmund. "Sometimes you have to adapt," he said. "I was more defensive with Bayern Munich when we went to Borussia Dortmund and won 3-0." That was in 2013.

When these two heavyweight managers met 13 months earlier, with the two clubs level on 17 points, City set up more conservatively than at any other time in Guardiola's reign and left with their first goalless draw and clean sheet on the ground since 1986. They should have snatched victory after Mahrez skied an 85th-minute penalty. About the previous seasons draw at Anfield, Klopp said, "You can see it as a compliment, but for sure it is not meant as a compliment! It's just a game-plan," said Klopp of his rival's approach last time out at Anfield. "I don't admire other teams, I respect them and I like a couple of things. The character of the team and the manager is pretty good, but the combination of speed and technique is always impressive in football. They have quite a few players who are good at that, organisation is pretty good. It's a good football team. But the improvements the boys made are obvious. For us it's a good sign that we can become closer, it's an important part of our development. There were games which we won where City had much more of the game than we had, but we scored the goals in the right moments. The result is the thing which stays in your mind, but the games were really good."

Guardiola assessed his approach last time at Anfield: "Sometimes you want to adapt to teams as good as Liverpool. Sometimes people have to recognise that we are playing the champions of Europe. Being defensive was not the plan, it was so good that they pushed us deep. They do everything well. You see the team, what is the weak point? They are a real complete team and we need this kind of rival. Last season when we won the league, we won the Premier League [against] the best contender I ever faced in my career. This was one of the biggest achievements we achieved as a club. Probably right now [Liverpool are] the strongest team in the world. Playing at Anfield, we know what it means for them and for all their rivals. [But]it's 90 minutes and we're going to try to follow the plan with thought in this game."

Guardiola compared Anfield to the Camp Nou and the Bernabeu, but he was undaunted. "It is never easy to win against a good team on a big stage," he added, "Everyone knows how hard it is to win away at Camp Nou or Madrid or Juventus, and at present Liverpool is probably an even tougher place to go. But I also know that last season we had a great chance to win, when we missed a last-minute penalty. So sometimes it can happen."

He welcomed the fervent scenes inside the famous arena. "I love it," said Guardiola. "I didn't like what happened in the bus outside the stadium but, in the stadium, when they support the team, it's perfect, it's lovely. That's why we're involved in this business, to be involved in this kind of experience, in these stadiums. They're an exceptional team and the stadium makes an influence. The history speaks for itself, it's something special, but I think it's more for the quality of the team and what they do, the quality of the players and the manager they have. I would say, right now, it's the toughest stadium in Europe to go to."

While Klopp rates City the best in the world, Guardiola currently rated Liverpool as the best in the world. "I said last season, when we won the Premier League, that they are the best contender I've faced in my career. That's why to win this league was one of the biggest achievements we've had as a club, and it remains the same. So, probably, right now, they're the strongest team in the world. The quality Liverpool have – if you play high, they make movements in behind, and they're so fast that, when you defend deep, they attack a lot of players, with Trent Alexander Arnold and Andy Robertson. They are incredible crossers, they have good headers in the box, they're incredible at the back, the second balls, with set pieces. After winning back-to-back titles, we need that kind of rival to help us take another step forward."

He would not concede the title even if they lost and fell nine points: "The season is long, there are a lot of games and situations that can happen."

Ederson out, Bravo in. Guardiola was bullish against a tidal wave of optimism for Liverpool's chances given the loss of their No 1 keeper, so influential for the defence. Pop commented: "He is out. We have another top goalkeeper and Claudio Bravo can do it too. He is an exceptional goalkeeper. He is an international goalkeeper. I have no doubts. Why shouldn't I be confident about my players? I see him every day in training. We won't lose because of Claudio. The red card the other day was because we lost the ball. Respect the guy. He is a top keeper, a career at a top, incredible level. He won the Copa America. He's a top, top keeper. The first season was a struggle a little bit in a new league; it was because the team was not in the top level. The problem was not Claudio. It's easy to point fingers. Why should I not have confidence?"

It was over 16 years since City last won at Anfield when Nicolas Anelka scored twice for the team managed by Kevin Keegan.

Since then, Liverpool won 13 times, with five draws.

Liverpool hadn't lost a game in the league since the 2-1 defeat at the Etihad Stadium on January 3. And lately they became masters of late goals. Forget Fergie time, ran the headlines, now it was KLOPPAGE TIME!

Would defeat, and a nine point gap be too much even for this formidable City side? The City boss commented: "I don't know. I don't know. The season is long. I just want my team to fight to the end. Liverpool are a team that lost one game last season, none this season, so you cannot believe that they will lose many, but the season is long."

Guardiola riled at the idea his team were "underdogs". He responded: "I've never gone into a game feeling like an outsider or an underdog, thinking I am not going to win. I am not going to take the bus to Liverpool thinking I am going to lose the game. That has never happened in my career. Always I try to believe that, if we do the special things we plan to do, we will have our chance to win. But I do accept that to win these type of games we will have to be at the top level. Definitely. We can't be half and half at Anfield because the way they play demands incredible attention in all the details for the whole 95 minutes."

Liverpool fan Sean Cox returned to Anfield for the first time since sustaining serious brain injuries in an attack by Roma supporters outside the ground in April 2018. Klopp was delighted: "It's great - I hope to be able to see him, to be honest. I'm not sure if it's going to be possible, but it's just wonderful. It's been 18 tough months for sure for the family, and for himself and his friends. Now that he's coming back, it's really nice. I'm sure that our supporters will make it a very special occasion for him, and I will try to see him as I would really like to. When it happened it was my lowest point at Liverpool. Something like this should not happen in general in life and it should not happen around a football game as well. We all know it's not finished yet and there is a long way to go. If we can give him the opportunity to come back to watch a really big game - and that he wants to do that - that for me, coming from a really low point, is one of my highlights since I have been here."

Media speculation City's bus would again come under attack. The issue was a sore point, memories still vivid how the barrage of missiles were thrown at their team bus before the 2018 Champions League quarter-final. City was in touch with Liverpool to stress the importance of being allowed an incident-free journey into Anfield. Klopp stressed: "I am a fan of fan power in the stadium, but that is senseless. If someone at Manchester City is concerned that is our fault and we all have to make sure that something like this never happens again. We all didn't throw a bottle, but it was one of us. All of us have to make sure we don't have not had a situation like that again. I wish I could say it would never happen again, but we all have to try and make sure."

Guardiola commented: "Hopefully it won't happen again, The police knew that then, I don't know if the police are dong something different."

Sunday, November 10 was a lovely bright, sunny, chilly day, with Saturday wins for Chelsea and Leicester, leaving City in FOURTH place, a hugely unfamiliar sight. It emphasised that it was no longer a two-horse race, and Liverpool faced more challenges from Brendon Rodgers and Frank Lampards teams. So, imperative for City to win at Anfield, or at least draw, but equally, even with a six point lead, for Liverpool at least not to lose. Perish the thought that Klopp would go into this game settling for a point, though.

A large crowd greeted the City bus as it pulled off Anfield Road into the stadium, there was jeering, gestures and the odd red flare but nothing untoward. Team news; Klopp: one expected change, Fabinho in for Lallana, resisting the temptation to start in-form Oxlade-Chamberlain, who made a habit of scoring against City at Anfield.

In fact Klopp made four changes from the Champions League win over Genk with Robertson returning at left-back, Henderson coming back into midfield, Firmino and Mané rejoining the forward line. Bravo started his first Premier League game for City in 18 months with intense focus on the 36-year-old Chilean. Rodrigo returns from a hamstring injury to replace David Silva, Angelino gets the nod at left-back.

November

SUNDAY 10 NOVEMBER - PL
LIVERPOOL 3
Fabinho (4), Salah (11), Mané (50)
MAN CITY 1
B Silva (77)

The clash of the Premier League titans may have taken place on a bright chilly Sunday in November but for most pundits a Liverpool win here would all but guarantee them the league, even if there were more than half the league games left to play. Following Saturday wins for Chelsea and Leicester, City lay fourth in the table, an unfamiliar sight under Guardiola. But it emphasised City's inconsistent start to the season having already dropped points to Spurs, Norwich and Wolves. So a win was imperative for City at Anfield while a defeat might be terminal for their chances of emulating those great Liverpool and United teams of the past by winning three titles in a row.

Large crowds greeted the City bus as it pulled off Anfield Road into the stadium; there was jeering, gestures and the odd red flare but nothing untoward. The team news revealed one expected change for Liverpool - Fabinho in for Lallana. Klopp resisted the temptation to start in-form Oxlade-Chamberlain, who made a habit of scoring against City at Anfield. In fact Klopp made four changes from the Champions League win over Genk with Robertson returning at left-back, Henderson coming back into midfield and Firmino and Mané rejoining the forward line. Claudio Bravo would make his first Premier League start for City in 18 months with an intense focus on the 36-year-old Chilean. Rodrigo returned from a hamstring injury to replace David Silva, Angelino gets the nod at left-back.

In a pulsating first half that lived up to its hype, City were often spectacular going forward, but Liverpool were clinical on the counter. The visitors dominated the opening few minutes, penning Liverpool into their own half and a cross looked to have struck Trent Alexander-Arnold on the arm before the ball was cleared downfield and found Mané, his cross was only half cleared by John Stones and fell to Fabinho who fired in from 25 yards. It was a smash and grab raid that highlighted City's weakness at the back and their uncertainty over stand-in keeper Bravo. City protests about the potential handball were turned down by VAR and Liverpool led against the run of play. #

On 13 minutes Liverpool broke again, Andy Robertson's cross finding Salah who headed home. Again VAR checked for a marginal offside against the Egyptian but again the technology favoured the home team. Conspiracy theories abounded on social media but there was no denying the fact that Liverpool were 2-0 up.

Klopp's team then managed the game, letting City have the ball and limiting them to very few chances although Angelino struck a post and Aguero missed a good chance. It promised to be a gripping second half with City looking quite capable of scoring plenty of goals, but Liverpool looked even more threatening on the break. The next goal would be critical and Liverpool added a third when Henderson's cross from the right deceived Bravo and Mané dived to head home. Yet City carried on pressing and there were multiple penalty claims for fouls and possible handballs all turned down by VAR.

Bernardo Silva did manage to score a consolation for City but in reality Liverpool had played their opponents to perfection, exploiting their weakness on the counter and their uncertainty at the back.

Of the first goal, Trent Alexander-Arnold told Sky Sports: "I think it might have hit my arm but it hit Bernardo Silva's first. You have to carry on playing, they complained but you have to keep on playing."

Former City captain Kompany, a Sky pundit for the evening, argued play should have been stopped in the Liverpool box, regardless of the final verdict. "You can argue about Bernardo's handball before - I don't think he knows anything about it and it's a natural position. But [Alexander-Arnold's] is a handball, that's not a natural position. Stop the action then and make a decision. You go which way you want to go, but my interpretation is that Bernardo's hand is in a natural position and Alexander-Arnold's isn't."

These games are often decided by millimetres and split second decisions and so it proved again. Back on 3 January, as Liverpool arrived at Etihad Stadium looking to open up a 10-point gap over City, and with the game goalless, Mané struck the post and Stones' attempted clearance rebounded off Ederson, forcing the defender into a dramatic last-gasp clearance. Goal-line technology showed the ball was 11.7mm short. Guardiola's side went on to win 2-1 condemning Liverpool to their only defeat of the season as City eventually claimed the title by a single point.

Clearly unhappy about the incident that led to the first goal

November

Guardiola said, "Ask the referees, don't ask me. Ask Mike Riley and the guys in VAR". During the game he had been furious as there was a second Alexander-Arnold 'handball' claim. Guardiola leapt up and down with rage wagging two fingers at the fourth official Mike Dean. The call not to award City a penalty was, according to the Professional Game Match Officials Board, because the appeal for handball against Alexander-Arnold "did not meet the considerations for a deliberate handball".

"What a load of rubbish! Absolute drivel," said Radio 5 Live pundit Chris Sutton as he was read the statement. "If I was a Man City player I'd be furious. In games that are decided by such tiny moments, that was a refereeing howler. There will be controversy. It did look like Trent's arm was in an unnatural position. I think Alexander-Arnold is a lucky, lucky boy. It should have been a penalty. I don't understand why it wasn't given. His arm was out, it hit him on the arm - it's a penalty. I just don't get it, with what we have been told about the handball rule that has to be the definition of a penalty. Why on earth does Michael Oliver not take it upon himself and look at it on the monitor? Later on he will see that decision and know that he got that wrong."

Robbie Savage, also speaking on BBC Radio 5 Live, added: "How on earth is that not handball? It's absolute nonsense. Go and use the pitchside monitor - it's a big error."

Guardiola had confronted Michael Oliver with sarcastic 'thank yous' at full-time as the pressure of a title race he was clearly losing seemed to be getting to him. Meanwhile Jürgen Klopp was having his own meltdown on the pitch! He refused to play to the Sky Sports cameras, clearly wanting a close up of his famous fist pumps to the fans, and beating his chest, waving them away, saying "not while you're here... I'm not a clown".

When the dust settled, the champions were fourth behind Brendan Rodgers' Leicester and Chelsea and the big question was could anyone prevent Liverpool from claiming their first Premier League title? Guardiola claimed he "does not know" as City's quest to become the first side since Manchester United in 2009 to win three consecutive titles was in tatters and it was still only early November!

"I am not a magician; I don't know the future," Guardiola said. "We have Chelsea at home next. We will try to beat them." He offered no comment on the big penalty beyond saying: "Ask Mike Riley and his people please" but then added, "Congratulations to Liverpool, they scored three, we got one but I'm so proud of my team, few teams can come here and play the way we did. We started incredibly well, we showed incredible bravery, they are the champions of Europe and it is the most difficult stadium in the world. We played like back-to-back champions. We cannot deny how good Liverpool are but the way we played, the personality, it was good."

Klopp called the frenetic game "incredible... really wild". Fabinho's opener met with a muted response but he explained: "The problem was the VAR. I saw the discussions before the first goal and I was just waiting. It is not the same any more but it is no problem. I can celebrate tonight. It was so tough to play, the intensity of the game was so clear. It was all worth it, really great."

Klopp was determined not to let any negative thoughts enter his player's head, with the inevitable 'it's yours to lose' stigma, and hoped this result gave his players the the confidence to go on after the latest international break. "We don't feel any pressure, to be 100% honest. The things that will now come up – we know about it. If you are with us, then nine points is a positive. There's a long way to go. Other people will 100% say – and have said already – that from now on Liverpool can only lose it. That's a very negative approach, but you can see it like this. But we don't care. I can promise you that we don't care. We were completely focused on this game – not the situation in the table and how many points we are ahead of City in the table. That's crazy. Nine points ahead of City, you cannot imagine that something like this would happen. But it's not important because who wants to be first in November? You want to be first in May. It's only November. We all know that but don't have to say it as it's clear. We will try and see what happens in the end. The pressure or whatever is not there yet. It will come, but, at the moment, it's just opportunity and go for it and do the work, throw all in what you have and let's see what happens. Each point we have we need to go through the most intense period ever."

KLOPP: "What a game. If you want to win against City you have to do something special and we had to be intense. When City started to control it more in the last 15 minutes, it was tense, but then you saw the quality and what the boys can do it. The boys did 75 minutes of unbelievable stuff. I feel sympathy for Pep [on the first VAR incident] but I did not see the situation, what I heard is that the ball hit first David Silva's arm and then Trent Alexander-Arnold."

PEP GUARDIOLA: "We lost - we'd liked to win but now we have to rest and prepare for Chelsea next. We played an incredible performance, I don't know how many teams can come to this stadium and play the way we did. They scored with the first shot on target, but we played incredibly well. There are three teams that have more chances to win the Premier League than us. We're in November so let's see what happens."

OTHER SCORES

FRIDAY 8 NOVEMBER
Norwich City 0 Watford 2

SATURDAY 9 NOVEMBER
Chelsea 2 Crystal Palace 0
Burnley 3 West Ham United 0
Newcastle United 2 AFC Bournemouth 1
Southampton 1 Everton 2
Tottenham Hotspur 1 Sheffield United 1
Leicester City 2 Arsenal 0

SUNDAY 10 NOVEMBER
Manchester United 3 Brighton & Hove Albion 1
Wolverhampton Wanderers 2 Aston Villa 1

SATURDAY 23 NOVEMBER – PREMIER LEAGUE

CRYSTAL PALACE 1
Zaha (80)
LIVERPOOL 2
Mané (47), Firmino (83)

Liverpool were often accused of 'luck' in securing all three points with a stoppage time goal but Klopp knows it's a reflection of the players mentality. Klopp's team had won 10 points from losing positions, the most in the Premier League this season and in total dropped just two points in 12 games. In the last seven games where they conceded the first goal, Liverpool went on to win six and draw the other, making them one of the game's most resilient teams. Klopp is often asked his secret is to grinding out results. Klopp and his players worked on the psychological aspect for years. "Of course it's all about that," Klopp told *The Athletic*, "but you can't just order it and then assume the boys will deliver it. If it was that easy then you could just tell them in the moment when you are 1-0 down with 10 minutes to play, 'you still have to believe'. You have to create something and what we have created all together started long ago. People now talk about it but I already feel uncomfortable talking about it because I don't take it for granted, not for one second. It's not that I'm thinking five minutes before we go 1-0 down "no problem, you can score". It's happened more often than not that we've come back which is good, very good, but [we are] not allowed to take it for granted. It's just that because it's happened so often, psychologically it's clear. If you do something good then it's absolutely likely that the next time you do it, it's likely that it will work out again."

For Klopp, talent was important, but it's inseparable from mentality. "You can have the best technical ability but if you aren't ready to show it then you can't make the best of it. It's no different in football than it is in normal life. The first step is to think you can do it. You want to do it, you want to achieve it, then you have to find a way to go there. It's constantly like question and answer, question and answer. Right, not right, trial and error. That's how we do it and in football it's no different."

As if to prove his manager's point, Roberto Firmino scored yet another late winner as Liverpool maintained their eight-point lead at the top of with a hard-fought victory over Crystal Palace as Leicester maintained the pressure in second place with an away win at Brighton. Klopp was preparing Salah, already stripped and ready to go on the touchline, to come off the bench just as Firmino scored, the manager then put his star striker back on the bench, and sent on Joe Gomez instead. Salah could only smile as he put his training gear back. Liverpool stretched their incredible run to 30 games unbeaten in the Premier League. Firmino poked in from a corner five minutes from time to restore his side's lead three minutes after it looked as if Zaha had rescued a point for the Eagles. Zaha's 82nd-minute goal was his first of the season and cancelled out Mané's 10th goal of the season just after half-time. Zaha wasted a great chance to score a second equaliser late on when he blazed over from close range. Tomkins had a goal ruled out in first-half stoppage time by the video assistant referee after Ayew was adjudged to have fouled Lovren.

Klopp hailed his team's 'exceptional' start to the season but made it clear they are only interested in winning titles, not breaking records. Should they remain unbeaten against Brighton, they could break their own record during the Merseyside Derby against Everton. "I have no clue about records," Klopp said. "We are not out there to break records but we are really there to get the best result in the full season. If on the way we break one of two records then good but winning the next game is much more important than people saying in 10-15 years that was the record set by this team. We really have a bigger job to do."

Guardiola needed to avoid his side being distracted by Liverpool although he felt one more defeat for City might be the end of their lingering hopes of a third in a row title. After coming from behind to beat Chelsea at home, he said: "Liverpool look unstoppable. I know it's far away with these numbers. My teams always try but we accept other teams can be better. So [if] we are going to lose the Premier League, we are going to try the next season. It's not the first time Manchester City in 100 years of history lose the league. If we don't do it, I'm not going to retire but I'm going to be disappointed.

"In these three years and a half, people can say we play good or bad but give up? That is not going to happen. My teams, always we try but I accept that the others can do better. If we lose, it's done. The line is so tight. I know we are winners and losers and that's all. But I think it's not a good message for society, for our kids, for our teenagers, showing them that just the winner is perfect. We are creating a depressed people, loser people. What is important is the effort, the commitment, the situation. In football I know we want to win but just win once and the other is disaster? It's not. It doesn't work in that way. That's why I said to the players relax, do your job, we will see in December, January, February, March and we will see what position we are in. If the position is far away, okay it's far away. We are going to try again next season."

ROY HODGSON: "The players should be congratulating themselves on taking a point from the leaders but it wasn't to be. I have praise for my own team for having a go, if you can be bold enough to praise your team when you're not winning. Throughout there was not an awful lot of clear-cut chances. That was testament to the defensive work we did throughout the team. The fact is you must take your chances and we only took one of ours. The late winner is a cruel blow but I have nothing to complain about from my side. I want to be positive, I think it was our best performance so far this season."

KLOPP: "At the end we won the game and it was deserved as well. There were not too many mistakes but the goal they scored was good. We have to bring plans together after the international break. I'm happy with the result and big parts of the performance because I know it's not possible to be brilliant every game."

OTHER SCORES

SATURDAY 23 NOVEMBER
West Ham United 2 Tottenham Hotspur 3
Arsenal 2 Southampton 2
AFC Bournemouth 1 Wolverhampton Wanderers 2
Brighton & Hove Albion 0 Leicester City 2
Everton 0 Norwich City 2
Watford 0 Burnley 3
Manchester City 2 Chelsea 1

SUNDAY 24 NOVEMBER
Sheffield United 3 Manchester United 3

MONDAY 25 NOVEMBER
Aston Villa 2 Newcastle United 0

November

WEDNESDAY 27 NOVEMBER - CHAMPIONS LEAGUE

LIVERPOOL 1
Lovren (65)
NAPOLI 1
Mertens (19)

Jurgen hugged opposing manager Carlo Ancelotti ahead of this game – there was a huge amount of respect between the managers - just as well as they faced each six times in the last two seasons. In one of those meetings - a pre-season friendly in the summer, Ancellotti left Jurgen a gift that, for once, had him lost for words -"My positive memory of the (friendly) in Scotland was the incredibly classy gesture from Carlo," Klopp wrote in his programme notes. "He bought a very lovely bottle of red wine and wrote a touching congratulations message on it, for what we had achieved the season before. I was suitably embarrassed in the moment he gave it to me, to the point I was lost for words. People who knowme well will tell you this is a very rare occurrence."

Salah returned as Klopp made three changes from the win at Palace at the weekend. Gomez and Milner in for Alexander-Arnold and Wijnaldum, Shaqiri on the bench for the first time since September after returning from injury. If Napoli were going to win at Anfield they were going to have do it without Lorenzo Insigne who was injured.

Klopp was booked just before half time for angrily complaining to the officials about an Allan foul on Mane in a frustrating first half where Napoli scored early. While it was a good finish from Mertens before the ball as played, Van Dijk was down injured and limping, fouled but the referee failed to stop the play. VAR looked at it, still a goal, then a second VAR check for potential offside. Still a goal. Fabinho was injured before the goal and replaced by Wijnaldum. Boos from the home fans for the officials as Klopp raced down the tunnel. Minamino put Salzburg 2-0 up in Genk at the interval. As it stood, Liverpool needed a point against Salzburg in Austria or they would be eliminated. On Fabinho's worrying injury Klopp commented: "I don't want to say what I expect. It's early and we all hope it's not too serious but it's pretty painful and in an area you don't want to have pain, around the ankle. The biggest thing [tonight] is the Fabinho injury, that's massive. He couldn't continue. We'll know more maybe tomorrow or the day after. It was an unlucky situation but that for us is the biggest problem, the other thing is just another football match, so let's just try and win that."

Already suspended for next match at home to Brighton, having picked up a fifth yellow card of the season in the Reds' 2-1 win over Palace, he had time to recover. Klopp was impressed with how Ancelotti set his team up to frustrate Liverpool. "The way Napoli set up, it didn't help that they scored, they could follow their plan all the time, we had to in-crease pressure all the time. We were not brilliant but we put pressure on them. I was not happy with the last 15 minutes of the first half. Second half it was just intense and of course it's not easy, they really defended the goal they had." With nine games scheduled for December, Klopp needed a dead rubber in the middle of it to give his players a breather. Lovren's headed equaliser secured the draw which an improved second half performance warranted, though it was a struggle. The dropped points left Liverpool requiring a draw from their last fixture against free-scoring Salzburg. "I am four years in, tell me when it was easy. I know how human beings are, people wished we could finish the group tonight and have a holiday game against Salzburg but it never happens, it will never happen. That is the situation.

"If we have ambitions in the Champions League we have to show it in Salzburg. Until then we have to show our ambitions in the Premier League. There are a couple of games to play until then and we have to be focused on them - and we will be, no doubt. Everybody here thinks, 'Oh my god, it will be tough' and it will be tough, that much is clear."

In the opening half, the referee twice stopped players taking quick free-kicks which Klopp took issue with. "I said [to the referee]: 'Don't do that,'" Klopp explained why he was booked. "He stopped the game twice and made a big fuss. There was an opportunity for both teams to have a quick restart but twice he [intervened] and had things to say [to the players]. So I said: 'Why did you do that? Please don't do that' and then I got it."

Liverpool announced Fabinho "suffered ankle ligament damage" and will be out "until the New Year". Klopp was not happy. "Losing a player of the quality of Fabinho is big. Really bad. It is bad news. Timeframe - we are not sure 100% but looks pretty sure he will not be involved in Christmas fixtures. We have to replace him and we can replace him. Now it's important that he does the right things and is back as soon as possible. Until then, we have to find solutions. We are not the only team with injured players and that's what we have to deal

November

with, and we will."

The Reds had 11 games over the next 34 days in the Premier League, Champions League, Carabao Cup and Club World Cup. Fabinho had started 12 out 13 league and all five European fixtures. Klopp was no stranger to final group games taking on 'knock out' proportions, as it had done in the two previous campaigns, so the game in Austria became a 'cup final' mind set again. "Everybody knows it's a final and we're prepared for that - Salzburg has to win against us."

SATURDAY 30 NOVEMBER - PREMIER LEAGUE

LIVERPOOL 2
van Dijk (17, 22)
BRIGHTON 1
Dunk (78)

In the Saturday midday game Newcastle came from behind twice to snatch a 2-2 draw as Manchester City dropped more points. Klopp could equal the club record of 31 games unbeaten set by Kenny Dalglish from May 1987 to March 1988 but he was more interested in stretching his lead over Guardiola to 11 points. Wijnaldum was making his 200th game for an English club, Gomez his 50th in a Liverpool shirt, and Klopp's team made no mistake romping into a two-goal lead thanks to Virgil van Dijk enabling the manager to bring off Mo Salah, still recovering fully from his ankle issue, needing game time to regain his rhythm at the same time needing a break, a difficult balancing act for Klopp who brought Lallana in his place. A little later he also took off Firmino to send on Origi. Then, a red card for Alisson!

From a long ball and with the keeper outside his area, probably intending to head clear, Trossard got the better of Lovren as Alisson jumped up and palmed away the lob – it was a straight red, the first Liverpool goalkeeper sent off in a Premier League game since another Brazilian Doni against Blackburn in April 2012. Alex Oxlade-Chamberlain was sacrificed to send on reserve keeper Adrian, who immediately conceded from the resulting free-kick. Quick thinking Dunk took it early, as Liverpool's players were still organising the wall. Adrian stood and watched at the left hand post as the low strike went unchallenged into his bottom right corner. From cruising to victory, Liverpool now faced 10 nervous minutes with ten men and a one goal lead.

Brighton continued to press as Mooy nodded into the path of Burn but he smashed it wide from a tight angle inside the box then Lovren jogged over to do up Adrian's shoelaces! The defence needed to pull their socks up as well! 'All I want for Christmas is a clean sheet', one fan tweeted. But he should have been grateful as Adrian pulled off a decent save to his left as Mooy was left in space in the box. And what a let off as Adrian gave every Liverpool fan at Anfield a heart attack as he spilled a routine save following a header from Gross in the box, Maupay was alert, ready to pounce on the rebound, but Adrian recovered just in time as it headed backwards toward the line; a fumble from a keeper who didn't look as though he had warmed up properly!

The crowd whipped up a rendition of "Allez, allez, allez" to rally their players, clinging on with four minutes of stoppage time as Brighton threw everything into trying for a last gasp equaliser. The fans held their breath when the board went up with four minutes left. Klopp was on the edge of his technical area, looking at his watch, and looking as nervous as any supporter as Liverpool saw it out, the final whistle greeted as if they had won the league, and they nearly had – they now held an 11 point advantage. The players celebrated with their fans who were singing deliriously. Klopp and Robertson were the last to head down the tunnel.

Klopp felt it was "unnecessary" for the game to come to an edgy conclusion. "It was unnecessary, of course, because we had unbelievable chances. Their keeper made some good saves. It was difficult this game because Brighton are a good football side. They put players between the lines. They put so many players there so it's difficult to defend. They had a lot of possession and we had to work really hard. I loved that the boys were prepared to do that after a busy week. We then had the red card for Alisson. Adrian comes in with cold feet and cold hands but made two really good saves. I think it was handball but I haven't seen it. There was no offside and then it is a tricky situation. He wanted 100% to head the ball but the other player got there earlier so we can't change that.

"Of course, life became more complicated with the red card and the change we had to make. We brought on a frozen goalkeeper, pretty much. Everybody sitting here is probably not really warm yet, and then you imagine you go on in shorts, a really thin shirt and some gloves which are not made for keeping you warm, and then, some people let the free-kick happen. You look a little bit silly in that moment, but that's what you have to accept. We kept on fighting and Adrian, especially, helped us a lot with two really, really good saves and crosses he caught... although with his cold feet he obviously couldn't [kick] the ball as far as he wanted. That kept it a bit interesting, but in the end it's only important that we won the game and that's what we did, and I'm really pleased about that. I'm very, very happy with the effort the boys put in again. I'm really happy and proud of the desire the boys showed. The red card made it a really special win, to be honest."

There was still no clean sheet, though and Klopp was far from happy with the referee allowing the free kick to be taken as his players were still in the process of organising the wall. "I think in a situation like this, when you have sense for human beings, you don't do it like this. It was very clever from Brighton but the keeper has just come on and is trying to set the wall. They are trying to get used to each other and the referee lets it go like this. We cannot change it but for me it's not 100% right."

With City dropping points and Chelsea also losing at the Bridge to West Ham, their first win there since 2001, it left only Leicester challenging Liverpool! The Premier League table even before December took on an incredible appearance. Not for Klopp though, any time to reflect. "It's how it is. But if Leicester win tomorrow we are eight points ahead. We don't think about these things. It was just to win this game – not that I don't think Everton can win there. We have one more day between now and the next game so we have to use that and then we try again. Results-wise, it's an incredible period, for sure. But we don't want to think about the last 14 games. We are concerned about the next one, that's next Wednesday against Everton, so that's a big one. We have to make sure that we are prepared for that because that will be another big fight, whatever result Everton get tomorrow.'

KLOPP: "Virgil was probably man of the match with the two goals but Adrian is for me – to come in to a game like this and make two saves." The manager was quick to point out that Lovren played well as well at the back. When asked again by his two goal hero, he said: "Oh come on, do we have to talk about individual players? He scored two goals, that's the story itself. He's good, really good, outstandingly good. But he has to be, he's a very talented boy, so he just has to use that talent and it would be a shame if he doesn't. So yes, incredibly important but if Virg plays the last line alone it would be pretty difficult. I think Dejan Lovren, who maybe doesn't have the headlines like this, but what he's playing since, he has all my respect, to be honest."

GRAHAM POTTER: "There were lots of positives for us. In the first 10-15 minutes we weren't quite as aggressive and didn't have the belief we needed. We gave a really good account of ourselves against a top team. We are disappointed because we came away with nothing but with the performance and the effort, we could have come away with something. We had good chances at 2-0 down. Virgil van Dijk was so powerful in his two actions for their goals and we weren't as good. That's the reality. But over the 90 minutes we put so much into the game and we need to take that forward and carry on improving."

OTHER SCORES

SATURDAY 30 NOVEMBER
Newcastle United 2 Manchester City 2
Burnley 0 Crystal Palace 2
Chelsea 0 West Ham United 1
Tottenham Hotspur 3 AFC Bournemouth 2
Southampton 2 Watford 1

SUNDAY 1 DECEMBER
Norwich City 2 Arsenal 2
Wolverhampton Wanderers 1 Sheffield United 1
Leicester City 2 Everton 1
Manchester United 2 Aston Villa 2

DECEMBER

In the week before the Merseyside derby Lionel Messi won a record sixth Ballon d'Or, while Virgil Van Dijk was second, a mere seven votes behind. Klopp said: "I see it slightly different and a lot of people see it slightly different but that's absolutely no problem. I have seen Lionel Messi so many times, probably 500 times in my life already, and he is the best player I've seen in my lifetime. But I can't remember a more impressive season by a defender ever. Honestly. So, it would have been right if Virgil had won it and I heard it was pretty close."

It was a proud night for Liverpool and their manager with three players in the top five and seven nominated overall. A review of how the votes fell show that Alexander-Arnold established a fan base in Sri Lanka, as they chose him as the best player in the world; he ranked 19th, two places behind Salah and Mané's attacking partner, Firmino. Wijnaldum came 26th, Alisson seventh. The nation of Bhutan voted only for Liverpool players - Mané, Van Dijk, Salah, Alisson and Firmino.

Ahead of the clash with Everton the Liverpool boss believed that Toffees boss Marco Silva had a "really good" squad but did not know "why it's not clicking so far". He felt for the under-fire Everton boss, "of course I have sympathy because I know how difficult the life of a manager can be. But the last thing Marco needs now is that I feel sorry for him – I don't. But I am really on his side because I know about the job. The table tells the truth at the end of the season, but if you go through the Everton squad, nobody denies that it's a really good one. They've had difficult injuries, especially the Andre Gomes one. Fabian Delph, too, is a very important player for them. There is a lot of pressure, of course, as Everton are an ambitious club and rightly so. They are not the only ones in this situation, this league is really difficult for everyone.

"Are managers given enough time? For me, yes. Generally, I don't know, I can only speak about me, I have never felt in doubt. And in my job or others, there is pressure to deliver. If it doesn't work out then they try something else. In general, the pressure and the decisions are made too quickly, of course. It happens because people think they cannot reach targets anymore."

Klopp, who has won five and drawn three of his eight derbies in charge, believed a win at Anfield could be the 'silver bullet' Everton were hoping for. "Remember we don't have to speak about quality and quality differences. Are we in a better moment in the table? Of course, that is obvious. But the stats, from my point of view, help Everton more than us because they want to strike back. They want do show they can do differently. They can solve a lot of problems in one game. It is a very important football game for us but that must be enough for us. We expect Everton at their best. It is a standout game for both teams. We have to make sure we are ready.

"For both teams it is a hugely important game. My first (Merseyside) derby we won 4-0 but I think they had a red card in that game but most of the time since I have been here the derbies have been tight results. We know we have to work extremely hard because all I saw against Leicester was them making life really difficult. That's what we expect. In the first few derbies there were some harsh challenges. Hard tackles are normal in football, but they were kind of over-forceful. That didn't happen in the last two or three games and as long as we can keep it on this level, everything is fine. Fight for it with everything you have in a football way."

WEDNESDAY, 4 DECEMBER 2019 - PREMIER LEAGUE

LIVERPOOL 5
Origi (4, 30), Shaqiri (15), Mané (43), Wijnaldum (90)
EVERTON 2
Keane (19), Richarlison (45+1)

Jürgen Klopp's team selection caused quite a stir as he left out first team regulars Salah, Firmino, Henderson and Oxlade-Chamberlain. Five changes in all. The big surprises were Shaqiri, Lallana and Origi. Alisson was suspended following his dismissal against Brighton so in came Adrian, Fabinho was injured so Milner was called up. Xherdan Shaqiri had managed just 11 minutes in the Premier League this season.

While Everton were delighted not see see Sala and Firmino, they would have been apprehensive at the sight of Origi, who had scored that freakish 96th minute winner to give Liverpool victory in last season's derby at Anfield. Everton hadn't won a league game against Liverpool

December

at Anfield since September 1999, courtesy of Kevin Campbell's strike. The Toffees had drawn nine and lost ten of their visits since. They hadn't won a Merseyside derby anywhere in their past 19 attempts when David Moyes' Everton beat Roy Hodgson's Reds 2-0 in October 2010. Klopp explained his reasoning just before kick off, knowing his team had eight games in December: "We can do it. I have to show the respect for the boys. I like the squad so we have to use it. That's the line-up for the day because we think it will be really intense so for this we need fresh legs. With the first whistle, it's a derby. It's an important game for both sides. In games like this you just try to fight as hard as you can and get the three points. That's what we will try. Thank god we are not into these kind of stats. I don't feel a little bit about the last game or the game before. I don't even know about my record against Everton. It's a very difficult game that's all I need to know. We are not thinking about the situation of the opponent. We need to show character. You know about the importance of a game like this but there are different ways to show it. It's to show that you are ready to give your all."

Klopp had a word of praise for Everton supporters: "I don't believe too much in coincidences. One of my first moments when I met Everton was at the Hillsborough memorial and the respect they showed. I appreciated it a lot. In difficult situations the people of this city stand together. That's a part where we are 100% united."

On the night all three of the players Klopp surprise selections were magnificent and some of the goals were world class as Liverpool were majestic racking up a 4-2 half time lead and eventually running out 5-2 winners, as records were sent tumbling. On recording a 32-game unbeaten record, Klopp said: "I would love that this number is in one season. That would be great! Last season we were nearly 38 games unbeaten but it was not enough. Nice number but not really interested in it."

Sadio Mané was man-of-the-match creating two goals with sublime passes, and scoring himself, although he might well have managed a hat-trick but had to be content with just the one, setting up both Origi and Shaqiri to set the Reds on their way. Mané was the only one of the famed front three to start and added a fourth as the first half ended 4-2 after Michael Keane and Richarlison kept Everton in it with two goals against the run of play. Wijnaldum applied the finishing touch in the 90th minute as Everton's winless run at Anfield extended beyond 20 years and left Marco Silva's job hanging by a thread, he would be sacked before their weekend fixture against Chelsea. Mo Salah was able to have the night off, Firmino and captain Jordan Henderson were introduced as late subs.

KLOPP: "All the goals were incredible, outstanding. Wonderful goals, sensational passes, super pieces of football. I loved it a lot! We needed fresh legs and I had to show my respect to the boys in the squad, that's all. They proved it. It is much more fun making changes, all of the boys are ready to deliver performances like this. It was a massive moment in my first season when Divock Origi got injured in the derby. It changed his career for a bit."

MARCO SILVA: "We cannot concede goals in the way we conceded. We knew everything about them before the match and how they like to play whether with Origi, Salah or Firmino, we know how they would play. There was a lot of mistakes. I am not the right person to answer about the situation, this question is for different people. We are making some mistakes which put us under big, big pressure. The type of mistakes we are making is because the players are playing under big pressure because of the position in the table."

OTHER SCORES

TUESDAY 3 DECEMBER
Crystal Palace 1 AFC Bournemouth 0
Burnley 1 Manchester City 4

WEDNESDAY 4 DECEMBER
Chelsea 2 Aston Villa 1
Leicester City 2 Watford 0
Manchester United 2 Tottenham Hotspur 1
Southampton 2 Norwich City 1
Wolverhampton Wanderers 2 West Ham United 0

THURSDAY 5 DECEMBER
Sheffield United 0 Newcastle United 2
Arsenal 1 Brighton & Hove Albion 2

December

SATURDAY, 7 DECEMBER 2019 – PREMIER LEAGUE

BOURNEMOUTH 0
LIVERPOOL 3
Chamberlain (34), Keïta (43), Salah (54)

As if to buck the trend, one minute Mané is top dog, the next he's benched! Klopp continued to rotate his squad, making seven changes from the Merseyside derby. Alexander-Arnold was rested, while the forward line was benched as Firmino and Salah returned up front. Alisson returned from suspension, while Keita, Gomez, Henderson and Oxlade-Chamberlain started as Liverpool retained their 11 point lead at the top with a comfortable 3-0 win at the Vitality Stadium.

Alex Oxlade-Chamberlain opened the scoring after a brilliant long-range pass from Henderson. Keita made it 2-0 before the break, slotting in with the outside of his foot after Salah set him up with a sublime back-heel. Keita then turned provider for Salah to extend the club record unbeaten run to 33 league games, winning 15 of 16 Premier League matches this season, as Klopp's team developed an air of invincibility.

Salah scored his 63rd goal in his 100th Premier League appearance - only Alan Shearer (79), Ruud van Nistelrooy (68) and Sergio Aguero (64) scored more in their first 100 games in the competition. Salah has scored more Premier League goals against Bournemouth (seven) than any other opponent, and has netted in all five of his appearances against the Cherries.

Even more pleasing for Klopp was their first clean sheet in 14 games and new Premier League goalscorers in Oxlade-Chamberlain and Keita - the 15th and 16th players to score in the competition for Liverpool this season. Oxlade-Chamberlain scored his first goal in 25 Premier League appearances for Liverpool. He last netted in the competition against Manchester City in January 2018, one year and 327 days ago.

Mané was an unused substitute alongside Origi. Klopp observed: "People were shouting for Divock and I understand that, but to bring him on to say 'thank you', we just have so many games. It was wonderful we didn't have to use Sadio Mané, but he's been playing all the time in the last couple of weeks. Ask the players if they are upset, but it's not difficult for me. I don't speak to Sadio, I didn't speak to Divock. I didn't speak to Hendo. I don't ask, I just have to make decisions and then next time everyone knows someone else will play. The boys are a really smart group who look at the schedule. They know how it is. If someone is angry or concerned that they are not starting, I can't help that. Next time everybody knows somebody else will play and then it's the next game and the next game so that's what happens now. Today we had 14 adult players plus Curtis and Harvey. That's our squad for today. The only players who are maybe back for Tuesday are Gini Wijnaldum and Adam Lallana to make it 16. We'll see how we start on Tuesday, I have no idea about that now. But we could give these two, plus Gini (Wijnaldum) and Adam (Lallana), so four players kind of a rest and hopefully they are all fit again for Tuesday and we will make decisions'

KLOPP: "It was a mature and professional performance - controlled, scoring wonderful goals. It was a super performance. It was what we needed. We didn't want to make it exciting again, so we wanted to control Bournemouth, absolutely, so nothing really happens any more. The players didn't like it too much, but I didn't want to see any unnecessary risks. We've hd so many games where we've had to chase to the last second because we were 1-0 down or it was 1-1. Then you have this really rare comfortable situation. The most used word in the dressing room at the moment from the boys when I came in afterwards were 'clean sheet, clean sheet, clean sheet, '...finally! Everybody was desperate for that. Now we have it, let's have it more often. [The injury to defender] Dejan Lovren was hopefully cramp but apart from that it was a perfect game. All round, nearly perfect day."

EDDIE HOWE: "I don't like to use injuries as an excuse, but there comes a time when you have to look at the situation and the teams we are playing. We lost another two players today. It is what it is. The squad is stretched. It is there to cope with the injuries but the difficulty for us is we are getting injuries but not getting players back. The mentality of the group is strong but damaged in confidence. We can always do better. We can always question ourselves and say we could have done better today, but the quality of the opposition was very strong."

With this result Liverpool were assured as being top at Christmas and Klopp was asked if he was going to be Scrooge-like in giving nothing away as he pragmatically shut up shop when 3-0 up, but he joked: "Christmas is after Qatar. I'm sorry but I can't think that far ahead." The day got better as the evening wore on as United won the

December

Manchester derby at the Etihad to leave the Citizens 14 points adrift of Liverpool.

OTHER SCORES

SATURDAY 7 DECEMBER
Everton 3 Chelsea 1
AFC Bournemouth 0 Liverpool 3
Tottenham Hotspur 5 Burnley 0
Watford 0 Crystal Palace 0
Manchester City 1 Manchester United 2

SUNDAY 8 DECEMBER
Aston Villa 1 Leicester City 4
Newcastle United 2 Southampton 1
Norwich City 1 Sheffield United 2
Brighton & Hove Albion 2 Wolverhampton Wanderers 2

MONDAY 9 DECEMBER
West Ham United 1 Arsenal 3

TUESDAY, 10 DECEMBER 2019 - CHAMPIONS LEAGUE

FT SALZBURG 0
LIVERPOOL 2
Keïta (56), Salah (58)

In the pre-match press conference in Austria, Klopp was far from happy with one of his answers in English was relayed in German. Klopp took over from the translator to provide proper translation. Klopp called out 's★★★' translator' after he misinterpreted Henderson's answer. The translator sat alongside him suggested Henderson said they would 'go easy' in their final group stage fixture. In fact, Henderson, who was asked about Liverpool's previous last match deciders in the competition, had said 'that doesn't mean it's going to be easy.' After Henderson finished, the translator got to work only to be interrupted by Klopp. In German, the manager said: "It's s★★★ when next to the translator sits a coach who speaks German. The question was if the Champions League title from the last year helps us because we have always delivered in situations like this. He [Henderson] doesn't talk about going easy in this game. We are aware of this challenge. He is speaking about all this normal stuff. You should really listen. Otherwise, I can do it by myself. It's not too difficult." Switching to English, he added: "I am in a competition mood already, I can tell you."

Chelsea were the last reigning champions not to reach the knockout phase back in 2012. Rather than perpetuate the negative, as usual it was emphasising the positive, as Klopp became animated at the prospect of doing something not even the great sides of the 1970s managed by reaching three European Cup Finals in a row.

Salzburg stood in their way, "Yes it is difficult but there is a job to do," he said when asked how the demands of such a hectic schedule of games affected his players. "We don't ask for excuses. We know our schedule. We know where we have to go. We played three days ago in Bournemouth a tough game, six days ago a very tough game against Everton. We play in another in four days a very tough game against Watford and then we fly to Qatar. We don't expect drops in performance. We don't accept drops — not just me, the boys too. We ask ourselves for the highest concentration. Then we will see what we get for it. We area group that is in the most intense period of our lives and we will try to enjoy it. It is difficult, no doubt about that — but there is nothing that can stop us."

Liverpool went through in the last group games beating Spartak Moscow and Napoli in the past two seasons. "We are ready for a proper fight," said Klopp. "I can't talk about special things. We know we have to give everything and that is what we will do. If Salzburg win the game they deserve it. If not, then we deserve it. We have to show that we deserve to go through. We are not typical Champions League winners. We are ambitious like crazy. We will run for our lives. We will fight for every challenge. This is the most important game in our lives, because it is the next one. This has nothing to do with the situation in the Premier League. We know our future. It's not that I expect us to go through, I expect us to play the best game we can play."

Klopp needed a plan to contain Erling Haaland scorer of 28 goals in 21 games this season, eight in the Champions League, only Bayern Munich's Robert Lewandowski had scored more (10). The Norway international, 19, came off the bench to score against Liverpool in his side's 4-3 defeat at Anfield. Klopp said: "I had a time when I had Lewandowski in my [Dortmund] team, they didn't listen to anything else in the press conference. I wish you could find something else you could talk about. How do you defend a very good striker? Try and stop balls into the box. He is a really big talent."

In the event the teenage sensation had chances but failed to become the first player to score in his first six Champions League appearances, van Dijk stopped Haaland from a one-on-one with Alisson after 15 seconds. Haaland was replaced in the second half, having had three shots and 23 touches. Liverpool kept a second clean sheet in a row, having conceded in each of the 13 matches before that.

"Jesse and his team worked great with their team and gave them a fantastic attitude; they used what they could use, but we also played very well in the spaces," said Klopp. "When we started to play more intelligently and use the spaces we had in the second half then we used our opportunities. We had 21 attempts on goal and we could have scored five or six times, so it was really difficult for Salzburg in the second half. But, once again, my highest respect for Jesse and his team." Liverpool kept a clean sheet in an away Champions League game for the first time in 11 matches, having conceded 18 goals in their previous 10. The only concern for Klopp was a hamstring injury that forced Lovren off in the 53rd minute. He limped to the team bus after-wards and it means Van Dijk and Gomez were the only fit central defenders. "It wasn't cool," said Klopp. "He played really well and was very important in those 55 minutes. We don't know how bad it is at the moment. We have to see."

Before the post-match press conference, Klopp turned to the translator and said in German: "Before we start, I'd like to apologise for yesterday. I know that it was unfair and even more so as it happened in public. It was completely stupid. I didn't like the way my answer was translated, but the way I addressed it was stupid. I should have done better and I'm sorry." The translator accepted Klopp's apology, with the manager joking that he should translate his apology into English.

★

In the draw for the round of 16 a few days later, Klopp was excited at the prospect of a special return to Madrid as Liverpool drew Atletico in the last 16 where they triumphed over Tottenham at Estadio Wanda Metropolitano. "It's an interesting draw. Before the draw I actually thought it would be Madrid - either one of the two clubs – and that's the way it is."

The draw brought back fond memories, and when asked if it will be special to make the return, Klopp said: "I think so, we'll see. I think we had the home dressing room in that game. Maybe we can ask them if we can have that dressing room again! It is fantastic. What can I say? I had one of the best nights of my life in this stadium. It was really nice. It was full with Liver-pool signs, but I think they've got rid of them."

Klopp believed Atletico would prove tough opposition and present a very different challenge to Tottenham six months earlier. "Madrid is the place where we only have fantastic memories, all of us, so that is great, but this time we play Atletico there and it is their home ground. It will be a tough game. Two teams who are used to playing intense football, different styles and slightly different organisation of course, but both are ready for intensity and that makes it pretty tough for both."

Klopp joked that manager Diego Simeone will not be celebrating after hearing the news. "A good draw, a difficult game - like it should be, but as we think and say most of the time, I don't think Mr Simeone is running through his living room and is happy that he got Liverpool. We have to go there to work and try our best. Then they have to come to Anfield."

SATURDAY, 14 DECEMBER 2019 - PREMIER LEAGUE

LIVERPOOL 2
Salah (36, 88)
WATFORD 0

Before the game against bottom club Watford, Liverpool honoured their greatest-ever manager Bill Shankly 60 years on from the day that he took charge. It was a fitting tribute, but also incredibly well-timed as Jürgen Klopp had signed a contract extension in the week, it was the perfect Christmas gift for Liverpool fans. Shankly's face adorned the match day programme with one of his famous quotes: "Liverpool was made for me and I was made for Liverpool". The same might now apply to the current boss! Klopp's message to his supporters appeared in the programme, "In a dressing room you don't look at someone and see colour, creed, sexuality or anything of that nature. You see a friend, a teammate, someone who you can help and someone who can help you. Someone that by working together, you can have better collective experiences than if you tried to do it on your own." It was the mantra of a manager who relied on the players who were not selected as much as those who were.

December

Again, Klopp might have tinkered with his line up, but the outcome proved to be just what he wanted, perhaps, though, not in the manner he would have liked. Mo Salah scored two vital goals, one just before the interval and one moving into added time to ease the team's nerves after a gutsy display by the bottom team under new manager Nigel Pearson. Salah's opener was a curler into the far corner. The second was dubbed the cheekiest goal of the season as his back heel flick nutmegged the defender near the goal-line. Salah scored eight Premier League goals against Watford; more than against any other team in the big 5 European leagues but none as unusual as this one.

Watford missed simple chances in both halves, Van Dijk almost passed into his own net following a mix up with Alisson and Alexander-Arnold was caught in possession on the right. Mané had a header ruled out for offside following a review by VAR, as The Reds worked hard for their victory with Alisson making smart saves after the break. Salah squandered other opportunities but Liverpool did enough to pick up their 16th victory of the season to open an 11-point gap at the top ahead of second-placed Leicester City, who faced Norwich later in the day.

VAR had changed Klopp's touchline behaviour. In the second half, with the score at 1-0, Mané's header from a Shaqiri cross was ruled out for a marginal, but correct, offside decision. Although he did not contest it, Klopp does not celebrate goals any more, in case they are ruled out. "I had no clue where it was offside, to be honest. I don't celebrate goals any more because you have to wait until somebody says it is a goal. I thought there was one pass before where maybe it was offside, but that Sadio was offside, I couldn't see."

Klopp confessed it was "not the prettiest game" but once again he was delighted with the attitude and application that has made Anfield such a fortress. He enthused: "At this stage you have to show resilience and I believe we did that today. We have so many games but we are happy with this. Watford had their chances but we scored ours. We could have made the game easier for us but it's intense to be constantly in charge of the game. We have to defend with passion not organisation sometimes and that was sometimes now, right? We have many more games than our opponent, who had a new set-up, Nigel Pearson, in the short time he's had with the Watford squad, did an exceptional job. This game was the next step for them.

"They had their chances but we had Alisson. We scored our goals but apart from that we had to fight. Could the game have been easier for us? Of course, if we had kept the ball smarter and moved it around a little bit. The boys are not tired but it is intense to always be in control of games, so I get that, we have to defend some moments with passion rather than organisation because that was not always perfect. But we did that. When we didn't Alisson was there, that is why we have 11 players. Ali was for 85 minutes of the game really doing warm-up exercises, but in these [other] five minutes he was really important and just showed what a goalie he is; he is unbelievable and helped us a lot in these situations. We had to fight, that's what we did and that's why we won. All good."

KLOPP: "It was not the prettiest game but I am more than happy with that. At this stage you have to show resilience and I believe we did that today. We have so many games but we are happy with this. Watford had their chances but we scored ours. We could have made the game easier for us but it's intense to be constantly in charge of the game. We have to defend with passion not organisation sometimes and that was sometimes now, right?"

NIGEL PEARSON: "I have already told the players our destiny is in our own hands and that intensity of performance and decisive counter-attacking and creativity at times will serve us well for the rest of the season, we need to emulate that. It's always hard to come to places like this. There is a bit of risk and reward. We knew we would have to absorb pressure. The disappointment was their goal came from our set piece and that is something we need to address. I think we put them under strain and caused them problems but they have unbelievable players. We need to reflect on the performance and that going forwards will serve us well in the fight. I have seen more positives than negatives today. We have to make things happen and hopefully people have seen encouragement today."

OTHER SCORES

SATURDAY 14 DECEMBER
Liverpool 2 Watford 0
Burnley 1 Newcastle United 0
Chelsea 0 AFC Bournemouth 1
Leicester City 1 Norwich City 1

December

Sheffield United 2 Aston Villa 0
Southampton 0 West Ham United 1

SUNDAY 15 DECEMBER

Manchester United 1 Everton 1
Wolverhampton Wanderers 1 Tottenham Hotspur 2
Arsenal 0 Manchester City 3

MONDAY 16 DECEMBER

Crystal Palace 1 Brighton & Hove Albion 1

TUESDAY, 17 DECEMBER 2019
CARABAO CUP FOURTH ROUND

ASTON VILLA 5
Hourihane (12), Boyes (OG) (16), Kodjia (35, 43), Wesley (90+2)
LIVERPOOL 0

There had been controversy surrounding this game and, following the EFL's refusal to allow Liverpool to postpone the fixture until January, Liverpool selected their youngest-ever starting line-up. Unfortunately the youngsters were overwhelmed as Aston Villa cruised into the semi-finals of the Carabao Cup. With the senior players in action at the Club World Cup in Qatar hours later, under-23s boss Neil Critchley led a side containing five debutants and which had an average age of 19 years, six months and three days. Meanwhile Villa made 10 changes from their Premier League defeat at Sheffield United, their vastly superior experience ensured they lived up to their favourites tag at Villa Park.

Liverpool began brightly but conceded two freak goals in the space of three first-half minutes to allow the hosts to settle. First, Conor Hourihane's free-kick from the right deceived Caoimhin Kelleher, and the Reds keeper then saw an Ahmed Elmohamady cross deflect off Morgan Boyes and loop over him into the left corner. Jonathan Kodjia added Villa's third with a cool finish after Jota's through ball, before the Ivorian swept in Elmohamady's cross from the right.

Wesley completed the scoring for the hosts, who reached the semi-finals of the competition for the first time since 2012-13. Five-times winners Villa head into a two-legged semi-final in January against Leicester City, although manager Dean Smith might view forthcoming league matches against Southampton, Norwich and Watford - the three teams below them in the table - as arguably of greater significance.

NEIL CRITCHLEY: "I thought we were magnificent. We were fantastic from the start, we had a couple of chances from the first whistle. We were really unfortunate to concede and then find ourselves 2-0 down. It was an incredible night and no-one wanted it to end. The support we had was unbelievable. The conduct of the Villa players was first class. For Dean Smith and John Terry to come in to our dressing room after the game and say the things they said... They said 'keep going, good luck' and wished us the best. A moment I will remember and the players will remember for the rest of their lives. Some of them showed the potential to one day play for us, or in the Premier League. They will know it was just part of their journey. My overwhelming feeling is one of immense pride."

DEAN SMITH: "It was probably the weirdest major competition quarter-final I've seen or been involved in. They started brightly, they've got some technically gifted young players. We were clinical, professional and showed a good attitude. It was a bit of a no-win for us apart from getting through to a semi-final. I must credit the players. Before the game I used the word 'attitude' - it had to be right today. Everyone expected us to win, we expected to win, but you've still got to do the job. Even though we were playing a young Liverpool team, we had James Chester who hadn't played for 11 months, it was Jonathan Kodjia and Orjan Nyland's first game of the season too. I thought Jota was a bit of a Rolls Royce for us tonight.

"Wesley needed that goal. He's got a little bit of unfair stick. He's a young player, he's got great honesty and attitude. It was a good finish. It will do him the world of good. I was brought up coaching U18s and U23s, Liverpool played really well tonight but they'll be disappointed with the result. They've got some starlets that will be performing at Premier League level in the next three or four years."

December

WEDNESDAY, 18 DECEMBER 2019
CLUB WORLD CUP SEMI-FINAL

MONTERREY 1
Mori (12)

LIVERPOOL 2
Keïta (9), Firmino (90+1)

Roberto Firmino scored a dramatic injury-time winner – five minutes after coming on as a substitute – to give Liverpool victory over Mexican side Monterrey and book their place in the Fifa Club World Cup final. The Brazilian striker, who replaced Divock Origi in the 85th minute, poked in fellow substitute Trent Alexander-Arnold's cross from close range in Doha.

Liverpool's Naby Keita had opened the scoring in the first half after an excellent Mohamed Salah through ball before Rogelio Funes Mori equalised. Manager Jurgen Klopp, had left under-23s boss Neil Critchley in charge of Liverpool's Carabao Cup quarter-final defeat by Aston Villa 24 hours earlier but was forced to name a makeshift starting XI due to injuries and illness in defence.

As a result, Liverpool looked vulnerable at the back and, despite taking the lead early on, could have fallen behind after chances fell to Monterrey's Dorlan Pabon, Funes Mori and Jesus Gallardo either side of the break. Keita also had more chances to score and was denied twice in the second half by keeper Marcelo Barovero. Funes Mori – the twin brother of former Everton defender Ramiro – shocked Liverpool fans when he pounced on a rebound to equalise three minutes later but the Premier League leaders were persistent, as they have been so often this season.

Salah kept the ball in play before teeing up Alexander-Arnold, who slid a cross behind the defence for Firmino to poke home, meaning Liverpool avoided extra time and a potential upset in Doha.

KLOPP: "All you need is Alisson Becker, Alisson Becker. He was there in the decisive moments. A really hard game and then you can bring on the boys. Wonderful goal, great game, super atmosphere. We have no clue about Virgil, we thought he would be fine. We will see. We have brought in a few kids and see what we can do line-up wise. We want to play the final and see what we can do."

ANTONIO MOHAMED: "For me, there was a red card, especially the first foul and the second. So I talked to the referee. Maybe a Liverpool shirt has more weight, therefore the Liverpool player wasn't sent off."

SATURDAY, 21 DECEMBER 2019
CLUB WORLD CUP FINAL

LIVERPOOL 1
Firmino (99)

FLAMENGO 0

Roberto Firmino struck in extra time to hand Liverpool a first Fifa Club World Cup triumph as Jurgen Klopp's side eventually ended the resistance of Brazilian champions Flamengo in Qatar. Firmino, who scored a dramatic injury-time winner against Monterrey to send Liverpool into the final, produced a composed finish in the 99th minute as the Reds became the second English side to win the tournament, after Manchester United in 2008.

In a dramatic conclusion to normal time, Liverpool had seen an injury-time penalty decision overturned after Sadio Mane went down under a challenge from Rafinha, with referee Abdulrahman Al Jassim reversing his initial verdict after checking the pitchside monitor following a consultation with the video assistant referee. Brazil forward Firmino squandered the opportunity to put Liverpool ahead inside the opening minute at Khalifa International Stadium, blazing over the bar before Naby Keita and Trent Alexander-Arnold also spurned early chances as the Premier League leaders made a blistering start.

Firmino agonisingly hit the post and Mohamed Salah shot narrowly wide shortly after half-time, but Flamengo responded well to early pressure in both halves and posed Liverpool problems - striker Gabriel Barbosa's attempted bicycle-kick typifying the Brazilian side's steadily growing confidence. Liverpool suffered an injury blow as Alex Oxlade-Chamberlain appeared to fall awkwardly on his ankle, and with the prospect of extra time approaching Jordan Henderson's powerful, curled strike from the edge of the box was superbly tipped over by Flamengo goalkeeper Diego Alves.

Firmino's breakthrough in the first half of extra time delivered huge relief for Klopp's side, and while Salah was denied by Alves soon after, the Premier League side were able to see out the second period

December

Another day, another trophy as Liverpool become World Champions

unharmed.

KLOPP: "The boys dug in again and massively put in a performance. They keep getting tested constantly - our life is like this. At the moment we pass test after test after test. We have to make sure we pass further tests as well. I struggle to find the words to express my respect for the boys. It was incredible. We did so many good things. I saw so many sensationally good performances and I am really happy. It was a very intense game for different reasons; it was not our best game we have ever played but it was enough to win. This was a wonderful night for the club. I said before I didn't not know how it would feel. Now I know it feels outstanding, absolutely sensational. I am so proud of the boys."

OTHER SCORES

SATURDAY 21 DECEMBER
Everton 0 Arsenal 0
Aston Villa 1 Southampton 3
AFC Bournemouth 0 Burnley 1
Brighton & Hove Albion 0 Sheffield United 1
Newcastle United 1 Crystal Palace 0
Norwich City 1 Wolverhampton Wanderers 2
Manchester City 3 Leicester City 1

SUNDAY 22 DECEMBER
Watford 2 Manchester United 0

Champions At Last!

Tottenham Hotspur 0 Chelsea 2

★

Following the triumph in the Middle East, Jürgen Klopp had his players ready for the crucial Boxing Day clash with title contenders Leicester and former manager Brendan Rodgers with one night's sleep after retuning from Qatar… and a nice cup of tea.

Klopp discussed how he had evolved into an English tea drinker. "You get used to different things, as I drink only tea now and not coffee anymore. I started with English breakfast but I changed. I like tea. It's not only black tea, it's a lot of different teas. That's cool. If you'd have asked me in Germany if I wanted a tea my answer would have been 'no I'm not ill.' I don't drink it with milk, not yet. A little bit of honey or something in it, that's it."

After a series of cup final defeats, the manager was now a cup final serial winner with three major trophies in the bag. Returning as world champions, he was eager to resume the quest for the title with a ten point lead. "We have developed at playing in finals. You get used to the excitement and still doing the right things. We have matured. We went there to Qatar to achieve something special. We did that, it felt brilliant. We went home, had a proper sleep and now we prepare for Leicester. I can't see opponents raising their game against us because we now have that title, because they do that already. I noticed it more than anything at Newcastle last season, but everywhere we go we are always a scalp."

The club were granted permission to wear their gold FIFA Club World Cup winners badge for one game after an appeal to the league immediately after lifting the trophy. Current rules allow only charitable messaging to be added to shirts in the middle of a Premier League season, anything different must be ratified by their board. The Reds argued that it will show English football in a good light. Real Madrid, world champions in 2016, 2017 and 2018, were granted permission to wear the badge in La Liga. Liverpool can wear the prestigious symbol in Champions League matches. For the FA Cup, Liverpool needed to submit a separate application to the FA. Manchester United were refused permission to wear the badge in the Premier League after they won the 2008 FIFA Club World Cup, the only previous occasion an English club has won the tournament.

While in Qatar, Everton hired Carlo Ancelotti as their manager, the one man who can claim a win against one of Klopp's full-strength Liverpool teams all season, with Napoli. "I like Carlo a lot and I wish him luck," Klopp said. "It will be nice to meet him at least a couple of times in the season, and I know I will see him early next month at Anfield, but to be honest I couldn't be further away from thinking about the FA Cup at the moment. We have three important league games to play first."

Pundits were sure the title race was already over at the halfway point, though Klopp was unconcerned. "People can think and talk about what they want. If anyone wants to think things are over before they are over we cannot stop them doing that, though it is not important to us. As a group we are pretty good at shutting the doors all around us to keep out the noise from outside."

Klopp said no top-flight coach had an issue with playing on Boxing Day but the spacing of games needed to be taken into more consideration. "People want it, in Germany it would probably cause a lot of problems in a private basis when a man wants to watch football on December 26th. We are not used to it. There is a break, everyone tends to slow down or switch off early beforehand. None of the managers have a problem playing on Boxing Day, but playing on the 26th and 28th is a crime. That is absolutely not okay and we still have it. This year we play 26th and 29th and it is like a holiday. I understand all those saying it should not happen. They are not moaning, they are telling. It is not for the spectacle. It would not be a problem to play 26th and 29th with more teams. There is no reason why more teams do not get more than 48 hours between a Premier League game. Obviously we can say what we want but no-one is listening. Every year is the same for the coaches with the 26th and 28th. Sports science gives you nothing to deal with this [schedule]. The body needs a specific amount of time to go again. That is science, but we ignore that completely. We just say: 'oh, they look strange running around again today'. We are not in that situation this year, but I understand each manager who mentions it from time-to-time - or pretty much always - when we see it coming up because it is just not OK but other people have to decide that."

Rodgers faced his last chance to mount any realistic title challenge, but only if Leicester inflicted Liverpool's first league defeat of the season.

"We will not get carried away," said Klopp on Christmas Eve. "It is exactly like in normal life. If you have a little bit of success and you get carried away by it you will quickly realise it is your last one. We don't get carried away for nothing, absolutely not. We're completely focused on the next step. I was always like this. I never in my life wanted to have a party before there was a reason. When there is a party for a reason I am in it 100 percent, but I do not have 20 per cent parties. So I can wait for it. There is no chance to get us in a mood where we could forget the things we have to do. The next time to prove that is Leicester on Boxing Day."

Klopp was fully aware of the threat posed by Jamie Vardy, who scored impressive goals against Liverpool. "We will try to stop him but they have quality running right through their team. Their league position does not surprise me when you look at the players they have and the fact that they do not have to play in Europe this season, but Vardy is a tough test for any defence. Since I've been in England he's always been in the top three scorers; he's really dangerous and hard to stop. We just try to avoid the passes to him. That is what we will try.

"Brendan has done an excellent job. Top-class team. Exceptional quality.'

Klopp still expected the main threat to come from City. "I think City moved the bar massively last season. The kind of consistency they showed in the last three years is incredible and difficult, very difficult to do. So they became champions two years ago and last year we helped a lot and they helped us as a lot as we tried to catch up with them. They did it in an incredible way. It has changed, it is not allowed to lose games anymore. It is difficult, obviously, but winning the Premier League should be difficult, it is such a strong league with all the teams you see now."

THURSDAY, 26 DECEMBER 2019 - PREMIER LEAGUE

LEICESTER 0
LIVERPOOL 4
Firmino (30, 77), Milner (Pen) (69), Firmino, Alexander-Arnold (76)

Jürgen Klopp's smile could not have been broader as his grip tightened on the title race following a Liverpool masterclass that overpowered nearest challengers Leicester City at The King Power Stadium to extend their lead to an imposing 13 points.

December

Asked if his side played better this season, Klopp replied: "We played an exceptional game against Manchester City, a super game against Arsenal and we have had a few better games. That was exactly the performance we needed, a little bit less good and we could have had problems. The boys were 100% in the game and that helped a lot. Champions League, Super Cup, Club World Cup. we want to talk about that much later in our lives and we have to win a few things then look back at how it felt."

Liverpool had been top at Christmas four times since they last won the league without going on to collect the title, but it didn't look like it would happened this time.

This was the biggest margin of victory in a clash between teams starting the day in the top two of the Premier League since league leaders Manchester City beat Manchester United 6-1 in October 2011.

Liverpool's Boxing Day advantage at the top was the joint-largest in Premier League history. 13 points clear of second-placed Leicester, more significantly, 14 clear of City with a game in hand. Liverpool had the joint-highest lead any team has had on Boxing Day in Premier League history - on a par with Manchester United's advantage in 1993-94, when they went on to become champions.

They had to drop 14 points over the remaining 20 Premier League games to give the chasing pack even a mathematical chance to overhaul them? It seemed highly unlikely. Not unless they had an injury to van Dijk, Mané, Sala and a few other key players, although they all seem key at the moment; in their last 45 Premier League games they had dropped just 13 points.

Again for Klopp that was one step, not the decisive one, "It is just a game against a really good football team. It is not about deciding whatever you are thinking about before it is decided. The only thing that changes is the numbers are different. It was 10, 11 and now it is 13 points. We don't feel it, we don't think about it we did not mention it once before the game. it is just not interesting. I can write the stories by myself. Never before in the history of British football has a team had a bigger lead and lost the lead. That sounds negative in my head and we are just focused on the next games. We have Wolves, Sheffield United, Everton, Tottenham and Manchester United, that does not sound like anything is decided. We try with everything we have to be ready. The number are not relevant."

Reflecting on the huge advantage, "It doesn't sound like anything has been decided to my ears. We are just trying everything we can do to be ready for our next games."

Klopp's side started 10 points clear of the Foxes with a game in hand - then produced a performance of such stature and dominance it overwhelmed the pretenders.

A slender one goal half-time lead, courtesy of Firmino's decisive close range far post header from yet another magnificent Alexander-Arnold cross, did not reflect their superiority, they could have scored twice inside the first minute through Alexander-Arnold and Mané, while Salah initiated a great break but was pushed too far wide, and Henderson had a shot deflected beyond the post.

Mané had a smart shot well saved before half time as Liverpool could have been comfortably ahead instead of a margin that always makes it nervy. Helped by a controversial penalty decision, they simply ran away with he game in the second half. Just at the point Leicester were enjoying their best spell, Soyuncu handled in the 71st minute, and substitute Milner scored from the spot with his first touch seconds after coming on. Milner, of course, scored the last minute penalty to beat Leicester at Anfield. Liverpool turned on the charm as the brilliant Alexander-Arnold set up another for Firmino, another pin point cross, for the Brazilian to scored with a cool finish. Then TAA cracked a perfect right-foot angled finish.

At one point Klopp was screaming instructions from the touchline due to their inability to keep the ball, He wanted them to conserve energy. Klopp said: "In the last 10 minutes, in this part of the season, you don't have a situation often where the game is pretty much decided. At 3-0 it was, at 4-0 it was 100%. I don't know exactly when we scored, but I think there were 10 minutes to go plus extra-time, so 13 minutes. But we were still sprinting and I thought, 'wow, how mad is that?' So I was really shouting out there, just wanted to keep the ball, so Leicester didn't attack us. There are a lot of things we have to improve - how we can manage the game in those situations, how we can play football, how we defended in the first half. There are so many things we have to work on."

On Firmino's run of form, the manager commented, "Bobby, in the last three games he has now scored four times. Before that, it was a bit like – I don't know exactly how – he didn't score that often and a journalist tells me then, 'Bobby Firmino didn't score for a while' and I don't even realise. When I think about Bobby, I don't think about scoring – I just think about how important he is. We had a little talk because, for the first time since I knew him, he looked a little bit concerned about that fact and I told him I am not interested in that number because he is the connector for our team. He is so important for us. He is not the only one who can play the position but he can play the position in a very special way. He doesn't have to come [to the manager] after every goal but this time we had this little thing where he thought I was calm enough to leave him on the pitch in these games, which I never thought about, so he thought he had to say thank you, that's all."

One of the big images of the Boxing Day triumph was the way Firmino threw himself into his arms of Klopp to thank his manager. Firmino delivered with four goals in his last three games. Firmino ran over to Klopp to celebrate after making it 3-0 with his second of the game, and the pair embraced again after the final whistle. Klopp stuck by him during just one goal in 16 games. "He doesn't have to come and do that after every goal but this time he thought I was calm enough to leave him on the pitch and he thought he had to say thank you," said Klopp.

Klopp's assessment of Henderson was encouraging after the captain suffered a knock after a challenge with Perez left him in pain and he was replaced by Lallana in the 82nd minute. Klopp replied: "Yes. [It was a kick] on the shin. It was bleeding but he told me afterwards 'I could have carried on!', so obviously it is not so bad this time."

Leicester lost a home Premier League game by a four-goal margin for the first time since a 1-6 defeat to Tottenham in May 2017. Firmino's second goal against Leicester was the 500th Liverpool had scored under Klopp in all competitions.

Liverpool won five consecutive Boxing Day matches for the first time in their league history, winning those games by an aggregate scoreline of 15-0. Liverpool have won three consecutive away league matches against Leicester for the first time in their top-flight history.

KLOPP: "I am happy about that. I appreciate it because I do not take it for granted and the boys have to do it every three days. We had big chances at the start of the game, did not score with them but stayed in the game and controlled it. It is was difficult for Leicester to get into the game, both teams felt the intensity of the season but we controlled it more and maybe Leicester were not as aggressive, maybe because of us and our positioning. We scored a first goal, super, super, cross from Trent Alexander-Arnold and Roberto Firmino can score from that situation. We struggled a bit with their build-up in the second half and we won the balls immediately and then scored the second goal, then the boys were flying. It looked really nice. 1-0 is not even a result, it was a moment and it could have been difficult when they had set-piece but that is OK, I don't expect a game like this to have a free run because they have so much quality and the season Leicester have had. We were very concentrated and the goals were absolutely nice and an important day for us."

RODGERS: "We played our last two games against two of arguably the best teams in the history of the Premier League. The players gave everything. It's a great learning game for us. Credit to Liverpool they played well. We just didn't have long enough periods with the ball. When you don't against a top team - world champions - it becomes difficult for you. They are going to be very hard to stop. They are a fantastic team, confidence is high. They have become winners and haven't lost many games in the past 18 months. To lose the games they would have to do - they now have got enough players, experience and quality to get the job done. They have a great cushion but that can go very quickly. They have the power and strength and now the big thing is the confidence. Having won the Champions League, Club World Cup and Super Cup, they have the feeling and the squad is very strong. They will be hard to shift in the second part of the season. People were trying to put us in a race with Liverpool but we know where we are.

OTHER SCORES
THURSDAY 26 DECEMBER
Tottenham Hotspur 2 Brighton & Hove Albion 1
Aston Villa 1 Norwich City 0
AFC Bournemouth 1 Arsenal 1
Chelsea 0 Southampton 2
Crystal Palace 2 West Ham United 1
Everton 1 Burnley 0
Sheffield United 1 Watford 1

December

Manchester United 4 Newcastle United 1
FRIDAY 27 DECEMBER
Wolverhampton Wanderers 3 Manchester City 2

★

Jürgen Klopp prepared for the final game of the year against Wolves at Anfield estatic about the attitude of his team, but still stoic about the way records were falling in their path. The club would proudly display the gold FIFA Champions Badge at Wolves for a one-off occasion in the Premier League.

On whether it was possible to go the entire season unbeaten, it was just not of interest to Klopp, who remained focus on the bigger prize "It is, it's massive. I am a while in the business already and if you had asked me if it was possible, I don't think [so]. At Dortmund I think we had 28, I don't know exactly, we will find out, and that felt already absolutely exceptional – but only in the review. In the situation – a colleague of yours asked me what I feel when the boys step onto the pitch and if I see this kind of swagger and stuff like this – unfortunately I can't see anything like this because I'm completely concerned about all the things of the game. I'm a very optimistic person but not before a football game; I know we can win it but I have never thought in my life we probably will win it. That makes life really uncomfortable sometimes. These numbers, I forget them now and if you tell me next time it will be again for me a big surprise the number is that high."

He was impressed by the sheer desire of his players to maintain their level, "I am blessed to have a very smart team, that's how it is. We don't mention it constantly. It's not that I have to tell them, 'Stay focused'. They are, they are. We have so many good characters in the team and they tell each other how to deal with it. There is nobody who is flying, not a little bit. But even that was already like this two years ago and we didn't have the same points tally. A few things came together, the quality and experience we made together. That we worked together longer obviously helps a lot, things are more settled and all that stuff. That's all good. Now we play three games in a row at home and one of them is in the cup, and I can tell already we need massive help from the crowd – massive – because the period is so intense and we need to use each source we can use for these games. Hopefully our people are rested enough to be at their absolute best because that's exactly what we need."

Klopp brought 22-year-old centre-back Nathaniel Phillips back from his loan at Stuttgart due to injuries to Lovren, Matip and Fabinho. "He's our boy, he's on loan at Stuttgart and is doing really well there. For people who don't know, Stuttgart pretty much should be, together with Hamburg, the best team in the second division. They are third in the moment, they want to get promoted obviously, and they unfortunately sacked the manager because they are not happy with third place so you see how ambitious they are. They are a football-playing side and Nat is doing there really, really well. He played, I think, 11 games. Now we have the situation that we have and we thought 'what can we do to help us a little bit?' and we asked Stuttgart if they would be ready to give him back to us for a while and they said 'OK'. I don't think we asked Nat, actually, but he looked really happy yesterday [Friday] when he was in the dressing room so it's just a nice story that we can do something like this. I hope that from Everton he will be available."

Just two days earlier, Manchester City had surrendered a two-goal lead in a dramatic clash with Wolves that left them 14 points behind Liverpool having played a game more. Guardiola's side were down to ten men after Ederson's 12th minute dismissal, as the champions unravelled. The title race was surely over...

On the huge gap, Guardiola admitted: "The advantage is too big, yes. It is big for a long time. It is not realistically to think about the title race. I have been asked the question for a long time and it is the same answer. We have to think of the next game and about winning our games. It's unrealistic to think about Liverpool, we think about Leicester. We have the chance to recover second place. I know the quality of my team but that's the situation."

Klopp's squad continued to remain focussed, that was the message to the fans, in his final programme notes of the year. "This group of players know they set their own agenda and their own benchmarks. They know they have the capacity to decide if going into a game we allow ourselves to feel fatigue or we choose to be fresh in body and mind. It's a choice we can make – we have the power to decide our own approach. I'm not stupid and we know what faces us in this particular period is a big, big test. But this is the Premier League and our ambition is to be the most successful team in it and that means

December

rising to meet every challenge. Talking about a particular subject is completely different to using it as an excuse. And these players have a 'no excuse culture' running through them. We will have setbacks, we will lose games, of course we will. This isn't because of failings we may have but because the quality of opponent is so high. But we will never look to external factors to explain it, no matter how legitimate they may appear.

"Our approach must always be about opportunity. To win the FIFA World Club Cup for the first time in our history was an opportunity and we took it. To come back to the fierce intensity of competition in the Premier League on the back of that – to this schedule – is an opportunity for us to perform if we choose to approach it as such, and we will. That is what I have seen from the players since we came back together in July and August. We set our agenda. We decide what is possible.

"It is in our gift to view the 'pressure' we are supposedly all under as a positive not a negative. Jordan Henderson spoke about this a lot last season and he was right. Replace the notion of pressure with opportunity. The right sort of pressure, which is linked to achieving something special, is a motivator and not a backpack to carry. Seeing pressure as opportunity can lift you up, rather than weigh you down. So this is where we are at as a team during this period. And it applies whether we win, lose or draw in certain games.

"This evening we face an unbelievably strong opponent and I really think it has the potential to be an amazing football match for those who love this special game of ours."

Klopp was asked as the game was live on TV just before kick off about a fabulous year, but time for reflection was not now.

SUNDAY 29 DECEMBER 2019 - PREMIER LEAGUE

LIVERPOOL 1
Mané (40)
WOLVES 0

Fans welcomed the players with a rendition of "We are the champions... of the world". This promised to be another tough game against a difficult opponent who had just completed a league double over Manchester City this season following a controversial 3-2 win at Molineux in which

City keeper Ederson was dismissed and VAR played a part in several key decisions. Yet Liverpool proved resilient and finished the year with a massive 13-point lead, plus a game in hand, following a single Sane Mané goal winner due, in no little matter, and two more controversial decisions that had seen the club dubbed 'LiVARpool' by rival fans.

Klopp said it was "a game where the crowd could be nervous and they weren't, so that's good". He added: "I think our fans are exactly like the team is. They are not interested in the moment. They don't want to celebrate now. We are a unit. We fight until somebody says it is enough. It is not about belief. It is not about knowing or wanting to know it's already done. That is just a game in the media. Can you imagine asking me if it is decided and I sit here and say 'yes, I think it's done'. That would be really crazy. It is not done."

He added: "Everybody asks me what it was like in 2019 – my 2019 team was brilliant but that's not important, we count seasons, not years. The 2019-20 season is not over. We are halfway there. There are 19 games to play. That's a lot and probably 19 of them will be like this tonight, for different reasons. We will be facing teams who will be fighting for the league with all they have, and the fight for the Champions League and Europa League has opened up again. We have to be ready. Who cares about points in December? We have just created a basis we can work with from now on.

"If it would be easy to win the amount of games we have done then more teams would have done it. It's not easy. We have to fight with all we have. I couldn't be more proud of what they did a gain to get that result over the line. It was just impressive. I'm really happy about that. But there is a long way to go for all of us."

Mané scored in the first half, slotting past Patricio after the ball bounced off Lallana's shoulder from a long ball into the box. After a lengthy VAR review for handball referee Anthony Taylor eventually confirmed the goal. Wolves then had a goal disallowed just before half time by VAR for a marginal offside by Moutinho after Neto shot into the bottom left corner.

Salah and Firmino came close either side of the break, but Jota had two big chances in the second half, a shot from a tight angle in the box which flew wide of the post, the second a gift from a rare van Dijk mistake which he hit straight at Alisson.

Klopp brought on Keita midway through the second half after

December

Lallana ran himself into the ground. Klopp observed: "I wasn't pleased with how we managed the game in the second half, not always. We had bad moments. Wolves weren't attacking as high anymore, we had passing options. There is no chance to recover in a game if you don't keep the ball. You have to do it when in possession. That's not a calm thing, it's a very lively thing. It's about being smart, play against movement and half spaces.

"Naby and later Millie helped immediately. You could see that. The other boys, my God. Adam and Gini. How they played today effort-wise, miles wise it was really great. But fresh players in the half spaces helped. Then we caused again problems but we didn't finish it off. It wasn't a game for two or three goals tonight. We just had to fight until the end. I have no problem for that."

Ironically, Sheffield United, who kicked off later at City, had a goal ruled out by VAR! City ran out 2-1 winners to remain in third place, 14 points behind the leaders who had a game in hand.

Liverpool finished the year as resounding favourites to win their first league title in 30 years unbeaten in 50 home league games, winning 40 and drawing 10 of games at Anfield. Liverpool ended 2019 with 98 points from 37 Premier League matches, their ratio of 2.65 points per game was the second highest achieved by a team in a single year in the competition, behind only Chelsea's 2.66 in 2005.

Liverpool fans had waited long enough to win the Premier League but with a 13-point gap they were pinching themselves. It was within touching distance. The old proverbial one hand on the trophy. Theirs to lose. The defending champions trailed by 14 points in third place, Leicester City 13 points behind in second, and a game in hand on both.

KLOPP: "It was a tough test and rightly so. Wolves are used to a tough rhythm of games. First half we were good and controlled the game, but I can imagine Wolves were not happy with the VAR decisions. However, the momentum went with them after that moment. We had nothing to do with the decisions. What can we say about the decision? For me, I was surprised when the whistle came for the handball. I thought it was a clear shoulder from the first second. But how can you be sure? So it took a while. After three minutes the decision was done. I saw immediately a kind of relief for a second, we are human beings so that's normal. But the next long ball we weren't there for the second ball, Adam makes a foul. Free-kick, corner, (Wolves) goal. It didn't count obviously but it brought the momentum to their side. They were really aggressive and really angry with us as well, we had nothing do with that situation but sometimes that's how it happens. The second half they changed a bit. We were not fresh enough in mind to react. Alisson wanted to make the game quick, and nobody else wants to it to be! Football is like life. Sometimes you are 100% ready and sometimes not. It was a big fight."

NUNO : "It was a tough game. First half Liverpool was strong. We stayed in the game, stayed organised and always the danger with the quality. In the second half we had good spells and created a lot of chances. We finished strongly. I am very proud of the players."

OTHER SCORES

SATURDAY 28 DECEMBER
Brighton & Hove Albion 2 AFC Bournemouth 0
Newcastle United 1 Everton 2
Southampton 1 Crystal Palace 1
Watford 3 Aston Villa 0
Norwich City 2 Tottenham Hotspur 2
West Ham United 1 Leicester City 2
Burnley 0 Manchester United 2

SUNDAY 29 DECEMBER
Arsenal 1 Chelsea 2
Manchester City 2 Sheffield United 0

JANUARY

Having masterminded an incredible start to the season, Jürgen Klopp welcomed in New Year 2020 knowing that Liverpool were already within touching distance of their first title in 30 years. With so much goodwill in the bank he was probably the only Premier League manager who could get away with playing a first team made up entirely of academy players in a fourth round cup replay against Shrewsbury Town that fell in the winter break. That extraordinary decision bore fruit as Liverpool's youngsters edged a tense replay 1-0.

It was clear that Klopp had transformed Liverpool into a relentless winning machine, articulating the view that when his team start rolling, they do so with such dynamic force that they are virtually unstoppable.

Trent Alexander-Arnold says the player buy into their manager's philosophy through a flexible tactical approach and instilling his immense passion into them.

Having won an unprecedented treble of Champions League, Super Cup and World Club Championship in the space of 6 months, Klopp's side were now seen as the best team in the world and were being talked about in the same breath as previous great Liverpool teams and the Manchester United treble team of 1999.

Alexander-Arnold said: "He gives us all a lot of freedom so it's very much the case that the players play to their strengths and are able to do that in different ways in the systems that we play. I think it's important that the team buys into that and the manager obviously understands what we need to do to win games. 'He's been like that for the time he's been here, so he's transformed the club in an amazing way and going forward there'll hopefully be a lot more success with him.

"You can see on the touchline and in his interviews after and before the games, he's so passionate about the game and passionate about winning. We see it every day in training and it's important for us that he gives us those messages. He's not only just helping us win, he's giving us the mentality to be able to overcome any circumstance during a game.'

Klopp openly applauded the 'bootroom' team he assembled around him and the owners for keeping the pressure off him. "I make it my job to have smart people around me and I am really skilled at listening to them," Klopp told *The Guardian*. "That makes life not so difficult, but I must say the people who own this football club have not put me under any pressure. I didn't have to win a title in my first season, or even the second. The steps we had to make were clear: we wanted to always be in the Champions League, because that gives the club the opportunity to develop, that allows the club to speak to different players. From that everything else has fallen into place."

"We're just over halfway through the season so it's important for us to keep our heads, keep focused and keep our mentality the same," said Alexander-Arnold. "That's what's been working for us, so nothing should change."

Youngster Sepp van den Berg was one of two signings last summer, after he was joined by Harvey Elliott. Van Den Berg played a key role in Liverpool's FA Cup replay against Shrewsbury. The Dutchman, who cost a mere £1.8m, revealed that the manager hugs every player when they arrive at Melwood, and explained how Klopp makes all his players feel "appreciated and valued".

He said "The warmth you feel as a young player at Liverpool is so special. I will tell you the best example of this. At other clubs you arrive in the morning and people will say 'good morning' or shake hands but here at Liverpool, you get a hug from the manager! Jürgen Klopp gives you a hug – and it's those special little things that made all the young players feel appreciated and valued. That kind of warmth from the manager gives us the hope that we are all on the path to the Liverpool first team."

The highly-rated youngster had the chance to join a host of other European clubs but chose Liverpool after meeting Klopp. "I had the chance to go to Bayern Munich, PSV Eindhoven or Liverpool. I was amazed that such big clubs wanted to sign me and I thought PSV Eindhoven was a brilliant option for me because I have been a fan from a young age. But once Liverpool came for me, I knew where I would go because I can only describe my feelings for the club as mega. It is such a big club – but at the same time it feels like a family club. Thanks to Klopp's approach and vision I am up against the best attackers in the world several times a week. He lets me train and play against Mo Salah,

January

Roberto Firmino and Sadio Mané. That is something I could only have dreamt of in the past. These guys really belong to the very best attackers on this globe."

In another example, recent signing Takumi Minamino was sat between Sadio Mané and Naby Keita in the changing room to help him settle in. While learning English, he spoke in German to Klopp and team-mates who understood the language. Mané and Keita, who both played for Minamino's former club Salzburg, speak German, and Klopp placed the Japanese star between them. "You know that you are part of the team, but because my English is not good enough yet their help has been really important," Minamino said. "They are still helping me on some occasions and during the first days they taught me the team rules, things like what time the meetings started and how the team functions on a daily basis. At the moment I speak a lot with the players who can speak German."

★

THURSDAY 2 JANUARY - PREMIER LEAGUE

LIVERPOOL 2
Salah 4, Mané 64
SHEFFIELD UNITED 0

Liverpool completed a full calendar year without losing in the top flight; 37 games, 89 goals, 101 points, impressive even by the incredible standards shown by Pep Guardiola's team over the past two seasons.

It took a touch of good fortune to take an early lead - George Baldock's slip allowing Andy Robertson to set up Mohamed Salah for a simple close-range finish in just the fourth minute. Salah's opener (03:25) was the earliest goal scored by Liverpool and conceded by Sheffield United in this season's Premier League.

A lot was being made of "luck" and VAR decisions, but its an old adage in this game, that you make your own luck, and nothing was truer than this ultra dynamic Klopp team, but nonetheless it was a constant thread of debate and idle chitter chatter, nothing more than something different to say other than The Red were an unstoppable machine marching on relentlessly toward their first title in 30 years.

Yet there was absolutely nothing fortuitous about this win, sealed

Sadio Mané, finishing at the second attempt after being played in by Salah. It maintained a 13-point gap after Leicester and City won on New Year's Day.

Klopp's side, though, dropped two points from a possible 60, so developing this aura of invincibility that would take some breaking. Liverpool's 18th consecutive league win and 51st top-flight encounter without defeat in a row at Anfield was another impressive series of stats.

Klopp labelled the congested festive fixture calendar as "criminal" as his side played six games in 17 days, but for vital points to continue the focus on the title he kept team changes to a minimum.

He made a late enforced, unforeseen alteration, bringing Milner in for Naby Keita, who injured himself in the warm-up, but it made little noticeable difference as the veteran utility player was superb alongside Henderson and Wijnaldum in midfield; the usual combination of stream rolling work-rate, unselfish and tireless movement and uncanny accuracy of passing providing the platform, with Virgil van Dijk on hand on the rare occasions Sheffield United were allowed a kick in the Liverpool half.

Salah scored one, but Dean Henderson made some important saves and the woodwork denied him when his chipped second-half cross floated past everyone to hit the inside of the post.

Firmino went close to his first Anfield goal since March with a curling effort just past the post and later in the second half failed to connect with Alexander-Arnold's low cross from point-blank range.

Chris Wilder was performing minor miracles on his low budget team, as only three sides in the country had a superior points-per-game record across 2019 - the leaders, reigning champions and West Brom, who had the joint most points in the Championship.

The no nonsense Wilder prepared his team with a final practice session on Stanley Park, the public park next to Anfield, when a dog joined them and urinated on one of their cones.

McGoldrick went close soon after Liverpool's opener with an effort that Alisson had to tip over, as the keeper was bedding down into a run of form that was making him an essential cog in the relentless procession toward the title. Lundstram had the ball in the net, but long after an offside flag had already ruled any potential goal out. Substitute McBurnie failed to convert from close range at the back post from a low cross. Alisson made his 50th Premier League appearance, his 26th clean sheet; among keepers in the competition's history, only Petr Cech (33) and Pepe Reina (28) kept more shutouts in their opening 50 starts.

KLOPP: "It's obviously good [to go unbeaten for a year] but the target was not to extend this [run], but to win the game. The best thing you can say when you play against Sheffield United is to keep the game not spectacular. We controlled the game. We played around their formation, played behind, in-between, broke the lines and had counter-attacks. All the things we want to have. The boys played sensational. You saw these glimpses in the game where we were a bit sloppy. They wanted two or three situations in which they could score in. We needed that concentration and that was incredibly tough but the boys did so well. Nothing ends. We have to make sure we are ready again. I am really happy and really proud of the boys. We should not take things like this for granted. The way we controlled Sheffield United was exceptional. In possession we were incredible, we were calm but lively as well. The goals we scored were exceptional."

WILDER: "Little bit drained - disappointed in our performance tonight, we never laid a glove on them. If there's ever an example of a team doing well and with the desire, that's Liverpool. The first balls, second balls, running forward, tackling, defending, being aggressive; they showed all those qualities. It's a great example for our team. Every time we tried to press they played around us with the quality they have got. All the stuff that gets talked about in academies, with young coaches - just look at what they did in terms of the basic stuff that gives you an opportunity to play and dominate. That's what they did to us. Not only technically, but tactically, they are a fantastic side. We have been well beaten. People talk about us having afternoons and nights like this when we came to the Premier League. We have not had that done to us all season until now so that's a small comfort. But it still hurts, we are still professionals. I believe if we played near our best we could have got something but we weren't anywhere near it."

Liverpool switched their attention to a Merseyside derby against Everton in the FA Cup, before going to Tottenham.

OTHER SCORES

WEDNESDAY 1 JANUARY
Brighton & Hove Albion 1 Chelsea 1
Burnley 1 Aston Villa 2
Newcastle United 0 Leicester City 3
Southampton 1 Tottenham Hotspur 0
Watford 2 Wolverhampton Wanderers 1
Manchester City 2 Everton 1
Norwich City 1 Crystal Palace 1
West Ham United 4 AFC Bournemouth 0
Arsenal 2 Manchester United 0

SUNDAY 5TH JANUARY
FA CUP THIRD ROUND

LIVERPOOL 1
Jones (71)
EVERTON 0

18-year-old Curtis Jones grabbed the Merseyside derby glory with a magnificent curling 25-yarder that eluded the outstretched arms of Everton keeper Jordan Pickford to inflict yet another defeat on the Toffees who remained without a win against the Reds since September 1999.

Klopp had the luxury of resting superstars such as Sadio Mane, Mohamed Salah, Roberto Firmino and Virgil van Dijk, survived the early loss through injury of James Milner, and yet still saw his side fully merit their place in the fourth round. Everton manager Carlo Ancelotti played virtually his strongest available side but the visitors paid for a lacklustre display and a succession of missed opportunities in the first half, when Dominic Calvert-Lewin, Mason Holgate and Richarlison saw efforts saved by Liverpool keeper Adrian. The Italian blamed a drop in his side's performance level during the match.

ANCELOTTI: "The line-up of Liverpool didn't affect our idea of how to play," he said. "We knew that Liverpool put in fresh players and that the intensity could be a high intensity, so I think the defeat arrived because we were not able to keep the intensity in the second half. We lost energy, we lost confidence, we were not able to build up quick from the back. We are going to speak and work together to find a solution to help improve the team. I know we have to work."

KLOPP: "I saw a sensationally good performance of a not very experienced team with a lot of players playing for the first time on this kind of stage, in front of this crowd, against the opponent. It was outstanding. I loved it - I loved each second of this game. If you want to be a Liverpool player, you have to respect the principles of this club. We cannot always play the best football in the world but we can fight like nobody else. And as long as we use our principles, we will be a difficult opponent to play against."

SATURDAY JANUARY 11 - PREMIER LEAGUE

SPURS 0
LIVERPOOL 1
Firmino 37

The best-ever start to a season by a club in Europe's top-five leagues "doesn't feel special somehow", according to Jürgen Klopp in his usual matter-of-fact, down-to-earth, totally focused on the end game.

Roberto Firmino's first-half goal opened up an astonishing 16-point lead over Leicester City with a game in hand with win No 20 from 21, as all the pundits were unanimous the race was as good as over with Klopp's team assured to finish first over the line. Their position strengthened as Brendon Rodgers team slipped up to a shock home defeat to Southampton.

Klopp, though, was not in the mood to reflect on records until the trophy was delivered. "We know about it and it is special but I can't feel it. When someone gives you a trophy it is done but until then you need to fight. It is only the start. We need to continue because our contenders are so strong. Pep will not give up. I will do the same. So far, so really good."

Klopp's teams stats were just mind boggling, 104 points across their last 38 Premier League matches, scoring in all 21, an impressive record maintained by Firmino, who turned Spurs' young debutant Japhet Tanganga and beat Paulo Gazzaniga with a sweet left-foot strike to give The Reds a deserved lead.

This was Liverpool's joint-best scoring run from the start of a season in English top-flight history, with the Reds also scoring in their opening 21 games in 1933-34. But they also kept six consecutive clean sheets in the Premier League for the first time since December 2006.

Liverpool were grateful for poor finishing from Jose Mourinho's side, without the injured Harry Kane. Son Heung-Min and substitute Giovani lo Celso missed excellent second-half chances

One of the threads of the campaign was that when not at their best, they found a way to win, this their 12th successive league win, dropping two league points from their first 21 games.

Firmino's neat 37th-minute sidestep and thumping finish emphasised that there is always someone in the front line to turn out a match winner.

Spurs claimed they should have had a throw-in before the goal but overall the better side won.

MOURINHO: "This is football. Sometimes you get more than you deserve. Sometimes you get less. This was an occasion when we got nothing when we deserved something. This is the best team in the world against a team in a difficult moment, with injuries, in a difficult part of the season. The boys were fantastic when we tried to change and create problems… 200% that the throw in for the start of the goal was our throw. I am confused with VAR because of that."

KLOPP: "It was very hard-fought because we didn't close the game down early. We should have been one or 2-0 up already when we scored. If you have a quality opponent like Tottenham and you don't close the game they will come back. Allison makes things look easy. It is not what we would have wanted. It is intense, you lose the ball and you are facing one of the best counter-attacking sides. We had Robbo (Andy Robertson) free two or three times and he didn't find a teammate, so we didn't help ourselves. We needed Allison for that today. We had a few dips defensively. Some games he has not had a lot to do with us winning the ball high early. It is good but there is no other chance to win games than to defend well."

OTHER SCORES

FRIDAY 10 JANUARY
Sheffield United 1 West Ham United 0
SATURDAY 11 JANUARY
Crystal Palace 1 Arsenal 1
Chelsea 3 Burnley 0
Everton 1 Brighton & Hove Albion 0

January

Leicester City 1 Southampton 2
Manchester United 4 Norwich City 0
Wolverhampton Wanderers 1 Newcastle United 1
SUNDAY 12 JANUARY
AFC Bournemouth 0 Watford 3
Aston Villa 1 Manchester City 6

★

Liverpool entertained their bitter North West rivals, Manchester United with a chasm of 27 points between them. Yet, it still felt like a defining fixture in their quest for their first title in 30 years against the only team so far this season to even hold them to a draw. Jürgen Klopp responded to Ole Gunnar Solskjaer's claim Manchester United worked out how to play against his runaway league leader by pointing to a noticeable shift in the last two fixtures. Solskjaer was indulging in a transparent and blatant mind games knowing the only time The Reds failed to win was at Old Trafford in October when they were held to a 1-1 draw, while their visit last season ended goalless. Solskjaer felt comfortable in publicly declaring he had found "a nice way of playing" against Liverpool.

Klopp was asked about Solskjaer's comments and questioned whether his team had found a nice way of playing against United.

"Hopefully," he replied with a smirk. Klopp believed the approach instead suggested the encounters represented a change in philosophy. "The games were not games you would imagine for United against Liverpool. In the past, there were good times for Manchester United and good times for Liverpool, there was usually one clear favourite but both teams tried to win it. In the last years, the away games especially were strange from that point of view. I heard Ole was confronted with the fact that I said United only defended. I don't know if I said that exactly, but probably it is true. It is strange when you play against a high, high-quality team – which United still is – and they play the way they play. That makes life really difficult. We had the same with Tottenham, after 70 minutes we had round about 70% possession. That's not normal, how can you expect something like that? And on the other side, the counter-attacks are of the highest level in the world for Tottenham and for sure Man United. I'm not saying they only counter-attack, but it's clearly a thing they want to do. If people want to see that as criticism, I can't change that. But it's not, it's just a description of the situation. If it's an open game, play football. If there is space there is space."

Liverpool had won 3-1 last season at Anfield, yet that was Klopp's only Premier League win over United. "We have to learn to deal with games like this in the right manner," said Klopp. "We did not too bad in the past but we still can improve. The game at United is a good example; we were not at our best in a game where we should be, because of the quality of the opponent. We were not bad that day but we were not at our best, and we have to make it more likely that we are at our best. For this you have to treat it like all very important games. For us the next game is always the most important; we know what a difference it makes to our supporters, and how important it is, but it's an add-on. We play all games for our supporters, not only these games. Liverpool is obviously the natural enemy of some clubs; we have more natural enemies than other clubs have, probably because of our history and how successful the club was. But I've said it before that we have to write our own history. That means we have to play the games our way."

United had only beaten Klopp's Liverpool twice in 10 matches since the German took charge but he had only beaten them twice. "This game is always built up like a mountain and stuff like that, and then we come here and they only have to defend," he said after Ole Gunnar Solskjaer's side held his to a 1-1 draw in October. "Since I've been in England it's pretty much been like that. We come here put it all together, attitude, tactical defensive shapes. Eight players defending with the quality of Man United, it's not easy."

Jose Mourinho said he was 'protecting' United when he said Klopp 'didn't like the menu' after seeing his side held to a draw at Old Trafford earlier this season. On punditry duty for Sky Sports for the fixture, he criticised Klopp for never winning at Old Trafford. "He didn't like the menu," Mourinho said of Klopp. "He likes meat and he got fish. United, with the limitations they have at the moment, they played with five at the back, were solid and didn't give the chance of transition. Jürgen Klopp didn't like the menu.

"They [Liverpool] missed quality to play against a team with a low block. They have a fantastic record of so many victories. But they have limitations against teams with low blocks. They can smash opponents that play the way they want to play against. Jürgen clearly has frustrations.

January

It's a fantastic situation for his team. But at Old Trafford - which is a special place to win - he [Klopp] never did it."

Mourinho was out of the TV studios and back in the dug out with Spurs and prior to facing Liverpool with his new Tottenham side, the former United boss was asked about the comments in his pre-match press conference. Mourinho was speaking as a pundit, not a manager, and that he felt a duty to protect United's impressive performance on the day. "In that moment I was not a football coach I was a pundit, I made that comment because I thought United did very well. I have been in similar positions as Jürgen is now, when you are the best team and used to winning. United were in a difficult moment and you praise the guys [who stop it]. In that match Solskjaer and the players did a very good job to almost win and I felt I had a responsibility to be protective of that."

When Mourinho was appointed at Spurs in November, Klopp spoke about resuming his rivalry. "Welcome back Jose, haha!" Klopp joked at a pre-match press conference. "It's nice to have him back. He was desperate, you can see that from the time when he was not in. Jose his heart is motivated, so that will be interesting as well!"

SUNDAY 19 JANUARY - PREMIER LEAGUE

LIVERPOOL 2
Van Dijk 14, Sala 90+3
MANCHESTER UNITED 0

16 points with a game in hand. 21 wins from the first 22 games. These were the formidable stats and represented an incredible achievement. It was almost too good to be true. The persistence from challengers was melting away like snowflakes, with dropped points for City and Leicester on Saturday and Sunday respectively, 64 points out of the 66 available this season, the one draw coming at Manchester United in October.

"We are here to work," commented a defiant and laid back Klopp. "It is as simple as that. It is a very positive atmosphere but I have to stay concentrated. We play on Thursday against Wolves. I am only interested in that game and nothing else."

But every game comes with its special challenge, and degree of difficulty, it is far from the walk in the park it would appear or the massive lead suggests. Late United pressure meant it was imperative to defend Virgil van Dijk's 14th-minute header with vigilance, commitment and total focus. Of course, it was all wrapped up in style in injury time when Alisson's long clearance set Salah racing clear to score and spark wild celebrations among supporters now convinced that 30 year was finally coming to an end.

Alisson's injury-time 'assist', Salah holding off the chasing Daniel James before rolling his finish beyond the keeper heralded a burst of "We're going to win the league" a theme song often heard before Sir Alex knocked them off their perch and had now returned as it rang around Anfield at greater volume and with greater conviction than it had for years, and since Liverpool narrowly failed under Brendan Rodgers in 2014. Alisson became the first Reds goalkeeper to assist a Premier League goal since March 2010, when Pepe Reina assisted against Sunderland; it was a special goal, a fitting conclusion to any game, anywhere any time.

Klopp refused to be goaded into deviating from his Groundhog Day response to all the hysteria, whether from the fans or the pundits. They can sing that," said Klopp. "I am not here to dictate what they sing. If our fans were not in a good mood now that would be really strange. Of course they are allowed to dream and sing whatever they want, and as long as they do their job in the moment we play, all fine. But we will not be part of that party yet. They've sung that a couple of times in the past I think. Everyone should celebrate - apart from us."

Firmino had a goal ruled out by VAR for Van Dijk's challenge on David de Gea, that split opinion on whether it was a legitimate challenge and the keeper was afforded far too much protection as he actually dropped the ball under minimum contact.

The United keeper also touched Henderson's shot on to the post and Salah missed an open goal from six yards as Klopp's team might have made life easier for themselves rather than waiting until the end to see out the win.

United had Marcus Rashford ruled out for a lengthy period with a back injury, and that was a big loss, yet United carved out chances of their own. Andreas Pereira turned wide of an open goal in the first half and Anthony Martial shot over from an inviting position after the break.

Strangely, with such a momentous points haul there was still anxiety

January

All eyes on the ball as Mo Salah makes sure of victory and removes any vestige of doubt about the destination of te league title

around Anfield in the closing minutes before the relief of Salah's goal emphasised by Alisson rightly running the length of the pitch to join in the celebrations after his long clearance 'assist'. There had been too many false dawns, too many big let downs, the anxiety was understandable.

With Van Dijk at the back, a perpetual threat up front, and a relentless powerhouse of rolling stock in midfield, this was the new force in the game, with the once mighty United now trailing Liverpool by 30 points, and justifiably so. That reflected the chasm in class and capability. Liverpool won consecutive home Premier League games against United for the first time since winning three in a row between September 2008 and March 2011. Liverpool became the first team since Arsenal in 2001-02 to score in their first 22 Premier League matches of the season - the Gunners went on to score in every game and win the title that season. Liverpool kept seven consecutive Premier League clean sheets for the first time since December 2006.

KLOPP: "It's a big relief, I was really happy with 85-90% of the game, we were brilliant. We dominated the game, especially in the first half. The energy they put on the pitch was incredible. On a normal day we would have scored three times in the first half and in the second half until 65 minutes we should have been more clear. But then United have obvious quality, played a bit more football and we had to defend. There were little mistakes here and there, we didn't use possession well enough and so the game stays open. Then we scored a wonderful, wonderful goal at the end, a really good feeling."

SOLSKJAER: "The players gave us everything. Today we hung on a bit at the start of second half, but the last 25-30 minutes we pressed them and pushed them back. I'm disappointed with conceding from a corner and with the last kick – but very many positives. I felt in the second half we performed really well against a good team and at a difficult place.'

OTHER SCORES
SATURDAY 18 JANUARY
Watford 0 Tottenham Hotspur 0
Arsenal 1 Sheffield United 1
Brighton & Hove Albion 1 Aston Villa 1
Manchester City 2 Crystal Palace 2
Norwich City 1 AFC Bournemouth 0
Southampton 2 Wolverhampton Wanderers 3
West Ham United 1 Everton 1
Newcastle United 1 Chelsea 0

SUNDAY 19 JANUARY
Burnley 2 Leicester City 1

THURSDAY JANUARY 23 - PREMIER LEAGUE

WOLVES 1
Jimenez 51

LIVERPOOL 2
Henderson 8, Firmino 84

Roberto Firmino's late winner extended the lead to 16 points with a game in hand and now had 22 wins in 23 league games. The Reds, who won their past 14 league games, became only the third team to go 40 games unbeaten in the Premier League. Liverpool amassed 67 points from a possible 69 – five more than any side in English top-flight history after 23 games.

Klopp was not feeling pressure about being so far clear at the top, "I don't think about it, I had to ask about exactly the amount of points, that's the truth, I really forgot in the week. I didn't think about it, I know we play Sunday at Shrewsbury, I know we play Wednesday at West Ham and I know we play Saturday. That's three games in seven days which is a lot. We lost Sadio Mané and that's the pressure I think about. All the rest is no pressure.

"We said it before it would be a really tough game, Wolves are doing so unbelievably well, they are so different to everything else you face."

Klopp suffered one of the biggest downsides to the campaign when Mané succumbed to a muscle injury in the first half, that looked like a consequence of the fatigue that the manger alluded to would eventually catch up with his players. "Sadio felt something in his hamstring. We don't know yet. We have to wait," said Klopp as the Reds faced three games in the next nine days - an FA Cup trip to Shrewsbury and league games against West Ham and Southampton. "That is tough and it's probably without Sadio," said Klopp.

Wolves made it difficult for Klopp before Firmino ensured another significant step towards the title. Henderson headed them in front from Alexander-Arnold's corner after just eight minutes but Wolves drew level six minutes after the break when Raul Jimenez glanced in Adama Traore's cross, the first goal Liverpool conceded in the league for more than 12 hours and it required important saves from Alisson to keep out Traore and Jimenez as there looked as if there was the possibility that Liverpool could lose their first league game in more than a year.

Firmino drilled home the winner with six minutes left, although substitute Diogo Jota then wasted a glorious chance to give Wolves a point in stoppage time. Manager Nuno Espirito Santo and his players looked dejected at the final whistle to be denied so late on as they pushed to become only the second team after Manchester United to take points off Liverpool this season.

Klopp praised his captain who scored the opener and set up the winner. "I am not sure when Hendo became involved in offensive set-pieces. He is normally the protection. It showed another side and he is in outstanding shape at the moment. He played an unbelievable game in a difficult game. He was helping people, shouting at people - but it is not about shouting, it is about what you say. He only asks of others what he expects of himself. We couldn't be in this situation without him."

Klopp had built a team that simply refuse to be go down without a fight, so it was almost as if it was no great surprise when Firmino made the decisive late contribution with Henderson in the best form of his career. Henderson delivered the crucial pass for Firmino's winner as well as heading the opener.

KLOPP: "We changed the system two or three times, we calmed it down. We had incredible chances in the first half and then at the end it was a magic moment from Bobby. The boys are human. It was a little bit up and down. We had discussion on the pitch, there was stuff to improve but set-pieces can bring us back in the game, a good bit of skill can bring us back in the game. Wolves were really strong but it's clear we could settle again. You just have to find a way to win and have someone who makes the perfect decision and that was Bobby again."

NUNO : "It was a good game. We played well. There is nothing to be disappointed about. Getting the momentum was important. We faced a fantastic team. This is the standards we want."

OTHER SCORES

TUESDAY 21 JANUARY
Aston Villa 2 Watford 1
AFC Bournemouth 3 Brighton & Hove Albion 1
Crystal Palace 0 Southampton 2
Everton 2 Newcastle United 2
Sheffield United 0 Manchester City 1
Chelsea 2 Arsenal 2

WEDNESDAY 22 JANUARY
Leicester City 4 West Ham United 1
Tottenham Hotspur 2 Norwich City 1
Manchester United 0 Burnley 2

SUNDAY, 26 JANUARY 2020
FA CUP FOURTH ROUND

SHREWSBURY TOWN 2
Cummings (65 (pen), 76)
LIVERPOOL 2
Jones (14), Love (og) (46)

There was a shock in store at Shrewsbury as Liverpool squandered a two-goal lead and looked set to be the victim of the latest FA Cup giant-killing.

January

Liverpool had cruised into a two-goal lead thanks to a first half Curtis Jones strike an unfortunate own goal just after the break from former Manchester United full-back Donald Love. But the introduction of Jason Cummings on the hour changed the complexion of the tie as he converted a penalty before tucking home the equaliser just 10 minutes later. In the final stages Liverpool were hanging on and deservedly earned a money-spinning replay at Anfield, becoming the first team in 2020 to score more than one against Klopp's men.

Shrewsbury boss Sam Ricketts said: "We carried out the gameplan superbly well. After 32 seconds in the second half most teams would have crumbled. In the end my players got at least what they deserved. I think it was there to win. We've had the better chances. It wasn't until Jason scored his first we were clinical."

The timing was unfortunate for Liverpool as any replay would land in the middle of their fortnight winter break, "We will respect the winter break" said Klopp, insisting that he and the first team would miss the replay and play the kids as he had done against Aston Villa and Everton earlier in the season.

WEDNESDAY, JANUARY 29, 2020 - PREMIER LEAGUE
WEST HAM 0
LIVERPOOL 2
Salah 35 (pen) Oxlade-Chamberlain 52

Jürgen Klopp doesn't feel as "though anything is done" despite hitting the 70 points mark before the end of January and moving 19 points clear as his team were serenaded from the field by the club's jubilant fans at the final whistle; finally they believed the title was heading for Anfield, and had secretly believed that to be true for some time now, but dare not shout it too loud, almost as restrained as the manager.

Mohamed Salah's first-half penalty and Alex Oxlade-Chamberlain's second-half strike delivered an astonishing 23rd victory in 24 matches with a 15th consecutive win to set a relentless pace no one could possibly live with, unbeaten in 41 league games as several top-flight milestones were within sight.

Yet, for Klopp nothing changed, he played down the significance of all the wonderful achievements as he refused to budge form his mantra of 'show me the silverware first'.

"I'm only happy about the three points," he said. "Tonight was a normal performance. I have no idea [if anyone will catch us]. The first target is to get the maximum points - there are still a lot of games. Yes we have 70 points, an incredible number, but so many things can happen. I'm not too much concerned about records. We had a record at Dortmund and Bayern beat it the next season. We don't feel as though anything is done, I promise you. We take a deep breath and then Saturday it's Southampton.

"I don't feel anything like that. I wanted to win the game but nobody was thinking it was 18 teams, let's make it 19. When you jump in the water you don't breathe for 38 games then you come up and look around. That's how we see it."

Klopp joked he would trust his Liverpool players with his kids. Klopp said West Ham's defensive mindset made the task harder but applauded the relentless ability of his side to get the job done regardless. "It's not a motivational problem for us," he said. "The difficulty was to get the rhythm, keep rhythm and to stay concentrated. I think their biggest chances we gave them.

"These boys I'd give them my kids to take care of them. I trust them 100 per cent but in these situations they still make these ridiculous mistakes. It's nothing to do with motivation. It's just staying concentrated when you are constantly in charge that's so difficult."

The Hammers made a reasonable start to nullifying a rampant opponent but last only until ten minutes before half time when Issa Diop's foul on Divock Origi allowed Salah to put the visitors ahead from a penalty and their first shot on target and while Manuel Lanzini's scuffed close-range shot and Robert Snodgrass' hurried effort represented good opportunities for the hosts. Declan Rice forced two excellent saves from Alisson, with Alexander-Arnold putting the rebound from the first against a post. Salah also struck the woodwork late on and Lukasz Fabianski saved from Naby Keita

Oxlade-Chamberlain's goal ensured a comfortable conclusion for Klopp's side, who could have scored again when Salah hit the post from 18 yards. The Ox's right-foot strike into the bottom left corner was initiated by Henderson from a West Ham corner and created by Salah's superb outside of the boot pass bisected a couple of home defenders to send him through on goal.

Klopp's side were far from their best despite dominated possession.

showing little end product until Salah's penalty. Virgil van Dijk and Joe Gomez were barely troubled in defence while Jordan Henderson provided a controlling presence in midfield with another in a string of outstanding performances.

Klopp's side had now beaten every team in the Premier League this season at least once, while Liverpool reached 70 points from just 24 games in the Premier League, the quickest any English top-flight side has ever reached this total.

Klopp registered his 150th victory as Liverpool manager in all competitions.

KLOPP: "If it was easy to win this amount of games a lot of other teams would have done it. It was a tough game. We've played some super games. We played a super game against United, Leicester super game. Today was a game. We still had to win it and we did. It was not a brilliant performance, against a side obviously that's insecure at the moment, but it makes it really difficult for us. A very important element in football is counter the counter, but for that the other team need to have counters and winning the ball back and using the space. We started pretty much each attack with a ball from a centre half against nine or 10 or 11. I wish we would have done better but I take it like it is because if it would be easy to win this amount of games and this number of points other teams would have done it. It's just really, incredibly difficult.

MOYES: "I thought the players did a good job defensively. We were playing against a really good team and we made opportunities and created chances against a tough team so overall I'm pleased. They're as good as there's been around. It's very difficult when you've been manager of Everton and Manchester United to say that but Liverpool are an excellent side."

FEBRUARY

SATURDAY FEBRUARY 1, 2020
LIVERPOOL 4
Oxlade-Chamberlain 47, Henderson 60, Sala 71, 90
SOUTHAMPTON 0

Liverpool opened up the biggest lead by any team in English top-flight history with an emphatic victory but Jürgen Klopp still insisted his side are "not even close to being perfect".

They now stood 22 points above second-placed City, who lost to Tottenham the following day. Liverpool also equalled City's record of 20 consecutive Premier League wins at home and only Bill Shankly's Liverpool team in 1972 had a longer winning streak on home soil in English top-flight history.

"We're not even close to being perfect. We just look to use our skills in the best possible way. The boys have done that for a while pretty good and that's why we have these numbers," said Klopp. "We didn't want a 22-point lead. We wanted 73 points at the end of today."

Four second-half goals extended their unbeaten run in the league to 42 games, 100 points from the last 102 available across two seasons, conceding just one league goal in their last 10 matches and 73 points from 25 games is a top-flight record. Only City had won more consecutive games at home in the Premier League, between March 2011 and March 2012.

Alex Oxlade-Chamberlain scored the opener just after half time - his second goal in as many league matches - when he drilled the ball low into the bottom corner.

Skipper Jordan Henderson made it 2-0 on the hour with a calm finish after being set up by Roberto Firmino.

Henderson then played in Mohamed Salah for Liverpool's third and the Egypt forward added a fourth from close range in the last minute. It was harsh on the visitors as they matched Liverpool for much of the first hour with Danny Ings going close in the first half and Shane Long denied by Alisson. Invigorated by a half-time talk from Klopp,

February

were quick out of the blocks in the second half and as soon as they scored the victory that most will have expected before the match felt inevitable. Without the injured Sadio Mané, Firmino and Salah delivered as Firmino produced a hat-trick of assists to take his total to 51 in all competitions for the club, while Salah scored twice.

Yet, it all hinged on who scored the opener, as the Saints thought it should have been them. Ings, who left Liverpool to join the Saints for £20m in July, had scored 14 goals in 19 starts heading into the match and he was a threat throughout. His close-range effort in the first half looked like it was heading in before it clipped the heel of Long and bounced away from goal. He was praised before the game for his tireless work ethic by Klopp, and he threatened early in the second half when he wriggled into the box before being stopped by a challenge from Fabinho. There were appeals for a penalty but it was reviewed by VAR, who decided Ings' evaded Fabinho rather contact from - although Hasenhuttl believed it was a foul. Immediately after the incident Liverpool went up the other end and scored the opener. Ings was substituted in the 70th minute, alongside Long, and was given a standing ovation by the fans of his former club. The Saints had 10 shots in the first half against Liverpool, the most the Reds faced in the opening 45 minutes of a Premier League match at Anfield since Chelsea in November 2014. Seven wins from their remaining 13 games would guarantee success.

KLOPP: "The readiness to improve in the game and learn from the game [is what we had to do to win]. The set-up of Southampton I could not give more credit to. What a strange result in the end. It's deserved because we score the goals, but what a team. They had too many shots on target and we had to change in the second half. That helped massively and when we are rolling it's difficult to stop. Even when it was 4-0 Southampton did not stop and I have so much respect for that."

HASENHUTTL: "Maybe the result is a little high but I would like to watch this game if we had gone a goal up. The best team in the world, for 50 minutes had no real chances and we had a massive one. It must be brave at that moment to say goal, so it's no penalty here at Anfield. The way we played was unbelievably good and I am proud and stand by our plan. It is a clear penalty but in such moments the game can turn in our direction. But in the end it was a deserved win for Liverpool. We played the best we can so I am very proud."

The first team squad would be given the night off for the FA Cup fourth-round replay against Shrewsbury, while their next Premier League match against Norwich City was two weeks later.

OTHER SCORES
SATURDAY 1 FEBRUARY
Leicester City 2 Chelsea 2
AFC Bournemouth 2 Aston Villa 1
Crystal Palace 0 Sheffield United 1
Newcastle United 0 Norwich City 0
Watford 2 Everton 3
West Ham United 3 Brighton & Hove Albion 3
Manchester United 0 Wolverhampton Wanderers 0

SUNDAY 2 FEBRUARY
Burnley 0 Arsenal 0
Tottenham Hotspur 2 Manchester City 0

★

Liverpool chairman Tom Werner admitted that he had to "pinch himself" to believe the standards being set by Jürgen Klopp's team as they surged into a record busting virtually untouchable 22-point lead, dropping only two points from their opening 25 games in their relentless quest to reach their Holy Grail of the first title in 30 years and first Premier League trophy.

Liverpool also reached the Champions League knockout stage, and the fifth round of the FA Cup with Klopp's Kids causing a sensation in a replay that the manager insisted it would be wrong to attend as he adhered to the inaugural Premier League mid winter break.

"I am pinching myself, but we haven't done the job yet," said Werner. "I keep saying to everyone I talk to that we really need to savour this because I appreciate the record we have achieved so far and I don't think it is going to come along quickly [again]."

Liverpool needed six victories from their final 13 games to end their wait for a 19th league title, and deliver the one trophy their fans desired above all else.

Klopp, though, perpetually brushed aside all the mind boggling records and focused on just one target - delivering the silverware, not talking about it until it's in the hands of captain Jordon Henderson.

TUESDAY 4 FEBRUARY 2020
FA CUP FOURTH ROUND REPLAY

LIVERPOOL 1
Williams (og) (75)
SHREWSBURY TOWN 0

Liverpool's youngest-ever starting line-up beat Shrewsbury Town to set up an FA Cup fifth-round tie at Chelsea. Just as in the first tie, a former Manchester United scored an own goal, with Ro-Shaun Williams' netting for the home side to send them through.

With the Reds' senior players enjoying the inaugural Premier League winter break, under-23s boss Neil Critchley led a side at Anfield containing seven teenage outfield players. At 0-0, Shrewsbury had a Shaun Whalley goal disallowed by the video assistant referee (VAR). Whalley thought he had given the Shrews the lead but his header was disallowed when VAR ruled there had been an offside in the build-up.

The visitors had come from 2-0 down to force a fourth-round replay but could not recover after defender Williams headed past his own keeper from Liverpool right-back Neco Williams' cross.

★

Players and managers are asked to sign all manner of things all the time, mostly in autograph books, pictures, the usual stuff. Jurgen Klopp was asked to sign the car of a fan's grandma. Reds German fans Michael Schulte-Karring, who followed Klopp since his days at Borussia Dortmund, is the 54-year-old dental technician's who wanted to meet his hero.

He said: "My grandma and grandpa bought the Volkswagen 1600 in 1971, but in 1998 my grandma gave me the car after I passed my dental technician master examination in Cologne. I used the car at my residence in Palma in Majorca and drove it on tours throughout Europe. In 2006, a number of children with cancer wanted to sign the car. I then started to collect signatures on it of solidarity in Europe for poor and sick people who need help. I don't know of a single German who can't identify with Anfield and its history. It would be my first visit to England and and an impressive 10 days in Liverpool for me and the car. My dream came true on the last day of a 10-day stay in Liverpool. The security of the Reds helped me with tips and let me park the car where it could be best seen. Many of them took pictures of the car or shot a video sitting in it." Then outside of Melwood training ground, Jurgen Klopp appeared. Michael said: "Our meeting lasted about 20 minutes. He asked me how long this mission had been running and I told him the story. He was thrilled with the car and signed it on the sun visor on the driver's side with the date '03.11.2019' and 'YNWA'.

Now just six wins away from being crowned Premier League champions, it was widely anticipated that the Liverbird would be eating the Canaries for dinner on the resumption of the Premier League after the so-called mid winter break. Not so Klopp who recalled the impressive performance of Daniel Farke's side in the season's opener when the Canaries took the game to Liverpool but ultimately lost. He said: "We scored four, they scored one, but they had much more chances in that game. That's what we have to think about. It was a really good warning and a good start in the season for us. It was early and we were not that consistent at that time. Now both teams are in a different situation but we will feel the quality of Norwich and we have to make sure they feel our quality."

As for the preconceived notion outside of Anfield that the title race was over, Klopp remained focused on the next game rather than entertaining title talk. "Norwich is obviously my first concern. We have prepared ourselves since Monday for this game. We didn't speak about anything else. We have no other chance than to make this game the most important game of our lives. Play it on Saturday and try with all we have to win it.

"People think it will be easy because they don't really think about it and they only watch the table but we know about the problems we can have - and we know about the problems we can cause them as well."

Farke coached at Borussia Dortmund, as did Klopp, and the Liverpool boss had every respect for his opposite number, and therefore would be taking nothing for granted. Otherwise, a shock would be a possibility. "I really admire that Norwich stick to their principles. It's really good football, super coaching. You can see all the patterns on the pitch, all the movements - that's from the training ground. They've caused 95% of all teams real problems. They've lost a lot of these games, that's why they're in the situation they are, but for me, on the outside, it looks like a club that really sticks together."

Farke wanted to be the first manager to beat them this season in the league. "No-one in the league has beaten them," he said. "They are one of the best teams in European history. It's a huge task and we know that. We have our strengths and if we bring our best football on the pitch, we can get something. We are not naive. The Manchester City game (3-2 win in September) showed when you're good in your topics, you can win. Liverpool are the best team in the world and we need to be there with an outstanding performance."

Klopp felt the break came at a good time given the condition of his players. "I was a player myself. When I look back it feels like I played through 80% of the time with pain. Nobody appreciated that because I played still bad so it didn't help. Nobody asked then. It is completely normal for a professional football player to play through pain. That's how it is. After that long period in December-January, there was no player in the squad who had no pain. Everybody had something. We sent players all over the world, we wanted them really to rest. I can see a difference in training. But it's not about seeing a difference against Norwich, it's about using this time for rest and recovery.

"The dream of a manager is to have a full week to prepare for a game. You have intense training sessions which you normally cannot have. Usually the most intense session is the game. So we use that week, we train hard. You don't really lose anything. You find your own rhythm again."

Klopp discussed City's game with West Ham being rescheduled in both clubs' winter break, just as his club's FA Cup replay. He said: "It just shows the problem with the schedule. It's the weather, nobody can change it. For us, it was never a standpoint against the FA Cup. It had nothing to do with that. It was just to make sure that we decided [on] a winter break so there must be a winter break. I can imagine it was really difficult organisation-wise."

Mane and Milner recovered from injury, and Klopp had no qualms about putting them straight back in. "Of course they are in contention. It looks like - and I hope it stays like this - apart from Shaqiri, Clyne and Glatzel, all players are in training. We have some good options. Hopefully it stays like this for the rest of the season."

Adrian opened up on what life is like under Klopp. "What Jurgen has achieved here is extraordinary. Just look how we are in the league. It is so easy working with him. So easy. He's always smiling, cheerful, optimistic. He's the manager but he behaves like any another member of the team. Him being close to us helps us believe in his methods. He's convinced us all of his leadership and abilities by being close to us and proving that whatever is on his mind works in the end.

"Klopp usually tells us that we'll face many problems during the games, so we must be able to fix them. Any team can surprise you with a new system, for example. He's there to guide us. He visualises football very well from the sidelines and transmits this knowledge to the players in a masterful way.

"Training sessions are intense. He does his job passionately and that's exactly how we perform on the pitch. Jurgen is not only a top strategist, but also a great person. The best group management I've seen. Next to the team through thick and thin."

On the Premier League's opening day, Norwich City at Anfield, Alisson had gone down with a calf injury. Klopp brought his new substitute goalkeeper off the bench, whispering in his ear: "Welcome to Anfield." Adrian had been at the club four days and trained with his new team-mates twice. As he was about to make his debut, did Klopp have anything else to add? "He hugged me. He showed me I had his trust. I felt like the schoolboy who has to introduce himself in front of his new classmates, but what can I say about Anfield? The way the fans embraced me in such a critical moment, losing one of their best players. They gave me total confidence."

Klopp hailed the return of "world-class" Fabinho needing him at his best again for the run-in. Klopp described Fabinho's return as "massive" and believed his absence earlier might help to keep him fresh. "It's massive. Massive to have him back. He was out for two months roughly, not the longest, but still enough to lose some rhythm. So we have to work hard to get that back and he is getting better and better. For us, he is a world-class player so of course it is a massive boost for us to have him back to give us more options. We had two or three if not four very young players on the bench [over Christmas period] so it is sensational news that he is back. And he trains very well too, so everything is getting better and better like normal. Will he be fresher for the run-in? Maybe, yes. It's been three or four weeks out and he was straight in again, he will be fine, he has not been overplayed in this moment, so that helps."

Philippe Coutinho had been linked with a return to Anfield and as he told *Sports Illustrated*, he was delighted with their success in his absence. "Liverpool is flying, and it doesn't surprise me. We've seen it already last year when they won the Champions League, but I'm also not surprised because of their fantastic squad and manager. I am so happy for them, because I have so many friends there, former teammates, so I'm just so happy for them, but that's all. I don't look back. I took another path, and now I am on another journey, much like everyone else. I'm focused entirely – just like them – on reaching my dreams. I'm happy with what I did in the past, and now I can only look forward."

Klopp stressed that Liverpool needed more information before deciding whether Salah could represent Egypt at the Olympics, a tournament for under-23 teams with three over-age players.

Salah was on Egypt's provisional 50-man list for the event, with its final on 8 August - the first day of the 2020-21 Premier League season. "Do I want to lose a player in pre-season? Of course not. That's clear," argued Klopp "But we have to consider different things. I will speak with Mo and all that stuff."

Asked if he felt Salah's accomplishments went under the radar after such a stunning previous season, Klopp said: "I don't feel that to be honest. The poor boy, everyone knows him still. If he scored 44 goals in three successive seasons then that would have been really cool and maybe we would have won the league last year! For the player, he is an exceptional character and he will never stop really. He wants to play and I am not sure how many games he has missed but that is just him. He is and became a natural goalscorer, that is how it is. I have no clue if he goes under the radar because he doesn't for us, obviously. This week we speak about Mo, maybe the week before it was Bobby and there are moments for sure when we spoke about Sadio Mane. There were moments maybe when two of them were not in the firing mood that much, but the other one finished the situations off for us. These kind of numbers are exceptional but it is not over yet so we don't really have to think about it."

Arguably the most sensational news on the eve of the return to football after the mid winter break was that of Manchester City being banned from The Champions League for two years for financial doping and the fall out including a call for the Premier league to dock points, and for the fifth placed team to qualify for next seasons Champions League under current UEFA rules.

Keita replaced Fabinho, Mane and Milner were on the bench. Top against bottom, 19 places and 55 points separating at Carrow Road as Klopp's team could go 25 points clear of City. Victory would give Liverpool the best record after 26 matches in the history of the top five European leagues. They had gone 42 top-flight matches unbeaten, putting them level with Nottingham Forest on the all-time list (1977-78), seven matches behind Arsenal's invincible record of 49 games (2003-04). Liverpool earned 100 points from the last 102 available, winning 33 of their last 34 and 73 points from 25 matches this season was a top-flight record.

OTHER SCORES

SUNDAY 9 FEBRUARY
Sheffield United 2 AFC Bournemouth 1
SATURDAY 8 FEBRUARY
Everton 3 Crystal Palace 1
Brighton & Hove Albion 1 Watford 1

SATURDAY, 15 FEBRUARY - PREMIER LEAGUE

NORWICH 0
LIVERPOOL 1
Mané (76)

The relentless march towards their first title in 30 years is "outstanding", said Jurgen Klopp. The stats made for astonishing reading:

- 76 POINTS AFTER 26 GAMES was the best record at this juncture in the history of Europe's top five leagues - something even the continent's great sides Barcelona, Juventus, Bayern Munich and Paris St-Germain were unable to achieve, but it also meant...

- UNBEATEN IN 43 LEAGUE GAMES, closing in on Arsenal's all-time record of 49.

- A MIND-BOGGLING 102 POINTS FROM THE PAST 105 available.

February

- 35 WINS FROM 36 GAMES - a 1-1 draw at United in October the only points dropped.

- WON 17 GAMES IN A ROW - one shy of City's record - 10 clean sheets in their past 11 games.

Yet again it was a late goal and after a narrow victory as Sadio Mane came off the bench on the hour as Klopp made a double substitution also bringing on Fabinho, to score the winner with 12 minutes remaining, athletically taking down skipper Jordan Henderson's perfect long range pass and cracking his shot in at the near post.

Mane scored the 100th goal of his English club career in all competitions, 25 for Southampton, 75 for Liverpool. Mane's goal was his 57th in the Premier League for Liverpool, but the first as a substitute. Klopp hailed Mane's "perfect" return as the wind and rain of Storm Dennis spoiled any chance of attractive football, and the Reds rode their luck en route to yet another league win.

But it was more like Storm Sadio which Klopp plans to unleash at full capacity in Spain. "It helps when you have such quality on the bench to bring on," said Klopp. "Yes Sadio could have started today of course but I want to have a free decision for Tuesday. You don't think they should play two games in such quick succession. The quality of the others is just too big that you have to push somebody through. It was perfect for Sadio to have a few minutes but it looked like he was ready, yes."

There was a huge debate whether Mane's physical contact with the first defender constituted a foul, but VAR did not overrule the referee's original decision to award the goal. On Mane's goal, Farke added: "I just watched it back shortly. When the referee doesn't give a foul it won't be overturned. It was also due to the quality of Mane - his control and then his second touch. It was smart movement from Mane and if the referee doesn't give a foul you can't see it overturned. We have already learned that VAR is not on our side."

Five more wins from their remaining 12 games to guarantee their first Premier League title, now a mammoth 25 points clear. "The gap is so insane, I don't really understand it," Klopp commented. "I am not smart enough. I have not had that before, had no clue how it happened really, it's just that we are focused on what we're doing, and it feels really good but that's it. It's outstanding, really exceptional but it's so difficult.

I go back into the changing room and we chat about the things, we have two or three minutes of analysis with me and the boys and I speak about the things at the end and then I remember to congratulate them because we won the game and were outstanding. I am like 'Oh, but congratulations. We won the game, another three points. That's the situation and you count the points and it's three more. Unbelievable. It's pretty special absolutely."

Chances were at a premium in a blustery first half, but Liverpool ramped up the pressure in the second period, Tim Krul making a stunning double save to deny Mohamed Salah's low shot and Naby Keita's close-range follow-up. Norwich could have scored on the counter as Alex Tettey's strike from an angle caught Alisson by surprise at his near post but the shot struck the foot of the upright. Lukas Rupp broke the offside trap in the first half and when faced one-on-one with Alisson, inexplicably decided to square towards Teemu Pukki instead of shooting and the keeper managed to claw the pass away. The lively Todd Cantwell struck the side-netting.

Yet, when Trent Alexander-Arnold dragged a shot wide from the edge of the box after just 13 seconds, a routine win looked inevitable, but the Reds had to battle hard once more. Once again it was the teams's ability to win irrespective of how. Again it took a long time to finally get the winner, yet Norwich failed to attempt a single shot in the first half of a league game for the first time under Daniel Farke, and the first time in any league match overall since April 2014. At the end the traveling fans sang "We Are Going To Win The League' with even greater conviction. "And now you are going to believe us!"

KLOPP: "I could tell in all the players' faces that they weren't nervous, they were enjoying it, and if one team was going to score it was going to be us. We protected against the counter-attack well too. It's really all about these wonderful football players. It's easy to talk about the wind and things like that, but on the pitch the boys have to deal with it. We played for sure two, three, four long balls too many and the formation wasn't prepared for that. So we weren't there for the second balls. Our positioning was not exactly like it should have been. Once we changed in this specific formation, and Cantwell reacting on him like man-marking. Then our midfield was sometimes surprised by the long balls of our centre-halves so didn't push up early enough. It was obviously much better in the second-half."

FARKE: "Performance-wise we were pretty good in many topics, sadly one topic was missing, to be clinical in our finishing. We had our chance in the first half. Performance-wise we can take a lot of confidence but sadly no points."

OTHER SCORES

FRIDAY 14 FEBRUARY
Wolverhampton Wanderers 0 Leicester City 0
SATURDAY 15 FEBRUARY
Southampton 1 Burnley 2
SUNDAY 16 FEBRUARY
Aston Villa 2 Tottenham Hotspur 3
Arsenal 4 Newcastle United 0
MONDAY 17 FEBRUARY
Chelsea 0 Manchester United 2
WEDNESDAY 19 FEBRUARY
Manchester City 2 West Ham United 0

★

Jurgen Klopp revealed that former Milan coach Arrigo Sacchi, who won the Serie A title and two European Cups, was his biggest inspiration. "The most important coach I learned from is Arrigo Sacchi. For all the things he did with his AC Milan, those things were implemented in our team. When I became coach, I didn't have time to look left or right but the basis of everything I do is what Arrigo did."

Sacchi managed the Rossoneri from 1987 until 1991, and again for a second spell in 1996-97, winning eight trophies and bringing 'Total Football', a Dutch concept, to Italy. His teams were known for playing a highly attacking 4-4-2 formation, as well as zonal marking and the offside trap.

Klopp had no plans to move to Italy: "I will not come to Italy, because I want to travel after my career. A good glass of wine, I will have fun with Arrigo. Either with Ancelotti or with Sarri. I love your country, the weather, the fantastic food. But to do my job, I will need to know the language and my Italian is not very good."

Klopp was often linked with a move to Juve, but it only extended to his respect for the club, not a desire to manage them. With Cristiano Ronaldo determined to inspire the Italian giants to European glory this season, Klopp believed the Old Lady to be one of the main favourites for the competition declaring Sarri's team was "the best I've seen in my life".

Maurizio Sarri responded: "Jurgen is one of the smartest and funniest people I've ever known and what he's doing here is shaking off the burden of being the favourites for the Champions League."

Sarri suggested that Klopp might want to change squads, but Klopp dismissed it: "I'm sorry, I didn't want to put Maurizio under pressure, I respect him too much. I don't play these mind games, but sometimes I don't think before I speak. I said I didn't understand why they weren't 10pts clear."

Before any clash with Juve, Klopp expected a tough encounter in the Spanish capital, scene of his finest moment in football. "I don't know exactly. We go there tonight obviously, which helps, we are in a different dressing room because we had the home dressing room for the Champions League final so that's already different. It's just a positive feeling, 100 per cent. Last time it was a massive game and this time it's a massive game, the only difference is there will probably be more Atletico supporters in the stadium but that's not too big. It's nice that we can come back that early, so all good."

The Reds flew out to Spain on Monday afternoon after a light training session at Melwood ahead of a return to the Wanda Metropolitano where they picked up the clubs' sixth European Cup in June, knowing it would be an intense battle with Diego Simeone's Los Rojiblancos, Liverpool's first competitive clash with Atletico since a Europa League semi-final nearly 10 years earlier.

Klopp talked of the quality of the remaining sixteen teams. "I really have no idea if we are the strongest team left in the competition. What I know and we showed last year is that we can beat the best. It doesn't mean we will, it just means we can, and that is the only thing I have to know. I have no clue if we can win the competition, but we should be ready to go for it. Just to fight for it, that is how it is. Then it is about luck in certain moments to win anything and that is what we will need for sure. There are so many strong teams out there. I said it before, Juventus was my favourite before the season, obviously I don't watch Italian football enough but if Juventus are not 10 points ahead

February

[in Serie A] then you can see there are some problems. Juventus have the widest biggest squad I ever saw in my life. Quality players, it is crazy. They can really play in different competitions and maybe there is a little problem that they are not so far ahead in the league. I think that is the main target but I don't know. PSG, when they are all fit...it is just a bomb. We don't watch that much French football obviously. We always say about Paris, 'yes but in France they have to win these games' but the quality they have is unbelievable. That is just a really strong team. Bayern getting more and more in again, The Bayern squad is massive, Dortmund is really really exciting, really exciting, so young, so fresh, so quick. And in the end, it is about who finds the right mood, in the right moment because quality will not be the big difference - who finds the right mood, the right desire all that stuff can win the decisive challenges and we will see who that can be. Barcelona you can never discount. Real Madrid, how can we sit here [and discount them], Manchester City, let's not forget, because the Champions League will be one of their big targets. Last year Man City was the best team in the world and we won the Champions League later, so now people are not happy with some things [at City] and we are it. But there is always another team which is at the moment the best in the world. We have no clue how far we can go and the only real problem at this moment is Atletico.'

Klopp wanted to join Real Madrid as the only clubs to successfully defend their crown in the competition's current guise. He added: "We don't feel like the winner of last season's Champions League, we are one of the contenders for this year. We want to be in Istanbul. You have to work your socks off and that's what we have to be ready to do.'

Pep Guardiola needed to win this tournament more so than ever before after the two season ban from UEFA, although Klopp stressed the need to reserve judgment on City until more information came to the surface but expressed his admiration and sympathy for a manager and a group of players who he insists are not to blame. "It was a shock when I heard it," Klopp told his post-match press conference at Carrow Road after their narrow win over Norwich to take them 25 points clear at the top. "I have no idea how these kind of things work or happen, but what I can say as a football coach is that Manchester City under Pep Guardiola play sensational football. That is how it is. I have always admired what he is doing, what they are doing and that will not end in this moment. One can imagine that it is really hard at the moment for the sports people; you trust your people, they tell you it is fine, but UEFA see things slightly different and now they have to deal with it. I have no idea what will happen next. I've seen a few things, obviously City will appeal, but I can imagine there will be much more information and people will talk about it. To be honest, I feel for Pep and the players, wow, because for sure they did nothing wrong, they just played football, and sensational football at that. Whatever Pep was, he helped each league to improve football. But then again, we all have to respect some rules. I have no idea if they did or not, but obviously UEFA sees it like this that they didn't, and we will see what happens."

Atletico boss Diego Simeone felt Klopp's team would be remembered as one of the game's greatest teams, "We are facing a magnificent team, really well-trained by a coach who is different and has different alternatives in his team. We have always spoken about great teams throughout time and I have no doubt this Liverpool is going to go down in history as a great team because it is different to teams that we have admired (in the past). This team is much more intense, more adaptable, and it makes me admire it as a rival."

Saul Niguez was full of praise for Klopp's "hunting dog" style, "They have those perros de presa [hunting dogs] in the middle who run, press. It's not just running for the sake of running: they do things that aren't normal and it looks disordered but it's ordered, mechanised. One comes out here and you think: 'That's mad, why's he there?' But the other man knows and comes from here. Klopp said they play with their heart, but it's planned too. One breaks out to press, wild, but they follow. It's very hard to escape when they come at you like that. It's incredible: they press like animals, because they know that even if they get turned there will be seven of them running like mad to get back. Liverpool are very complete, a great team in every area [but] they find it hardest when you're deep because they're very, very, very good in transition. I watched them against Norwich and if it wasn't for Mané's extraordinary control, they don't win. They've won lots of games they could have drawn or lost, which tells you something about what they have inside. It's not luck. It's work, sacrifice, not giving up a single ball for lost."

Klopp compared himself to Diego Simeone using a classic Arnold Schwarzenegger film reference. "People say I'm emotional on touchline, but if I'm level 4 then Diego is level 12. I'm the kindergarten cop

February

compared to him!

"I don't know him well enough to know his managerial style. But he was a world class player and I wasn't, that's obvious. I don't know the biggest difference between us."

As for the tie, he said: "This is one of the most difficult fixtures in the life of a football player. Really well organised, squeezing results. They are in a transition period, that's normal, but they are fighting with all they have. It's really difficult. Atletico haven't played as bad this season as people are saying. A result machine. Diego's teams are always world class organised, that makes him one of the best. We have met once or twice, exchanged some messages after big defeats or big wins. It's our first competitive meeting, it will be interesting!

"Some our best games (in CL) were away. Bayern away was one of best games I've witnessed. Barcelona was, even though we lost. We are a proper threat. That doesn't mean it will be like that again. If there's one team where you have to be at absolute best, it's Atletico. They give you absolutely no presents. If you work as hard as possible, you have a chance. If you don't do that, you have no chance. There's a reason they were in so many European finals. Atletico are a clear, proper machine. Whatever happens, they are there. They close you down and counter-attack. If you are not focused on your attacking, you won't have a shot on target. Atletico have speed, aggressive, have a clear philosophy. I know we are in the country of tiki-taka, but I admire things like that. For me, it's all fine.

"But they haven't played against a team like us. We shouldn't forget that. We are organised as well, we play football, we have different aspects of game. We want to be in Istanbul. When you are in the final it's nice, especially when you win it. We see ourselves as a team who can go to finals, who can win the competitions. We're not the only one, but one of them. As a team, we have the chance to do something. We try to show this.

"Always we struggle a bit in the group stage and then knockout we were quite convincing, so hopefully it will be like this."

Klopp dismissed the recent media criticism of Simeone as results took a dip: "That's football. Eight years, seven probably successful. You lose good players, that's tough, you have to change the team and bring in new players and they have to get used to the philosophy. That takes time."

Klopp commented on Trent Alexander-Arnold being put forward as the Worlds No1 footballer: "I have no idea if Trent will win the Ballon d'Or, but thank you Cafu for being a really nice fella! Cafu obviously thinks a right-back should win it! I couldn't admire Trent more. It's a very positive message from Cafu but can only cause problems if it's 'Klopp says this, Klopp says that'. He has big potential, but if Trent can win Ballon d'Or, I have no idea.

Klopp's sign off line, having build up PSG: "The biggest favourite in the competition is PSG. Now they have the pressure!!!"

TUESDAY, 18 FEBRUARY 2020
CHAMPIONS LEAGUE (LAST 16)

ATLÉTICO MADRID 1
Saúl (4)
LIVERPOOL 0

Liverpool's defence of their Champions League title hung in the balance after Saul Niguez's early strike gave Atletico Madrid the lead going into the second leg of their last-16 tie at Anfield.

Klopp was furious with the play-acting and time wasting, but it was an incident leading up to the only goal on the night that got him in trouble with the referee. While Klopp said he had no complaints about being booked he he explained: "It was too much. I am pretty sure, was it a throw-in for us before the first goal? That doesn't help to stay calm. All human beings make mistakes."

The Reds were limited to two clear chances and no shots on target. Salah headed wide, and Henderson's hooked shot flew just wide of the far post. Klopp replaced Mane and Salah with Origi and Oxlade-Chamberlain but neither made an impact. Klopp brought on Origi for Mane for the second half, but the hero of last year's final managed one moment of quality when he hooked in a cross for captain Henderson, who fired wide.

Klopp substituted Mané for fear the Senegal forward would be sent off after being targeted having received a booking late in the first half for catching Sime Vrsaljko with a flailing but accidental arm. Several players surrounded the referee asking for a second yellow card when Mané was caught up in an innocuous incident moments later, and Klopp confirmed the striker was replaced as a precaution. "It is obviously a part of football that I don't like. The plan tonight was to get Sadio out of the game with a second yellow card. I was afraid that Sadio's opponent would go down if he took a deep breath on him or something. I don't want to have this situation and that is why I took him off. He was targeted. It was clear.But I deserved my yellow card.

"It is only half time but you need to be really strong as a referee in this atmosphere. Already in the first 30 minutes three of their players went to the ground I don't know what for. Nobody to blame. I am fine, 1-0 down at half time we have the longest half time break and we will use that. Welcome to Anfield. It is not over yet."

Klopp's skipper came off injured in the 80th minute, replaced by Milner, to cap a forgettable night. "It was hamstring which I hope was precaution. I am not 100% sure but we will see. He was not too concerned, but enough to go off obviously." said Klopp.

Three-time finalists Atletico, who were on a poor run of form, held on to a fourth-minute lead when Saul turned sharply to fire home after a corner came off the boot of Fabinho. Robinson said: "The corner just ricocheted, it was tight but onside. We gave them the best possible start and that gets the fans behind them and then they start falling over and getting under the skin a bit. We put in a decent performance and we know we can be better. We've got a second leg to put it right. They celebrated as if they won the tie after the game.'

Minutes before kick-off Klopp referred to Atletico having a similar "intense DNA" to his own side - and they were at their intense best. The Reds was confronted with almost a mirror image - a team that relentlessly pressed and got numbers forward on the counter. Simeone, dressed again in all black, was his animated self on the touchline - barking orders and occasionally rousing the home crowd.

"I have no problem with the result," added Klopp, who has never lost a European two-legged tie with Liverpool. "I saw so many happy faces at Atletico, but it's not over yet. I'm not sure what we have to be in the second leg. They were going constantly to the petrol station and we drove with one tank. I'm not sure if Diego Simeone saw a lot of the game because he was continually animating the crowd."

Since the start of last season, Liverpool lost six of their 10 away games in the Champions League; no side has lost more away from home in the competition in this time, they were level with Red Star Belgrade).

Saul gives Atletico an early lead in Madrid

Two of Liverpool's three defeats in all competitions this season came in the Champions League, also losing 2-0 at Napoli in September 2019, the third defeat being their 5-0 loss to Aston Villa in the EFL Cup in December 2019.

KLOPP: "It was not exactly what should happen but it happened. It was the fight we expected and the atmosphere we expected but I love so many parts of our game. It is only 1-0 down at half time and the second half we play at our stadium. We lacked in the final third. They defended with all they had - their defending in the box was incredible. When you are 1-0 down with a team like this who only want this kind of result - 0-0 would have been good for them. They are coming to Anfield and we know our fans will be there. Atletico fans who can a get ticket... 'welcome to Anfield.' Emotions are important. Tonight they were obviously completely on the side of Atletico, but I am really looking forward to the second leg. We speak from time to time about the power of Anfield and the power a stadium can have and tonight you saw that. It's half-time and we're 1-0 down. The second half will be played in our stadium and they will feel it."

SIMEONE: My side started winning when we came up the road and our bus turned at the roundabout leading to the stadium. We saw players who believed. Something beautiful woke up in us. The crowd and the side were a block as one. It enthused us. Winning breeds winning. The best way to feel strong is to win and that's what we want to do. It was a very important win for the club tonight. In the eight years I've been here, I've not seen the crowd like that for the whole game. It was really emotional. The feeling that came out of the people, the reply of the people, I've rarely seen from our fans at this level. They were there the whole game. It made me want to put my boots on and go on the pitch.'

MONDAY 24 FEBRUARY - PREMIER LEAGUE

LIVERPOOL 3
Wijnaldum (7), Salah (66), Mané (79)
WEST HAM 2
Diop (10), Fornals (52)

Liverpool now faced the double blow of a rare defeat, a 1-0 set back in the first leg Champions League tie against Atletico, and returning with captain Jordan Henderson suffering a hamstring injury

Henderson was in the form of his life, with three goals in his 34 appearances "We have heard of different hamstring injuries in the Premier League - Harry Kane for example - but it's not that bad," said Klopp. Kane had surgery on a torn hamstring that wrecked his season. Klopp added: "It could have been worse, it was a hamstring. [Henderson] will be out for three weeks or so, which is not cool but how we see it is we were still lucky.'

Liverpool's lead had been cut to 22 points with City winning their game in hand against West Ham, and then won at Leicester, with Guardiola, tongue in cheek, commenting: "We are seven points clear of third, and 19 points from Liverpool right now so maybe we have a chance to beat them!"

In fact, City could be 28 points adrift by the time they next played at United, with Liverpool having three before then, but for Klopp the next one was the most important and Hammers posed a question mark that didn't exist until defeat in Madrid. Klopp wanted that winning feeling back straight away, "We have to put it right to get the other feeling back. I don't think we lost how it feels when we won a few games."

Klopp pointed out the difference in the dressing room when not experiencing defeat, and how it hurts when defeat showed its face. "The difference is massive. Much more than three points, it's from sunshine to the hardest rain and that's how it should be. If you really want to be successful, then it has to feel really bad, and that's how it felt. So we want to put it right even though it is a different competition. We lost the game, there's absolutely no positive in that but if there's any help in that result it's that you felt a defeat. Nobody thought: 'Oh, in the league we're fine.'"

Mane was surprised at being hauled off at half-time against Atletico but Klopp explained to the player had he had "no chance" of avoiding being sent off. "I asked if he was surprised, and he said yes. He said he was not nervous at all and he could deal with it. It's good that the player sees it that way but I saw it different. My honest opinion, I don't think he had a chance. We need Sadio physical. Sadio doesn't foul, but he has contact with his opponent. And both situations, I would say, were made up. It's part of the game, I don't like it too much. You cannot avoid situations, but the one they created a minute before half-time, with eight players around him pushing him in the ref's direction, I didn't believe we could finish the game with 11 if we kept him on the pitch. He was exceptional again, caused problems and I would have loved to have him on the pitch. He's fine, completely fine. He's rested, which is good again!"

Klopp had no intent to drop any points, as his team proved surviving a night of more struggle than usual and even faced defeat at 2-1 down with 22 minutes left! Yet, once again, somehow they did what was needed to win, and this victory equalled the English top-flight record of 18 successive wins, set by Manchester City from August to December 2017. Liverpool had won their last 21 home Premier League games, equalling the English top-flight record for consecutive home wins, set by the Reds themselves between January and December 1972 under Bill Shankly.

On equalling City's record winning run, Klopp said: "I never thought it would be broken or equalled. We did it and I cannot believe it happened to be honest. I like a lot tonight that everything positive helps. When we equalised the stadium was rocking and that helps us. Whatever will happen this season is an effort of all of us. I could not be more thankful or appreciate the support we get. So far so good.

"I said at the beginning we want to write our own stories, create our own history. Obviously, the boys took that really seriously and that

February

is all cool but just not too important at the moment. It's so special. The numbers are incredible, so difficult. We are just in the situation and want to recover and prepare for the next game."

The title was now four games away, maybe fewer if City dropped points. Klopp said: "You see City playing and this is the team in world football that are able to win all their other games. We have to keep winning. We need to be ready and it is a home game for Watford [next]. It is not about shining but the hardest work. As long as the boys are ready to work hard I am not concerned but it is still a job to do."

Liverpool took an early lead when Fabianski failed to deal with a Georginio Wijnaldum header after a wonderful cross from Alexander-Arnold. The fans sang "Now You Are Gonna Believe Us...."

But that ditty had to be put away for much of the game as the Hammers hit back through Issa Diop's header from a corner, which should have been kept out by Alisson. When substitute Pablo Fornals swept West Ham into the lead nine minutes after the break Liverpool were grateful for another Fabianski error, allowing Salah's shot to slip through his legs in the 68th minute. Alexander-Arnold notched his second assist for Mane's winner nine minutes from time, slipping his pass over a stranded keeper. Alisson produce a crucial late block from substitute Jarrod Bowen, who was clean through, but the ball struck the side of the keepers face as Allison was big and brave to stop him.

Liverpool soared to an unstoppable 22-point lead but missed the driving force and leadership of Henderson but when they fell behind with the clock ticking, Klopp made a decisive substitution, replacing Keita for Oxlade-Chamberlain, who immediately charged forward, and unleashed one of his hallmark 30-yarders off target but it lifted a nervous crowd. Keita finished the first half with the most successful tackles, the second most complete passes and an 86 percent pass completion rate, but gave the ball away cheaply a couple of times. Oxlade-Chamberlain brought an extra something.

West Ham fans may have arrived at Anfield to protest about their owners running of the club, but left proud of the way their team ran Liverpool as close as anyone this season, but one man shone above all the rest and it was the right full back the pundits were raving about yet again. Justifiably so. Only Cesc Fabregas (20y 134d) and Wayne Rooney (21y 63d) have reached 25 Premier League assists at a younger age than Liverpool's Trent Alexander-Arnold (21y 140d). Since his Premier

League debut in August 2014, Liverpool's Andrew Robertson has registered 27 assists in the competition, more than any other defender in that time.

KLOPP: "I liked a lot how we started, exactly how we wanted to. We scored a wonderful first goal. But then we weren't good in second ball situations. We have to pick them up much more often. We struggled in this situation and that gave West Ham a good feeling. We didn't defend set pieces really well at all. It's normally a strength of ours. West Ham knew they had a way to stay in the game with the second balls and the set pieces. As long as the opponent thinks there's a chance it makes it difficult. We lost a little bit of patience in the first half. After they scored a second, we found our feet again but we knew the counter would be dangerous for us. I didn't feel any nerves around Anfield. I don't think anyone in the stadium thought it wasn't possible. There was only 51 minutes on the clock, that is a long time. We were a bit lucky, Mohamed Salah's goal, Lukasz Fabianski will normally save and then the Sadio Mane goal was a little bit lucky with the deflection. The best goal we scored was disallowed, that was a really nice goal. I couldn't have wished for a better position to go into these last 11 games. The Champions League final [against Tottenham] helped a lot to know we are able to [keep winning]. I said after, it was the worst final I played with a team but we won! We learned in that season to do the right things again and again. It's long ago. We had to work on that, consistency, staying in the game, using different situations. The set-pieces brought us back tonight. Getting the momemtum back again - because we had a couple after each other. You need to have different ways. There were so many things we could do better but to reach this number of games, you cannot be brilliant all the time. We just try to make the best of what we have. I am pleased with the attitude we showed. The crosses were a bit too hard from Andy Robertson and Trent Alexander-Arnold but we had super situations so all OK. But even at 2-1 down I didn't feel any nerves around Anfield. I don't think anyone in the stadium thought it wasn't possible. There were so many things we could do better but to get to this number of games unbeaten, you can't be brilliant all the time."

MOYES: "We can take a lot of positives. Before the game nobody will have given us a great deal of hope. I thought for large periods of the game we had a chance. I felt as if we'd done a good disciplined defensive

February

performance at Manchester City. I felt tonight we could maybe try and go another way and see if we could get a result here, but it's not easy because Liverpool have so much ammunition. In the end, it wasn't good enough."

SATURDAY 22 FEBRUARY
Chelsea 2 Tottenham Hotspur 1
Burnley 3 AFC Bournemouth 0
Crystal Palace 1 Newcastle United 0
Sheffield United 1 Brighton & Hove Albion 1
Southampton 2 Aston Villa 0
Leicester City 0 Manchester City 1

SUNDAY 23 FEBRUARY
Manchester United 3 Watford 0
Wolverhampton Wanderers 3 Norwich City 0
Arsenal 3 Everton 2

★

There was certainly something in the air ahead of the next game at lowly Watford; perhaps not the coronavirus! Liverpool were attempting a record-breaking 19th straight league win against a Watford team scrapping for their lives under new boss Nigel Pearson - some sages thought it might not be quite as easy to navigate as it looked on paper. In the build-up many focused on the inevitability of a Liverpool win to go with the other 18 on a relentless run that had left them just weeks away from winning that elusive 19th league title.

The build up was dominated by the idea that if the Premier League was halted by Government decree to avoid gathering at sporting events as part of a preventative package of containment then would the entire season be deemed 'null and void' or would games be played behind closed doors. It doesn't get more surreal than that.

The Reds were taking the spread of coronavirus 'seriously'. Games in Italy had been postponed, the entire weekend games in Switzerland were called off, and Liverpool fans were told to self isolate after passing through the country on the way home from their Champions League knockout game against Athletico Madrid. Arsenal and Newcastle United instructed their players not to shake hands at training.

Jurgen Klopp said: "For pre-season we haven't thought about

changing anything because of coronavirus. It is all dictated by medical staff. We take it serious but we cannot avoid anything. It is not a football problem, a society problem. Hopefully the smarter people find the way. We cannot do anything different, we take it seriously but we haven't told anyone not to shake hands. We cannot do more than we are here. We haven't been told we cannot play so we will. We take it serious but we don't go crazy with it."

To add to the feeling there was little to talk about as Watford posed zero threat, the opening gambit at the Klopp media briefing was that Klopp described himself as a half official Scouser at the start when asked about it being the Global Scouse Day. He also laughed about the promotional video for coconut milk featuring some of his players and he thought it was so funny he sent it to his friends via WhatsApp. Well, Jurgen does have a sense of humour. But I watched the video and thought it anything but funny!

After all the nonsense preamble, the important business for Klopp was to prepare to win another important game, no thought from him it would be easy. Liverpool were on course to break the league's record points total of 100, set by City and this was the 19th game they could win in a row to set a new all time record, one which would last for some time.

Klopp insisted his squad still had room for improvement, and he was not taking Watford for granted, far from it, building up the opposition as he normally does, praising the work of Watford's relatively new manager Nigel Pearson who, although had not got the results in recent games, had extracted excellent performances form his team. Klopp had not met him or gone up against any of this teams, but was fully aware of his motivational skills and the impact he was having at Watford, if not in terms of results, but in terms of performance. No way was he taking them lightly.

Klopp also dismissed suggestions that a 'weak' Premier League contributed to The Reds amassing a 22-point lead which they can stretch to 25 with City involved in a Cup Final. Such remarkable dominance created a debate about the current strength of England's top flight. Klopp believed City's midweek Champions League victory at Real Madrid indicated the strength, not weakness, of the Premier League. "I couldn't care less," Klopp said of the debate. "I don't think that any Liverpool supporter should have any concern for things like

February

this. If other people think like that - if they really think City are not as good as they were - then I can say they are. They have scored a few more goals than us but have conceded a few more than us and if you look why it is clear they have been missing some players. The other teams are really strong too. Yes, Bayern Munich beat Tottenham and Chelsea [in the Champions League] but they are both unbelievably strong over a season. They have had some problems, that's all true, but in the moment that you play them you don't feel that they have these problems. We have no influence on the points they have, apart from the games when we played them. And these games are always proper games whether it is Tottenham, Chelsea, Arsenal, City or Manchester United. That is clear and while we have won most of those games so far they were always difficult. So that says nothing about the [lowering] quality of the Premier League, especially when you look at City's win over Real Madrid. They are one of the best teams in the world maybe at the moment and they were clearly better so that shows as well how strong the league is. When we played Watford, Norwich and West Ham they didn't look like teams in the bottom three."

Klopp stressed: "There is so much more to come from us. It's really nice that we are so far away from perfection and still can get results. That means we have a lot of space for improvement and that's exactly what we will do, this season and for sure next season as well."

But few were listening. Everyone thought it would be a foregone conclusion that Liverpool would sweep Watford aside as they had done with everyone else. Yet Klopp knew going for this enormous record brought its own pressures. "People will talk about the game number 19 and it's a proper opportunity for Watford to give us a real struggle, but we know that. I thought weeks ago that Watford away would be one of the tough ones. I'm looking forward to it and it will be important to them, but we have to show it is an important game for us. We have to be 100 per cent ready fro these fights. That's what I love about my boys, when it's not clicking they don't lose desire, it's the other way around. It will be tough and very physical. Watford will show how much it means for them and we have to show what it means for us. We have to fight foe each blade of grass to win."

The build-up continued with Klopp confessing that he was unaware his skipper was stopping the players talking about winning the title. Oxlade-Chamberlain revealed that Henderson had strong words with any team-mates who mentioned the possibility of claiming the title. Klopp insisted that the skipper was not acting on his orders as he reiterated that his squad remained focused on winning one game at a time. "I didn't know Hendo had banned that! It is just how we see it. I can't imagine they sit in the dressing room and discuss it before I come in because when I come in I see nothing of that situation. I don't see anyone wanting to talk about it and Hendo telling them to shut up. It is just focusing on the next game. I don't think that is too difficult but I can imagine what it is like because I meet people who want to talk about it and who say: 'Unbelievable. You're going to do it.' Stuff like this but it doesn't bother me. I don't care. I can imagine people think like this but there is only one team who can make it happen or not and that is us. That is what we try to do and we try to do it by being 100 per cent focused on a specific game, and that is now Watford. I have no problem with people talking about [the title] but I don't think about it. So why should I speak about it?"

Klopp confirmed Henderson, Milner and Shaqiri would miss the match but all three were making progress but in the absence of his midfield skipper he didn't accept that Keita and Oxlade-Chamberlain were competing. Keita had not lost any of the 34 Premier League matches in which he had featured and his individual on-field numbers regularly look good indicating he was doing better than the perception. "They're not competing against each other and hopefully they don't see it like this. It's not like this," Klopp explained. "They offer naturally different things. Naby can play better, obviously, and has played better. But that wasn't the reason the (West Ham) game was like it was. Then Oxlade came on, really fresh and with his natural skill, having direction, speed, it's a different player. In different situations we need different players and they all are exceptional. Until the change, we were more fixed in positions. It wasn't flexible enough or unpredictable enough, we were too easy to defend, we didn't really come through. In other situations we were too high on the wings and were hit on counter-attacks."

The West Ham game had been the first time they had been behind in a Premier League match since November 2nd at Aston Villa. Klopp observed: "I watched the game back, and in that game being 2-1 down helped us a little bit because the direction after that, a lot of things were different. I didn't know it was the first time since Villa, but the boys reacted well and that's the only thing we have to know. Some people used the word complacency, that they saw glimpses of that. I didn't see that at all. Complacency? It's a long season and the concentration level can drop from time to time in all teams, in games and between games. How much the boys fight for a result is exceptional. There is no fear about anything, but we also don't take it for granted that there will just be one or two goals up.

"This game (Watford) will be tough. I said it, 100 per cent. I don't want people to think we are going to win 6-0. It just will not happen."

Well, Jurgen was right about that!

SATURDAY 29 FEBRUARY 29 - PREMIER LEAGUE

WATFORD 3
Sarr 54, 60, Deeney 72.

LIVERPOOL 0

Such was the level of expectation of Jurgen Klopp's whirlwind leaders making English football history that press accreditation for the game had been oversubscribed, with hundreds of media outlets keen to cover the moment Liverpool broke City's all-time record. More than a hundred packed into the old stadium with just one angle on the agenda - Liverpool making English top-flight history, with a record-breaking 19th win in a row on their relentless march towards the title

This was supposed to be a non contest, there could only be one winner. Instead the assembled press pack watched Liverpool's first top-flight defeat since they were beaten 2-1 by eventual champions City on 3 January 2019 - a gap of 422 days.

Of course, it had to happen at some time, the phenomenal run came to an end... but at second-from-bottom Watford? No way! It was one of the biggest shocks of the season by far. The only team that could match Preston North End and Arsenal's record of going unbeaten through an entire league campaign had finally succumbed to a team that started the day in the relegation zone and had not won in their five previous outings.

Afterwards the microphones in the press conference room within the bowels of Vicarage Road picked up the sheer volume of celebrating Watford fans (and perhaps fans of all the other clubs!) outside the ground nearly drowning out Klopp. Asked if he cared that Liverpool could no longer emulate Arsenal's Invincible season of 2003-04, or indeed match or better their 49-game unbeaten run in the league, Klopp replied, "Not really, because I don't think you can break records because you want to break records. You break records because you are 100% focused on each step, the record is the result of the performance and we didn't perform today. The boys have already so many records. Why would they want any more? We don't want to be greedy. We can't be the best ever Premier League team because tonight we just weren't good enough. Maybe we can set another record in the future. It was clear that at some time we would lose a game. We didn't wait for it but it was clear that it would happen. Tonight it happened. I see it rather positive. Because from now on we can play free football again. We don't have to defend or try to get the record we just can try to win football games again. No (we didn't see this result coming) it's normal. A lot of people will say that but congratulations, I didn't.

"When we look back in 500 years, we'll say Liverpool nearly did it – but that's not my concern. We don't think it's not important because we won so many games. But we don't think as well it's the biggest catastrophe in the world of football. We don't have to defend or try to get the record – just try to win football games again. What the boys did so far is exceptional but it's not over. We'll go again.

"We've never estimated the situation wrongly, we never thought it's easy. These boys are working constantly extremely hard. It's just the result of how the boys played. But of course sometimes a little knock is important. A kick up the backside? Why not? So I don't see anything negative in that. From time to time if you are not good enough you need to see effect. So restart. Maybe the longer the run goes maybe it becomes more important. But I didn't see that today. Now it is over. We can start again with whatever we did before. And we will. We cannot say now we will react in this way or that. We have to show it in the next games.

"You cannot win the amount of games the boys have done if they are easily influenced by the outside world, and we will see how they react. But I don't know because I've never won 18 games in a row and didn't lose 44 first time in my life. So maybe it becomes more important the longer the run goes on but nothing has changed. Sometimes we score late goals and sometimes we are influenced by misfortune or whatever.

February

Ismaila Sarr was the unexpected hero on the night as relegation battlers Watford pulled off the biggest surprise of the season

I'm not bothered but I'm not sure how other people think about that What the boys did so far is exceptional. How they react we shall see."

As for his team selection for the next game, the Chelsea cup tie, he added: 'You'll find out after how this result has affected my thinking."

Nigel Pearson praised Klopp for his 'gracious' reaction. Shortly before the full-time whistle, Klopp went to the Watford dugout and shook hands with his counterparts, with Pearson full of admiration for how the Liverpool boss handled an unexpected defeat. Asked what Klopp said to him, Pearson revealed: 'Well, look, he was very, very gracious. I think there's a lesson for everybody. When you're in the sort of position that they're in, I think he showed a lot of dignity, I think he showed a lot of humility and he just congratulated us. Fair play to him for doing that. Let's be honest, they are an incredible team and he's done an amazing job there. It doesn't matter what exactly it is that's said, I think what is more important is that somebody in his position is able to show respect to his peers. He comes out of it, I think, with an awful lot of positives and so do his players by the way, who were very gracious in defeat as well.'

Liverpool's hopes of remaining unbeaten for an entire Premier League season were ended by Ismaila Sarr scoring twice while captain Troy Deeney added a third in a sensational second-half display that defied all the odds. But Liverpool were poor, not just one of their stars, but all of them! They managed just one shot on target.

The Reds had won their past 18 Premier League games and another at Vicarage Road would have made history as the longest winning run in the English top flight. It just didn't happen, but there was no luck, no VAR, other than a deserved win by the much better team; Watford!

Watford had enough chances to seal victory in the first half alone and only a superb save from Alisson denied Deeney, and it seemed that as the half ended goalless their chance had gone, and that Klopp sent his team out early for a second half that ought to have been all-Liverpool after a managerial pep talk to get them going.

Instead, Watford took a deserved lead when Doucoure squeezed a cross in from the left for Sarr to stab in. Minutes later Sarr was put through on goal by Hughes and the winger calmly lifted the ball over Alisson for the second. Troy Deeney completed a famous victory, curling into the back of the net from the edge of the area after an error from Alexander-Arnold.

The Reds remained 22 points clear but with City now having a game in hand, they were not going to relinquish their grip on the title, but it was such a shock, everyone would be waiting to see how they would react.

A superb run of four wins in five games at the start of Nigel Pearson's reign had lifted them from the foot of the table and out of the relegation zone but five games without victory prior to the visit of Liverpool had dropped them back into it. Yet, performances had been good and they were boosted for this game by the return from injury of Sarr.

Recent performances by Liverpool had not been quite at the same extraordinary level fans had been accustomed to seeing; scraping past Norwich, losing to Atletico and a comeback against West Ham that owed everything to a goalkeeping howler. The pairing of Virgil van Dijk and Dejan Lovren looked vulnerable, in comparison to the Van Dijk-Gomez partnership. Lovren made his first Premier League start since 7 December but the Croatia international struggled to deal with the pace and trickery of Sarr and the power of Deeney.

Lovren also started the last time Liverpool lost by three goals - the

February

2017 4-1 defeat by Tottenham. He was not alone, even van Dijk made a number of uncharacteristic mistakes, while no one could say they hit their true form.

Liverpool were supposed to set a new record to be proud of, a new mark in the history of the game. Instead the game produced a barrow-load of unwanted stats:

- Watford became the first side to beat Liverpool in the Premier League since City in January 2019, ending the joint-longest winning streak (18) and the second longest unbeaten run (44) in English top-flight history…
- Liverpool's loss was the biggest margin of defeat for a side starting the day top of the Premier League since November 2015 (Man City 1-4 Liverpool).
- Watford's victory was the biggest over a side starting the day top of the top-flight table by a team in the relegation zone since Leicester beat Manchester United 3-0 on November 23rd 1985.
- Watford secured their first top-flight victory against a side starting the day top of the table since the final day of the 1982-83 season, also beating Liverpool that day (2-1).
- Liverpool failed to score in a Premier League game for the first time since March 2019 (0-0 v Everton), ending a run of scoring in 36 consecutive league games.
- Liverpool conceded more than 2 goals in consecutive Premier League games for the first time since December 2016 conceding as many goals in their last two league games (5) as they had in their previous 14
- Liverpool had just one shot on target in a Premier League game for the first time since February 2019 in a goalless draw against Manchester United (1)
- Liverpool ended a 44-game unbeaten run in the Premier League just five games short of Arsenal's top-flight record.
- Klopp's side were the third Premier League team to manage more than a calendar year without losing (Arsenal - whose 49 games included the entire 2003-04 season) and Chelsea (from October 2004 to November 2005) are the others.
- The Reds fell 14 games short of AC Milan's remarkable unbeaten

Serie A run from May 1991 to March 1993 - a sequence of 58 games lasting 672 days. Liverpool's record is the fifth longest in Europe's top five leagues, behind Milan, Bayern Munich, Arsenal and Juventus.

- They fell way short of the British record of 62 league games unbeaten by Celtic between November 1915 and April 1917. The Glasgow club almost matched it again two years ago when they went 56 Scottish Premiership games - and 69 domestic matches - without defeat from May 2016 to December 2017.

NIGEL PEARSON: "To beat the best club side in the world is testament to how we played. It's such an important win for us. They are such an outstanding side, we had to get our performance right - as close to max as possible - and I thought we thoroughly deserved the win. We threatened with the ball and defended with discipline, energy and commitment. I want the players to enjoy this and I want it to galvanise our season .Every single one of them out there today delivered what they were picked to deliver - and that's what really pleases me, more than anything else. I think that performance surpassed everything else we've delivered so far. You've got to earn the right to beat a side as good as Liverpool. The players were fantastic today in terms of cohesion on the pitch - we showed a lot of discipline when we didn't have the ball, but I also felt we caused them problems throughout the game by being committed when we had it.'

KLOPP: "3-0 is a bit harsh but we had a big hand in that. They did exactly what they wanted to do, we did not. That's how football works. The first half was a tough one, a lot of second balls, running here and there, we had the ball a lot but we didn't come in the right positions to cross, the right positions to finish, against a really good, organised side, with a top set-up for this game. You have to accept it, it's not so easy, but it's the proof we were not good enough tonight. It's always very difficult. We have to accept if after. In the game you have to fight. We were 3-0 down but we still tried, there were no silly situations where somebody got frustrated and tried to kick someone. If you win good, if you lose, try to do it in the right manner and do it like a man. A lot of things (went wrong) obviously, We couldn't create clear enough chances against a very complex side. I don't think we felt the game really. We tried, we tried, we tried, but at the end we crossed from the wrong spaces. When we crossed we didn't have the positioning in the box. So, that was the first half. I really thought we started much better in the second half because we could adjust a few things but then they scored the first goal and from that moment pretty much everything went wrong because I have to see the goals back. The first one you lose one of these challenges but it's routine for them. The most important thing is congratulations to Watford, well deserved. That's what should be the headline. The first half there were football things that didn't work out for us and overall we didn't create enough and that's what leads to a defeat. But it's just one football game and we have to admit that Watford was the better team. Everybody is fighting like crazy and we fought the whole season like crazy. Tonight we lost that battle. What can I say? That it's not acceptable? We feel the defeat. Absolutely it's the opposite of what we wanted to happen. We feel that and now we have a chance to show a reaction."

Social media reaction was predictably humorous with Bundesliga title challengers RB Leipzig, sending a GIF of Liverpool transfer target Timo Werner looking shocked by the result as he checked his phone, while the official Arsenal account tweeted "Phew" as their Invincibles tag was still safe for another season!

OTHER SCORES

FRIDAY 28 FEBRUARY
Norwich City 1 Leicester City 0

SATURDAY 29 FEBRUARY
Brighton & Hove Albion 0 Crystal Palace 1
AFC Bournemouth 2 Chelsea 2
Newcastle United 0 Burnley 0
West Ham United 3 Southampton 1

SUNDAY 1 MARCH
Everton 1 Manchester United 1
Tottenham Hotspur 2 Wolverhampton Wanderers 3

★

For the manager there seemed no point in ranting and raving at his players just to make himself feel better after the shock 3-0 defeat at Vicarage Road ended a 44-match undefeated run and prevented a new Premier League record of 19 successive victories.

After their poorest performance in over a year, Klopp gave them a calculated assessment of where they had gone wrong after re-watching the match as he appreciates what they have achieved this season. He would be an "idiot" if he now began to doubt them. "It can happen that I get angry with the players, but I didn't get angry with the players in this meeting. If you need to analyse, you analyse and analysis is not really emotional. It is looking at the facts and we were just not good enough. That is the easy answer. From a common sense point of view if I go in that meeting and shout at them like they have lost the last 10 games in a row because of a bad attitude that would be really strange. I am not interested that after the meeting I feel better. I am interested in the boys getting the right information and it can be more emotional - I would not say angry - or less emotional.'

Klopp was confident they were ready to, in one of his favourite phrases, "strike back". He said: "There was no applause. They don't come to me and say, 'That was a great meeting boss'. Of course, they want to strike back. This is an exceptional group of players. The situation we are in is special. Who can give us advice? We came through an incredible long period with incredible performances, sensational football, wonderful goals, great success - until this point. I am not a little bit in doubt about the character of the boys and I would be a real idiot if I would be to be honest because they deserve my trust, my faith and they don't lose it after a bad game."

Klopp planned wholesale changes, but probably would have made virtually as many even if they had beaten Watford. Having already beaten Chelsea twice this season in the league and the Super Cup, Klopp named changed teams in previous rounds, and in the fourth-round replay win over Shrewsbury, Liverpool's youngest ever side was led by Neil Critchley, who just announced he was joining Blackpool.

Klopp said: "The defeat has nothing to do with the line-up. Do we want to win the game more because we lost the last one? I don't know because we want to win games constantly. This is the most important game we have because it is the only one we play and we have to win it if we want to go through. It will not be easier for us because we lost the last game and so there will be more motivation. We never really think about lesser pressure or whatever. We are Liverpool, we always have to deliver. We play at Chelsea but everyone expects us to win. We have no clue what Chelsea are doing, they don't know what we are doing. We

February

always play with a team which gives us the best chance to reach the next round. We don't really think, it is not less pressure than before, it is just last 16 of the FA Cup and we want to go through and hopefully everyone can see that."

Asked whether the end of their unbeaten league record could have a destabilising effect, Klopp added: "That's over now, we can concentrate on football and we will do that. It didn't distract us and no one can tell us how best to deal with runs like this because not a lot of teams had it.

I was not happy with the performance (at Watford) but it was always clear there will be a moment when it could happen and now it has happened."

Klopp launched an impassioned defence of the 30-year-old Lovren, under fire more than anyone from the fans for his performance at Vicarage Road. "It's not fair, but that's the world. If anybody gave Dejan Lovren the blame for our defeat then I can't help these people. A lot of times in my life I speak to people and they know less than I do about football, that's okay as I'm a well-paid Premier League manager and I should know more than most people. But on that level, I can't discuss it.

"It was a massive challenge for him to play against Troy Deeney. So many other centre-halves would struggle in this specific situation, Joe has had problems as well. Losing the first ball is never the problem, because Troy cannot score from there, so it's about formations around that. Both Dejan and Joel Matip have played sensational games for us in this position but you need to be healthy and fit and when you are fit you need rhythm and that is the most difficult thing to get in football. Dejan is an outstanding centre-half. You tell me one player on Saturday night who played his normal level and I would be really surprised. It's not because two players didn't play the week before."

Asked if there was a loyalty towards some of the younger players Klopp replied: "It's not about loyalty, these boys are our boys, if we win the FA Cup in the end they would be involved in all the celebrations. From the Shrewsbury team there will be boys in the squad, but if they start we will see. It's a different situation than the last round." James Milner and Joe Gomes were available, and like it or not, whoever Klopp left out it would be perceived as a reflection of that shock Watford defeat.

Klopp responded to headlines that coronavirus could mean abandoning the season, curtailing their title. Supporters aren't "silly enough" to believe the story, suggested Klopp.

Klopp said: "I don't think our fans are paranoid. I think people who are not interested in us bring up these stories. I can't believe Liverpool fans are thinking about it, and I speak to Liverpool fans. Anybody wants to ask me about that and how much sense it would make to delete the results of this season and who plays Champions League next year, would be really interesting. It's a nice story, but when I saw it first, I thought wow, somebody thinks something like that? Liverpool fans aren't silly enough to believe these things."

Klopp dismissed the notion that he might now take the FA Cup more seriously. "I'm not sure if you saw that but we go really hard in all the games. So if you invest 100 per cent, how can you invest more? How can I take a risk with a player who played on Saturday, with all the little bits of information from everywhere? No, I can't. So if I think a player played now X, Y and Z and we need another option, I will do it. I want to win this game. It's not because I don't take this game seriously and think, 'Yeah! Send the reserves out against Chelsea and whatever!' We are not like this. We just try to do the best all the time. Sometimes you see it. Sometimes, maybe, you don't see it. We cannot fight more for the cup competitions than we do already. One cup competition that we proved we take really seriously in the last couple of years is the Champions League. The FA Cup? It's nothing to do with us not wanting to go to the final. It was just because [of] draws, performances…

"Team selections? They were always reasonable. There was always a good reason for it. Now we lost a game, we cannot be invincible, so now that is done and we can lose a couple more? I don't understand that. We play Chelsea with all we have. Then Bournemouth, with all we have. Then [Atletico] Madrid with all we have. Then Everton, then Crystal Palace or FA Cup, right? It will be with all we have. Nothing else. 100 per cent. That is us. What we really blame ourselves for is that you didn't see it on Saturday. We didn't see it. That is where we are really critical of ourselves. But it doesn't mean in the future we will not do it anymore. That is what we want to be. We want to be very, very intense in a good way."

MARCH

TUESDAY 3 MARCH
FA CUP FIFTH ROUND

CHELSEA 2
Willian 13, Barkley 64
LIVERPOOL 0

In the event the manager made seven changes: Gomez returned, while Lallana, Adrian, Origi, Minamino and teenagers Jones and Williams started. Alisson, Alexander-Arnold, Lovren and Wijnaldum were left at home, not even in the squad. Klopp explained his multiple changes: "I wanted a team that's naturally looking forward to the tie. We were counting the days, pretty much, going into a tie and trying everything. Fresh legs, we want quality, positivity, we want a lot of things. We could have had a different line-up as well, I'm not sure, but I decided for this and I'm really happy with it to be honest and I like the team. They had no time for showing a response, really. A lot of the answers I gave to the questions, it's already done. We lost the game, yes, and it felt really not good, I can tell. But it's over and it is a different competition. We have to play as good as possible, that's the plan."

By the end the three first choice forwards were on the field but it was to no avail, Klopp's team lost their third game in four across all competitions. Liverpool suffered their second successive defeat of this stellar season without a single goal, yet they had their chances, especially in the first half.

Klopp was not concerned about the momentum of the season being stalled. There was no crisis. No need to panic. He explained: "Well look, it went our way for so long because we defended so well. Teams usually don't get a lot of chances against us. No, we have to admit that in the last three games we've conceded too many goals, that's true. This was completely different today from Watford. But I'm not worried about momentum. Momentum is not something you go and get and then just have it. You can lose it but then you have to go and get it again. We have always the chance to get it back. So I'm not concerned about momentum. We never thought it would be an easy season, period, game tonight; nothing. It was always difficult. We did well tonight but we weren't good enough. The performance tonight was completely different from Watford. Against Watford it was really bad, but tonight was not bad, it was a really super intense game. That performance tonight I'm not concerned about, that's football. We made seven changes, that's why we made them. There would be a lot of sprints and a lot of spaces in midfield. There would be a lot of accelerations in midfield. Losing 2-0 is not cool, but is relatively easy to explain in this case. We made two massive mistakes around the goals. Adrian made a super save a second or two before, and this ball is really flying, a really good shot from Willian and he can't make that save. But before that we lost the ball, and that's the problem.

"It wasn't the biggest shock, that's football. I liked our reaction and liked the way we played with some good stuff, it was a super intense game and both teams were really running like mad. It was clear it would be difficult but we had our moments, we had our chances especially when we shot three or four times. Conceding the second one didn't help and it was a bit more difficult to take. Chelsea then defended with all they had and threw their bodies in, a really, really physical game, but we couldn't score. We're out the competition – it's the opposite of what we wanted."

Adrian gifted Willian the opener after 13 minutes when he fumbled a 20-yarder claiming he was unsighted having just pulled off a wonder save from the same player. Recalled keeper Kepa Arrizabalaga made a string of saves including a triple save in the same move that brought the Stamford Bridge crowd to its feet. The Spanish number one had been left out of games of late following several howlers but appeared to be unbeatable in the first half hour despite concerted Liverpool pressure.

The game was settled after 64 minutes when former Everton midfielder Ross Barkley surged from inside his own half on a solo run before beating Adrian with an emphatic strike. Mount hit the top of the bar with a 25-yard free-kick, while Olivier Giroud's close range shot was brilliantly tipped on to the bar by Adrian as Chelsea repeatedly caught the visitors on the break. Meanwhile Liverpool had plenty of possession but couldn't manage a shot on target after the 31st minute. In truth the scoreline flattered the presumptive league champions on a night memorable for the debut of 18 year-old Billy Gilmour who dominated midfield for the hosts.

KLOPP: "I would really like if you stop mentioning it (the Watford loss). But we deserved to lose because they scored twice and we made massive mistakes for both goals. After that it was a completely open game, we had three-four shots in a row in the first half and Sadio Mane was close to finishing but the intensity of the game is why we made some changes. We needed fresh legs and then it needs to settle a bit but conceding does not help. The boys reacted well, I liked it but the second goal is a problem and Chelsea defended physically well. We are not unlucky in these moments, we looked good and Adrian made a superb save initially before the first goal. We have to be ready in the moments. We played Chelsea and they play in counter-attacks and that is OK, in moments they struggled with us. A lot of parts of the performance I really liked. We know we have to improve, it is not about destiny, not about not clicking here or there, it is all about us and we have to take it in the right way. It is not the best three weeks of the whole season but it is a chance to make it the best three weeks now and that is the plan. We are not interested in Atletico Madrid, it is all about Bournemouth. They are fighting with all they have and they did really well against Chelsea. Nobody has to feel sorry for us, we will win football games and that is what we want to do on Saturday."

LAMPARD: "I'm really proud. Liverpool are the best team in the league and what they are doing is incredible. So for us to put in a performance like that, the effort, the quality was something special. We know we've got a long way to go but you have to celebrate those moments."

★

Liverpool released a statement on the growing threat of coronavirus after Merseyside recorded its first case with suggestions fixtures would be played behind closed doors to follow the lead of Italy's Serie A. Within days the Italian government confirmed all sporting events would take place without fan attendance until April 3. The club were in dialogue with UEFA over the use of mascots for the Champions League tie with Atletico, having decided there would be none at Anfield when the Reds hosted Bournemouth aiming to go within three wins of the title.

A Liverpool statement read: "In recent weeks, there has been a rise of confirmed COVID-19 (novel coronavirus) cases around the world. We have several new measures in place across LFC operations to help prevent the spread of the virus and protect the health of our employees. We have taken pro-active measures including cancelling any staff travel to high risk countries and reminding everyone of good hygiene practices through notices in/around all our sites. We have also activated a health questionnaire screening for all external visitors to all our training facilities, our office locations and other community facilities that we use regularly. For supporters planning on attending Anfield there will be hand sanitisers and/or antibacterial handwash in all the washrooms at Anfield as well as additional information posters reinforcing the official medical advice for everyone to take personal responsibility for excellent personal hygiene. We are also taking matchday precautionary measures and will not have any mascots on the pitch. Any supporter displaying symptoms that are consistent with the virus should ensure they familiarise themselves with the Chief Medical Officer's advice on self-isolation. We will continue to take the best advice from the relevant authorities and will update supporters with any further developments."

Jurgen Klopp was questioned after the Reds were knocked out of the FA Cup to Chelsea. "I'm concerned like everyone else, I live on this planet and I want it to be safe and healthy, I wish everybody the best absolutely. But my opinion on coronavirus is not important."

Then the Premier League and EFL ordered pre-match handshakes between both teams and officials will not take place until further notice. The measure came after the government asked the Premier League "to step up its contingency planning". Several clubs have instructed players not to sign autographs or take selfies with fans.

Klopp reacted: "My answer will not change. Of course we get information every day and we trust the things the Premier League tell us. So, that's what we need to do – handshakes or no handshakes. Mascots or no mascots, to decrease the probability of infection. As I said after the Chelsea game, people with more knowledge than me will make decisions and we hope and trust that they make the right ones."

His first question in his pre-match media conference, will captain Jordan Henderson be fit to face Bournemouth at Anfield on Saturday? Good question as he had been badly missed. "No. Jordan has a chance for Atletico Madrid but not for Bournemouth." Klopp confirmed. More bad news Klopp confirmed his goalkeeper was out, not only of the league game, but the Champions League last 16 second leg against Atletico Madrid with a muscle injury. "[Alisson] had a little incident before the Chelsea, we thought nothing of it - the plan was he was going to be on the bench anyway. And then we thought 'come on, we don't have to take any risks' so left him out of the squad. Then he had a scan the next day and they found something, so now he is out. We'll see how long. Next week for sure and then we'll see. It's a small muscle in the hip region. You could all do your work with it, he being a professional goalkeeper can not. We have to judge the situation. I would say after the international break, 100%. Whatever we can get before that we will see." Keita was back in training after a similar problem and could return after a two-match absence.

Klopp was working to make sure two defeats didn't become three. "Winning gives you confidence, losing costs you confidence, so that's completely normal that you start thinking about things. One defeat feels like two defeats, so it's not a massive difference, It's just how you get back on track immediately – the results track, if you want. We have to work really hard and we have to fight back. It will always be like this and it will never be different. And that's what we have to do on Saturday as a unit with our supporters and not just waiting for the perfect moment.

"People say it's a difficult situation but I think it's an interesting one. This is where I do my work and it's my job to help the players get back to where we want to be and where we think we belong. I'm not in the mood to create headlines but I am also not blind so I can see that we didn't score or create much in our recent games. We know for sure that we could have done better in a lot of moments bit that doesn't mean we'll never score again or that our opponents will score with every chance they have. That's not how it is. The boys want to respond in the right way and they know that if they perform at their highest level it will be difficult for Bournemouth

"We had a big meeting after Watford and Chelsea. I said after the [Chelsea] game I liked a lot of the game. We conceded two goals, one after a counter-attack and one after a super shot – it was a tricky ball Adrian usually saves and if you don't lose the ball beforehand, it was two situations we didn't like. It was an intense game otherwise, completely fine. Difficult to say when you've lost but it is the truth. We had two big moments where we could have scored – in the game against Chelsea where we won a couple of months ago we scored in these moments. That's the difference. After Watford, I thought now we have to talk in a more detailed way and we did. I saw a reaction from the players [at Chelsea]. So we just carry on. I cannot make a meeting where it is the same. It doesn't work. The opponents were strong, us not so much.'

One record Liverpool that survived the defeat at Watford was the record 22 games unbeaten at home. Asked how big a part the supporters played in the team's dominance at home, Klopp responded: "I realised a while ago how big the influence and impact the support is at Anfield. They have given us nothing but good things. They are not even the slightest bit responsible for the not so good things that have happened. Everyone knows what we need to do. We need to play our passes and try different things. To win games, you have to take risks, and I'm sure the atmosphere will be as good as possible.

"We never really thought about statistics but in this moment it doesn't really feel like we won the last 22 and that's how defeats change things. We would never ignore the things that have happened to us, results wise or injury wise. We have to create an atmosphere again, use that atmosphere and then have the right mind set – our people as well, because it's not only is that we lost as a team but our supporters lost them as well. It's about a reaction and fighting back with an atmosphere that's really exceptional. It's not about records, it's about creating the biggest possibility of winning the next football match."

The Cherries were in the drop zone on goal difference but Klopp was impressed by the way Howe's side can take advantage of a set play. "Bournemouth are especially dangerous at set-pieces. I think they have scored 50% of their goals like this from set-pieces, which is impressive, so we have to respond there, play football and force a way through. We have to be perfectly protected because of the threat of a counter-attack through Josh King and Ryan Fraser. That's what we have to do and it wouldn't have been different if we had won. We want to fight and that's what we have to do."

March

SATURDAY 7 MARCH - PREMIER LEAGUE

LIVERPOOL 2
Salah 24, Mane 32

BOURNEMOUTH 1
Wilson 8

Jurgen Klopp picked a strong team, the only unexpected change recalling James Milner at full back for the rested/injured Robertson, there was no place for Lovren in the squad. With Anfield packed, Klopp said: "This is a chance to change the situation with football. We have to fight, get back on track and made it as difficult as possible for Bournemouth. Robertson is something between rested and injured. He would have started but he felt something, he will be fine for Wednesday. Not only we - as a team - lost three of the last four, our supporters lost them as well. Now it's about the reaction - really fighting back with an atmosphere that is exceptional. Look, you cannot hope for momentum - you have to work for momentum. That's what we want to do. In the moment, we are completely focused on nothing else than the game tomorrow."

Milner was caught on camera during the pre warm up coaching tactical advice, illustrating how much senior players like Henderson were missed during the mini-dip. As they stretched going through their exercise routine on the itch Milner said: Those reactions straightaway, as soon as you lose it, bodies around it, everything we do, highest tempo today, and we play out of that area. You score, we score, they score, we lift it again." It was easy to dish out advice, but the captain led by example with a goal line clearance that effectively won the game for the hosts.

It was a landmark game for Salah, his 100th Premier League appearance for Liverpool and he had scored in all five of his Premier League appearances against Bournemouth - seven goals in total. Salah loves to score to Anfield - 13 of his 15 Premier League goals this season coming at home. Eddie Howe knew it was going to be a daunting midday task, "We know this is probably the ultimate test this season. We've got to rise to it, embrace it and attack it. We're not going to win by playing okay, or playing at 60 or 70%, we can only do it if we excel. The most important quality we can have this week is belief."

The sun was out, The Kop was in full throttle voice, dozens upon dozens of flags, Liverpool's players walking past their opponents without shaking hands. Instead each player greeted the other with a nod! There was a growing sense within Anfield that what would have been billed as a routine assignment had taken on much greater significance, a defining moment in the pursuit of the title.

When Bournemouth took an unexpected early lead, there was a sense of 'here we go again' and the possibility of Liverpool blowing yet another late title race from fans hardened by previous set backs. They fell behind in controversial circumstances, Callum Wilson slotting home Jefferson Lerma's low cross after appearing to shove Joe Gomez in the build-up. VAR saw no infringement and the goal was given. Klopp was furious with the decision to let the goal stand but urged his side to come roaring back. Later the manager questioned the application of VAR, he was in conversation with fourth official Mike Dean immediately following the goal. "Mike Dean I'm sure saw it was a foul but it's not his job to intervene anymore. It's VAR. And then VAR hides behind the phrase 'not clear and obvious'. It makes no sense. It it's a foul, it's a foul. If it's no foul, it's not a problem. But when it's that clear, nobody felt comfortable about that. Not the ref, nobody. Everybody knew something happened here which is not okay. That should be easy to sort with someone watching it on a screen. I understand 100% Bournemouth sees it different but it was a clear, clear foul."

Having lost three of their past four games in all competitions, there were palpable nerves inside Anfield after falling behind early but the team soon hit their stride as Salah equalised following a mix up in the Bournemouth back four, the Egyptian beating the keeper low to his left after Mane had dispossessed Jack Simpson deep inside the Cherries' half. It was Salah's 70th league goal for the club in just his 100th league game. Within 8 minutes Mane latched on to van Dijk's perfectly-weighted through-ball to complete the turnaround. Klopp was so relieved to see his side take the lead that he let out a huge roar in the direction of the linesman nearest his dugout.

Yet Bournemouth were never out of the contest and 12 minutes from time they caught the Anfield rearguard cold, as Ryan Fraser was clean through and lobbed Adrian. The ball looked destined for the net but captain James Milner somehow got back to effect a clearance the biggest cheer of the afternoon. From then on the home side kept possession and wary eye on their opponents. The win was far from convincing but at this stage of the season the three points were all the mattered.

Jurgen Klopp didn't object to doing it the hard way, in fact, even thought it had some merit! "Imagine we had won against Watford, won in the FA Cup and against Atletico in the end becoming champions whenever it will happen - and everybody would say, 'Yeah, champions'. So if it happens, it will feel really special. If it happens."

Well, it will happen, and yes it will be special. Certainly on top of the Super Cup and the World Club Championship. This is a Treble worth celebrating, a new chapter in the club's history, and one to be proud of. Liverpool were finally on the comeback trail, not just in this match, but for a little run that gave their detractors an inch in which to criticise.

Of his aggressive celebration in front of the linesman the manager said "Yes, that happened. Would I do it now? No. But in the moment I just don't understand how that could be a goal. This shows the problem of VAR that still exists – it's not a system, it's a human being and the rules. Does anybody in the room think it was not a foul? (Nobody puts hand up) So it was a foul. Ah. Touch was enough to make Joe struggle, it's a foul, nothing else. They scored a goal in the next situation, the ref let it run so that's why we have VAR, so they can have a look.

"VAR made really difficult decisions in two games on the same matchday the other week. So how it is possible somebody sits there and doesn't see it? Yes I celebrated in that direction (of the assistant referee), I'm not happy about it, but I didn't say anything while I was celebrating."

The Reds were grateful for that stunning goal-line clearance from Jame Milner to prevent Ryan Fraser from hauling Bournemouth back on level terms in a nervy second half. Racing back, the 34-year-old defied his age as he stretched to pull off a spectacular goal-line clearance that had Klopp purring with delight. "The biggest chance fell to Bournemouth, we have to admit that. Milly saved our life in that situation with a really long, long, long, long big toe. Great."

Invited to lavish more praise on Milner, Klopp amusingly rolled his eyes. "I hope I haven't been short of praising Millie in the past. Why would we extend the contract of a 34-year-old by two years if he's not incredibly important to everything that we do?"

Sadio Mane almost added a third with a cracking 25-yard strike that cannoned back off the bar and the crowd were soon signing 'now you're going to believe us...we're going to win the league'. The anticipated chorus rang out around Anfield, more in relief than in triumph. They were three more wins from the title!

Liverpool kept the ball in the corner close to the end and the crowd encouraging it! What tension. It's unexpected from Liverpool but until they have got their hands on that trophy, they won't care. Talking about 'hands', the players were shaking hands at the end. Really? Not taking Government advice then?

Klopp's joy was clear to see at full-time as he performed his trademark three fist pumps in front of the Kop. The fans begging him for more as he left the field, he repeated it in front of the main stand! "I was in good spirits after the game," said Klopp. "I was absolutely happy about the result, the three points and the performance. I knew it would be tricky. The decision of the ref around the goal made it even more tricky for us, obviously. We wanted to fight back before the game and then we had to after that decision. The way we played after going 1-0 down was exceptional. When you get a decision like that and a goal like this, there are other teams in the history of football who would slip, but the reaction of the boys I loved. We fought hard, played super football, the strikers played really good together, they were connected. We had some super situations. We deserved that today. The attitude and reaction to different knocks I liked a lot.

"Now, we have three days to prepare for another difficult game. In a wonderful stadium and a sensational crowd that was, I think, the best 12:30 pm performance of our crowd since I am here. I loved it, so let's make sure we are ready for that."

Liverpool held on to register a record 22nd consecutive home win in a league season, surpassing the club record set in 1972, between January and December, under Bill Shankly. Shankly - a three-time title-winning manager - had achieved 21 straight home successes to hold the record prior to Klopp's exploits. Asked if he was aware of the record, Klopp reacted: "Oh yes. I will never compare with this fella. Great, I think it was 23 [22] today. We didn't think about the number before the game, but after the game we can think about it for a couple of minutes. It's nice. It's absolutely nice. It's special, not normal. And the game today is an example: we have to fight hard. We are not geniuses, but we can really fight until the end of the season, and then we'll see what we get for it.'

Shankly's team began and ended their record run against the same opponent – Crystal Palace. A 4-1 win over the Eagles in January 1972 and a 1-0 triumph against them in December that year book ended the original record. What a coincidence as the current Liverpool team started their streak with a 3-0 win over Bournemouth in February 2019 and broke the record against Bournemouth again on March 7, 2020 Both of the record runs have spanned across two separate top-flight seasons. Shankly's side lost out on the title by a solitary point in 1971-72 (in an era when only two points were awarded for a win) but continued their home winning streak into 1972-73, when they went on to clinch the league. Klopp's team also lost out on the Premier League last season by a solitary point! And were now three wins away from matching Shankly's team's achievement and winning the title the following campaign.

The biggest of Liverpool's past 21 home league victories were 5-0 routs of Watford (February 2019) and Huddersfield Town (April 2019). The largest wins in the 1972 streak were also two 5-0 scorelines – against Newcastle United in March and Sheffield United in September of that year. Both of the runs also saw exactly 13 different Liverpool players score at least one goal. In 1972, the range of scorers stretched from John Toshack (14 goals) and Kevin Keegan (eight) to Phil Boersma and Bobby Graham (one each). The current run has seen scorers from Sadio Mane (19) and Mohamed Salah (18) down to Naby Keita and Joel Matip (one apiece).

In 1972, only one substitution was permitted per match by any team – and Shankly made just two across all 21 wins combined in his record run. As a result, only 17 players were used in total, eight of whom featured in every single match. Klopp, by contrast, has used 23 players in equalling the feat, only four of whom have played in all 22 victories – full-back Trent Alexander-Arnold and Dutch duo Virgil van Dijk and Georginio Wijnaldum.

KLOPP: "I know what the boys are able to do, but I am not the one that is playing, they are. We have said before, confidence is not something that you get, put in your pocket and keep for the rest of your life. It comes and goes. You need that feeling where things work out. You have to fight hard, that's always the main thing to do, but we have 82 points now, which is really nice. We have to carry on fighting. Give everyone a proper fight and that's what we did today. But then we wanted to fight back before the game, so we had to fight really back. We did that, put them under pressure, did a lot of good stuff, had really good situations, scored wonderful goals. We're not geniuses, but we can really fight and that's all we have to do until the end of the season. Three wins to go? No, no, it's Atleti 100 per cent. That's a tough one, as we know. Of course, they will not come here and try to play a friendly game. It will be the opposite. Today helps, 100 per cent. Maybe [there will be] one or two players coming back - we will see - and then with a good line-up and with Anfield, we'll try to change it."

EDDIE HOWE: "We gave it a go, we started really well and looked a threat on the counterattack. Their two goals came from the transition, they punished us when it counted. We made a mistake for the first goal, and the second was similar – we had the ball, seconds later we are conceding. We gave everything to it but came away with nothing. Losing Steve Cook was a big moment, and Phil (Billing) couldn't really move at the end. We couldn't have a full assault at them. It was a very, very good performance after a very difficult start. There are situations that really don't help like the first goal.

★

Manchester United completed an unexpected league double over Manchester City for the first time in a decade as Anthony Martial's first-half goal and a last second strike from Scott McTominay gave them victory at Old Trafford. City's normally reliable Brazilian goalkeeper Ederson gifted Ole Gunnar Solskjaer's side both goals, allowing Martial's routine near post shot to squirm under his body from a quick and clever Bruno Fernandes free-kick on the half-hour and then, with seconds left, threw a clearance straight to McTominay, who showed great technique to send a long-range finish, struck first time, into the net in front of a delirious Stretford End - a win that left Liverpool with a 25-point lead meaning they required just two more wins to secure their first league title for 30 years. City were lacklustre at Old Trafford as they sank to their seventh defeat of the Premier League campaign, making it the most league games lost in a single season in Pep Guardiola's managerial career.

March

City now faced home games against Arsenal and Burnley to get themselves in shape for the Champions League last-16 second leg meeting with Real Madrid, in which they held a precious 2-1 advantage from the first leg in the Bernabeu. Guardiola's side, champions in the previous two seasons, were scheduled to play twice before Liverpool's next league game, the Merseyside derby. If they win the derby and beat Palace at Anfield on Saturday March 21, they would be champions!

Unless, of course, City lost one of their next two home games, which would be highly unlikely.

OTHER SCORES

SATURDAY 7 MARCH
Arsenal 1 West Ham United 0
Crystal Palace 1 Watford 0
Sheffield United 1 Norwich City 0
Southampton 0 Newcastle United 1
Wolverhampton Wanderers 0 Brighton & Hove Albion 0
Burnley 1 Tottenham Hotspur 1

SUNDAY 8 MARCH
Chelsea 4 Everton 0
Manchester United 2 Manchester City 0

MONDAY 9 MARCH
Leicester City 4 Aston Villa 0

★

In the build-up, Jurgen Klopp wanted the Anfield crowd to sweep his team to victory, told his players to counter the opponents 'dark arts' by playing beautiful football, and was agitated by a persistent Madrid based journalist pestering him about coronavirus.

"Not a lot of the Atletico players have played at Anfield before and that is what we want to use," stressed Klopp. "Our crowd will be our advantage and we have to use it with the performance on the pitch. It has to be exceptional because they defend deep and have counter-attack threat. Each player can be dangerous. I have the highest respect for them but there are always ways and we have to find them tomorrow night. We have to show we have really learned from the first game."

Klopp insisted that Atletico's cynicism would not prevail at Anfield and told his players how best to responded to the inevitable provocation with purer football. Klopp criticised Madrid's gamesmanship in the first leg, where they targeted Mane and tried to get him dismissed. "Sadio did nothing wrong, absolutely nothing, and I still thought in the next situation it will be like this (red card). If it was always that easy for you to get out the best player of the opponent then there is something wrong with the game. If the player does nothing wrong but it's still possible... Wow! Everyone (from Atletico) runs against his elbow or whatever (to feign injury) - that should not happen."

Klopp withdrew Mane at half time in Madrid, but would not do that in the second leg. He told his team the perfect response is play beautiful football. "We spoke about that already but we will probably mention it again. To ensure your best players stay on for 90 minutes? Yeah, that would help 100 per cent. In a similar situation in the second game probably wouldn't do the same. You need always a referee who is aware of situations like this, we cannot do it by ourselves. We expect a really 'experienced' performance from Atletico, let me say that. In all different departments they are experienced and we have to deal with that. But there is another area of football where we can be better, better than the first game and better than Atletico but we have to show that tomorrow night. We need higher speed in different moments, better switches in different moments, we need braver football in different moments, we need to play around the formation, behind the formation, play through the gaps."

Klopp was unsure about the benefit of playing matches behind closed doors but his club respected any decision taken as "there are things that are more important than football." The coronavirus had already spread to more than 80 countries, with sporting events around the world impacted by Covid-19. Klopp was asked about the possibility of playing games without fans – a move now common place on the Continent but yet to be implemented in England. "There are things that are more important than football. I think we realise that again in this moment. What we need is time to find a solution for that. How can we win that time? By avoiding different situations. I don't know enough about how much it would help with [closing off] football games. The problem with football games is if you are not in the stadiums, then you go watch it closely together in rooms and I'm not sure which is better in this case, to be honest. I mean that. Whatever will be decided, we will respect. We all have families, we are parents, we have kids and friends, which we want to do well. For that, it's clear we will accept that, but I don't know how much sense it will make. If people think it will help, then we will do it."

A Madrid-based reporter pressed Klopp on whether he feared his squad could be infected by the virus given the major preventative measure in England has been the prohibiting of pre-match handshakes between both teams and officials by the Premier League and EFL.

"Are you from Madrid?" Klopp replied, "you live in Madrid – are you not concerned?"

The journalist retorted that he does not play football, with Klopp saying: "That's not that special. Football is just a game." He added: "In this moment, the players are all healthy. Why should we worry? What we do by not shaking hands is sending a sign. It's good for you, it's good for me, that we don't shake hands now. It's important that 22 completely healthy players are sending this sign for society. Playing football is just a game. We are not the society, we are only are part of society and we should all be worried in the same time. That's exactly what I don't like – you sit and ask me this question, but you flew from Madrid to be here. So stay there – they've closed schools and you're obviously concerned. But you think football is worth it to travel or whatever. So that's our common problem – we play football, but we cannot stop it [the spread of the virus] with football. We do what we have to do."

Captain Jordan Henderson was back. He had not played since suffering a hamstring injury in the first leg but Alisson was out for the defending champions. Klopp planned surprises, "If you play predictable Atletico's defence will go for the next six months without (a problem). If you prepare situations where it is not that easy to defend the more often you are in situations where you can score and that's what we have to do. If you are afraid of going out you cannot play with freedom and we need this freedom. We need to play free. Knowing they are really good at defending, defend their counter attacks, get the ball back, use the space they create in this moment. There are a lot of opportunities for us but against a quality team they are difficult to find. But we know about them at least and now we have to make sure we can show them as well."

Liverpool had lost three of their past five in all competitions – more than the rest of the season combined! But the 2-1 win over Bournemouth took them to within two wins of the title. City were due to play Arsenal in the league at the same time as Liverpool's tie but the game was postponed due to the virus.

Atletico had won three of their previous 11 games in all competitions so were outside the Champions League places in La Liga. Liverpool had never lost against Atletico at Anfield in two previous European meetings, drawing 1-1 in the Champions League group stage in 2008-09, winning 2-1 in the second leg of the Europa League semi-final in 2009-10. On each of the previous two occasions Liverpool lost away in the first leg of a Champions League knockout match, but still progressed to the next round - against Chelsea and Barcelona in the semi-finals in 2006-07 and 2018-19. Klopp had yet to lose a home Champions League game with Liverpool who had not lost a two-legged knockout phase tie in the Champions League since Chelsea beat them 7-5 on aggregate in the 2008-09 quarter-finals.

Just prior to kick off Klopp commented: "We had a meeting in our hotel, my last words... I don't know, it's really not that important. If you look at a tie like this where they win the first leg, then for 95% of the teams in the world they will think it will be tough for us tonight. There are a few teams with still a chance though and that's us. We know a lot more about the opponent now and what we need to change. We have to use the atmosphere, we have to accelerate in small spaces to make big spaces and we have to do a lot of things that we are good at that we didn't show there."

On his captain's comeback he added, "He has looked really good in the last few days. He's rested and full of desire to play football. It's very important that we have a proper passing game from that position. It's a complex thing tonight, we have to show a complete performance. I heard [Alvaro] Morata had some issues. Diego Costa, I saw warming up when we played there and he was like a kid, so excited to be involved in a game like this. We know that Atletico can be quite annoying. We can be quite annoying, so it's a good fit for Diego Costa as well."

March

WEDNESDAY, MARCH 11, 2020
CHAMPIONS LEAGUE LAST 16

LIVERPOOL 2
Wijnaldum 43, Firmino 94
ATLETICO MADRID 3 AET (AGG 2-4)
Llorente 97, 105+1, Morata 120 +1

It was dry but extremely blustery, Jurgen doesn't like the wind! But the heavens opened as the teams walked out on to the pitch. The downpour failed to dampen the electric atmosphere with a rousing version of 'You'll Never Walk Alone'. Klopp and Simeone elbow tapped instead of shaking hands. Earlier when Klopp and his players emerged from the tunnel, he angrily yelled "put your hands away" to fans. The Reds were jogging onto the pitch to go through their warm-up. Some fans tried to get a high five from Alexander-Arnold and Salah. Klopp - trailing behind his players - was incensed as he gestured at the supporters.

Liverpool's hold on the Champions League ended after drama in extra time - and a catastrophic blunder by Adrian. Not even Roberto Firmino's first goal at Anfield this season at the start of the added 30 minutes could save them.

Wijnaldum's first-half header was scant reward for Liverpool laying siege to the Atletico goal for much of the first 90 minutes and when Firmino scored early in extra-time, the Kop sensed another memorable victory, but Adrian's dreadful clearance allowed substitute Marcos Llorente to pounce with a low finish to score Atletico's crucial away goal. Llorente struck again with another composed finish in the 105th minute and former Chelsea striker Alvaro Morata added insult to injury with a third in the dying seconds to send Atletico through to the last eight.

Atletico's first goal killed the Reds momentum, but Klopp refused to blame Adrian. "He's a man and he knows that's how it is. We will not blame him for a second – what you (the media) do, I don't know, but stay respectful, that would be really nice," said Klopp, who lost his first two-legged European tie since becoming Liverpool manager in the club's first home European defeat since 2014. "He did not want to do that, he saved us in so many moments when he played. Since he's here, he had super performances. This goal didn't help tonight but that's how it is. I said, if you lose a game you always lose for some (different) reasons."

In contrast to Adrian's blunder Jan Oblak forged a formidable barrier for Atletico, making an astonishing 11 saves and claimed countless crosses. Just when The Reds finally established a measure of control through Firmino's goal, Adrian hacked out a hopeless clearance and Llorente profited to make a mockery of all the stats in Liverpools' favour, including allowing Atletico just 28% of the ball. Liverpool had 34 efforts on goal!

Liverpool surrendered their long unbeaten home record as well as the tie, but the Kop stayed behind them singing "We shall not be moved". Klopp applauded the Kop. He found it difficult to explain the goals Liverpool conceded and he criticised the style of play from Atletico but promised his team would bounce back again as Henderson talked about the bitter disappointment felt in the dressing room. Having reached the final in the last two seasons, winning a sixth European Cup, it was a frustrating end to Liverpool's brilliant run in the competition.

"Nothing, no impact," insisted Klopp. "Come on, we tried everything. For two-and-a-half years we had an exceptional ride in the Champions League, we had party after party after party in the Champions League pretty much. And tonight was a party, everything was set, it was great – crowd exceptional, the stadium, everything showed up in the best way. I realise I am a really bad loser, especially as the boys delivered a super game, fought hard, played well and scored wonderful goals. But we lost. That's it. No impact on anything. Atletico won both games, they are deservedly in the next round so from now on we will watch the Champions League instead of being part of it. But everybody knows we will come again and go again. Thank you to everybody who helped us on that ride. But now it's over, I cannot change that any more. Now we have more time to prepare the Premier League games.

KLOPP: For the score to go 2-1 was not cool, it was a blow but it's not a big problem. The second goal was a bigger problem. After the second goal the legs were a bit tired. Everything that looked really natural in the first 90 minutes became a bit stiff. The crosses did not have the same quality We wanted the first time crosses like for the first goal, which was brilliant and the boys forget to do that.

I am completely happy with the performance. It's so difficult to play a side like this. I don't understand with the quality they have the

March

Llorente ends Liverpool's hopes of retaining the European Cup following an Adrian howler

football they play. They could play proper football but they stand deep and have counter attacks. We accept it of course but it doesn't feel right tonight. I realise I am a really bad loser, especially when the boys put such an effort in against world class players on the other side who defend with two rows of four. We know in the last two years we had some lucky moments in the Champions League, you have to, to reach two finals, but today it was everything was against us in the decisive moments. I'm searching for the right words. Our main mistake was to not score the second goal five minutes earlier. We scored it in extra time and not in the 90 minutes. The 90 minutes were exceptional, the boys played a wonderful game. You saw all the goals we conceded you should not concede them. We lose in a specific way, it's always different but it's difficult to explain those goals to be honest. We caused them more problems than probably people thought after the first game. Against a defensive set-up like that, to cause a team that many problems is really exceptional, so I loved that. We will come again and go again but now we are out."

SIMEONE: He stopped every situation he had today but we also made it hard for their strikers to shoot. He saves games for us. Messi wins games for you up front and in goal people can win games for you as well. Oblak does that. Our fans will remember this and his performance for a long time.

THE PREMIER LEAGUE SHUTS DOWN

When he was first asked about Coronavirus prior to the Premier League shut down, Jurgen Klopp was pretty blunt with the media. "I wear a base cap and have a bad shave!" The world was entering 'unprecedented" circumstances, and the Liverpool manager didn't feel it was his place to comment on it; it was far too serious. He stressed that this was not the territory for a football manager to be making profound statements or observations. How would he have insightful knowledge about such issues?

"Unprecedented" is over used in general terms as much as "world class" is overused in football terms but this was an historic chapter in football, as it was, indeed an historic chapter in world affairs. The pandemic exercised the minds of scientists and politicians, who were armed with the facts as they developed, as this become something out of the normal domain of sport, irrespective of whether it was the national sport of importance to so many.

Not since the likes of Bill Shankly, Jose Mourinho, in his prime, or Brain Clough, the People's Choice to be be England manager, has anyone come close to Klopp in being in tune with the fans. Yet, unlike The Special One, his most endearing characteristic is that he is a man of the people, almost 'ordinary'. Even fans outside of Anfield gravitated toward him because he is so genuine. Klopp has become the most recognisable and respected manager in the world, but it hasn't changed him.

Initially, the government insisted they must not move too early to prohibit large gatherings but former health secretary Jeremy Hunt criticised the decision to allow football and horse racing to continue as normal as "surprising and concerning". Measures announced by Boris Johnson included advising anyone with a "new, continuous" cough or high temperature to self-isolate for seven days. Testing would only focus on identifying people with the virus in hospital - closing schools or cancelling sporting events at this point could do more harm than good, should people tire of the restrictions. But the Scottish Government advised the cancellation of gatherings of more than 500 people, while

The Premier League Shuts Down

Ireland shut schools

Hunt said the UK was in a "national emergency", with just four weeks until it reached the stage that Italy were then at. "You would have thought that every single thing we do in that four weeks would be designed to slow the spread of people catching the virus," he argued. Susan Michie, professor of health psychology at University College London, suggested "nobody has the right answer".

The effects of the virus were felt around the globe. Canadian Prime Minister Justin Trudeau and his wife Sophie were in 14-day isolation after she tested positive. Australia stopped gatherings of 500 or more people, not including transport or schools. Ghana and Gabon reported their first cases, while India recorded its first death. However, just eight new cases were reported in China.

When Arsenal's visit to Brighton was cancelled after manager Mikel Arteta tested positive, the Premier League suspended the competition, but it was felt it would be for three or four weeks - not, as it turned out, nearly four months!

Klopp backed the decision to postpone the Premier League and, in a letter to the clubs fans wrote: "The decision and announcement is being implemented with the motive of keeping people safe. Because of that we support it completely."

Klopp message to supporters followed the Premier League's decision to postpone all football activity until April 3 at the earliest with Liverpool two games away form landing their first title in 30 years. But for Klopp he made it clear to the fans, that football had to wait.....

I don't think this is a moment where the thoughts of a football manager should be important, but I understand for our supporters they will want to hear from the team and I will front that. First and foremost, all of us have to do whatever we can to protect one another. In society I mean. This should be the case all the time in life, but in this moment I think it matters more than ever. I've said before that football always seems the most important of the least important things. Today football and football matches really aren't important at all.

Of course, we don't want to play in front of an empty stadium and we don't want games or competitions suspended, but if doing s it helps one individual stay healthy - just one - we do it no questions asked. If it's a choice between football and the good of the wider society, it's no contest. Really, it isn't.

Today's decision and announcement is being implemented with the motive of keeping people safe. Because of that we support it completely. We have seen members of teams we compete against become ill. This virus has shown that being involved in football offers no immunity. To our rival clubs and individuals who are affected and to those who later will become so, you are in our thoughts and prayers.

None of us know in this moment what the final outcome will be, but as a team we have to have belief that the authorities make decisions based on sound judgement and morality.

Yes, I am the manager of this team and club and therefore carry a leadership responsibility with regards to our future on the pitch. But I think in the present moment, with so many people around our city, the region, the country and the world facing anxiety and uncertainty, it would be entirely wrong to speak about anything other than advising people to follow expert advice and look after themselves and each other. The message from the team to our supporters is only about your well-being. Put your health first. Don't take any risk. Think about the vulnerable in our society and act where possible with compassion for them. Please look after yourselves and look out for each other.

You'll Never Walk Alone, Jürgen

Liverpool implemented government advice and welcomed the Premier League statement to postpone all games, including Premier League, FA Cup, academy and Women's Super League fixtures in the best interests of players, staff and supporters: "The club has implemented its own precautions across its sites to minimise the spread of the coronavirus by minimising contact where practicable and reinforcing the official medical advice for everyone to take responsibility for excellent personal hygiene. Ticket and bookings already purchased for the postponed Premier League fixtures may still be used for the rescheduled dates, which will be announced in due course. If supporters are unable to attend any of the rearranged dates then a refund process will be announced at the time the revised fixture dates are announced. Liverpool FC Foundation has also announced the LFC Legends game against Barça Legends on Saturday March 28 at Anfield has also been postponed. More details regarding the Legends game can be found here. The Foundation and Red Neighbours are also reviewing the delivery of their community programmes in the best interests of everyone involved. Anyone displaying symptoms that are consistent with coronavirus should ensure they familiarise themselves with the chief medical officer's advice on self-isolation. We will continue to take the best advice from the relevant authorities and will update supporters with any further developments. Click here for the latest government advice on coronavirus.

The Premier league statement read: "Following a meeting of Shareholders today, it was unanimously decided to suspend the Premier League with the intention of returning on 4 April, subject to medical advice and conditions at the time. Premier League Chief Executive Richard Masters said: "Above all, we wish Mikel Arteta and Callum Hudson-Odoi speedy recoveries, and everyone else affected by COVID-19. In this unprecedented situation, we are working closely with our clubs, Government, The FA and EFL and can reassure everyone the health and welfare of players, staff and supporters are our priority. Despite the challenges, it is the Premier League's aim to reschedule the displaced fixtures, including those played by Academy sides, when it is safe to do so. In this fast-moving environment, further updates will be provided when appropriate."

Sir Kenny Dalglish insisted that the Premier League season must be completed, and declared that only those with an "agenda" wanted it declared null and void. Dalglish was adamant the league campaign had to be completed. He said in the Sunday Post: "What must definitely not happen is for the 2019-20 campaign to be declared null and void. That would not be fair, and any person with football at heart would admit that would be totally out of order. In Scotland, would it be fair to say to the Premiership leaders, Celtic, that all of their efforts in the past nine months over 30 games count for nothing? "The same would apply to Dundee United in the Championship. Would any person without an agenda really think it would be the most-sensible outcome to deny Liverpool their chance of winning the title after doing fantastically well in their 29 league games so far to build up a 25-point lead over Manchester City with nine games remaining? Of course not. Nobody can allow the hard work to count for nothing. So let's do away with any of this talk, and try to use our time and energy wisely. I've been in football for more than 50 years and I know what goes into it. The season must be completed."

The Premier League and the English Football League was postponed further until April 30 but the season was extended 'indefinitely' following a crisis meeting with all 20 clubs. The FA confirmed that the current season would be extended 'indefinitely' until it is completed. In total, there were still 92 Premier League fixtures to be played. A statement from the FA said: 'The FA's Rules and Regulations state that "the season shall terminate not later than the 1 June" and "each competition shall, within the limit laid down by The FA, determine the length of its own playing season". However, our Board has agreed for this limit to be extended indefinitely for the 2019-20 season in relation to professional football. Additionally, we've collectively agreed that the professional game in England will be further postponed until no earlier than Thursday 30 April. The progress of COVID-19 remains unclear and we can reassure everyone the health and welfare of players, staff and supporters are our priority.'

Space to complete the domestic season had been made available after UEFA earlier confirmed that the summer's European Championship would be played next year instead.

Rio Ferdinand believed Liverpool should miss out on winning the title as the season should be voided while there were suggestions that the remaining games should be played behind closed doors. But Ferdinand believed that would create problems if fans then congregate in large numbers to celebrate against Government advice to keep away from each other. 'I just think the Premier League should be void. Void it,' Ferdinand said on Instagram. 'I know there's going to be a lot of Liverpool fans going, "oh, Rio, it just because you used to play for Man United". I just don't see a way that can be done where health isn't compromised. Simple as that. All this behind closed doors business – you're still going to have players there, are the players not part of society? There are players who are going to go down with the illness who might not have recovered, or catch it from someone then it spreads to other players. It won't be fair, it's not a level playing field. I just don't feel it's right. There are going to be people in the stadium, security, it puts everyone at risk. All this, "oh we're going to win this" or "so-and-so might go down", you've got to put those type of things to one side. This is about life and death situations, about society in the wider grand scheme of things. Football ain't that serious in that sense. Listen, we all love it but it ain't life or death, when it comes to matters like this, you've got to put people's heath before anything. Start the season, clean slate, once all this health situation has been sorted out we can start the new season but I don't see it happening in that time. Now if we wake up one morning in the next month and it's all gone and the country can get back to normal immediately then we can have a conversation about that. But I don't see that happening, not from what we're being told. And the experiences that other countries who are two or three weeks in front of us, we're not going to be in a place to do that. PSG vs Dortmund the other day, behind closed doors but outside there were thousands of fans out there.

'Imagine Liverpool win the league, which they would, do you think those fans after 30 years of hurt will sit at home and say "well done, guys"? They'll be out, I'd want to go out. Not everybody is sensible in situations like that. People will go out trying to celebrate and go crazy because that's what football does, it brings out emotions and people sometimes act out of character. A team who survives relegation in the Premier League, do you think those fans won't go out to celebrate? Sheffield United qualify for the Champions League or Europa League, think their fans won't go bananas? PSG's fans the other day, it wasn't a massive game, knockout stages of the Champions League, it wasn't a trophy, and their fans were going bananas. That's football. I think it'll be silly to do that and put these fans in a position that will do stuff that's not right for society in general. Just void the whole season. It's a shame because a lot of effort has gone into it. People have invested a lot physically, emotionally, financially. But it's bigger than that.'

Liverpool FC issued mental health advice to their players, telling them that what happens with the title is out of their control and they should focus on minimising infection rates. A presentation by the club's sports psychologist Lee Richardson offered advice on breathing to ease anxiety levels. The self-help document 'Mental Health & Well-being' contained a section 'Acceptance and Control': "What happens with the decision of the Premier League or the direction the virus takes next is out of our control. All we can control is our behaviour and our response to the challenge of keeping the most vulnerable safe and minimising infection rates. In focussing on the controllable and in accepting that which we cannot control, i.e. Premier League, government response, we give ourselves the best chance of overcoming the psychological challenge of keeping perspective. As the manager has said, football is not the most important thing. The health and safety of us all is far more important.'

Players were encouraged to 'breathe with their bellies' should they become stressed, with an emphasis on using the diaphragm. Richardson recommended starting each day with a breathing regime should they be feeling anxious. 'As you know, good regular teeth-brushing promotes good dental health and in the same way good regular diaphragm breathing promotes good mental health,' he says. In a section on 'Managing Isolation', players were warned of the dangers of boredom and told to establish daily routines and use the opportunity caused by the crisis to spend time with family.

They were advised not to focus on the news or social media and to raise any concerns they may have with the club. Retaining a sense of humour was encouraged, but they were informed that many people will be losing loved ones so they run the risk of causing upset should they post anything which could be seen as insensitive on social media. They were reassured that 'we will come out of the other side of this'. They are told that normality will return but also to be 'realistic that this will not be for some time'.

Sadio Mane made a donation of 30m CFA francs - 45,000 euros (£41,000) - to the national committee fighting against coronavirus in his home country of Senegal, while players contributed to a £50,000 donation to Fans Supporting Foodbanks - a joint initiative between Liverpool and Everton to tackle food poverty in the Merseyside area.

Klopp was reduced to tears after watching footage of NHS staff singing You'll Never Walk Alone. The video, shared on social media by Labour MP Mary Foy, showed a number of healthcare professionals working together to help tackle the escalating pandemic, before those involved join together for a rendition of YNWA. An emotional Klopp was touched by the enormous sacrifices of healthcare workers. 'My English is not good enough to say. It's extraordinary, it's great. I think yesterday I was sent a video of people in the hospital just outside the intensive care area and when they started singing You'll Never Walk Alone I started crying immediately. It's unbelievable. But it shows everything, these people not only work but they have such a good spirit. They are used to helping other people, we need to get used to it because usually we have our own problems and stuff. But it's their job, they do it day in and day out. They bring themselves, if you want, in danger because they help ill, sick and seriously handicapped people, so I couldn't admire them more and appreciate it more, I really couldn't.'

The Premier League Shuts Down

Klopp and his players sent a heartfelt video to medical staff. At the start of the four-minute tribute, Klopp said: 'Hello. Myself and the staff of LFC would like to take this opportunity to deliver a message to say thank you to all the incredible people who work in the health services, all the health workers, if you want, out there. It's unbelievable what you are doing and on behalf of all of us at LFC I would like to say thank you. Or how we would say in Germany, vielen dank.' Klopp's message was followed by further tributes from each individual member of the playing squad, including skipper Jordan Henderson, Mohamed Salah, Virgil van Dijk and Sadio Mane while at home self-isolating.

Klopp confessed that it had been difficult to prepare for the second leg Champions League clash with Atletico as the pandemic was taking hold in the Spanish capital. The Reds lost the first leg tie 1-0 but there were doubts whether the match at Anfield would go ahead with other games in Europe cancelled or taking place behind closed doors, while Madrid was already beginning to shutdown before the fixture and all La Liga had already said that games could no longer go ahead with supporters in stadiums. Yet, thousands of fans were able to travel to Merseyside in a crowd of over 50,000 people. 'It is two weeks ago, but it feels like it is ages ago that we played Atletico and Thursday was a day off. I remember, we all knew about the situation with coronavirus around the world but we were still 'in our tunnel', if you want, and until then it didn't really arrive into our mind in England. We played the Bournemouth game on Saturday, we won it, then Sunday City lost, so the information for us was 'two wins to go'. But then on Monday morning, I woke up and heard about the situation in Madrid, that they would close the schools and universities from Wednesday, so it was really strange to prepare for that game, to be honest. I usually don't struggle with things around me, I can build barriers right and left when I prepare for a game, but in that moment it was really difficult. Wednesday we had the game, I loved the game, I loved what I saw from the boys, it was a really, really good performance other than the result – we didn't score enough, we conceded too many, that's all clear, but between these two main pieces of information it was a brilliant game! Thursday [we were] off and then Friday when we arrived it was already clear this is not a session. Yes, we trained, but it was more of a meeting. We had a lot of things to talk about, a lot of things to think about, things I never thought before in my life about. Nobody knew exactly – and nobody knows exactly – how it will go on, so the only way we could do it was to organise it as good as possible for the boys and make sure everything is sorted as much as we can sort it in our little space, in the little area where we are responsible, really. That's what we did in a very short time, then we sent the boys home, went home ourselves and here we are still.'

Klopp kept tabs on his players in the team's WhatsApp group and their social media posts. James Milner and Alex Oxlade-Chamberlain kept fans entertained with the former pretending to cut the grass with a pair of scissors and the latter posting a dance video.

'I didn't cut the grass but I tried the dance of Ox! Not as bad as you probably think!' Klopp joked. 'It's very important in these times that we all show we take this situation seriously, but we are human beings. You have to keep your own mood up and you have to keep the mood up for other people. If the boys do anything on Instagram, as long as it's in a legal frame I'm overly happy about it – it just shows they are still cheeky and all that stuff. I like it, I like it a lot. I like the line-ups they do. All these things are really funny. It's good.'

Speaking to Liverpool's official website via a video call from his home, Klopp said: "The only way to get football back as soon as possible, if that's what the people want, the more disciplined we are now the earlier we will get, piece by piece by piece, our life back. That's how it is. There is no other solution in the moment, nobody has another solution. We have to be disciplined by ourselves, we have to keep the distance to other people. It is a difficult time for all of us, but from a personal point of view an interesting one as well because I've never had a situation like this and was never that long at home. From a personal point of view, I am really good, but like everybody else, [I am] concerned about the situation around us, of course. There are so many people out there that have much bigger problems so it would feel really embarrassing to myself if I was to talk about my 'problems' – I have the problems every person in the world has in the moment. That's the lesson we learn in this moment. In the future, in 10, 20, 30, 40 years, if we look back and then the conclusion is that this was the period when the world showed the biggest solidarity, the biggest love, the biggest friendship or whatever, that would be great. So in the moment when you go through a phase or a period like this it's not possible to see that, especially not for the people who are ill, but there will be a point in the future, a moment in the future when we look back and hopefully then we can see it like this."

Liverpool players posted updates, entertaining fans on their social media pages. Oxlade-Chamberlain released a video of himself dancing with his partner - Little Mix singer Perrie Edwards - while team-mate James Milner played up to a joke of him being boring by pretending to cut grass with a pair of scissors. "We spoke a couple of times, we have a really intense, big, big group chat - the whole of Melwood are in that," Klopp said. "The boys are really lively in that, the boys are just interested in what everybody is doing, comments on what everybody is doing - if Ox (Oxlade-Chamberlain) is on Instagram or whatever. So, that helps a lot. The mood is good. I didn't cut the grass but I tried the dance of Ox. Not as bad as you probably think. It's very important in these times that we all show we take this situation seriously, but we are human beings. At the moment we are at home and when you are at home, you cannot do something to help outside. We are not health workers, we don't work in a supermarket. You have to keep your own mood up and you have to keep the mood up for other people. If the boys do anything on Instagram, as long as it's in a legal frame I'm overly happy about it - it just shows they are still cheeky and all that stuff."

In an interview with Liverpoolfc.com via video link, Jordan Henderson stressed there were far more important matters than missing football as he detailed how the squad were keeping in contact and the steps to ensure they were ready, physically, to return to action when safe to do so. "Yeah, it has been different, it has been challenging at times, especially when you've got three kids running around the house! But at the same time I feel as though I'm in a luxury position if you like, in terms of I've got a garden, a nice house that the kids can go and run around and play in, go in the garden and play. I understand a lot of people might not have that luxury. I'm surrounded, obviously, by my wife and kids, so it makes it a lot easier. But there's people out there who are a lot worse off who are suffering more than I am and my thoughts really just go out to them. It sort of puts everything into perspective a little bit.

"Football isn't even in the thought at the minute. Of course myself and other players will be wanting to get back as soon as possible and be chomping at the bit to go and play football. But at the same time, you understand that there's bigger problems and bigger things going on in the world. We just need to do our best to support our families, stay safe and just keep listening to what the authorities are telling us. And hopefully this period can finish sooner rather than later and everybody can start some normality off again sooner rather than later.

"It's a totally different test. My biggest downs in my career up until this point were obviously injury, I would say. That was the hardest thing for me to deal with personally, but this is a different challenge. The time that I've spent with my family and my kids over the last couple of weeks is something that I've never been able to do before, so I'm just trying to take a lot of the positive things around it. I've really enjoyed being with the kids every day, helping them with their school work and things that I wouldn't normally do. I've just tried to do it as much as I can and enjoy it. But when it is 24/7 it can be challenging at times as everybody will know! But I've just tried to enjoy this period that we're going to get. I know it will be for a long period, of course, but just stay positive and try to enjoy it as much as I can because I've never really had a block of time like this to be with the kids and my wife for a long time."

As for the new virtual training methods, Henderson observed: "We've been given some programmes and stuff by the club, of course, and things that we need to do. But I suppose it's like the off-season in that sense – just [be] given a programme, follow that over the holidays. But with us having a newborn, I haven't really had a set time every day, I've just been doing it off the cuff. Whenever I get a period of time in the day, I go out and do my work that I need to do. So far, I feel as though I've been keeping in decent-enough shape.

"We've got a big WhatsApp group and things are getting fired in quite often, so everybody's sort of staying in contact and chucking different videos in and different challenges that we can do. There has been a lot of contact with the lads because normally we're spending every day together and travelling together and all sorts of stuff. To not see each other for a long period of time is strange, especially at this time of the season. But at the same time, when we have the off-season, again, it's pretty similar to that. It's just the time that we're at and the stage that we're at in the season that it is a little bit different. Now we're in the house and you can't really do anything else, it is a bit strange.

"I think it is important to stay in touch with people, especially the lads. Some people cope differently to others. Some of the lads are on their own who I've spoken to, which must be really difficult. Most

The Premier League Shuts Down

of the lads have family and kids and stuff, which will make it easier – maybe a little bit more difficult at times! But overall a lot easier when you've got family around you and people around you. But when you're on your own it must be so difficult, so I've touched base with those lads and they seem OK but it's only been a couple of weeks and we've probably got a few more months to go at least.

"You want to go out training every day, you want to play football every day. So to have that taken away so suddenly is difficult. But this period, I'm sure at the end of it it'll make people appreciate things a lot more and not take stuff for granted as much. There's definitely a period to learn and to take things from, and at the end of it I think we'll be a lot better off. But at the same time, I understand there's a lot of people going through pain and suffering – and our thoughts obviously go out to them. But all we can do is just keep listening to what we've been told. And like I say, hopefully this doesn't last too long. But in the meantime, we've just got to stay positive, try to help each other and stay together, which I've seen a lot, to be fair, on social media. [There's been] a lot of support – especially to the NHS and rightly so for the work they're doing, which is the most important thing. Football is so small in this situation, so we've got to sort this situation out first and then whenever that is, we can start talking about football and looking forward.'

As the leader in the dressing room, the captain was mindful it was an especially tough time for the foreign players. "You might feel alone but the lads and the people at the club will make sure that they feel supported in everything that they do and the programmes and stuff. I think we're going to do stuff as a group as well. I think that will start to happen a little bit more often where we're doing maybe sessions together like on FaceTime or different apps that you can use so everybody is doing it together. I think that will start from this point going forward just to try to keep everybody in touch. It helps support the players that are finding it a little more difficult on their own"

The players had been helping out as much as they could, with food banks for example as Henderson added: "It's an important time for everybody to come together – not just our club but everybody in the country and in the world. It's important that everybody comes together and we try to just listen to the advice that we've been given to make sure that this virus sort of goes away sooner rather than later and everybody can get back to some sort of normality soon. It's a time to come together and help each other. I'm sure there's other ways of doing that, especially supporting the NHS and the work that they're doing – you can see how much support they're getting from the whole country, so that's really important as well. But for us as players, [I'm] thinking of different things that we can do all the time. I'm sure the lads will help, which we have already with the foodbanks, but if there's anything else then I'm sure the lads will be on board to do so.

"The football will resume at some point. The great thing that there's been about this group of players is focus. Whatever challenge has been put in your way, you've always met that head-on... It is important. This is why we keep doing the work that we've been given, keep doing the training stuff because there will come a time – whenever that is – that we need to go back and start training and play games pretty quickly. I'm sure all the lads are doing the stuff to keep ticking over for when we are ready to go back in when it's safe for us to do so and we can start the Premier League again – that's all we can do really.

"We're missing the fans, that's for sure! I would just say stay safe, of course, stay inside and keep listening to all the advice that the government and the authorities have given us. If we do that, this will sort of pass quicker than we hope. But just try to stay positive. It's a perfect sort of chance to use our song that we sing every game in terms of You'll Never Walk Alone – it's the perfect opportunity for that. I've seen stuff on social media where the nurses were singing along to it, but stuff like that is really powerful. This is the time where it's not just words, you've got to use it as best we can as people and as human beings. But just listen to the authorities, do your bit, do what you can and hopefully this will go sooner rather than later and everybody can get back to some sort of normality and look forward to what the future holds.

★

Liverpool became the latest Premier League club to place some non-playing staff on temporary leave after Spurs, Newcastle, Bournemouth and Norwich were heavily criticised when they furloughed non-playing staff. Staff affected would receive 80% of their salary through the government's job retention scheme and the club would make up the difference. A Liverpool statement read: "Even prior to the decision on staff furloughing, there was a collective commitment at senior

The Premier League Shuts Down

levels of the club - on and off the pitch - with everyone working towards a solution that secures jobs for employees of the club during this unprecedented crisis. There is ongoing active engagement about the topic of salary deductions during the period matches are not being played to schedule. These discussions are complex and as a result the process is ongoing."

The decision was criticised by former Liverpool players Jamie Carragher and Stan Collymore. Carragher tweeted: "Jurgen Klopp showed compassion for all at the start of this pandemic, senior players heavily involved in Premier League players taking wage cuts. Then all that respect and goodwill is lost - poor this, LFC." Collymore wrote on social media: "I don't know of any Liverpool fan of any standing that won't be anything other than disgusted at the club for furloughing staff. It's just plain wrong. Fellow football fans, furlough is for small business staff to keep those small businesses from going bump! Every Premier League owner has serious cash, and makes money from skyrocketing values of clubs, so what aren't you getting about your owners dipping into their pocket?" In February, the club had announced a pre-tax profit of £42m and increased turnover to £533m. Last year they spent £43m on agents' fees.

Health secretary Matt Hancock said Premier League players should "take a pay cut and play their part" during the pandemic. Since then, Premier League clubs have said they will ask players to take a 30% pay cut in order to protect jobs. All 20 top-flight clubs agreed to put the proposed "combination of conditional reductions and deferrals" to players, during a video conference call between the Premier League and players' union the Professional Footballers' Association. The Premier League would advance £125m to the EFL and National League, and give £20m towards the NHS.

The Liverpool statement added: "While our priority from the outset has been to focus primarily on the health and wellbeing of our players, staff, supporters and local community, the club has also committed to playing as full a role as possible in the Premier League's ongoing response to the crisis. As such, we welcome yesterday's announcement from the Premier League which confirmed the provision of support for the National Health Service, the EFL and National League and a commitment for the 2019-20 season to resume only when it is safe to do so."

A member of staff who works at Liverpool, and did not wish to be named, told BBC Sport: "The club call their staff their family - I'm not feeling like a family member. Why is a club that turns over [millions of pounds] using a government scheme for its staff, when other businesses are more in need of it? I feel disappointed and I'm feeling that this government scheme could be used by businesses in trouble." The member of stuff added that they were "disappointed, especially after Everton said they were not doing it".

Liverpool said they were aiming "to protect the best interests of the club and our staff in both the short term and the long term, with all such actions being undertaken following various internal discussions". The statement continued: "In some instances, further measures will follow only once all parties are in a position to proceed and updates will be provided as and when this is the case."

Within a few days, Liverpool reversed the decision to apply for government assistance after furloughing staff and were "truly sorry" for coming to the "wrong conclusion." A letter from CEO Peter Moores now insisted they would find "alternative means" to cover furlough costs.

Dear Liverpool supporters,

First and foremost on behalf of our ownership, Fenway Sports Group, we would like to emphasise the thoughts and concerns of everyone are with those suffering from the dreadful COVID-19 pandemic and the families of those affected.

We would also recognise and pay tribute to the heroism of the incredible health service and key workers locally, nationally and internationally. All other worries should be placed in that context first.

Allowing for perspective in these unprecedented and harrowing times, it is important to address an issue we, as an organisation, have been involved in since the weekend.

We have consulted with a range of key stakeholders as part of a process aimed at achieving the best possible outcome for all concerned. A range of possible scenarios were considered, including but not restricted to: applying to the Coronavirus Job Retention Scheme, which pays 80 per cent of salary and guaranteeing the 20 per cent payment; applying to the Coronavirus Job Retention Scheme with a guarantee to reimburse monies received at a later date; and, thirdly, finding an alternative means to cover our furlough costs. It is as a direct result of this extensive consultation and our own internal deliberations at various levels throughout the club that we have opted to find alternative means despite our eligibility to apply for the Coronavirus Job Retention Scheme. We believe we came to the wrong conclusion last week to announce that we intended to apply to the Coronavirus Retention Scheme and furlough staff due to the suspension of the Premier League football calendar, and are truly sorry for that. Our intentions were, and still are, to ensure the entire workforce is given as much protection as possible from redundancy and/or loss of earnings during this unprecedented period.

We are therefore committed to finding alternative ways to operate while there are no football matches being played that ensures we are not applying for the government relief scheme. We would like to acknowledge the great army of staff and casual workers who work tirelessly to ensure Liverpool is a club that operates to the highest of standards.

But in the spirit of transparency we must also be clear, despite the fact we were in a healthy position prior to this crisis, our revenues have been shut off yet our outgoings remain. And like almost every sector of society, there is great uncertainty and concern over our present and future. Like any responsible employer concerned for its workers in the current situation, the club continues to prepare for a range of different scenarios, around when football can return to operating as it did before the pandemic. These scenarios range from best case to worst and everything in between. It is an unavoidable truth that several of these scenarios involve a massive downturn in revenue, with correspondingly unprecedented operating losses. Having these vital financial resources so profoundly impacted would obviously negatively affect our ability to operate as we previously have. We are engaged in the process of exploring all avenues within our scope to limit the inevitable damage. We thank the many amazing people in our club, at all levels, who are committed to helping us do just that, despite the complexity and unpredictability in the world and our industry. We would also like to take the opportunity to thank those who have engaged with us in a productive fashion, none more so than our supporters, their representatives, particularly Spirit of Shankly, the Mayor of Liverpool, Joe Anderson, Metro Mayor, Steve Rotheram, local MPs Dan Carden and many other individuals, with whom we have had much valued dialogue.

Stay safe. Peter Moore Chief executive officer

★

Sir Kenny Dalglish tested positive for coronavirus and was admitted to hospital but showed no symptoms, his family announced. Dalglish was in for treatment of an infection which required intravenous antibiotics and was routinely tested for coronavirus after being admitted. "Unexpectedly, the test result was positive but he remains asymptomatic," the Dalglish family said. The statement added: "He would like to take this opportunity to thank the brilliant NHS staff, whose dedication, bravery and sacrifice should be the focus of the nation's attention at this extraordinary time. Prior to his admission to hospital, Sir Kenny had chosen to voluntarily self-isolate for longer than the advised period together with his family. He would urge everyone to follow the relevant government and expert guidance in the days and weeks ahead. He looks forward to being home soon. We will provide further updates as and when it is appropriate." Sir Kenny was soon released, and told supporters via his column for the Sunday Post that "I'll be resting but I am feeling fine, thankfully."

Klopp reflected in his message over video link, "I had the opportunity to text immediately with one of his daughters and we spoke about it. She was quite… not relaxed, but she was fine and said it looked all well—and two days later we heard he was released from hospital. It's good news—very good news—and I hope he is doing well still. We all know Kenny and we love him. We just sent him all our thoughts and prayers in that moment, but maybe he didn't need it, which is even better."

News spread throughout the squad by their WhatsApp group, and echoed the sentiments of many during that time when someone close was affected as Klopp commented: "It was a real shock three days ago when I heard about it first. The boys were sent a message in our WhatsApp group and everybody was like, 'wow'. What you feel in that moment is a massive difference if you know somebody who got the virus, or if you don't know. In this moment, it was like, 'Wow, one of us has it' and it was really crazy. We all know this terrible disease is causing heartache all over the world, but this was the first time for many of us someone we have such a personal connection to was affected to this extent."

The Premier League Shuts Down

The longer Klopp was away from his players, the more it hurt. They trained remotely, with a variety of workouts hosted via video link bringing the squad and staff together. The sessions enabled the squad to work as a group as they maintained fitness and Klopp said the social aspect of the video calls should not be underestimated. "When we have these training sessions, I could have never imagined I would enjoy it that much but it's just the moment when I see the boys again and that changes everything. For a minute, for an hour, for two hours, however long the sessions are - the boys are all in good spirits; you feel immediately why you miss them so much, because it's just an exceptional group. You want to be together with them, you want to be closer to them than you can be. These are the closest moments, so I enjoy these sessions a lot. It's getting worse, the longer it takes. I accept the situation 100 per cent like it is but the longer you don't see somebody you like, the more it hurts. That's the situation we are in at the moment."

The club video chats encouraged players to interact but Klopp insisted they remained professional. "Some people may say it's like a normal meeting or normal session we have - but it's not like this. I like that as well. That's the best thing of having this situation in 2020 - we have this technical opportunity. Imagine if we would have had that in the '80s - not because of football, because of all the social contact and interaction we can have and use now. That makes a big difference."

Klopp filled his time at home watching YouTube videos of Liverpool lifting the Champions League trophy and sent it into the players' WhatsApp group chat and ordered a new running watch. 'There's not a lot of good things at the moment, but it has given me time to do a lot of things, different things. I have learned a lot of new things in this period. I am in charge of the dishwasher, which is nice actually, I am the master of that little machine now and I did my first scrambled eggs. I was impressed by the scrambled eggs but I haven't had the opportunity to make another, but the challenge for next week is, I am 52 now, but I cannot tie a tie but next week we will learn to tie a tie. After this week I will know how to tie a tie, that is the challenge. And it will probably take a whole week because my hands are completely useless usually so it should be funny.'

Klopp normally watched 'silly films' like Waterboy and Dumb and Dumber but he used this time to step out of his comfort zone 'My other son is here with us, he was here when the lockdown started so he is still here and every night one of us is in charge of the remote control. We watch a lot of Downton Abbey. I never watched the Marvel movies before but I watched Ironman and stuff like this, which I enjoyed as well, it's a nice popcorn movie and you don't have to concentrate too much.'

Isolation gave Klopp time to reflect, speaking to old friends on his phone, which he admitted has 'surprised them how much I'm on it'. He said: 'We have a class mates group and because I don't have any pictures here, they are all at my mother's house, I never thought about getting them. But my cousin, who was in my class with me, she started sending baby photos of me and then I asked in the class mates group if they had any more and then there were sending them in like crazy. I had a wonderful day to be honest. I was laughing so hard, a lot of nice memories came up and it was a wonderful thing to do and now I have all these pictures, which is nice. I looked crazy strange when I was young as well. It will be a big laugh for some, in hard times if people can laugh about that, then I'm happy about that, no problem.'

Jurgen's wife Ulla Sandrock was praised for a generous act of kindness in her local supermarket where she handed out £1,000-worth of food vouchers to staff. Ulla visited the Waitrose store in Formby and gave staff on the shop floor vouchers worth £50 as a thank you in appreciation to supermarket staff who were working as normal. Ulla distributed 20 vouchers worth £50 each.

Later managers at the store requested all vouchers be handed to them so they could be shared evenly across the whole team. One staff member said: "This was an incredible thing to do. Typically, Ulla didn't want to make a fuss, or receive any recognition, and just wanted people working in shops to get the recognition they deserve." A spokesman for the store told the Liverpool Echo: "Our Formby team is incredibly grateful for the support and understanding shown by everyone who has visited our store, but we would always respect the privacy of our customers."

Klopp said that the lockdown was not unusual for him, as he rarely ventures further than the club's training ground. Klopp said: "My life didn't change too much to be honest, I can't usually go out, my private life if I can go to Melwood for 8, 9, 10 hours then it will be the same because at home it's always the same we don't go in restaurants and things like this, so it's not changed too much. But of course I miss, the boys miss football. I miss for everybody else that they can have their normal life, so it's not important how I feel because I get used to the lockdown, private lockdown if you want. But I can imagine for the people out there it's much more difficult."

The pandemic put Liverpool's first title celebrations on hold. But Klopp remained calm in the crisis and said: "We know what we want and the first thing that we want is that everybody is safe and healthy. If football can help in some departments with lifting the mood, then we have to start training. But I don't know when that will be."

★

Liverpool paid tribute to the 96 fans who died at Hillsborough on the 31st anniversary of the disaster. The club remembered supporters who lost their lives at the FA Cup semi-final with Nottingham Forest on April 15, 1989 despite being in the midst of the coronavirus crisis. Liverpool tweeted: "We stand together today as a family to remember the 96 Liverpool fans - men, women and children - who so tragically lost their lives at Hillsborough. We are together in spirit today to offer our love and support on this very difficult day. You'll Never Walk Alone."

Players and club staff observed a minute's silence in memory of the 96. Club flags were flown at half-mast across the club throughout the day. Klopp said in a video message: "Today is the most significant date for our football club each year. The plan was for us to be together at Anfield but this is not possible, the only thing we can make sure is we are in each other's thoughts. Believe me you have our thoughts, you have our prayers and most of all you have our love. You'll never walk alone."

Liverpool captain Jordan Henderson sent a message to all those affected by the Hillsborough disaster on behalf of the players. "Today was a day when as a club we were all supposed to be together at Anfield to honour the lives of 96 people who went to a football match and never came home. The fact that we are unable to do so will make this anniversary especially hard for the families and survivors of Hillsborough. I'm not one for making speeches, but on behalf of all the players at Liverpool I just want to let everyone affected know that you are in our thoughts today.

As ever, we are together in spirit even if we can't be together in person. You'll never walk alone."

Coronavirus deaths in Liverpool were blamed on the March 11 Champions League tie attended by more than 52,000 at Anfield including 3,000 from Madrid, where a partial lockdown was already in force. At first there was no confirmed link between the match and any coronavirus cases, according to the government's deputy chief scientific adviser, Angela McLean, who said it warranted further investigation. "It will be very interesting to see in the future, when all the science is done, what relationship there is between the viruses that have circulated in Liverpool and the viruses that have circulated in Spain," she said at the UK government's daily coronavirus news briefing in mid April to a question from the Liverpool Echo.

Liverpool city council's director of public health Matthew Ashton previously told The Guardian the match should have been called off. The mayor of Madrid, Jose Luis Martinez-Almeida, said it was a "mistake" to allow thousands of Atletico fans to attend. "It didn't make any sense that 3,000 Atletico fans could travel to Anfield at that time," Martinez-Almedia told Spanish radio station Onda Cero.

Latest figures at that time showed 246 people had died with coronavirus in Liverpool's NHS hospitals. Madrid was one of Europe's worst affected cities. Spain had the second-highest number of confirmed infection cases in the world, behind the US, figures from Johns Hopkins University as the country's death toll climbed close to 21,000. Chancellor Rishi Sunak rejected claims the government was too slow to cancel large sporting events in the days before lockdown. The Cheltenham Festival, along with Liverpool's Champions League match, went ahead in the second week of March. There were 251,684 racegoers in attendance across the four days of the Festival, while 68,500 watched the Cheltenham Gold Cup on 13 March.

Strict limits on daily life - requiring people to stay at home, shutting many businesses and preventing gatherings of more than two people - were introduced on 23 March. "There is often a wrong time to put certain measures in place, thinking about sustainability and everything else," Sunak said. "At all parts of this we have been guided by that science, we have been guided by making the right decisions at the right time, and I stand by that."

Ever since the Champions League tie there was growing concern that fans from one of the early European epicentres of the pandemic were allowed to travel to Anfield, even after Spain had closed schools and banned mass gatherings. Two days later the Premier League suspended the season. Toward the end of May it emerged that the two major sporting events in March "caused increased suffering and death", the scientist leading the UK's largest Covid-19 tracking project said. Data gathered from millions of volunteers found coronavirus "hotspots" shortly after the Cheltenham Festival and Liverpool's Champions League match against Atletico. Professor Tim Spector said rates of cases locally "increased several-fold". The government said many factors could influence cases in a particular area.

Although some European countries had already staged events without spectators, or completely called them off, sports governing bodies in the UK were taking their cue from Boris Johnson who declared in early March that people should "as far as possible, go about business as usual". On the first weekend in March, there was a full programme of football in both England and Scotland, five horse racing meetings, and Six Nations rugby at Twickenham between England and Wales - which the prime minister himself attended. Yet, a forthcoming Six Nations match in Dublin had already been postponed, along with the Chinese Grand Prix and football matches in virus-stricken northern Italy.

The UK government's stance remained consistent. Just 24 hours before Cheltenham opened to 250,000 spectators on 10 March, Culture Secretary Oliver Dowden rebuffed growing calls for a ban on mass outdoor gatherings. He told the BBC: "There's no reason for people not to attend such events or to cancel them at this stage." But Prof Spector from King's College London said "people will have probably died prematurely" because of the decision.

Figures seen by the BBC Radio 4's File on 4 programme show Liverpool and Cheltenham were among the areas with the highest number of suspected cases. The figures come from the Covid-19 Symptom Study, with an estimated 5-6% of the population, aged 20 to 69, having symptoms in those two regions.

On 11 March - the second day of the festival - the World Health Organization declared coronavirus a pandemic. Later that evening, Liverpool hosted Atletico, visiting fans allowed to travel to Merseyside and mingle in bars and restaurants, despite, at that point, Madrid accounting for almost half of the country's confirmed cases. Liverpool supporter Joel Rookwood, who was ill for eight weeks, believed he contracted Covid-19 that evening, and recalled how when goals were scored, spectators were oblivious to the risks. "The celebrations were some of the most physical that I've experienced," he said. "People were jumping all over each other." The Spirit Of Shankly said it raised concerns about the arrival of fans from Madrid at a council-chaired safety meeting two days before the match but were told it would go ahead in accordance with government advice. Liverpool would not have been able to unilaterally call off the match, that decision would have had to come from Uefa. Prof Spector said: "I think sporting events should have been shut down at least a week earlier because they'll have caused increased suffering and death that wouldn't otherwise have occurred."

In a statement, the government said: "There are many factors that could influence the number of cases in a particular area, including population density, age, general health, and the position of an area on the pandemic curve."

★

Chairman Tom Werner admitted the club made a mistake with the decision to furlough staff, but hoped the quick U-turn showed their commitment to the club. The backlash from fans and former players led FSG to reverse their decision within 48 hours, reminiscent of when they changed their stance on raising ticket prices to as much as £77 — which led to a mass walkout at Anfield in February 2016. 'It's better to admit a mistake than to dig your heels in,' Werner said. 'Hopefully people will know that all we really care about is trying to support the fans and support our players and our club in a way that is sustainable.'

Werner approached 10 years in charge as he waited for football to resume. 'It's a terrible situation we're all in. Someday, hopefully, there will be a vaccine and we can return to the joy of being in a stadium and watching the elegant play of great football players. The most important thing is safety and the Premier League are working on protocols. But there's a hole in so many people's lives. Football is central to their dreams and their hopes. Certainly, as regards to Liverpool, we are playing magnificent football and we are just a couple of matches away from winning the trophy. But I do put it in perspective.'

Liverpool had been on the brink of administration when FSG

won the battle to buy the club from Tom Hicks and George Gillett. With Klopp's side winning the Club World Cup, the European Super Cup and the Champions League, Werner added: 'The 4-0 win over Barcelona was the single greatest sporting event I've ever seen. The reaction our supporters had in the stadium that day and around the world is something that I'll remember for the rest of my life. I thought I could never imagine experiencing anything like (the parade that followed the 2-0 win over Tottenham in the final). Then somebody said, "Well if we win the Premier League, this parade will be dwarfed". I'm looking forward to a parade when we can all congregate again.'

Liverpool wanted to put on a title parade for their supporters when it was safe to do so.

PROJECT RESTART

Liverpool mayor Joe Anderson's outspoken remarks that resuming the Premier League was a "non-starter" did not go down well with the club as "Project Restart" was put into operation. The Mayor feared a "farcical" situation with fans congregating outside Anfield - even if Liverpool clinched the title at a neutral venue.

The Premier League told its clubs only "approved venues" would be used, raising the possibility of matches being played at neutral grounds, with the league hoping to restart on 8 June as "Project Restart" envisaged the season resuming behind closed doors because of social distancing.

Liverpool were "disappointed" with Anderson's comments. Anderson, Liverpool's first directly elected mayor, told BBC Sport: "Even if it was behind closed doors, there'd be many thousands of people who would turn up outside Anfield. There's not many people who would respect what we were saying and stay away from the ground, a lot of people would come to celebrate so I think it's a non-starter." Asked about whether playing at a neutral venue would help, he said: "Even then, I guess that a lot of people would turn up outside Anfield to celebrate and I understand the police's concerns around that, so there's a real difficulty here for us. I think it would be really difficult for the police to keep people apart and maintain social distancing if they were going to celebrate outside Anfield. It would be farcical. It's difficult for us to try to stop people gathering in parks when the weather has been good, especially young people. And I fear people would just ignore it. The police are right to be concerned about that as we are here in the city, and public health officials are also concerned about that, so we'd ask the Premier League and government to take into account all of these concerns that we have."

In a statement, Liverpool said: "As well as a lack of evidence to support such claims, we would also point to recent discussions with mayor Anderson relating to the possibility of any behind-closed-doors football, which concluded that it is important that key stakeholders across the city continue to engage and work collaboratively. In recent weeks, we have engaged with supporters' groups who have informed us of their determination to respect social distancing measures and, in the event of a resumption of football being announced, we would continue to work with them and other key stakeholders in keeping with our collective desire to achieve this crucial objective. As part of our ongoing operations, we are in regular contact with the mayor and his office and we hope these conversations can continue."

Anderson added: "I think the best thing to do is to actually end the season. It isn't just about Liverpool - they've clearly won the league - they deserve it, they should be crowned league champions. The bottom line is, though, this is about health and safety and people's lives and I think football should have to come second in regards to making a choice here."

More than 300 people had died from coronavirus in Liverpool hospitals at that time.

Senior medical directors of the FA, Premier League, Rugby Football Union, England and Wales Cricket Board and the British Horse Racing Authority held talks in the first of a series of meetings to discuss the feasibility of a return. Culture Secretary Oliver Dowden, England's deputy chief medical officer Jonathan Van-Tam, UK Sport CEO Sally Munday and a representative of the Sports Ground Safety Authority were also be on the call. Sports leaders were asked to give evidence to MPs at a Department for Digital, Culture, Media & Sport select committee hearing on Tuesday on the impact of the crisis on sport.

The return of Premier League football would lift the spirits of the nation, according to Dominic Raab at his media briefing early in May. The government would only give the green light for it to resume when it is safe to do so. Project Restart was looking for ways to resume the season. The First Secretary of State said: "I think it would lift spirits of the nation and people would like to see us get back to work and children can go to school safely but also past times like sport. I know the government has had constructive meetings with sports bodies to plan for athletes return to training when it's safe. I can tell you that the culture secretary has been working on a plan to get sport played behind closed doors when we move to second phase so that is something we are looking at. Of course, the key point though, we can only do it when the medical advice and scientific advice is that it can be done safely and sustainably but certainly that is something under active consideration." Raab refused to confirm when fans would be allowed to return to games. "I can't look too far into the future because there are various ways to get control of virus and defeat it for good - a vaccine is certainly one of those. Therapeutics is another. I think we are waiting to see how effectively international test tracking and tracing can be. That is also an option, but whether it's a combination of test tracking and tracing and other social distancing measures within what is possible in a sporting environment. We want to see whether behind closed doors - what the options are for doing that. So it's worth taking a close look at that, seeing whether it's possible to do it safely, but as ever taking the scientific and medical advice about how and when to proceed."

Raab told BBC Radio 4's Today programme: "Well, I'm absolutely open to that (resuming the Premier League) and horse racing too. And, I know that both the Premier League and racing are working on how this might be doable in a safe way, but that safety has to be paramount."

★

Premier League clubs agreed to stage one of the return to training protocols allowing teams to start training in small groups. Players had to observe social distancing rules, and contact training was not permitted as the first stage "has been agreed in consultation with players, managers, club doctors, independent experts and the government". The Premier League statement added: "Strict medical protocols of the highest standard will ensure everyone returns to training in the safest environment possible. The health and wellbeing of all participants is the Premier League's priority, and the safe return to training is a step-by-step process. Full consultation will now continue with players, managers, clubs, the PFA and LMA as protocols for full-contact training are developed."

Klopp insisted that his side deserved to be crowned champions, even if the season was curtailed. With the prospect of null and void firmly off the table, he spoke out about how unjust it would have been if his side wasn't awarded the title. "There was talk that people wanted to declare the season null and void. So you thought: 'Huh? We have played 76 per cent of the season and you just want to delete the thing?' That would have been something that I personally would find unfair, to just say that it didn't happen. We are first in the home table, we are first in the away table. It is a season in which we should become champions.

"Dealing with the crisis is the most important thing. But that doesn't mean that certain things are of no importance at all just because they are less important. I think there are worse things in life than not becoming champions. A lot of people around us have big problems. People die, it always happens, but at the moment because of a virus that we all didn't know and for which nobody could be prepared. We cannot prepare for everything, but also have to react often. That's the biggest part of my life, reacting to things that I didn't expect.

"People say: 'How can you think about football, in moments when people are dying out there?' Nobody does that, but like every other branch of business, we have to prepare for the time afterwards, because it will come of course. When it comes to football, that means that we will start training at some point and to make sure everyone is safe, unique measures are taken. As they were made in Germany, they are now being taken in England. The training centres of the English professional clubs will be the safest. There are no places to be infected at all."

The Bundesliga became the first in Europe to resume, behind closed doors, on Saturday 16 May. One of the games on the day of relaunch was the derby between Schalke and Klopp's former club Dortmund. Champions Bayern Munich, four points clear at the top, travelled to Union Berlin. Most teams had nine games to play, with the final weekend rescheduled for 27-28 June. The season resumed under strict health protocols that banned fans from the stadium and required players to have Covid-19 testing. Around 300 people, including players, staff and officials, were in or around the stadiums during match days. The league had been suspended since 13 March; clubs returned to training in mid-April with players working out in groups. Christian Seifert, chief executive of the German Football League, held a news conference where he said despite the empty stands and other restrictions, "it was crucial to resume play". The Germans went ahead despite 10 positive results from clubs in the top two divisions following the first series of coronavirus tests - and two in the second series. Chancellor Angela Merkel eased some restrictions, allowing shops to reopen with the country seeing fewer than 7,000 deaths.

German football continued despite France's Ligue 1, the Netherlands' Eredivisie and Belgium's The Premier League was still waiting confirmation of the details of their restart. Union Berlin centre-back Nevan Subotic told BBC World Service Sport: "It is a precarious situation for all of us. It is going to be impossible to come out of the league with positive remarks, it is just going to be a lot of risk management and trying to get to a finished season with the fewest casualties. We are not going to have games with fans and for me that is what makes it special. Playing football is fun and is challenging but what makes it exceptional is the community aspect of it. That is gone and I don't want to pretend like it is not a huge thing. It is a huge thing and it is what makes it special. Therefore what I will definitely enjoy is the first game back with fans inside the stadium. I am looking forward to that and that is my end goal."

Seifert sounded a note of caution reinforcing the fact that this was quite a fragile situation, saying "we're playing under probation" adding that they had to prove that their health and safety concepts were working on every single match day. The Premier League, La Liga and Serie A were looking on to see if Germany can make it work.

As the Bundesliga was the first major European league to restart, Klopp followed along by watching his home country's latest matches; no hugging during celebrations, but the biggest difference from normal play was that there were no fans in the stadiums. "It will be like this for some months, but this doesn't mean that football won't stay the marvellous sport that it is. Everyone started to play without fans surrounding them and we love football not for the atmosphere that there is at the stadium."

One player and two staff at Watford and Burnley assistant manager Ian Woan were among six positive Premier League tests, the other two at a third club, the details were not been revealed. Players and staff who tested positive self-isolate for seven days. Of 748 players and staff from 19 clubs were tested with Norwich City testing a day later.

Before the news about Watford's positive tests emerged, captain Troy Deeney said he would not return to training because he feared for his family. "We're due back in this week. I've said I'm not going in," Deeney, 31, told Eddie Hearn and Tony Bellew on the Talk the Talk YouTube show. "It only takes one person to get infected within the group and I don't want to be bringing that home. My son is only five months old. He had breathing difficulties, so I don't want to come home to put him in more danger." Burnley said Woan was "asymptomatic" and "currently safe and well at home".

"The Premier League is providing this aggregated information for the purposes of competition integrity and transparency," it said in a statement. "No specific details as to clubs or individuals will be provided by the league and results will be made public in this way after each round of testing."

Clubs were permitted to test up to 40 personnel and some did not use their full allocation, while some samples were still to be processed. As well as training in small groups of no more than five, sessions must last no longer than 75 minutes for each player. Social distancing must be adhered to. Official protocols sent to players and managers included corner flags, balls, cones, goalposts and even playing surfaces disinfected after each training session. Ongoing measures in further guidance include twice-weekly testing as well as a daily pre-training questionnaire and temperature check.

REDS READY TO RESUME

Jurgen Klopp's players were "eager as five-year olds" training in their gardens ahead of the Premier League return, ready to go again to be finally crowned champions as the BBC announced their Team of the Season and Manager of the season ahead of the restart.

Incredibly, seven of the eleven came from Anfield, however, considering their exceptional season, it was hardly surprising. Manager of the Season? Really, there was only one candidate.

Liverpool's preparations were well underway with an intensive training programme as Klopp said: "The boys have a lot of work to do, physical work because we all expect to go again. I don't know exactly when but we have to prepare for that - that is what the boys do. When we come back together again, we have to make the best of the situation we have. We don't know how long we will get to prepare for the games, so in that moment we will just try. When we give the boys a challenge to do in their gardens you can see in them they play really like five and six-year old boys. There will be busy times coming up - hopefully - but we are prepared for that. We are so recharged I can tell you - you can use my energy to light up different cities in my home area! So that's 100 per cent possible and that's how it is at the moment."

Klopp gave his players detailed video analysis showing his squad highlights of past glories…and ones still to come. They included their Champions League final triumph and December's World Club Championship win.

Speaking to Fox Sports Klopp said: "We have to make sure that we will be physically ready again. Then there is the technical thing and the tactical thing. It is the tactical thing we probably work most on at the moment with a lot of videos we send the boys - we send them videos of what we did well, what we didn't do well and what we want to do in the future. We remind ourselves of things we have achieved in the past and want to achieve in the future. There are a lot of things we are really looking forward to do again. It is the little things, you appreciate the little things so much more in this moment, the little things you can do."

Klopp said the players maintained their strong bond throughout the lockdown: "We immediately created a chat group just a very lively one! There are around 60 people involved, all the Melwood staff, and I told them I don't want that anybody feels alone for a second in this time. Whatever happens we will go through it together."

The first thing Klopp wanted to do when he saw his players again was to give them one of his famous bear hugs, but it wouldn't be possible. Klopp spoke about the measures that would be necessary to ensure their safety. 'Honestly, I would like to give them a hug. It's been a long time since I've seen them and I like them a lot. Though that probably won't be allowed so we'll leave that till much later. But we have to be professional from the first day, we have to check first the individual status and then once we know that, from that point we can start.' Liverpool allowed players to train in isolation at Melwood but a maximum of three permitted to enter the grounds, with no coaching staff present

Arsene Wenger insisted Liverpool 'are champions in everyone's head' irrespective of whether they are officially awarded the Premier League title. 'Jurgen has done extremely well because that club has waited 30 years for this title, and when you think they have such a massive difference [points gap] to the second team, Manchester City, as well – 25 points, it's absolutely massive. No matter what England will decide, Liverpool are champions in everyone's head, I think.'

Klopp exerted no pressure on his players to produce whirlwind football. "Football is a game where everyone is pretty much in the same situation we play against another team and we don't have to be at our all-time best we have to be at our best possible and that's exactly the same for the other teams. Whenever we will start we will have had the same time for preparation and our job was always, and always will be, to use the situation you are in.

We will be in as good a shape as possible."

Klopp was delighted to return to Melwood with players being phased back in small groups to restart training. "Lockdown has been as good as possible it's not exactly what I want to do but it's what we all have to do so we try to make the best of it. We are in close contact. We started 8 weeks ago and now you feel everyone is desperate to get back to a 'new' normal life. I have missed the boys the most because we have created a group there not only the boys but all the people at Melwood because we have a really good relationship and we became friends over the last four and a half years. We see each other pretty often with Zoom and those things but it's still not the same and going back to Melwood and doing all the things we usually do is something I really miss."

He joked that the biggest lesson during lockdown is the extent that Gary Neville is opinionated, outspoken on a range of topics, in particular how the Premier League should restart, the affect on lower league clubs and the Government's response to the crisis. "I didn't learn a lot in lockdown, other than Gary Neville has an opinion about absolutely everything. It is incredible."

Being isolated made him realise how connected society is. "I didn't learn a lot but I have known myself for 52 years and I knew I can deal with difficult situations before. This is a difficult situation, not only for me or my family but for every single person on the planet. I am quite proud how we as a society have dealt with it. We are not perfect, we will always make mistakes but I think we have learned how connected we are to each other."

Klopp brought smiles to three club supporters in isolation by surprising them by dropping in on their Zoom calls. In March, Liverpool launched an initiative with the aim of helping people to stay connected during the pandemic. Liverpool released a video that showed Klopp checking in on an LFC Foundation volunteer, Brett Duffy. In the zoom call, Klopp reminisced on his early days as a coach. Duffy is currently studying at Liverpool John Moores University. Klopp said to Duffy, "When I started, I had to do all the analysis myself so I know it's quite intense! In the end, you give it to a head coach and he says 'yeah interesting' and puts it away. You look in good spirits still, that's important. That's how the boys are, that's how I am, and so we will go again and we will be back."

Klopp also caught up with Darren Smyth. In January, Smyth had undergone brain surgery on his birthday and was isolating after a cancer diagnosis. Smyth informed Klopp that he was at Anfield to watch the Merseyside derby in December 2018. He also shared how he "marvelled at the atmosphere" inside the stadium after Divock Origi scored a stoppage-time winner. In reply, Klopp said that they might have been celebrating in different places within the stadium but both of them felt the same amount of joy. Klopp commented that football is all about these moments that can never be forgotten. At the end of the call, Klopp invited Smyth to Anfield to share a beer in his "food room." He also asked Smyth to stay strong, as the latter was due to have lung surgery later in the year.

The third fan surprised by Klopp was Noah Smallwood, a young boy suffering from Perthes disease that affects the patient's hip. Noah was scheduled to undergo an operation at Alder Hey. Klopp called it the world's best hospital and assured Noah that he is in the best hands. Klopp invited the kid to Kirby, Liverpool's new training ground.

Klopp insisted his club would do everything to guarantee player safety as he was 'over the moon' as a handful of players returned to Melwood for the first time since March 13. The club went to great lengths to adhere to the strict social distancing rules, setting up a one-way system in the complex to ensure nobody crosses paths. Every member of the playing, coaching and medical staff were tested at the club's Kirkby Academy on Sunday. 'I was over the moon,' said Klopp. 'I always said we don't want to rush anything, but I don't think it is rushed. It is for the first step, for this kind of social distancing training and we have five players. We do whatever we have to do, we do whatever we can do to stay safe.

'But also we have to keep other people safe and still be able to play football. I'm really looking forward to seeing the boys but it's still strange and different because we cannot be really close to each other. But we will see, it's getting better.'

For the previous two weeks, players were permitted to go to Melwood to do running sessions on individual pitches but now a group of five were able to work together. The return to non-contact training "felt like the first day at school", according to Klopp. "I woke up even earlier than usual and then I realised it was my first day. It felt like the first day at school - for me, it was 46 years ago, but it must have been similar. I dressed myself in my uniform again - and for the right reason, for going to training."

Klopp was "really happy" to see his players again and that they were all in "good spirits" and "good shape".

"Yes, the group is there. They are all fit and hopefully it stays like this, of course. From a sports science point of view, it is a proper challenge to prepare for something when you don't know when it will happen. That's 25, 26 or 28 players when for one moment, you should be ready – but that's the job to do. It's how it is. I enjoy these problems much more than the problems I had [with training] in the last few weeks, so it's our job and we will find a solution for that. The league decided they would let us start training, the protocols from the league [are] brilliant. It is not easy to do, to fulfill all that, but we did it and so now we are here and we can start training in a very, very safe place. Then hopefully for all of us we will get good news because that always would mean the development was in the right direction for the whole country and then for the league as well. We prepare for the future; when the future will start, we don't know yet."

June 12 was penciled in for a return, amid speculation it might need to be pushed back a week to get players fit. "We don't know exactly how long we have, but we have some time to prepare the rest of this season and already the next season, because I don't think there will be a massive break between the two. It's a pre-season for us. We don't know how long and we will not have test games or friendlies. Maybe we can organise it between us when we are allowed to, but it will not be the same like in other pre-seasons. Then we have to make sure we are as fit as possible for the first match; even for the second; and probably, 100 percent, for the third. Or whatever, it depends how long we will get."

Klopp was glad his players had a "real rest" during nine weeks off in lockdown, as opposed to two or three weeks of holiday per year. "Of course, you cannot rest when you are worried about the situation in the world, not in the same way like you do on a proper holiday."

Official protocols stated corner flags, balls, cones, goalposts and even playing surfaces were disinfected after each training session. Klopp said the the protocols were "brilliant" as his side were able to train in a "very, very safe place". He added: "Then hopefully for all of us we will get good news because that always would mean the development was in the right direction for the whole country and then for the league as well."

No player was forced to train if he did not feel safe to do so, Klopp said, after their first training session for more than nine weeks with 10 players on a sunny day at Melwood that he expected all his players to show up but they were under no pressure. "It's their choice so that's clear," said Klopp, who had two more training groups later on. "I said before the session 'You are here on free will. Usually you sign a contract and then you have to be in when I tell you. In this case, if you don't feel safe, you don't have to be here'. There are no restrictions, no punishment, nothing. So it's their own decision and we will respect that 100%. The boys are fine. We would never put anybody in danger to do what we want to do. Yes, we love football, and yes, it's our job but it's not more important than our lives or the lives of other people."

Klopp felt "like a policeman, pretty much, wearing my uniform" as he set off for Melwood, with nobody allowed to shower or change at the ground. Groups of five trained on separate pitches but Klopp said "it looked like football".

Klopp and Pepijn Lijnders were among the first to head into the training ground, and with preliminary fitness tests already having been conducted the squad kicked off with fitness and ball work, similar to early days of a typical pre-season, albeit at an accelerated rate, "It's a pre-season for us. We don't know how long and we will not have test games or friendlies, not really. Maybe we can organise it between us when we are allowed to, but it will not be the same like in other pre-seasons. But, no, it's a pre-season. Today we started with training, good things, not the highest intensity but the boys look in good shape. We don't know exactly how long we have, but we have some time to prepare the rest of this season and already the next season because I don't think there will be a massive break between the two. We don't know exactly but we should prepare for a rather shorter break between the two seasons. It means that's our training period, so use it."

Klopp described the first sessions back as "absolutely perfect," as the squad retrain the "little things" that are lost with an extended spell out of practice. He noted that this 'pre-season' is likely to benefit the next campaign as much as the one already underway, as he anticipates a much shorter break between seasons than usual. "I didn't see all the boys yet, I only saw 10 of them and the coaches, which is a good start,

I would say. They all look in good spirits. The weather is brilliant here. Melwood is prepared for us; all one-way roads through the whole area and everything is prepared and set. We are ready to go and it was really nice to be back.

"Melwood was busy through the whole period, not with training but the chefs were here cooking for the players and stuff like this, delivery services, and all this kind of stuff. So, a lot of things happened here at Melwood but not the football stuff. So now coming back and seeing how it is prepared is brilliant. Ray Haughan did an outstanding job to put all the people pretty much in place. As I said, it's all one-way roads. If you are in the wrong place and have to go to the toilet you need nearly half an hour, but that's how life is in the moment. It's all different but we have to get used to it and then we have to use it. In the moment when you got used to it, then you start with the right things. Today we started with training, good things, not the highest intensity but the boys look in good shape. The sessions were perfectly organised, it is all about football. It's little things, getting used to the pitch, boots and ball, turns, passes, half-passes, softer passes, running, little accelerations and stuff like that. Little finishes, not proper shooting but little finishes, all this stuff. It looked really, really good, I have to say. If anybody was worried from our fans, you don't have to – the boys are in good shape.

"It is easy to entertain the boys usually, to be honest, because you throw a ball there and say, 'play' two goals, a ball and the boys are entertained and they do some stuff, which always you can use. Pre-season is always the most creative period of the year, but now because we are not allowed to play small-sided games or in general [have] challenges, that cuts out two very important things in football, but it's no problem. We know that, it is for all the same, so yes, we have to be creative so that we are entertained and don't get bored by our own sessions and for the boys as well. It is always easier if you enjoy something, if you enjoy the things you do, you are ready for more intensity – and, of course, we have to increase intensity. So, for that there will be a few things.

"I don't think anybody ever wrote a football book and thought about a pandemic in that moment and said, 'OK, it is not allowed to be closer to each other than two metres', so that is not there and we have to be creative and we will."

Klopp was encouraged by what he has seen in the Bundesliga and hoped the Premier League could follow suit. 'It's a little step. From a personal point of view, I can say it's a massive boost because I really love being together with (my wife) Ulla in the house and having time for different things but I'm a football manager and I want to be together with the boys. Now I can at least have them piece by piece, five pieces by five pieces, so I really can't wait. That football is closer to coming back I think is really a good sign for people as well. I hope that we are now in England on the right side of the thing.'

Klopp enjoyed having football back on his screen and he is already no stranger to viewing without fans because he likes to watch without the sound on! 'Look, I love it. In this part I'm a strange person; when I watch football – other games, not our games – I watch them most of the time without sound because I don't want to hear the commentary, I'm just interested in the game. So now for me it's completely normal to watch other football games. I love the game, I'm interested in what they do and stuff like this.'

Ultra groups protested against resumption behind closed doors. Klopp sees little point in debating it with fans facing potentially a year before they can attend games again. 'I know, football behind closed doors, of course it's not the same. Why do we have to mention it? We all love it when we have contact, when we get cheered up by the people, when they push us through the yards and all that stuff. We love that but we cannot have it. Why would you think always about something you cannot have in the moment? Use the thing you have in the moment.'

Klopp was confident his players would be back just as strong as where they left off, but would miss the fans. "When we start, it goes really again for everything," said the Reds boss. "The competition will make the intensity. So it's not about 'oh, Liverpool have to win two games'. By the way, we have to win two games when we start – it's not 'only two', it's two. We have to win them. We have to do it, unfortunately, without the best boost in the world and the best kick in your ass in the right moment in the world, from the Anfield crowd. But that's how it is. It's 100 per cent (that) the perfect package of football is a full, packed Anfield stadium, two really good teams, big fight, super goals and at the end Liverpool win. That's the perfect matchday. So, a lot of these things are possible but Anfield will not be packed for a while. So that's what we have to accept, that's the only thing. I know, football behind closed doors, of course it's not the same. We all love it when we have contact, when we get cheered up by the people, when they push us through the yards and all that stuff. We love that but we cannot have it. And it looks like it will be possible – and it is in Germany already possible – to play behind closed doors."

The worry was that players could take longer than they have to get back to match sharpness after the two-month lay-off. But Klopp insisted: "That football is closer to coming back I think is really a good sign for people as well. I always said we don't want to rush anything, but I don't think it is rushed."

The Premier League was "as confident as we can be" about restarting in June, said chief executive Richard Masters. Players resumed training on the day it was announced there had been six positive tests across three clubs. "We've taken the first step," commented Masters, "It's great for everybody, including the fans, to see our players back on the training ground." Masters said it was "flexible" whether they would return on June 12 as planned. Culture Secretary Oliver Dowden said phase two – the return of contact training in elite sports - could get government approval "later in the week." The Premier League would not take this next step until it is safe to do so. "We wouldn't have taken the first step to get back to training if we weren't convinced we had created a very safe environment for our players," Masters said. "It is the first step and we have to be sure when we go to contact training we have completed those processes."

Elsewhere, Chelsea midfielder N'Golo Kante trained at home, Watford captain Troy Deeney declined to return to training. The Premier League hosted video conference calls "to provide health reassurances" to club captains and managers before training recommenced. "We have done everything we possibly can to make return to training as safe as possible," Masters said. "We think it is safe to return. We have to respect players' decisions not to return to training. I would be comfortable to return to training."

Liverpool could have a trophy presentation "if we can find a way of doing it", but there remained concerns about fans gathering outside Anfield, and Masters said crowds of supporters was "a concern". The Premier League wanted "to play out the season as much as possible at home and away venues". He added: "We're talking to the authorities about that. I do believe we can appeal to fans not to congregate outside football grounds or go to other people's houses to watch football matches in contravention of government guidelines."

Playing at Anfield and lifting the Premier League trophy without any fans will be "pretty strange". Jordan Henderson said Liverpool fans "make a huge difference and we all know that. Of course it would feel different because if you win any trophy and receive it without any fans there, it would be pretty strange. It is still not over. We still have work to do and we still need to perform at a high level right the way until the season finishes because we want to finish as strongly as we can to make sure it is a full season.

"After that, whether we win it or whatever, then [receiving] the trophy and the fans not being there... you just have to deal with it when it comes. Hopefully it does happen. We are still in a very good position. It will mean we have won the Premier League and we will all be very happy but then we can look to the future - and whenever fans are allowed back into the stadium, I am sure we will have some sort of celebration together."

Liverpool and other clubs returned to training with strict protocols in place, including training only in small groups, but Henderson said the measures were "amazing" and made the players feel "safe". He said: "We have had programmes to follow, so some of us are probably fitter than before we went into lockdown. The lads have looked really good physically and I never really had a doubt that that would be an issue. When you go back, it is a bit different with the type of training, getting used to the ball again, longer passing and shooting and the sharpness of twisting and turning, the change of direction, you need to get used to it. After a few weeks of full training, we will be right back where we left off, hopefully."

In the latest round of Premier League testing, two individuals were positive, including Bournemouth goalkeeper Aaron Ramsdale, taking the total number of cases to eight from 1,744 tests carried out. Henderson added: "My opinion is that as soon as everyone is comfortable and as soon as it is safe to do so, we are guided by the experts and doctors on what they deem safe to do. For us at Liverpool, it has been really good. It has been great to get back and everyone has felt comfortable and safe, otherwise we would not have gone in. Hopefully that is the case throughout the Premier League."

At the end of May Premier League clubs unanimously voted to resume contact training as 'Project Restart' moved to phase two. Players were be able to "train as a group and engage in tackling while minimising unnecessary close contact," a statement said. Discussions continued on plans to resume the season when "conditions allow", it added.

This was a significant step towards the resumption of the season, but brought heightened risk of transmission with 11 v 11 close-contact training. Social distancing was still needed off the field, as players and staff had to actively opt-in to agree to the strict requirements - but also the added risks - that come with entering this phase.

Premier League players and staff continued to be tested twice a week for coronavirus. At this point toward the end of May, eight tested positive after 1,744 tests. The decision to return to contact training was agreed following consultation with clubs, players, managers, the Professional Football Association, the League Managers Association and the government. Plans for the third phase of Project Restart included a step towards normal training and build-up to competitive games.

Kylian Mbappé heaped praise on Jurgen Klopp by describing his side as a winning machine. The Ligue 1 champions were trying to extend their star forward's £600,000-a-week contract beyond the summer of 2022. Asked about Liverpool's remarkable Premier League campaign Mbappé paid tribute to Klopp for his side's ruthlessness. 'This season, Liverpool have been a machine in the Premier League. They have made winning look easy but the truth is that it is never easy. Performances like they have been having don't just happen. To be as ruthless as they have been would come from lots of hard work in training and from having a very good manager.' Reports in France claimed he was "very flattered" Klopp reached out to his father, Wilfried, to discuss a possible transfer.

GHOST GAMES

South Korean side FC Seoul fined a record £67,000 for filling their empty stands with sex dolls during their K-League match against Gwangju FC. Around 20 dolls were placed in the stadium with some wearing face masks and the team's colours while others displayed t-shirts and placards with the logo of SoloS, a sex toy seller. The mannequins, most of them female, but some male, were placed in the arena as a substitute for fans.

The Premier League season would restart on 17 June with Aston Villa v Sheffield United and Manchester City v Arsenal. The Premier League announced the starting date with the the two games in hand.

A full fixture list would then be played on the weekend of 19-21 June. There were 92 fixtures still to play. The Premier League, suspended on 13 March, restarted 100 days later after Leicester City's 4-0 win over Aston Villa on 9 March, but with all games behind closed doors

At the point of deciding to re-start, 12 tested positive after 2,752 tests across the league. Premier League players and staff continued to be tested twice a week, with the capacity increased from 50 to 60 tests per club for the fourth round of testing. Any tested positive would self-isolate for seven days.

Plans for the third phase of Project Restart included a step towards normal training and build-up to competitive games. Gary Lineker was among those who tweeted their delight at football's return. But Arsenal fan Piers Morgan was more apprehensive that their first fixture back was against high-flying Manchester City. London Mayor Sadiq Khan expressed concerns that football's return may allow the virus to spread, especially if supporters gather outside stadiums. He told LBC: 'We don't want to inadvertently give an opportunity to the virus to spread'. Khan called upon the police and councils to ensure social distance guidelines were followed.

Four games would be broadcast, free to air, live on BBC Sport, the first time since the Premier League's inception in 1992 that games will have been shown live by the BBC. "This opportunity creates an historic moment for the BBC and our audiences," director of BBC Sport, Barbara Slater said. "At a time when sports fans across the country are in need of a lift, this is very welcome news." There were plans for additional Match of the Day highlight programmes. Every one of the remaining 92 Premier League games would be broadcast live across Sky Sports, BT Sport, BBC Sport or Amazon Prime. Sky Sports made 25 free to air, including the Merseyside Derby on the first weekend of the 19-21 June. The last time a live, top-flight league football match was broadcast on the BBC was during the 1987-88 season.

Liverpool could clinch the title with victory in their first game back should second-placed City lose to Arsenal. The game in which Liverpool could secure the title could be held at a neutral venue. Deputy Chief Constable Mark Roberts wanted up to six matches moved at the request of local police forces, including the Merseyside derby and Manchester City v Liverpool. Roberts discussions with the Premier League had been "positive" with a "shared focus on the priority of public health".

"We have reached a consensus that balances the needs of football, while also minimising the demand on policing," said Roberts. "The majority of remaining matches will be played, at home and away as scheduled, with a small number of fixtures taking place at neutral venues, which, contrary to some reports, have yet to be agreed. The views and agreement of forces which host Premier League clubs have been sought and where there were concerns, the Premier League has been supportive in providing flexibility in arranging alternative venues where requested. This plan will be kept continually under review to ensure public health and safety and a key part of this is for supporters to continue to respect the social distancing guidelines, and not to attend or gather outside the stadiums."

In a statement, the Premier League said it's "ambition is to complete all of our remaining fixtures this season home and away, where possible". It added: "We are working with our clubs to ensure risks are assessed and minimised, while co-operating with the police at a local and national level. Discussions with the National Police Chiefs' Council and UK Football Policing Unit have been positive and are continuing. We are prepared for all outcomes and have a neutral venue contingency."

"The situation will change our celebrations obviously as well but the stadium," Jurgen Klopp added, "we didn't hear that yet. I heard that there is still talk about it, I'm pretty sure that we can solve the situation here as well in Liverpool. I heard a day ago a really good phrase about that we have the best home fans in the world, and now we need the best stay at home fans in the world. That's how it is.

"We waited a while for this situation and it's not done yet. If we had not stopped the league, or it would not have happened, the silly null and void stuff, then it was clear we were already champions. We wanted to play anyway and now we are really desperate to play because we want to become champions on the pitch that looks like that we can do that. Wherever it will be we don't know, we hope it will be at Anfield but we don't know and that's not important. Most of the people on this planet never have the chance to become champions of the Premier League. For us, it looks like we have the chance so we take it."

Klopp believed that it would be an "exceptional" day when Liverpool get the title sealed, regardless of where it is won. He accepted the situation was "not perfect" but promised a big celebration when it's safe to do so. "In the moment for me, whenever it will be, in an empty stadium blah, blah, blah, with all the thoughts and prayers and love from the people all around the world it will still be an absolutely exceptional day in my life. Yes it's not be perfect but we knew for a while it would not be perfect so we are already used to that. We just want to have it and then we will see how it feels. I am pretty sure it will feel pretty good. Absolutely. Usually you have a 50 per cent chance if you become champion that you will not become champion in your own stadium.

"Who cares? That's really not too important, we just want to be together in that moment and we will see how much close contact is allowed until then and we will use each inch of that for sure, but only if it's allowed. Then there will be a moment in our life when we have time and the opportunity and it's allowed to celebrate together then we will have a moment, and we will celebrate it in the right manner. Whenever that will be, then we decide how much we enjoy it then."

Serie A was scheduled to return on 20 June, the country's sports minister Vincenzo Spadafora confirmed. Serie A was suspended on 9 March, with Juventus leading the table by a point with 12 rounds of matches remaining. The FIGC intended for the top three divisions to be concluded and that if any of them should restart and then stop again, a shorter alternative of a play-off would be devised.

Massimo Cellino, who owns Serie A bottom side Brescia, said resuming was a "crazy decision". "It's too much for the players," he told BBC World Service's World Football Show. "We stopped [training] for two months. It is dangerous to restart it playing three games a week. So I'm worried about injuries and the hot weather which is going to be terrible in Italy more than Germany." But Udinese and Nigeria defender William Troost-Ekong said: "It's lifted everybody's spirits, As long as we can do it in the right way without too many risks and setting the right example for the country, I think it's a good thing to be doing."

Ryan Giggs took inspiration from Liverpool as Wales manager. 'I think what we have seen this year is Liverpool are a fantastic team, managed by a great coach Jurgen Klopp and, it pains me to say it as a United fan, but they have been fantastic this season. Obviously they'll go on and, whatever way it is, they'll win the league and deserve it. They've had two brilliant seasons actually, last year pushing Manchester City all the way (last season). They're a great team to watch. There were

Project Restart

certain things that I've taken out of the way that Liverpool play, and taking it on to the way that I want to do with Wales. Hopefully United will bridge that gap and catch them up. But you have to give credit where credit is due and Liverpool have been fantastic this season.'

Troy Deeney believed the season had lost all 'integrity' and that the eventual title win will always be overshadowed. The Watford captain was one of the leading voices in opposing Project Restart, opting not to make a return to training unwilling to risk the health of his five-month-old son, who has had breathing difficulties. While talks with Premier League bosses and England's deputy chief medical officer, Jonathan Van-Tam eased his fears, Deeney was still adamant that the current campaign should've been written off and that Liverpool's long wait for a Premier League title will be sullied. 'I believe that when it comes to the integrity of this season anyway, it's already gone. I feel sorry for Liverpool because no matter how it plays out, they deserve to win the league. They deserve to get the trophy. But no matter how it plays out, even if we play all the games, it's still going to be the year spoiled by the pandemic. It's not going to be that year that Liverpool won the league being the best team and, you know, it's 30 years they haven't won for. So I do feel sorry for Liverpool and their players and Jordan, but in terms of integrity, there's no way you could say that this is a viable competition. It's like running a marathon, 20 odd miles, stopping for two months and then sprinting the last bit and going: "Ah, that was a good time that."

'I saw some comments in regards to my son, people saying: "I hope your son gets corona." That's the hard part for me. If you respond to that, people then go: "Ah, we've got him" and they keep doing it. In a time where it's all about mental health and everyone says "speak up, speak out, please speak", Danny Rose spoke out and I spoke out and we just get absolutely hammered and battered for it. So people see that and go "woah" and it's not just us that gets it, the missus gets direct messages and you'll be walking down the street and people will be like: "Oh, I'm at work, you go back to work".'

Jamie Carragher suggested Klopp could use their final games as preparation for next campaign in lieu of a full pre-season. The Reds could theoretically have five or six games left with nothing to play, and Carragher felt they could be used as "preparation" for the 2020/21 season as there will be a shorter break between campaigns. "Listen,

Liverpool have won the league. Gary just joked before about Liverpool losing every game; I honestly think Liverpool would still win the league as Manchester City would have to win all theirs. Jordan Henderson has come out plenty of times in interviews to say 'it's not won yet, it's not won yet.' Players know they can't say it publicly because there's nothing worse than just saying it and coming across as confident and cocksure. You never take anything for granted. The position Liverpool are in, it's just what game it happens in. I think the Liverpool players now, it's just get it won as quickly as possible. It's an interesting one from Liverpool's point of view because if they do win the league in the first couple of games they are one of few teams who have nothing to play for, so it's a case of how Jurgen Klopp approaches it. Will he use it as a preparation for next season to use his squad? There won't be as much of a break. That will be interesting."

Brendan Rodgers "had no strength" after contracting the coronavirus in March. Rodgers was the second Premier League manager to confirm he had Covid-19, with Mikel Arteta testing positive in March. Rodgers suffered with "breathlessness" before fully recovering from the virus. "I could hardly walk and it reminded me of walking up Mount Kilimanjaro. We had a week off when we were supposed to play Watford [14 March] and then the week after that, I started to struggle. For three weeks I had no smell or taste. I had no strength, and a week after, my wife was the same. We were tested and both of us were detected with the virus. It reminded me of when I climbed Kilimanjaro. The higher you went the more you suffered with acclimatisation and the harder it was to breathe. I remember trying to run for the first time [after becoming ill] and it was hard to go 10 yards. I had no real appetite and it was a weird sensation of eating food without ever tasting and smelling what it was. It has made me really appreciate being fit and healthy."

Rodgers said it was "brilliant" to have the players back together.

"It was good to have that contact again and to be near them. The last couple of days we have split into groups of 12, which is not normal, but how they have adapted has been really nice. The rhythm of it [training] has changed but I'm really pleased with them physically and it's like they have never been away."

Troy Deeney raised concerns over the increased risk to black, Asian and minority ethnic (BAME) players. But Rodgers said none of the players at Leicester have "given us any inclination that they do not want to play".

"I feel safe and we are very lucky in football that we are being tested twice a week," he added. "One of the key things about keeping this virus away is being in the open air and that is where we are all day, so we are very fortunate. When we go to stadiums we won't be in the same changing room. We will be in four or five different areas so that is an example of adaptation."

Domestic competitive sport behind closed doors was announced by the UK government as 'phase three' guidance paved the way for live sport to return on 1 June for the first time since mid-March with individual sports assessing the risk, consulting athletes, coaches and support staff. Horse racing was among the first to resume, while the Premier League was due to restart on 17 June. "The wait is over. Live British sport will shortly be back on in safe and carefully controlled environments," said the Secretary of State for Digital, Culture, Media and Sport, Oliver Dowden. "This guidance provides the safe framework for sports to resume competitions behind closed doors. It is now up to individual sports to confirm they can meet these protocols and decide when it's right for them to restart." Speaking at the daily UK Government coronavirus briefing, Dowden added: "Football, tennis, horse racing, Formula 1, cricket, golf, rugby, snooker and others are all set to return to our screens shortly."

The key protocols that must be adhered to:
- All competition delivery partners and user groups involved, from the teams and athletes, to the support staff, officials and media, must travel individually and by private transport where possible.
- Prior to entering the competition venue, they are expected to carry out a screening process for symptoms. Anyone with known or suspected Covid-19 will not be permitted to enter and should be placed, or remain, in isolation.
- Social distancing maintained by all groups where possible. This includes the competing athletes and support staff on the bench and field of play, such as during any disputes between players and referees, or scoring celebrations.
- Dressing room usage should be minimised. However, showers can be used.
- Competition delivery partners and elite sports organisations should appoint a named Covid-19 officer to be responsible for oversight of

all planning and communications.

Premier League chief executive Richard Masters "welcomed" the decision, adding: "We have provisionally planned to restart the Premier League on 17 June, but there is still much work to be done to ensure the safety of everyone involved. If all goes well, we will be thrilled to resume the 2019-20 season in just over two weeks' time."

The government announced that people will be able to exercise outside with up to five others from different households, provided social distancing guidelines were followed; people who play team sports can meet to train together and do things like conditioning or fitness sessions, although physical contact was not allowed. It allowed parents to accompany their children to coaching sessions carried out on a one-to-one basis or in small groups.

Declaring the season null and void was never a possibility in Jordan Henderson's mind. When asked if he was worried that Liverpool could be cruelly denied the title, Henderson responded: 'Not really. I think obviously for us we still think we've got work to do, and we have. We've got nine games left, and we want to win as many of them as possible. I was always under the impression that, not only for us but for the rest of the league, it needed finishing at some point. We're all back training now, so we've been working hard. It's been good to get back, get some good sessions in. It sort of eased us back in again, a little bit of light training, some decent sessions. And then obviously, we went into the bigger group now and full-contact training, so that's been really good.'

Seeing his team-mates on a daily basis filled him with joy, 'That's been brilliant, just being back and obviously training. Seeing the lads on a day-to-day basis again and just having that banter. You do miss it, so it's nice to be back and hopefully we can just continue like this until the games get played again.'

Klopp said of being able to have the whole group together: "It's absolutely brilliant, a massive difference. The weather is just outstanding, it means all the things we have to do outside – we don't have changing rooms here, that makes it all slightly difficult – but with the weather it's absolutely no problem, it's rather nice to do it this way. So, we enjoy it a lot. We could work on all the things we wanted to work on. The first week was already really good with the small groups, I enjoyed that as well, because it was just important to get on track again, to get used to the pitch and ball and boots and all that stuff. And now we work on tactical things, that works really well.

"The boys are still the same really good bunch of boys – and that helps a lot. We are in a good moment, we enjoy it. Hopefully we can make progress in the next two or three weeks, there are a lot of things that need to be organised still, obviously. We need to get hopefully a couple of [bits of] information but we take it like it is and use each second we are together."

Social distancing, hygiene protocols, one-way systems, temperature checks on arrival and strict measures on access to the various areas of the training facility were just some of the health and safety procedures. "It's [been] a massive organisational challenge, to be honest," said Klopp. "What Ray Haughan did in that department is unbelievable – where we can park, where we can walk and all that stuff. When you make the step from 10 players of two groups of five, to nearly 30, that's massive. And we still have to stick to the same things. So, we are fully concentrated when we come in here, let me say it like this; that we do the right things, that we get the temperature tested and all these things. It's not like it usually is. It's completely fine but it's just when you come here it's not like, 'Yippee!' – you think, 'Where do I have to drive, where is somebody who gets my temperature?' and all that stuff. That's how it is in the moment."

Klopp described this period as being similar to a pre-season schedule in terms of the training work being done with players to raise their match fitness and sharpness. "We don't have to be match-fit now. We try it with increasing intensity, day by day, but we have to be fit on the 19th or 20th, whichever day they will give us against Everton, I think. That's the moment when we want to be at 100 per cent. It's roundabout three weeks until then, that's good. We want to use that and we will. It's our pre-season; how I said, we don't expect a long break in between the seasons, so this is a very important period for us. We never had nine weeks without football training in our lives – since we played football, pretty much. That's all different but interesting as well. We enjoy the situation, that's really all good. And it makes all the difference for us, to be honest, to come together and have this hour or two here together. You get this contact, feedback as well on the pitch directly, not via a computer or a screen. It's a massive, massive lift."

"That's what we were all waiting for," Klopp said of the news of the provisional restart. "But now it's always like this. You were waiting for that, somebody tells us we could start, that's good. Now we know, from a training point of view, what we have to do when and when we have to be at 100 per cent in the best way, how we can train in different intensities. That was very important. Now, of course, it's more and more interesting when we play where, the times are really important because we will see how we can organise the travel stuff. So, the situation keeps us busy, that's absolutely OK. But on the pitch everything is fine, that's really great. Around, we organise it as good as possible and use the situation.

"I have missed it so much it's unbelievable. I know it's not the most important thing in life but it is my passion. I hope the people are looking forward to it because we are."

Klopp insisted there was still "a lot of work to do" and Liverpool "want to win as many games as possible" as he was taking nothing for granted. "It's nice to think about it but we are not champions yet and we know that. We know we are close but close is not there. There are 27 points left for us and we will try everything to take them all. We are still not champions. We have to play football games and we have to win them. We don't want to stop winning after two games or whatever it is. I don't see results written in the stars; we have to work really hard."

Henderson pointed out that playing at Anfield and lifting the trophy without fans present would be "pretty strange". Klopp said celebrations with fans would happen eventually and "there will be a parade" when it is safe for supporters to gather in large numbers.

"If we become champions, whatever celebrations are possible we will do as a team internally and with all our supporters in the moment we are allowed to do so again. I can promise that if it happens, there will be a parade as well. Whenever. Who cares! We only need one day when everybody is able to come and then we will do that."

Mark Roberts, the national lead for football policing, said six matches could be moved at the request of local police forces. Those fixtures included the Merseyside derby as well as Manchester City v Liverpool. Merseyside Police said "in relation to crime and disorder" it had "no objections" to the derby being played at Goodison Park, and it would be "ready to provide whatever policing is required of us". Klopp "would love" to play their home games at Anfield but there was no advantage when crowds are absent, as shown by results since the

Bundesliga resumed. "We will not have the help from the crowd but no team will have that so where is the advantage? Whoever we play it is the same situation which is why I'm not too worried about it. We have tried to simulate the situation by training in the stadium and getting used to it. If you look at Germany, they have not had a lot of home wins. If the alternative is not to play at all, then I will play wherever you want. I don't care."

Henderson and Mane benefitted from the enforced break as their bodies have been able to 'rest'. Klopp's players returned to training "in good shape", some able to rest "for the first time in ages" following heavy schedules. "Some of them were better than last summer after a shorter break. When we start, we will have had four weeks - three weeks of contact training together - and that should be enough, it has to be enough. You never know after a summer break how you will be when the season starts again and it is a little bit similar to this time.

'It's like a summer break, just much longer because usually the players don't have that long off but we were in contact constantly. The boys were busy, the boys came back here and looked great. We did tests with them and some of them were better than last summer. It was not the break you want because it was stressful, mindset wise, nobody knew how it will be. That's not a holiday, we were all worried about the situation but the body could rest for the first time for ages for some of my players.

'Jordan Henderson or Sadio Mane have had two weeks off in the last two summer breaks. From that point of view was good. But the challenges after that long period with no football, they trained pretty much everyday, but without football how would it be? That looks now in the moment really good.

"From the first match, we all play for absolutely everything."

Klopp instructed his players to wear face masks and gloves whenever they ventured out during lockdown. "It feels 100% like a secure environment, but we can never be sure there will be nil infections because we still have a normal life. The boys are massively disciplined. It has been nearly 11 weeks already which for people in this age is a true challenge. It is for all of us a challenge, but for them especially. We go to petrol stations, we need fuel, we need food; stuff like this. We wear face masks and I do not understand why everyone in England, especially in close areas, is not wearing a face mask and gloves. It helped in Germany a lot. I am not an expert but it helped there a lot. We told the boys wherever they went, I wanted them to wear face masks and gloves so just from that point of view, nothing can happen. Humans are [at] the most risk from humans. That is how it always was. We are all our biggest enemies sometimes, so we have stay disciplined and we will."

Klopp was surprised more people in England were not wearing face masks as the country eased out of lockdown and while his players were being safeguarded back in training, the rest of society were not being more vigilant. Klopp went on to discuss the club's preparations for the season. "The environment itself, the training ground [and] around the matches, that will be 100% safe. Everybody is doing everything you can imagine so nothing happens there. These young boys physically are in incredible shape. I am not worried about them; if I was, I would not be here."

Klopp backed Liverpool fans to behave sensibly around the games that could see his team crowned champions with the first fixture back the Merseyside Derby with Everton confident it would be staged at Goodison Park, after asking Liverpool City Council to convene their Safety Advisory Group. Klopp said: 'We will speak to our supporters, 100 per cent. But our fans will not make something negative out of it. If we win, we will have our celebrations as a team. If it happens there can be a parade in the future, we only need one day when everyone comes.'

Klopp led a sing-a-long with his players to wish club legend Steven Gerrard happy returns on his 40th birthday. Players and coaching staff gathered at their Melwood training ground to pay tribute to the Anfield icon on his special day before a training session. Klopp marked the occasion by signing 'Happy Birthday' along with his entire squad in a number of different languages, as is now custom under the German manager, in a video posted on the club's Twitter page.

The training session focused on a series of 11vs11 scenarios to increase their readiness for match situations. The players took a moment during the workout to show their support for the racial justice protests taking place across the United States, and in London by taking a knee in the centre circle and posted "Unity is strength" on social media following the police killing of George Floyd.

The two sides donned home and away kits as Mane rounded Adrian for one goal before Keita held off Joe Gomez for a second. Assistant coach Pepijn Lijnders said: "We wanted to give the players the feeling of playing and competing without a crowd. We are just going step by step back to our way of playing, knowing that we have to work hard in training and be really committed to our principles to reach the same level that we had. Today was an important step in that direction; firstly getting familiar with the process around the games and secondly giving our squad playing time and competition very close to the environment that we will have in the future."

Klopp promised he would do "whatever is in his power" for the club to celebrate a first title in 30 years together with supporters when it is safe to do so, insisting the club must control how the accomplishment is defined to them. "I never thought 'oh in the year we can become champions this happens' and maybe it's kind of a destiny," Klopp told The Anfield Wrap from Melwood during an interview conducted over Zoom. "This club went through so many difficult moments in the past. This situation is still absolutely doable from a football point of view. It's not perfect. Of course it's not perfect. But we decide what it means to us."

Pointing to his head and then his heart, Klopp continued: "We decide what it means for us here and here. We will celebrate it together and if it's not allowed and not possible for that moment, then we will do it at an appropriate time. We will wait and then we will come together with millions of people to celebrate. If anybody thinks 'oh, they're a little bit crazy,' I couldn't care less. If it will happen, it would have been an absolutely incredible ride with all the things that happened last year (missing out on the title to Manchester City by a point) and before that losing the Champions League final (to Real Madrid in Kiev). It would be an exceptional celebration. Most people will never, ever forget these tough times. We have more time to find the right moment to enjoy it together. And then we can say like three or four weeks before 'make sure that you are all ready' and we do it. Then we can show again how special we are as a club, and that we don't care what others think about us, if they say that we are a little bit mad or whatever. We just enjoy ourselves and celebrate what we are, who we are and what we've won and that would be my absolute dream. So I really can't wait. I can promise, whatever is in my power, I'll do to make sure that we'll have a proper parade – whenever that will be."

He indicated the club's desire to make sure they are the pacesetters again next season. "There's a lot of yards still to go. We want to go for everything. We want to go for the maximum points we can get. That's how it is now. This could be the most special season, with or without Covid-19. We have to make sure that we just stay on track, because the next season will come up and we have to be ready for that as well. Other teams will work to have what we have so we have to give ourselves this chance again."

GAME ON

In this "unprecedented" season, this was the first, and no doubt last, time anyone sees a "pre-season friendly" at the start of June.

Jurgen Klopp was pleased with the shape his side after they thrashed Blackburn 6-0 behind closed doors at Anfield. Sadio Mane, Naby Keita and Takumi Minamino all scored in the first half, Joel Matip and Ki-Jana Hoever got second half goals before youngster Leighton Clarkson scored their sixth. Klopp was full of prise for the new boy, "It is just so nice. Not only the goal, but when you see the situations when he came on, I think the first pass was between the two strikers, he got it in the No.6 position where he is calm, turns and passes the ball out." Klopp praised a number of the other academy players who featured, adding: "We can teach the boys a lot, but they have to bring a lot. Obviously the basis for Leighton is not too bad and Jake [Cain] did really well, as well. All of the boys. For Sepp [Van den Berg] it is always hard for centre-halves. We have four, so sitting outside [but] he looks really promising in training sessions. Ki-Jana, centre-half and right-back and looks really good. You see them – when Harvey [Elliott], Curtis [Jones] and Neco [Williams] played, it looked good as well. It's coming, it's nice and nice they are here and training with us. The way we play helps the players to feel safe; everybody is defending and you should never feel alone in a big area where you have no chance to sort the situation. That's what I really like and for the boys it was really good. Klopp also enthused about his players' general approach, "It looked really good. Shape is important, form and things like this are important of course, but it is attitude. It is work-rate. It is things like, "are you ready to go for these kind of things? In the first game, we don't have to be football-wise on our highest level, but we need to show that we are ready for competition, that we are ready to defend, that we are ready to find solutions to solve problems or find solutions for difficult situations. That's what we have to be – and I saw that today. The boys really did well and that's how they've looked since we've been back – and how they looked before we were away, so [it's] so far, so good."

Klopp added, "It was not only a workout; for us, it was a really important test. It looked really good, obviously. It looked really good, pretty much from the beginning. Yes, you have to get used again to playing against a deep-defending side and stuff like this. Blackburn had a playing build-up from time to time, so we could work on the high press as well. So [the] counter-press was brilliant, the football was really good, the goals were nice and it was a really good afternoon. I am really thankful that Blackburn came here and we could do that, so I wish them all the best. We wanted the players to go for 45 minutes [but] because of a few little issues we couldn't do that, so we didn't have enough 'first-team players', I would say, so that's why we decided to let three players go for 60 minutes. That's ok. It looked really good, obviously. It looked really good, pretty much from the beginning."

Klopp was 'completely okay' playing with no fans, "Yes, it's different, of course. You need to get used to it, but I like it. After three times, it is completely okay. I thought before – and I don't have experience in this area – that it would be really awkward, but we have to create our own atmosphere in the games. We have to be lively as well, we have to be animated and stuff like this. Being positive about the things that have happened and so on, that's how you can create an atmosphere – and it's what we have to do as well. Apart from that, it is Anfield."

Klopp says that it is not just the new atmosphere in the stadium that needs getting used to, but there are so many new off-the-field practices. "Everything is different. The boys now go home and they didn't have a shower. It was raining before the game, so that would have been funny if there had been really hard rain and then you drive home in your own car and you didn't have a shower. Our meeting was here in the boardroom. We want to have it like this, we can organise it differently at Anfield when we play here, but we have no clue how it'll be at away games and we need to create as awkward-as-possible situations just to not be surprised. We want to focus completely on football and whatever happens around the games, we just take it like it is."

It was a chance to test some of the new protocols that were finalised that week by the Premier League; players were encouraged not to spit or clear their noses and not to break social distancing during goal celebrations, no ball boys or girls, sterilised replacement balls. The new normal in the Premier League. While everyone involved in German football had to wear masks, until they actually played, players were exempt from masks even in the changing room or on the bench, although the fourth official as well as doctors and physios had to wear them. Players and coaching staff were told not to encroach on the referee or his assistants during the game, and technical areas would be zealously policed by fourth officials.

Players would emerge from the tunnel in small groups, the pre-match line-up was abandoned and the fourth official and medical staff wearing face coverings. There would be a minute's silence to remember those who died with coronavirus before the first matches. Heart-shaped badges in tribute of frontline NHS staff would be worn on kits.

Clubs agreed to a range of medical and operational protocols for the restart of the season with strict limits on those allowed into stadiums on match days and grounds will be split into zones, including the tunnel and pitch side. Only 300 people would be in each stadium, with no more than 110 in the 'red zone' including players, club staff and officials.

There was deep cleaning of corner flags, goalposts, substitution boards and match balls before and after each fixture. Some extra disinfection, such as of the substitution board after it is used, would take place during matches and at half-time, while other work was carried out during drinks breaks if they were permitted by the league. The medical protocols stipulated how squads and coaching staff must travel to and from games, observing social distancing. Clubs were encouraged to fly on longer away trips to limit use of hotels, and every player and coach would be temperature checked before they arrived at the stadium. Players would use hand sanitiser when they entered and left the field.

There would be strict limits on the number of people permitted at stadiums on match-days and grounds will be split into a green, amber and red zone, with the latter area which includes the tunnel and pitch limited at 110.

Mandatory one-minute drinks breaks in every half to ensure players were able to rehydrate from personalised water bottles. The precise timing of the water break was at the discretion of the referee, but expected towards the midway point of each half and take place even during night matches for hygiene reasons.

Where road travel was more practical ahead of local derbies for example the multiple coaches were likely to be used, while some clubs altered the lay-out of the coaches they normally use to facilitate social distancing. Some clubs were striving to produce programmes to avoid disappointing collectors, which could be ordered on line. The Premier League rolled out the slogan "Support your club. Stay safe. Follow at home". The slogan was an echo of the Government at the start of the coronavirus lockdown that read: "Stay at home. Protect the NHS. Save lives". Clubs reminded fans not to congregate at a stadium during a match, hoping the remaining 92 fixtures would be played on a home and away basis although the situation remained under review.

A YouGov poll showed ongoing worries among the public as nearly half of the country - 48 per cent - believed that top-flight resumed too soon with 39 per cent of football supporters didn't feel the season should be resuming in just five days time. Only 26 per cent of the nation felt it is the right time for the Premier League to be returning with concerns over the pandemic still very much lingering. Two per cent of the public and four per cent of Premier League fans felt the season was coming back too late.

For the first dozen games Premier League players' names would be replaced on the back of their shirts with 'Black Lives Matter'. The Premier League supported any player who choose to 'take a knee' before or during matches. "We, the players, stand together with the singular objective of eradicating racial prejudice," read a statement. In a joint message from all 20 clubs, players added that they were committed to "a global society of inclusion, respect, and equal opportunities for all, regardless of their colour or creed". A Black Lives Matter badge featured on all playing shirts for the rest of the season alongside a badge thanking NHS staff.

Despite al the focus on the restart, there was quite a bit of activity, comings and goings at Anfield. Nantes signed Pedro Chirivella on a free transfer after his contract expired at Anfield. The 23-year-old had moved to Liverpool in 2015 from Valencia's academy but made just 11 first team appearances in his five years with the Reds, with most of those coming in cup competitions. Owen Beck signed his first professional contract following in the footsteps of his great uncle Ian Rush. Beck, a left-back, thrilled his uncle with the news. Liverpool legend Rush tweeted 'First pro contract @OwenBeck10 very proud!' The talented youngster had been called up by Wales at U17 level. Beck joined Liverpool from Stoke when he was an U13 player. Loris Karius was back and prepared to stay and fight for his place at Anfield. The 26-year-old keeper cut short a mediocre two-year loan spell at Besiktas. "I'm not in a pressure situation at all, I don't have to change. I can move forward in training at Liverpool. As the second-choice goalkeeper in England you know that you get your chances. I am currently at the best club in the world, play for titles, have the highest level around me every day in training. I am fully aware that I am in a good position to be in Liverpool. I have great conditions there.'

Jadon Sancho was a revelation at Borussia Dortmund, tracked by a host of elite teams but Steve McManaman didn't want Liverpool drawn into a bidding war. "Klopp will bring players in, particularly when those out of contract leave. It's just a matter of timing, but with the team they've got at the moment - why would you spend nearly £100m on a 20-year-old? I don't mean it disparagingly. Sancho might suit Liverpool and he'd definitely suit Manchester United. I've watched him lots of times and he's having a wonderful season. Ideally I think he should stay at Dortmund where he's already playing Champions League football and flourishing."

Timo Werner had been a long standing target but the German striker was about to join Chelsea. McManaman believed Stamford Bridge was a better destination for the 24-year-old. "He will want first-team action all the time and you simply can't guarantee that at Liverpool. The main thing for Klopp is to keep a strong and professional core of 18 or 19 players who are full internationals but have the right mentality if they're not playing. I think most people get that, but it's hard to bring in a £60m player and say: 'You're probably not going to play every game, we've got people who are just as good as you.' Nowadays new signings want to come in feeling they're going to be first choice in the team."

But the main focus was the restart as there was massive interest, fascination, trepidation, to a large degree and mixed feelings. A Norwich City player was one of two to test positive from the latest round of 1,200 Premier League tests with Norwich beating Spurs 2-1 in a friendly at Tottenham Hotspur Stadium. Spurs confirmed they had no positive tests and said the Canaries player had "no close contacts" with their team. The unnamed player self-isolated for seven days, missing the restart. There were now 16 positive results from 8,687 tests in total.

"It'll be fantastic when it happens but the fans are not going to be there," Steve McManaman observed, "Further down the line, the fans will be allowed in, they can celebrate properly then and have a parade round the city. But you saw the reaction of the fans when Liverpool brought home the Champions League. If they win the league after 30 years, they will celebrate, but it won't be the same as being at the ground and celebrating with the team."

McManaman reckons this new generation of Liverpool players can become the dominant force in English football for years to come. "It's one of the best, if not the best team, in Premier League history," he said. "I know Arsenal's 'invincibles' went undefeated, but until the season was was stopped Liverpool had more points. You need success again next year though. Then you can see if if they're one of the greatest ever Liverpool sides.

"This will be some team if you can then put them alongside Bill Shankly, Bob Paisley and Kenny Dalglish in the history books.

When you talk about really great teams they need to have longevity. And that's the hard part, doing it a second and third time. Liverpool have had sides that have done exactly that on many occasions. Klopp has already won the Champions League, so you hope this is the start of a dynasty for Liverpool."

Klopp's side could comfortably surpass City's record points tally of 100 from 2017-18. The Reds could reach 109 if they won all their remaining games. "Their league record is phenomenal," McManaman said. "Great teams go on to win then win again and be serial winners, but in a one-off season, Liverpool will go down as the best really. It's a great game first up. It's a derby match so they'll have to be at it straight away, they'll have to hit the ground running. And I think they will now say 'we've got nine games left, we want to beat Manchester City's record'."

Jordan Henderson warned against complacency. "We need to be prepared. We need to be raring to go and not get caught cold coming out of the blocks. There's still a lot of work to do and a job to be done. Although we're in a very good position, I still feel that we have got to perform at a high level and finish the season off well. We are still very focused and very determined. For the players it will be different playing in a big game in a stadium where there's no crowd because you can hear everybody talking but we have to embrace it and have the right mindset. The intensity can still be at a high level. If you have the right mindset the intensity can be as high as you want it to be. In that sense, when we return, I expect the intensity to be high and the football enjoyable to watch. When you were little and you used to play for your school there was no crowd watching then really, so you've just got to enjoy your football and appreciate that we are able to go back doing what we love doing. We've got to embrace that and make the best out of the situation that we can.

"If we do manage to do our job properly and get over the line to win the league, then that would be amazing. I'm sure Liverpool fans are desperate for us to get back playing and we as players can't wait to get back playing and finish the job off as best as we can. Although it will be strange to have no fans, winning the Premier League would still be something that we've all dreamed of and something that we all want really badly. It won't take anything away from that."

Henderson was worried about swearing as games in empty grounds make it easier to hear what is being said on the pitch, without the chanting from supporters to drown it out. Henderson advised teammates and his ever-enthusiastic coach to watch their language. "We've got to adapt to that situation and try to keep the swearing down to a minimum! I'm more worried about my language when I'm playing! I don't want to be having to apologise to everybody after every single game so I need to be careful, especially in the heat of the game. I'm sure the manager will have to be careful with his language as well. But he'll also know we can't blame the crowd for not being able to hear what he's saying at certain times of the game."

Klopp wasn't the least bit concerned about when they would celebrate the title properly, maybe with a bottle of beer and this time try not to look as though he is about to topple off the bus! He said: "Most of the people on this planet never have the chance to become champions of the Premier League. For us, it looks like we have the chance so we take it. Then there will be a moment in our life when we have time and the opportunity and it's allowed to celebrate together then we will have a moment, and we will celebrate it in the right manner. Whenever that will be, but we decide how much we enjoy it then."

JUNE

In Merseyside derby history there had been two previous 7pm kick-offs, the first was an FA Cup fifth round tie in March 1967 watched by 106,000; 60,000 at Goodison Park, plus a big screen at Anfield watched by another 46,000! This historic, surreal "Project Restart' had fewer than 300 people dotted around the old 'haunted' arena, played out to a so quiet that a saxophone could be heard coming from somewhere in the vicinity of the stadium, with Joy Division's "Love Will Tear Us Apart" and Gerry Rafferty's "Baker Street" high on the play list.

Jurgen Klopp stressed that football is "not like riding a bike" as no one could be sure how each team would reappear after more than 100 days of lockdown. The Reds were embroiled in one of the best campaigns in Premier League history when the league was halted in March, although they had suffered their only real sticky patch of results at that time. Even so, they went into this Merseyside derby 22 points clear, two wins away from the title, their first for 30 years, their first Premier League title. "I expect us to be in a good shape," said Klopp. "I don't know if we are 100% but Everton have had the same time [off]. It is all about being ready to face problems in a game and finding solutions. In nine weeks not doing anything you can lose almost anything. The players trained every day but we don't train them for a specific moment as we had no idea until a week before that training would start again. Training is completely different if you just want to keep fit or be in the best shape for a specific day. We kept them fit until we knew until we go again and the boys don't lose a lot. Unfortunately it is not like riding a bike. We have to bring 11 or more players together to have the same idea in the same moment."

The 236th Merseyside derby arrived an astonishing 103 days since Liverpool last played, in their home second leg against Atletico Madrid in the Champions League, which saw them exit the tournament they won the previous May. Everton had not beaten them in 21 attempts in all competitions - a record run for either side in this fixture. "Everton will be highly motivated," said Klopp. "Starting a derby in a normal season would be interesting, and now it is our short season it is very interesting. It is a special game for different reasons."

From the players' perspective Trent Alexander-Arnold commented: "If you can imagine your ultimate dream and being so, so close to it - two steps away from it really - and someone saying 'you need to wait over 100 days then you might get it'. It was quite frustrating, but the league position hasn't changed, our mentality hasn't changed and that is to win every game, push boundaries, break records, win the league and be remembered." Not only that but Liverpool fans would have to wait before celebrating as any parade had to be delayed because of restrictions on large gatherings. "You have to wait so long to win the league, then when you do it, you have to wait so long to celebrate it properly," added Alexander-Arnold, who grew up in the Liverpool suburb of West Derby. "The things we see on that day, though, will hopefully be things we will never forget."

Trent said he would auction the boots he wore in the Merseyside derby to raise money for the Nelson Mandela Foundation, which strives for "freedom and equality for all". His boots bore the message 'Black Lives Matter', which replaced player names on shirts for the first 12 matches of the restarted season. "'Do your talking on the pitch.' I've always loved that sentiment. But now we need to speak up in other ways as well," Alexander-Arnold wrote on Twitter. "It can no longer just be our feet where we express ourselves. We have to use our profile, the platforms we have and the spotlight that shines on us to say, it's time for meaningful change. While we have this opportunity, where people are listening - let's speak, let's educate, let's campaign and let's promote the message that better education brings change. This is the moment of change. This is the moment to say enough is enough. This is the moment to make sure it stops now. Racism is a fire that is now burnt out."

Klopp believes society should look to football and follow its lead with regard to how the game handles racism. "I think equality should be in all parts of society, not just in football. You can see at each level there are so many smart people out there and the last thing you should look for is the colour of someone's skin. Being smart has nothing to do with your skin colour, it has only to do with who you are and you don't have to be smart you can be likeable, lovable, you can be funny or whatever. It has nothing to do with your skin colour. For us in football it is the most natural thing. I struggle a little bit to talk about it because we live it completely different. For us they are all the same, absolutely the same. So if there is one thing you can learn from football it is this."

Klopp was hopeful football had learned lessons during the pandemic, most important of all: "We never want to play behind closed doors again". He hoped the sterile atmosphere of an empty Goodison Park would not deter his players from performing at the top of their abilities, "No one should compare [performances with and without fans] because none of the famous European nights at Anfield would have happened without the supporters. You can't comeback - OK you can comeback - but it is not as likely [without fans] and the reason for this habit of things like this happening at Anfield is the crowd of course. There is no doubt about that. The holy grail of what you dream to happen in your career is to be in front of a packed stadium and to score a decisive goal in the last second in your home ground. We've known for a while it will not happen like this and you only have to remind yourself a little bit we all started playing football without crowds and we loved the game anyway."

Everton had a raft of injuries in midfield, with Schneiderlin, Jean-Philippe Gbamin and Delph out, defender Mina and Walcott sidelined but Andre Gomes was available. Alisson was fit after a hip problem. Salah and Robertson overcame fitness concerns.

Mark Lawrenson's prediction: "I am expecting Liverpool to be the team trying to set the pace but it is optimistic to expect the kind of performance that has put them so far clear at the top of the table. As good as the Reds' front three are, they are only brilliant when they are really sharp and I don't think they will be. I would not be surprised if Everton are cautious, play three at the back and sit in a little bit - they don't want to get torn apart - so because of all that I can see it being a close game. But the way Liverpool's season has gone so far, I am still going to go with them to find a way of winning. We already know they are capable of doing that when they are not at their best."

Manchester City's 3-0 victory over Arsenal on Wednesday meant Guardiola's side held on to the trophy for a few more days and Everton breathed a sigh of relief as they avoided the possibility of seeing their rivals winning the title at Goodison Park. The Reds, though, can equal their longest top-flight unbeaten streak versus a single opponent of 19 matches; Liverpool are unbeaten in 21 matches against Everton in all competitions (W11, D10), a record run without defeat for either club in this fixture. Everton had not won the second league Merseyside derby of a season since 1987-88, a 1-0 victory at Goodison Park.

Everton went three league matches without a win, but were unbeaten at home in the past seven league games, although behind closed doors if was proving, as it did in Germany, that home advantage counted for little. Their tally of 18 points under Carlo Ancelotti was only been bettered by Liverpool, Manchester City and Manchester United during the same period.

Ancelotti, as manager of Real Madrid and Napoli, had won all three competitive home matches as a manager versus Klopp, then managing Borussia Dortmund and Liverpool, by an aggregate of 6-0. Liverpool's defeat at Watford in their most recent Premier League away fixture ended a run of eight successive victories on the road. They could lose four successive away matches in all competitions for the first time since April 2012 under Kenny Dalglish.

Liverpool's record of 27 wins, one draw and one defeat was the best by any club after 29 matches in the history of the top five European leagues. The Reds required 19 points out of a possible 27 to break City's top-flight record tally of 100. But Liverpool had conceded six goals in their last three league fixtures, following a run of letting in just one in 11 matches.

Origi had scored five in seven against Everton in all competitions. He needed one to draw level with Robbie Fowler's Merseyside derby total of six while Firmino failed to score in any of his nine Merseyside derby appearances in all competitions.

Klopp pondered what he would tell his players just before the game, in the final pre-match briefing, knowing that he had quite a few selection issues and his team lost four out of six games before football was suspended. The Reds were beaten in both legs by Atletico Madrid as they went out of the Champions League, while Chelsea knocked Klopp's side out of the FA Cup.

Liverpool also suffered a surprise 3-0 league defeat at Watford, their two wins between 18 February and 11 March coming against struggling West Ham and Bournemouth.

Klopp said: "The rest should be different because all the games are different. It's obviously a specific situation. I have an idea of what I will tell them, but there are still a few hours until then. A few things can go through my mind, but in the end I've done it a few times so I should be fine. You cannot win the game in the meeting, I think you can lose it. I'm not sure but I think if you say completely the wrong things then maybe you can lose it there, but you cannot win it. In the end, we have to give the right information and the boys have to do the job."

Jamie Carragher compared Klopp to Shankly, in that supporters hung on his every word and has a 'special quality' to say the right thing. "Like Shankly, the supporters look to what Klopp says about every situation – and he always finds the right words. Jurgen claims he doesn't prepare what he's going to say, but I don't know if I believe him. He has a great ability to communicate, he has this special quality to say the right thing. He brings people with him – and makes people believe in him. Throughout the pandemic, he didn't ever say anything that crossed the line. It wasn't ever about wanting Liverpool to win the league and not being worried about what the world was going through, although he was so close. He always said the right words – not only for Liverpool fans, but for football. Klopp can be very funny, but, on the flipside, when something serious happens, it feels like he is the go-to manager for the league. He always nails what needs to be said and how people are feeling."

SUNDAY JUNE 21 - PREMIER LEAGUE

EVERTON 0
LIVERPOOL 0
Attendance: approximately 300

There were shock selections as top scorer Mo Salah was relegated to the bench along with Wijnaldum and Matip was preferred to Gomez with Keita in midfield and Minamino in attack making his first Premier League start. Henderson failed to make the squad, replaced by Milner. Everton gave a first Premier League start to 19-year-old Liverpool-born forward Anthony Gordon. Klopp explained, "Mo, Robbo and Shaq were the only three who couldn't train all the time. Mo is ready for the bench, we have to listen to the medics. Now we are here. This stadium is a bit calmer, it is good."

A police helicopter flew over Goodison Park, there was a strong police presence around the stadium, although there were very few fans gathered outside. Police horses were in Stanley Park but it was quiet. Grey skies over Merseyside after a blustery day of sunshine and showers as Liverpool's players got changed in a portakabin erected in the car park behind the Sir Philip Carter Park Stand on arrival and entered in a corner of the stadium while Everton emerged from the usual tunnel.

Inside the stadium it was also quiet as Klopp strolled on the pitch wearing a bright red Liverpool mask. Kenny Dalglish was sat in the stands after his recovery from coronavirus.

There was heavy rain as Everton appeared on the pitch accompanied by the Z-Cars anthem. As featured in all the preceding games, there was a moment of reflection for those affected by coronavirus before the players and referee Mike Dean took a knee to support the Black Lives Matter campaign. Mane was so eager he forget about the pre match ritual and instead charged up the pitch. Realising his error, he jogged back to his own half and took the knee. Millions watched around the world at this powerful anti-racism statement.

The referee also took a knee, but Mike Dean arrived back from lockdown with a new grizzly grey beard and was immediately and mercilessly mocked on Twitter. One Twitter user wrote: "Lot to take in with the derby in an empty Goodison Park but Mike Dean reffing it with a lockdown beard is on the top of my thoughts." Another said: "Mike Dean in a full beard you just know he's going to misbehave." One added: "That beard has aged Mike Dean about 20 years." One even joked: "Tremendous amount of respect for Mike Dean's lockdown beard, the master of making the story all about himself." While another said: "Is that Mike Dean or an obsessed sea captain chasing a white whale? That beard makes it hard to tell." Another even tried to get it trending, tweeting: "Surely Mike Dean's beard will be trending soon. #mikedeansbeard".

James Milner pulled up injured just before half time so Joe Gomez came on, as there had been numerous injuries in the opening series of games. Since the Premier League resumed, there had only been three first-half goals in 11 Premier League matches, and this was no different, it was goalless at the interval, Salah was already warming up midway through the first half but it was Oxlade-Chamberlain on for Minamino in a like-for-like switch to play on the right flank.

AT half-time Mark Lawrenson on BBC Radio 5 Live observed: "It feels like someone has got the players out of a freezer and they've not quite defrosted yet."

Klopp made a double change. Origi and Wijnaldum on, Keita and

A minute's silence was observed for the victims of coronavirus before each Premier League game.

Firmino off after Everton sent on Sigurdsson for teenager Gordon. Then with around 18 minutes left, Klopp was forced to make his fifth and final substitution with Matip going down with an injured ankle, Lovren was on. So, no chance of bringing on Salah even for a final flourish.

    A close range flick by Calvert-Lewin was smartly saved by Alisson but it fell to Tom Davies whose first time attempt rolled against the post and away after being partly blocked by Gomes desperate lunge. Liverpool just about survived as Richarlison wiggled his way into a shooting position before forcing Alisson into another smart save as Everton saved their best to last and almost snatched victory, although Fabinho free kick forced Pickford to tip it over. Liverpool had dominated possession but produced few chances, with Matip heading wide from a free-kick.

    Ancelotti's predecessor Marco Silva had been sacked after a 5-2 derby capitulation at Anfield in December but the hugely successful Italian made a huge the difference. Everton were superbly organised defensively. Klopp admitted his side rode their luck during their largely disappointing draw. "We are not too snobby to accept a point in an away game like this at Everton. It was a real fight. Both teams showed they understand it's a derby even without a crowd. It was intense, physical, and all players were really involved and really in the game. I liked our defending and high midfield press but we didn't have enough chances for the possession we had. We were dominant but they had the biggest chance and that's how it is. We were lucky in that moment. It came out of the blue, but apart from that, we were in control. We didn't have a lot of chances; most of the time we were dominant but they had the biggest chance - that's how it is. In the end, Everton defended really well and we were not smart enough to use the space we had.

"You saw the derbies we had here before - they were never really better, I have to say! The point is one we deserve. When I think of all the derbies here, they looked pretty similar - the result is similar. At Anfield the games are slightly better. Each team is fighting like crazy so in the end there is not a lot of football. There is space for improvement for us here at Goodison; I like football when it's slightly different but that's how it is; we had a proper fight, it was intense and we were ready for that. The players were really in the game, so that's good. I really liked our defending.; the high press, midfield press, counter-press good. We won a lot of balls. Everton were well organised so we had to run a lot but we looked fit and ready.

"I liked the intensity level of the game from my boys, the high press, but I didn't like too much the rhythm - but we cannot force that. I saw four weeks (of) training sessions and I was happy. It was just a difficult game. Physically we were ready, which was important. The defensive stuff was there, I liked offensively but you need moments. If you score in a moment it can change a situation. The performance level was OK, we played a year ago in April here, we've played in December here - the games look always the same. We have to respect the opponent as well and Everton were here to make our lives difficult and they could have won the game. A point is a deserved result."

Klopp lavished praise on his keeper Allison for his vital late save from Calvert-Lewin: "We should not take it for granted. Absolutely outstanding. That is what a world class goalie is - nothing to do for pretty much 90 minutes and then he was there. He saved us a point, it was not the first one."

Ancelotti said: "It was not an open game because we did not want an open game. The performance was good against a strong team. We showed good personality and character. A draw is fair. Honestly we were really close to winning but it was a tough game, difficult game.

We performed really well. We were focused, we sacrificed. We had opportunities to score at the end. Liverpool played a good game, they had more possession but defensively we were really good. Offensively we tried to build from the back. They pressed really high and it was difficult to find a solution from the back so we decided to play more long ball."

Klopp explained his decision to substitute Minamino at half-time, suggesting it was all part of his pre-match plan. "Before the game I already had the idea that I wanted to change early. I just wanted to wait a little bit until somebody had lesser fresh legs. We will use the opportunity that five changes give you. Taki played well, he was in the game, in the beginning it was a bit difficult. But then there was no need for a second change. Naby also did really well. It was a good performance and it was nothing to do with Taki's performance. It was purely my idea"

Klopp learned a lot about the physical condition of his players. "We know more now about the physicality, so far so good. But I saw Crystal Palace yesterday and they look like a well-oiled machine so it will be a tough job. Of course we want to make more chances; we have to more clear in situations - pass the ball, shoot in the right moment, more crosses. The second half we started to do that better but Everton defended really well; they tried to take care of Sadio Mane and Trent Alexander-Arnold and we were not smart enough to use the space for somebody else. That's normal when you begin to play again but a lot of things were very good.

"Now I know we are ready because you don't know 100 per cent if we did enough (during the break), but we can involve fresh legs on Wednesday. Now we've got three days. Crystal Palace looked good on Saturday and we have to make sure we are ready for Wednesday. Alex Oxlade-Chamberlain was lively, Naby Keita looked absolutely good.

Matip endured a "really painful" problem with his big toe, while Milner was likely to be back in time for the trip to City. "Milly felt a hamstring a little bit, but we had this in the past. Milly is not often injured and hopefully it is not serious. He is smart enough to show up in the moment when he feels it, so hopefully it was the right moment. Maybe not Wednesday, but after that I would hope [he is available] Joel was unlucky and we had to make a quick decision. It was a situation with Richarlison and he bent or stretched his big toe. I don't think a lot of people have had that; it is really painful, but hopefully it settles, the pain settles and then we will see. I hope nothing serious has happened, but I don't know yet."

Klopp overtook Bob Paisley' record of ten games unbeaten in Merseyside derbies. In Klopp's 11 derbies as Reds' boss, he had seven wins and four draws, with an aggregate of 18-5. The goalless draw does mean, however, that the last three derbies at Everton have ended similarly, with the last derby goal scored at Goodison being Mane's dramatic late winner in December 2016.

The most important record was one which Liverpool already held, the longest unbeaten run in the history of the derby. The Reds hadn't lost to Everton since 2010, extending their run to 22.

Only a few supporters gathered before kick-off and a small group took photographs of players as they drove out of the stadium on to Goodison Road less than an hour after the final whistle. It was all so much of an anti-climax, long forgotten as the next days could finally bring that title.

The point left the Reds 23 points clear at the top of the table. Only in the unlikely scenario of City dropping points at home to Burnley on Monday, Liverpool could still win the title on Wednesday against Crystal Palace at Anfield.

OTHER SCORES

WEDNESDAY 17 JUNE
Aston Villa 0 Sheffield United 0
Manchester City 3 Arsenal 0

FRIDAY 19 JUNE
Norwich City 0 Southampton 3
Tottenham Hotspur 1 Manchester United 1

SATURDAY 20 JUNE
Watford 1 Leicester City 1
Brighton 2 Arsenal 1
West Ham United 0 Wolves 2
AFC Bournemouth 0 Crystal Palace 2

SUNDAY 21 JUNE
Newcastle United 3 Sheffield United 0
Aston Villa 1 Chelsea 2

MONDAY 22 JUNE
Manchester City 5 Burnley 0

★

Jurgen Klopp was eagerly looking forward to the first game back at Anfield, determined to consign the Merseyside derby to the past, and to look forward. He explained: "The derby was an example. We took it like it is. We aren't thinking about it any more." As for the Anfield return without fans, "It's still a home game, we know where things are. It feels already good when you walk into our dressing room. We want to see it as a home game on the pitch as well."

Klopp accepted it would be a surreal atmosphere, though, on match day without their fervent fans to raise the temp. "It will be very different. We trained for four weeks, we knew it (was coming). Football isn't the same without fans, 100% wouldn't be the same game without them. It is a period without them and we have to make the best of it."

Klopp was confident there would not be a large gathering of fans, if indeed, any fans, gathering outside of Anfield for the first game back.

He also wanted to play City at their ground, as discussions continued whether the Manchester police would permit it, particularly if it turned out to be the title decider. Klopp argued: "The whole period we are in showed the massive majority of people behave responsibly. I wasn't worried about it." After initial fears from authorities over Liverpool's return game at Everton, no supporters congregated around Goodison Park, with Merseyside Police praising fans of both clubs for "coming together" in staying away. For Klopp, it was a "good example" of why the clash with City can and should be held in Manchester, particularly due to the infrastructure around the Etihad. "Maybe I don't know enough about the history of English football that I could be concerned about the City game against us. The City stadium is pretty well-located to close it down, if somebody would be there it would not be close to the stadium. But I don't see that, the whole period which we are in showed that the massive majority of people really behaved responsibly and serious, and took the situation how it is. The discipline level is probably higher than ever before, so I was not worried about that.

"I know football fans since I'm five years old, and 98 percent of them are completely fine and have the same view on life as I have and love similar things that I do. In this moment in time I was not worried

June

about that, but maybe I don't know enough about it. I hope that we can do it there. Sunday was a good example, 100 percent." But the situation was being played out while lockdown was being eased, but there was still a remote chance of the competition being halted if there was any outbreak of the virus among the players. The Premier League announced that just one positive test from the 1,829 that were carried out on players and club staff between Wednesday and Sunday at the outset of Project Restart.

The backdrop to the return of football to Anfield could not be more stark as the players or club staff member who tested positive self-isolate for a period of seven days, likely have to miss the next round of fixtures. A statement read: 'The Premier League can today confirm that between Wednesday June 17 and Sunday June 21, 1,829 players and club staff were tested for COVID-19. Of these, one person has tested positive. Players or club staff who have tested positive will now self-isolate for a period of seven days. The Premier League is providing this aggregated information for the purposes of competition integrity and transparency. No specific details as to clubs or individuals will be provided by the League and results will be made public after each round of testing.'

The easing of lockdown was the background to Liverpool's return to Anfield, but ahead of it City ensured that it was not going to be a procession to the title as Phil Foden and Riyad Mahrez both scored twice as City thrashed Burnley to ensure Liverpool had to wait a little longer to wrap up the title. Three first-half goals ensure City enjoyed one of their most comfortable wins at the Etihad Stadium, with Foden's superb long-range strike breaking the deadlock before Mahrez's double just before the break. The Algerian's fine solo effort made it 2-0 before he added another from the spot after Ben Mee fouled Aguero, with the penalty being awarded by the video assistant referee. It was all too easy against a Burnley side that did not name their full complement of substitutes for their first game since the restart after several players' contracts were not renewed for the last portion of the season.

Foden played a starring role in the rout, starting the move that saw Bernardo Silva tee up David Silva to make it 4-0 soon after the break, and then adding a fifth himself after Jesus helped on a David Silva cross. Guardiola's side were 20 points behind the leaders with eight league games remaining.

Burnley issued a strongly worded condemnation during the game after a plane carrying a banner reading 'White Lives Matter Burnley' was flown over the ground shortly after kick-off. Burnley "strongly condemned" those behind a banner that was towed by an aircraft over Etihad Stadium during Monday's match. The aircraft circled over the stadium just after kick-off. Burnley and City players and staff had taken a knee in support of the Black Lives Matter movement moments earlier. "Burnley strongly condemns the actions of those responsible for the aircraft and offensive banner," said the club. "We wish to make it clear that those responsible are not welcome at Turf Moor. We apologise unreservedly to the Premier League, to Manchester City and to all those helping to promote Black Lives Matter." Burnley added that the banner "in no way represents" what the club stands for and that they will "work fully with the authorities to identify those responsible and take appropriate action". Burnley captain Ben Mee said he and his teammates also condemned the banner. "We're ashamed, we're embarrassed," Mee told BBC Radio 5 Live. "It's a minority of our supporters - I know I speak for a massive part of our support who distance ourselves from anything like that. It definitely had a massive impact on us to see that in the sky. We are embarrassed that our name was in it, that they tried to attach it to our club - it doesn't belong anywhere near our club. Fans like that don't deserve to be around football." Both Burnley and City were wearing shirts with the players' names replaced with 'Black Lives Matter'.

"The club has a proud record of working with all genders, religions and faiths through its award-winning community scheme, and stands against racism of any kind," added an official Burnley statement. "We are fully behind the Premier League's Black Lives Matter initiative and, in line with all other Premier League games undertaken since Project Restart, our players and football staff willingly took the knee at kick-off at Manchester City."

Blackpool Airport suspended banner flights from its base. In a statement, Blackpool Airport manager Stephen Smith said: "Blackpool Airport and Blackpool Council are outraged by this incident. We stand against racism of any kind and absolutely do not condone the activity, the message was offensive and the action reprehensible. The decision to fly the banner was taken entirely by the banner flying company without the knowledge or approval of the airport or Blackpool Council. Due to the nature of the activity, banners are not checked before take-off and the content is at the operator's discretion."The incident was reported to the police yesterday evening [Monday] and the Civil Aviation Authority has been notified. Blackpool Airport are investigating the banner operator in question and further action will be taken by the board tomorrow [Wednesday]. Following an emergency review this morning, Blackpool Airport will suspend all banner towing operations at the airport with immediate effect and we would suggest that other airports should also consider this approach in light of what has happened at Blackpool."

Looking ahead to the game against Crystal Palace, Mark Lawrenson expected a lift in performance, "Liverpool huffed and puffed against Everton, and we saw a few things that we suspected already. Takumi Minamino is a work in progress, the Reds miss Andy Robertson at left-back, and they can be short of a spark in attack when Mohamed Salah is absent. Salah will play in this game though, and that is one of the reasons I think Liverpool will win. I am expecting to see at least another 25% from the Reds, and even if they don't play well, I don't see Palace scoring."

Palace were no pushovers, having won their last four games, without conceding a goal, and were now joint-eighth with Tottenham. "I'm really proud of the team's performances throughout the year," said Roy Hodgson. "It's tremendous the players are getting credit for the season they have had. It was nice to restart as we did but it was no surprise to me."

Only bottom club Norwich had scored fewer Premier League goals than Palace but the Eagles had kept cleans sheet in their last four games. "I'm very, very happy with how our defence has performed," said the former Liverpool boss, "We've been tight in most of our games. It's not just the defenders though - particularly against Bournemouth we saw the forwards contributing to the defensive effort too."

Hodgson was back at Anfield. "You relish facing Liverpool because it proves you are at the top level of football in England. These games are the flag-ship of football. Of course, we would prefer to face Liverpool in front of a packed Anfield but we have come to terms with the circumstances as they are."

Klopp added: "It would be cool if we can just play our game at the highest level against Palace. It will be difficult, but we have to make it as difficult as possible for Palace. I don't need these games for players to prove themselves. I know everything about my players, I don't need to see them in a specific game to perform to plan with them or not. Decisions like that are made over many moments - two or three games won't make massive difference. The game we won 4-3 against Palace was pretty special. They know how to find the target. We will have to stop them. Losing to Palace (in April 2017) was not a good feeling. I didn't think it was going to be the start of a big run. Roy is doing an incredible job at Palace, organisation is really high and are physically strong."

Klopp admitted to feeling totally abandoned at a packed Anfield during his first encounter with Palace. That was the night of November 8, 2015. It couldn't be more different now, the contrast when the same opponents five years ago, which marked his first defeat as Liverpool manager. Seven games into his Anfield reign, a Scott Dann winner highlighted the size of the job he inherited. Fans streamed out of Anfield long before the final whistle: "I felt pretty alone!"

Now he would be feeling alone in a vastly different way with no fans streaming INTO Anfield! Asked if he would feel less alone now, even in an empty stadium. "Definitely. Definitely," he replied. "It was on that day I felt literally alone because so many people left the stadium, and I think it was important I made a statement that night that things had to change. I have never felt alone again since that night – and even without the fans I will not feel alone when something special happens, whenever it happens. They had to think about it and thought 'Okay, we are not just there for the start and for 80 minutes of the game, the team needs us for 95 or 100 minutes or however long it will go'. That was important. We had to change and people had to change. Supporters can change as well, if they want to help. Losing that night to Palace helped because I could make that kind of statement after the game. It was not planned but I felt that moment helped us to come closer together. The supporters had to think about it, they had to know that the team needs them right to the end. That was so important. A lot of things have changed since then, but obviously they worked it out and may that continue forever!

"It was a cold night against Palace, I remember that, but I don't know too much about that time any more. The only thing I know is that the team we had at the time, and the team before that, was the basis for what we have now. They created the mood that we could build on, even if the mood was not that good in the moment. We had to use the fact that people wanted to change things.

If people don't want to change and think everything is fine because a new manager is coming then nobody is bothered. The situation was our starting point and losing to Crystal Palace that night maybe helped more because I could make this kind of statement (about the fans) after the game."

Since Klopp's first Liverpool defeat his squad has changed for sure; only one player who started that night, Adam Lallana, is still at the club, although not for much longer and only seven of the limited squad he inherited were still there, including Henderson, v Milner, and Firmino. Klopp said: "We didn't have a massive masterplan and think, 'We have to sell him, him and him and bring in him, him and him.' The only thing I know is that team was the basis for what we have now – they created the mood that we could build on, even if the mood was not that good at that moment. We had to use the fact that people wanted to change things. Losing to Palace that night was our starting point and maybe helped us. The team at that time was not so bad but I'd say the team now is a pretty good one!"

Klopp provided an update on injuries. "The two guys, Milly and Joel will not be available tomorrow. We have to figure out exactly how long it will take, but tomorrow they don't play. There will be injuries, 100 percent, we all have to make sure the boys are in the best possible shape." Klopp was asked about the new Premier League rules with five substitutes rather than three. "It will be massively important in the streak of 5-6 games in a short time. We will have to make subs at specific moments. That's sports science as well, we can't just close our eyes as well."

Robertson and Salah were back as expected. Klopp added: "He trained yesterday completely normal, will train today completely normal I would guess so he's available – what I make of the lineup you will have to wait until tomorrow. It is the same with Robbo, he trained yesterday as well completely normal, so that's the same."

Minamino was likely to make way for Salah but Klopp praised him, "There were a lot of good parts to his game but no-one is interested when you don't win. A lot of things in his performance were good."

If Liverpool beat Palace and City win at Chelsea the next day, their meeting on 2 July could turn into the title decider and the venue was still to be confirmed. However Klopp was not thinking of City and that match potentially deciding the title: "I haven't thought about it. We can prepare properly for it but I'm not analysing it yet. I'm completely 100% concentrating on Palace. I don't analyse City now, I don't think about City. I'm completely in the Crystal Palace game, I don't know about destiny too much – we have to play football games and we love that by the way, and if we win all the other teams can do what they want they cannot catch us, so we don't have to think too much about it, we just have to play football.

"It's not about catching or whatever, I didn't finish that season before we started so it's now 20 points we have as an advantage. The only thing I realised when I watched the game last night is how is it possible that anybody is 20 points ahead of this team? It's pretty much unthinkable, but we must have done a couple of things really well that we can have the situation but I don't think about City can catch us or whatever, I think about Palace.

"If you are not with us you make something bad of this, what I said and make a big headline of it, 'City cannot catch up' or whatever that's complete bollocks because that's not what I said. What I mean is I'm only concerned about what we are doing in the next game and not what City are doing. I watch them and respect them a lot, I've said that plenty of times and yes they look like they will win all the games they still have because they look really strong, but that's all. They were always strong, we are not so bad so let's think about that."

Klopp admired City's performance but when asked if he considered the possibility, however remote, of not now winning the title, he was pulled up by the club's press officer for saying "complete b★★★★★★★". He was also asked about top clubs wanting to expand the Champions League, which he pointed out that he was not involved in any talks on that subject, and thought it was time to be reducing layers work load not increasing it. "That's a load of bollocks as well!" Thats got a laugh, and quite a bit of approval on social media. But mind your language Jurgen! But, in reality, he was not "bothered" about the when.

"I thought it would be a cool thing to be a champion with Liverpool one day, when this will be I don't have a lot of influence, we try to improve day by day, month by month and year by year and it worked somehow. Now we are in the best possible situation to do it. Whenever it will happen this season I am not too much bothered about, to be honest.

"Of course, I would like to do it as early as possible just because it would mean we would win the next two games, that's the only reason for it. Apart from that, from a historical point of view looking back I don't think a lot of people will look back at when it happened, was it matchday 32, 33 or 34? That's not too important. I don't see it like this, it would be nice if we win it [as soon as possible] then I won't have to answer questions on it! We are really fine with the situation. The first game back, the derby, was pretty special because these games have a specific history.

"The first game back, the derby, had a specific history. We are fine with our start. Not overly happy, but now we have the second game. It would be cool if we could just play our game on the highest level."

★

WEDNESDAY 24 JUNE - PREMIER LEAGUE
LIVERPOOL 4
Alexander-Arnold 23, Salah 44, Fabinho 55, Mane 69
CRYSTAL PALACE 0

"We may be apart physically but we will always be together". So said Jurgen Klopp in his programme notes. After 104 days Liverpool were back at Anfield requiring five points for the title. But without their fans.

At 6:40pm, a convoy of 20 Mercedes people carriers rolled into view carrying each member of the Crystal Palace playing staff resembling an episode of 'The Apprentice'. Palace had flown from London in the morning, arriving at Liverpool airport just before noon, before a pre-match meal in the nearby Titanic Hotel and the game. They would head straight back to London – individually, by road – after the game to avoid an unnecessary overnight stay.

Once the Palace squad entered through a door usually reserved for hospitality guests, to avoid any potential contamination, three coaches carrying Liverpool's squad cruised through Anfield Road. greeted by 23 fans and 15 police officers.

Back on March 7 Liverpool were last in the Premier League at Anfield. Jordan Henderson's social media to post was a message saying: 'bring the noise tomorrow, Reds!'. The only noise this time was the buzz of a police drone, surveying the local area, and one fan shouting: 'Come on Reds! Come on!'

Just as he was at Goodison Park, Kenny Dalglish was alone in the stands at Anfield, a survivor of the virus. Sir Kenny, 70 next year, swapped the chill of Goodison for the warmth of Anfield, with summer back. As plain old Kenny, he had been the manager the last time the title came to Anfield back in 1990.

John Barnes was pitch side for Sky TV, and he said of his surroundings: "They've done a great job, it's clean, and empty! It's going to be surreal like at Goodison Park because of course in a Merseyside derby you expect the phwoar of the crowd and at Anfield. In terms of the way it looks, you can see the pictures of the flags, it looks great, but of course what happens on the pitch is the most important thing today. I saw Crystal Palace and they look like a proper-oiled machine. They have four clean sheets in a row, so it will be a tough job 100 per cent, I know that. But that is how the Premier League is always, so no problem with that."

Anfield seemed as intimidating as ever despite the absence of fans, the stands saturated with the red of their supporters banners and messages, and when YNWA sounded over the sound system the players felt their fans presence, it seemed to inspire the players; while flat at Goodison, they were brimming with energy here.

The fans tuned into their TV sets sensing an occasion of enormous significance. the team news reflected the manager's mood. Out went Keita, Minamino and the injured Milner and Matip for Wijnaldum. In came Salah, Gomez and Robertson and what Klopp considered his first choice team.

Klopp said he hadn't yet seen all the flags and messages draped around the stadium, but was eagerly looking forward to seeing it. No doubt he didn't look at all the social media around his team selections.

Typically, Klopp's selection received a mixed reaction.

As You'll Never Walk Alon rang out inside an empty stadium, it was hard not to feel the emotion, the passion, and the commitment of the fans were there in spirit. Liverpool were sharper, quicker, and piling on the attacks, with a couple of shots wide, but their first goal since the return was a question of time. Palace's slim chances disappeared when dangerman Wilfred Zaha limped off, apparently he had not looked good in the warm up, but battled on for a while before giving up. Without

June

the outlet he provided, the home team were never going to be troubled, and Alisson was a spectator thoughout the first half.

Liverpool might easily have won a penalty when Firmino tried to dink the ball past Gary Cahill and he wanted a penalty for handball. Cahill's hand was high, it was handball, but the defender was very close and VAR ruled no pen. But that first goal was coming....

On 23 minutes Liverpool were awarded a free-kick 25 yards out and after much discussion, Trent Alexander-Arnold was allowed to take it. The result: absolute perfection as he curled it into the top corner. Alexander-Arnold had been directly involved in 30 Premier League goals since his debut in August 2016, five goals, 25 assists, that's at least five more than any other defender in that time. His goal came in time for the first drinks break; it could be champagne as the title was getting ever so closer!

A second wasn't going to be far behind but in the mean time the other full-back hit the post. Andy Robertson's free-kick this time caused trouble, as Hennessey flaps it down, he hit it on the bounce, but it's deflected slightly against the post. Virgil van Dijk almost sneaked it over the line, but somehow Palace got it clear. Palace were clinging on hoping for half time with only one goal deficit, but that wasn't going to happen.

On the stroke of half-time Fabinho provided the assist for the the crucial second and is mobbed by nearly every other player. He receives the ball just over halfway, comes under pressure but lofts the ball with perfect weight over the head of the retreating Patrick van Aanholt for Salah to control on his chest. The finish is superb, weighing up the keeper's position and planting it wide of him.

Fabinho continued his masterclass with a long range strike early in the second half. As sweet a rocket as you will see anywhere, any time. Robertson played it square, megging referee Martin Atkinson in the process and Fabinho cracks it first time 30 yards out into the corner. A brilliant goal!

Sadio Mane puts the icing on the cake in the 69th minute finishing a superb move involving all of the front three at blistering pace and great accuracy. Townsend had lost the ball 70 yards from his own goal, Mane played the ball inside to Firmino, who in turn found Salah, who is in his own half but slots Mane away with a brilliant first-time long range pass out of reach of the last defender. Mane streaks clear, opens up his body and bends it into the bottom corner.

Now, Klopp could afford to bring on the kids, and he did. Keita, Oxlade-Chamberlain and Minamino came on, as did Elliott and Williams, and they all shone.

Mark Lawrenson on BBC Radio 5 Live: "Sunday's performances and tonight's were polar opposites. They didn't cope with the behind closed doors aspect on Sunday but they are going to win the league. It is a surreal experience but it certainly didn't stop Liverpool tonight, they were back on it."

Crystal Palace had arrived at Anfield accompanied by talk of European qualification after four straight Premier League wins but this was a harrowing night, they simply had no answer to Liverpool as they were ripped apart at regular intervals. Having kept four consecutive clean sheets Palace conceded as many goals against Liverpool in this game as they had in their previous six Premier League games combined. This was Liverpool's 20th win at Anfield in all competitions this season (23rd home match), making them the first club in Europe's big-five leagues to win 20 home matches in 2019-20.

Liverpool had now scored 100+ goals in all competitions for a third consecutive season, the first time they have done so since 1986-87.

Klopp enthused, "Imagine if this stadium would have been full today and all the people could have experienced it live. I don't think the game could have been better because my boys played like everybody was in the stadium. The atmosphere on the pitch was incredible. [Before the restart] I said I would like to see the best games behind closed doors ever because, hopefully, we won't have to see them again. That was the best counter-pressing game I have ever seen. We needed the first goal, but Palace didn't change their approach but we felt 'free' after the first goal.

"We tried hard to tell the boys how good the Everton game was apart from the last third. Today was a reaction and I liked the game so much. 4-0 up in the 87th minute and four players chasing one Crystal Palace player like it's the only ball in the world, I like it so much, wonderful result and a wonderful game. The boys are in good shape and in a good mood and it was important we showed our supporters we are still here and we do not want to wait.

"It was a brilliant game. If you are involved in this, if you are as close as I am to these boys then you can't be happier than I am. The way they played, the passion we showed was so exceptional, there was moments that I couldn't believe it. Especially after being 4-0 up and still showing it. That's important too, that's not doing it because we have to, it's doing it because we believe it's the right thing to do. I'm so happy that we showed that we do it for the people even when they're not really here. in this moment I am in a really good mood.

"The game was exceptional. From talking about football, it was exceptional from so many points of view. It is so difficult against a 4-5-1 but how we pushed them back! The free-kick of Trent? Exceptional. The second goal? Wonderful pass from Fabinho, sensational finish by Mo. The third goal was then Fabinho… yes! He scored already against Man City like that, he showed he can do it. But then we score the fourth goal. What a pass from Mo! Sadio finishes the move off, exceptional. There were so, so many good things about it even when we did not score.

"When the kids (Neco and Harvey) came on, they were involved immediately and they could have scored. This game will last in my mind for a while. This is where we want to be. This is what we have to show against each and everybody. Tonight was a big step, that's clear. We've all still got to play seven games, if we play like this it's really not nice to play against us."

Roy Hodgson admitted: "We didn't need to make any excuses really, but it's a Liverpool team in incredible form. They were so aggressive, so good in winning the ball back, we had no opportunities to put our foot on the ball and ask them some questions. They have been excellent. It's just a question of when it's mathematically impossible for anyone to catch them. They aren't going to lose any matches. They are going to keep winning. Their determination and desire in a game they could easily have taken it easy in, you didn't see them taking it easy. Even in the last four or five minutes they were desperately chasing the ball down and looking to score again. That attitude is why they are going to be champions. The big question is by how many points it's going to be. I can only congratulate them on a wonderful season, a wonderful two seasons really. No doubt Jurgen will be looking forward to the day he can celebrate in front of all the fans."

Palace were without former Liverpool striker Christian Benteke through injury and lost Zaha early with a muscle problem, but to be fair to Hodgson he didn't make that an excuse because he was honest

Trent Alexander-Arnold celebrates the goal that effectively sealed the title in front of a deserted Anfield.

enough to concede it wouldn't have made much difference. "It didn't help, did it," said Hodgson. "It was always going to be hard when they play with such intensity and power to get hold of the ball. We really couldn't retain possession because they pressurised us so well. Any attacks we would have liked to have mounted fizzled out. It means it was constant pressure on our midfielders and back players. The second goal was quite decisive one, that put them very much in the driving seat and as a result a third goal put the game to bed and left us hanging on and making sure it wasn't more embarrassing than conceding the four goals. Up until 3-0 it wasn't like they were creating chance after chance, but they were winning the ball well and we couldn't establish any possession."

Salah said: "It was great to win like that and it was a great performance. All the players are motivated to win the league and we are motivated to play the best football behind closed doors." As for his super strike he gave full credit to Fabinho for creating it, "I give him all the credit, I just run the space and it was a great ball. To have a game like Everton can happen at any time, we were not in top shape but we had to react and we did well today."

Salah relished the prospect of his first title, "I feel great and since I

June

came here I said I wanted to win the Premier League. We haven't won for a long time. Two points to go to win the league, it's great. Last year we had a chance but Man City also played really well and deserved it. It's our time to win the league."

The outstanding Trent commented: "The lads have done really well. It was a difficult game and we were disappointed to only get the draw at Everton, but for the first game back at Anfield, it couldn't have gone any better. It's two points (we need); it's quite close but a lot can happen. We have worked hard for this as a team and this is what we have always dreamed. Hopefully we will get it across the line.'

Rekindling the fabulous free kick and comparisons to David Beckham, he responded: "I have been practising a lot and I had a few against Everton which I was disappointed not to score with, but it's always good to get the ball rolling for the boys. The comparisons with the best free-kick taker in Premier League history are very nice but there is a lot of work to do. It is quite close [the title] but we know a lot can happen in the Premier League. We have worked hard for this and this is what we have always dreamed of. We are in a good position so hopefully we can get over the line soon. We have to focus on ourselves, we are not hoping Man City drop points, we know it's our hands. We still have to go to City next week and get a result."

Manchester City now had to win at Chelsea the following day to further delay the inevitability of Liverpool's coronation. But Guardiola had said in his media conference earlier in the day that he was more focused on the FA Cup quarter-final with Newcastle than worrying about playing Liverpool or beating Chelsea to delay their coronation. That brought a wry smile form Klopp. "They are brilliant. Pep should play poker and the football they play is unbelievable. We are different and we have to be, but we are good as well. There are different ways of playing football and I like them both."

The players smiled sheepishly when asked if they would be glued to their TV sets at home fingers crossed that Chelsea deliver the title sooner rather than alter but they would be watching.

Klopp had to watch, he explained: "I have to watch the game tomorrow because we play them one week later. That's being professional and doing my job. I watch the game not to prepare a celebration but because we play City a week later and also Chelsea. This game is a really important game to watch for plenty of reasons. Whatever happens we have no influence on it so I have no interest. I am pretty sure the game next week against City is a must watch for every football fan on this planet because whatever will be decided two really good teams face each other. I watch the game tomorrow night to know what City is doing and what Chelsea is doing when we play them. I have nothing to do with any other things. We don't plan things like that, we want to play this game tonight. We wanted this result."

★

With every Liverpool fan now cheering on the Blues of Stamford Bridge, it was comforting to remember that Chelsea had form. They'd done it before, and not so long ago. Leicester City's Jamie Vardy organised a house part for his team-mates as they watched Chelsea deliver the title to the King Power. Then, they were the most unlikely champions, the 500-1 outsiders. Now, Liverpool had been the champions elect for the longest period in football history. they looked like champions since Christmas, arguably even before, but were forced to put it all on hold for three months.

They were not going to care if they won the title sitting at home watching on TV or whether they would take the title from the reigning champions the following Thursday when first and second were due to meet.

City boss Guardiola was putting on a brave face about the prospect of Liverpool coming to The Etihad to take the title from them. Maybe he would prefer it all to happen at the Bridge. Either way he seemed unperturbed as he insisted there would be no extra significance if Liverpool were to win the league at their stadium. "It doesn't matter, they are already champions".

Graeme Souness knew the destination of the title had long since been decided as he praised Klopp for their intensity against Palace. "They're sensational. Ninety-seven points last year... their consistency levels are off the chart. They deserve to be champions, you could have given it to them at Christmas. Week in week out, they play with such a high tempo and such aggression. For the manager to get that out of them, they've been sensational. Liverpool to a man tonight were determined to show the derby game was a hiccup. Tonight they were bang at it, so professional, they were never going to do anything tonight other than be convincing."

June

Jamie Redknapp hailed the Reds' performance, describing the Anfield club as a 'brilliant machine' with special praise for goalscorers Alexander-Arnold and Fabinho, 'He's [Alexander-Arnold] a fine young man, he says the right things and is so composed when he talks and when he plays football. At his age taking free kicks and corners, he's an exceptional footballer. He just gets better all the time. The fact Robertson and Salah didn't play against Everton, you see the difference they make. Fabinho was the best player today, his goal, his assist for Salah, there were so many positives. When I think about Fabinho, he's great at shielding the ball. But that pass was exceptional, the way he lifts it over the defence. It just shows you he's got a lot more than what you see in his game. It's what you expect from Liverpool, they don't let you have a second, they're just a brilliant machine."

It all sounded like an appreciation of the newly crowned champions by the Sky pundits as Sky were preparing for a special programme the following night on how Liverpool won the title should City drop points at the Bridge. Souness believes that despite the contrasting styles of Klopp and Guardiola, they would dominate domestic football and European game for years. "He [Klopp] wants to play a certain way, high tempo, aggressive football. He's got players he's getting the very best out of. They're both great to watch. If you're playing Liverpool you have to be ready to go to war, they're going to get in your face. They're not silky midfielders, they're all warrior types. They'll want to bully you from the start. City will want to play triangles and pass around you. Liverpool today were fantastic. Because there's so much good football from Liverpool, you forget how hard they work. Pressing is not just about being willing to run around and sprint around, it's about anticipating.

"If you're making a direct comparison between the two teams, they both have top goalkeepers, you'd rather have Liverpool's back four and then City's midfield, then toss a coin for the attackers. It's a different type of football, both great to watch. Who would I rather watch? Liverpool today were fantastic and, against Arsenal, City were fantastic. We're enjoying a purple patch. I think these are two special teams in the time of the Premier League. These teams could dominate European football as well."

Frank Lampard aired his Liverpool alliegences, calling them "we", and recalling he had just signed when The Reds last won the title 30 years ago. "I couldn't respect City more. Their football team is unbelievable, I really like the football they play a lot. We are different, we have to be different, we cannot be like Man City. We can be just as good, and that's what we want to be, and we probably celebrate different things when they happen on the pitch. That's completely fine and we respect that. It's like the analogy of Messi or Ronaldo, which one do you prefer? They're both brilliant at what they do. Man City play through midfield more, they like a possession-based game. Liverpool are different, they get it up to the front three and magic happens, like that last goal [against Palace]. That's what it's all about for Liverpool, they've got so much pace going forward. But you can't say either is wrong, they're both great to watch and a joy in their own right. Some like Ronaldo, some like Messi. It depends on the type of football you like."

Frank Lampard would happily play a part in crowning Liverpool champions for the first time in 30 years, but only because it would mean his side have taken points from City as his team need points to consolidate their place in the top four. Infact Lampard was keen to catch Leicester in third. "I have had absolutely no thought of Liverpool's situation, it makes no odds to us at all," said Lampard. "We respect Liverpool and Manchester City as two fantastic teams, in the last two to three seasons they've been dominant, but we can only look at what this match means for us."

Chelsea had famously played a big part on the night Leicester clinched the league in the 2015/16 season, coming from 2-0 down to draw 2-2 against Tottenham in "The Battle of the Bridge" with nine Spurs players booked. "I don't think you can compare a Chelsea-Tottenham game to potentially stop Tottenham winning the league," added Lampard on the rivalry between the London sides. "I am aware of the situation, but I can only focus on us. We have a job to do and our job is to go up against one of the best teams in the world over the last few seasons and try to get a result."

Having 'stolen' RB Leipzig star striker Timo Werner from under Liverpool's noses, the least Chelsea could do was to hand The Reds the title on a silver plate.

CHAMPIONS AT LAST!

Liverpool broke two records simultaneously that would have been improbable if not impossible to envisage not long ago, and a record that will, presumably, never be surpassed. With seven games remaining, The Reds landed the title in the fastest time, beating a handful of previous winners by two clear games. Yet, they also had to wait the longest, well into the month of June, the longest season in history, so they were the latest ever to be clinch the title.

Liverpool's 30-year long wait was finally over after Manchester City lost 2-1 at Chelsea to confirm the Reds deservedly landed their first Premier League title. Jurgen Klopp's side needed one victory to seal the league but City's failure to win at the Bridge, meant they won the title exactly the way Leicester did, when Chelsea beat Spurs and their players had to watch it out as did the Liverpool players in a local hotel where they were celebrating along with their manager.

Liverpool's 19th top-flight title and their first since 1989-90 was achieved with one of the most formidable teams in the club's history. Despite being urged to "stay home" by the city's metro mayor Steve Rotherham, thousands descended on the club's spiritual home to celebrate. With a heat wave many thousands packed the streets, it was hard to persuade Liverpool's faithful to stay away. Many of the supporters who congregated at the club's ground wore face masks and some lit flares.

A number of players, including Alisson, Virgil van Dijk, Alex Oxlade-Chamberlain, and Andy Robertson celebrated together watching the Chelsea-City game. Klopp, wearing a Liverpool shirt, commented: "It is unbelievable. It's much more than I ever thought would be possible. It's an incredible achievement by my players and it's a huge joy for me to coach them. I haven't waited 30 years, I have been here for four-and-a-half years, but it is quite an achievement, especially with the three-month break because nobody knew if we could go on. I know it is difficult for people in this moment but we could not hold back. We will enjoy this with our supporters when we can."

Suggestions the season might be null and avoid angered Liverpool fans but the Premier League's return enabled them to cap their stunning success. Because of the measures in place the Reds would not be able to celebrate with their supporters immediately, at least not in the traditional sense. The next time they play will be at the side they have beaten to this season's title and who pipped them so narrowly last campaign, Manchester City, who will be giving them a guard of honour.

Following their defeat at the Bridge, Pep Guardiola congratulated Liverpool on their title success. With City's 100-point total for a season one of numerous records Liverpool can still break, the clash between the new champions and the deposed champions would still have a bit of bite.

Klopp's side produced one of the most memorable campaigns in Premier League history, amassing 86 points already, with a record of 28 victories, two draws and a single defeat from their 31 games. At one stage they led the table by 25 points - a record gap between a side in first and second in English top-flight history.

Liverpool's triumph represents a huge moment for their fans, who grew accustomed to success in the 1970s and 1980s, including a run between the 1972-73 and 1990-91 seasons in which they only failed to finish first or second in the league once. In the past 30 years, winning three FA Cups, four League Cups, a Uefa Cup and the Champions League twice - the latest coming last season under Klopp - as well as three Super Cups and one Club World Cup, the title was elusive. Since Kenny Dalglish led them to the First Division championship, they have had to endure three decades without league success, during which their record tally of titles was surpassed by rivals Manchester United, who have 20.

During that dominance Sir Alex Ferguson famously revelled in having "knocked Liverpool off their perch". The Reds have come close during that time to restoring themselves to the top of the English game, finishing second in the Premier League on four occasions. Gerard Houllier (2001-02) and Rafael Benitez (2008-09) both took them close. In the 2013-14 season, Brendan Rodgers' side looked as though they were going to take the crown but a late-season slump - synonymous with a Steven Gerrard slip that enabled Chelsea to score and win at Anfield - saw them fall agonisingly short. Last season, they racked up a stunning 97 points, losing only one game all campaign, but had the misfortune of coming up against an even better City side, who beat them to the title by a point. No side had ever achieved so many points without winning the league.

The appointment of Klopp has been pivotal to Liverpool's resurgence. He arrived at Anfield in October 2015 following the sacking of Rodgers and with the club 10th in the Premier League, having led Borussia Dortmund to two Bundesliga titles and the 2013 Champions League final, and with a reputation for fast-paced, high-pressing attacking play, which he described as "heavy metal football". His four full seasons finishing positions: fourth, fourth, second and now first.

Prolific front three Mohamed Salah, Sadio Mane and Roberto Firmino all arrived during Klopp's reign. The trio have scored a 211 goals in less than three seasons (92 for Salah, 65 for Mane and 54 for Firmino). The additions of world-class goalkeeper Alisson and centre-back Virgil van Dijk were essential in completing the team. As Klopp enjoyed a couple of beers to calm his nerves before the Chelsea game, according to Robertson and Milner, interviewed with their Liverpool shirts, they too were enjoying the celebrations hoping to persuade their boss to have a couple of days off.

Klopp is the only Reds manager since Dalglish left (including the Scot himself during a second spell from January 2011 to May 2012) with a win percentage over 60. "The last two years and since Jurgen's come in has been very positive," Dalglish said "He's been fantastic and epitomises everything Liverpool football club stands for. Whatever they got, they have deserved it. Onwards and upwards. We have a lot more happy days to look forward to as long as Jurgen is here.

"I'm very pleased for everybody connected with the football club," Dalglish added. "Jurgen has done a fantastic job. The highlight has been the camaraderie within the team and the way everyone has helped the team. Last night's game was a huge example of that. They played with tempo and never gave Crystal Palace time on the ball. It's the whole feeling within the club, you do not win anything without a great dressing room, and they have that."

★

Jurgen Klopp enjoyed a beer or two and a much debated 'dad dancing' session as part of the hotel celebrations that went on long into the night. "If I want to dance, I'll dance. I don't do it for the boys. We were in a good mood, so it happened not for the first time at an evening event. The boys know that I like a dance from time to time. Last night was a good moment in my life so I expressed that on the dance floor as well. I don't know what dance it was, honestly. I dance. I do that from time to time. We were in a good mood, the music was good. The reason for coming together was the right one, which is why we came together. I was always a better dancer than a football player. Unfortunately I couldn't make my life with dancing."

Klopp became the first manager to win the title and Champions League in his first four full seasons in Premier League history, so no one is going to begrudge him a bit of silly dancing as he celebrated along with his players. The Liverpool manager was involved in more emotion with his family as he wanted to share getting over the line for the title with those closest to him even though separated by the ongoing coronavirus pandemic.

"I called my family 10 seconds before the final whistle. We had a Facetime call," he said on Friday afternoon when he was finally able to compose himself. "I told them I loved them, they told me they loved me. It's sad I can't be with them. I told them to leave it on. It was a really nice moment. I cannot answer all the messages I got but I can read all of them and that is what I will do in the next few days."

Klopp composed himself after looking highly charged, emotional and did a Gazza and cried during his round of media interviews immediately after Chelsea bet Manchester City at the Bridge to deliver the clubs first title in 30 years. Klopp wiped away a tear when he was live on Sky Sports and gave his reaction to the news to Liverpool legends Kenny Dalglish and Graeme Souness. He was brought to the height of his emotions as he watched the match at the Bridge with his players as he confessed: "It was really tense, the 90 minutes of the Manchester City game you can imagine. I didn't want to be involved really. But when you watch it and you are involved then you hope and then the big chances Chelsea had with a penalty situation and all that stuff it was quite intense. So the team is downstairs [in a hotel], we obviously watched the game together, for tonight, we will enjoy this moment and it is the best thing I can imagine. It is more than I ever dreamed of. This is a safe place and that is what we wanted from tonight to let the boys have this together. I know it is still difficult out there but we couldn't go back, we had to come together. We were together at the game already

A clearly emotional Jurgen Klopp couldn't continue his interview with Kop legend Kenny Dalglish.

and we had to come back to a hotel for recovery and stuff like this.

"It is very important. We need pictures for them and we have a lot of pictures from the season and now we have pictures tonight from the celebration and we will create pictures from the celebration for all our supporters. Then we will be together and enjoy this properly the way we can, but tonight, we made the best of our situation I would say. We all do that together, it is a mix of the history you have created and it is what we are compared with, rightly so. I think we found a nice way to get rid of it a little bit because we had to write our own story.

"But anyway, that gives us a lot of power. It is the atmosphere in and around the club, the intensity level, how everyone lives football at this club. And then it is 100 per cent a really good hand in choosing the players we kept and brought in. It is a wonderful mix. They are all winners without doing it 15 times in the past. But now they are here together, we can start winning together. It is so incredibly difficult but it is possible with consistency and that drives us. We knew, three years ago, we played a really good season and I think we finished fourth and it was clear that we lack consistency. But you cannot ask for that and the boys create it, you have to work on that and you have to convince everyone and that is what we all did, together. But of course, from time to time you have to help them a little bit with a few words. It is a big moment and I have no real words to be honest. It is such a big moment,

I am completely overwhelmed. I never would have thought it would feel like this and it's just big. Sorry, gentleman, all the best."

He also stressed that while he was dedicating the title to legends like Kenny Dalglish and Graeme Souness who were also being interviewed on Sky, he also dedicated to the fans, "I can only tell you it is for you out there. It is for you. Incredible." When the raw emotion and the sharing such a special moment with his players had subsided a tad, Klopp described the winning moment they all revelled in and shared when speaking to the clubs official website. Asked if he could sum up his emotions, he responded: "No, unfortunately not because if I tried to start talking about it [how I feel] again I will start crying again and that doesn't work really well!

"I am completely overwhelmed; I don't know, it's a mix of everything – I am relieved, I am happy, I am proud. I couldn't be more proud of the boys. How we watched the game tonight together, we knew it could happen, it couldn't not happen, we didn't know. We want to play football and we are really happy that we are allowed to play again – then when it happened in that moment, it was a pure explosion.

"When we counted down the last five seconds of the game, the ref counted down a little bit longer than us so we had to look at two or three more passes! Then it was pure... I cannot describe it. It was a really, really nice moment. Directly after it, I felt so empty inside – I cannot believe it, I am really not happy with myself in the moment that I feel like I feel, but it's just a little bit too much in the moment.

"I will be fine, nobody has to worry. I actually couldn't be happier; I couldn't have dreamed of something like that and I never did before last year, honestly. We were not close enough three years ago, a year ago we were really close... what the boys have done in the last two-and-a-half years, the consistency they show is absolutely incredible and second to none. Honestly, I have no idea how we do that all the time. Last night, a very good example – we played a game like the stadium is fully packed and everybody is shouting 'Liverpool' or whatever constantly. It is a wonderful moment, that's what I can say."

Klopp was inevitably required for a press conference the next day, when he said: "The players wanted to write their own history and stories so they were ready not to compare us with those great figures in this club. We were unbelievably good last year and smashing this record

Champions At Last - Jordan Henderson, Joe Gomez and Virgil van Dijk celebrate

is absolutely exceptional. It is really difficult to get there.

"Last night I was absolutely overwhelmed and didn't understand anything, what happened with my body, what happened with my emotions. I realised it was obviously really big, I knew that before but I don't think you can be prepared for a situation like this. I was not. Maybe you can, but I wasn't and so it hit me full, in my face, and when I've had similar situations you know that it's nice but it's intense as well. I don't feel the pressure too much before it happens - but when it happens the amount of relief shows how big the pressure was before. I was just not able to speak. Usually it's a good moment to have a speech to the players but I was just not able to do it - I was completely overwhelmed, I was crying too much last night."

On whether he will get a statue like previous title-winning managers, Klopp joked that one was really not needed. Bill Shankly and Bob Paisley already been honoured at Anfield alongside founder John Houlding, while Sir Kenny Dalglish has his own stand – and former captain and Liverpool legend Steven Gerrard recently spoke of his desire to see Klopp with his own. "He deserves to be mentioned in the same breath as those iconic managers," Gerrard explained but Klopp joked: "They all got theirs when they were not here anymore. People can do that but I still want to live for 30, 40 years, but I'm not interested in statues!

"I'm the manager of this team and we won the league, people see this pretty positively obviously and I am pretty positive about that as well but we don't have to compare me with these iconic figures. I don't know exactly how long Bill Shankly was at the club but what he did where he picked the club up from the Second Division and then Bob was his assistant and won pretty much everything. And Kenny played for this club, became the manager, player-manager and was immediately successful as a manager which is incredible – so from my point of view there is no comparison possible. I am here since four-and-a-half years ago, came from Germany over here and tried to do my job. I love the city, love the club, yes that's true, but there's no comparison possible and especially not needed."

On comparisons with Liverpool managerial legends, he went on: "I don't see it that way. It's not too important. But if people want to see it like this, I'm not the guy to tell them to stop doing that. But they are really icons. What Bill and Bob did is just incredible and in very difficult times - people had nothing and they lifted and built this city. Kenny was player-manager - it's unbelievable, I don't think there is any story that can compare with that, just incredible. Since we use our history in the right manner, since we don't compare any more, since we are just happy about it, build on it, since then we can do what we do now.

"The history is no burden any more. It is the basis for what we are doing. Last year we had 97 points so we were really close - it's not like it's been up and down with us. Here's the second year now where obviously we are pretty good. Winning all the time, that's really difficult because the other teams are too good for that. They have a good chance to improve of course as well - we have to be better, they have to, we will, they will and then we will see who is best. We have to bring in new things, other teams will defend us differently, we have to adapt but that is normal in life and in football. But the consistency, if we can keep it that would be a massive achievement already."

Klopp again reserved praise for the fans: "I know it means the world to them – it means the world to me. It's massive and what I love is when you have a successful football club in your city it gives the whole city a lift. I am really happy for our people. It means absolutely everything to me. It's the only reason why we play football. This city is a very emotional city that went through a lot of hard times, like the club had to go through, and having these good moments is essential. Having a successful football team in a city always lifts the mood in a city so it helps everything. At this moment in time, in the biggest crisis our generation has probably ever had, it's so important that we don't forget that there is something we can really look forward to."

Klopp was confident Liverpool will not lose the hunger for silverware. "We won some stuff but they are still humble and as long as they stay humble we have a chance of being successful." Well, a haul of the Champions League, Super Cup, World Club Championship and the title wasn't bad inside 12 months!

Reflecting on his start at Anfield in October 2015, Klopp recalled, "Without knowing it at the time, the most important thing I said to the players was that we have to create our own stories and own history. When I came in, I had to tell them not to compare themselves with anyone any more, some of the fantastic people who played for this club and won everything in the past. We needed to get the opportunity from our supporters to find our own way, and this is only possible because people never lost patience with us in any moment. We got rid of the heavy backpack. I took it off that day and never got it back."

Most important for Klopp is his relationship with his players. "I have a very good relationship with all my teams but the mix of skill sets that these boys bring in here, plus the personality they bring, is absolutely exceptional and only this combination of things makes it possible. They are really a bunch of top boys and I am really happy to be part of this moment. They are all individuals and different and that's good, but they have no real selfish characteristics as well."

Chairman Tom Werner and owner John W Henry penned an emotional letter. The figureheads behind Fenway Sports Group were keen to emphasise the role Jurgen Klopp had since he joined the club. "There can be no disappointment in winning the Premier League!" commented Henry. "You never stop learning in football and we had a lot to learn. We made a lot of mistakes and I'm sure we will make more but there is a team operating at many levels with a focus. The harder the road became, the more effort these young men expended. When I look back on this season, when I'm in a retirement home in 10 years, it won't matter. I'll just be able to reflect on an achievement. When we first got involved with the club 10 years ago, we dreamt of this moment."

Werner commented, "All of us were so delighted because this has been a long march. I know that our supporters struggled for 30 years to reach this pinnacle. My first thought was to just share that moment with our supporters because without them, the club is nothing. As Jürgen said, our supporters provided such an incredible contribution to winning the league – not just this year, but every year. My hope is that all of us who are supporters of the club can take a moment today and this week to safely celebrate what is a remarkable achievement.

"I didn't have the pleasure of knowing or watching the great football of Shankly and Paisley, so I don't really want to compare Jürgen to previous managers. I just know that the league is extremely competitive and when we first became involved in Liverpool over 10 years ago, we were not even thinking about winning the league. Our dream was to just become top four and make it to the Champions League. He has just created such an atmosphere at Liverpool that there's no alternative except to win. He has created such an atmosphere. One of the things that I'm just joyful about whenever I watch the team is how many players contribute. It doesn't just lie on the shoulders of our wonderful striker or our wonderful goalkeeper. So many players contribute – from Henderson to Firmino, to Oxlade-Chamberlain, to Wijnaldum, to Fabinho, to Van Dijk. I also enjoy their joy because I saw a video of them last night celebrating together and you could just feel the camaraderie that this club has. We celebrated this as a club.

"People have asked about which World Series [at Boston Red Sox] that we've won was the most meaningful. It's like comparing one child to another. You love all your children. We were all in Madrid last year and winning the Champions League was special, but this is really magnificent because it's the culmination of 30 years of trying to win the Premier League. The key was the ability of Jürgen to ask so much of everyone, every match over the last two years and their ability to respond."

Asked about what's now next for LFC, Werner commented: "As I said, we want to undersell and overdeliver. We hopefully would be ensuring another period of sustained success. The competition is fierce and I know our rivals are working tirelessly to upend us. But we've got such talent in place as Jürgen, as Michael [Edwards] and the team on the pitch. One of the things that stuck with me this year was their hunger for winning. I don't think that will be diminished. They're such a good group of players. I have such fondness for them as individuals off the pitch. They're humble, they're kind, they enjoy each other's company. You could see that in the videos when they were all celebrating. It's a lot to ask them to stay at this extraordinary level but it is our goal to continue to play with this quality."

Jordan Henderson's Zoom call was hit with a host of requests to join after BT Sport accidentally opened the door for people to join the call, although no one actually managed it. "Amazing. I didn't want to talk about it till this moment. It's amazing to finally get over the line. So happy for all the boys, the fans, the club the city. I'm a little bit overwhelmed right now, amazing feeling. So proud of what we've achieved."

Henderson discussed the differences between winning it on the pitch, and watching on TV. "When we won the champions league it was a different experience being on the pitch. Then watching the game tonight and the final whistle going being with everyone, all the staff, another moment in our lives we'll never forget. I can't really describe it. I said after the CL final it wouldn't be possible to do that without the manager [Klopp] and it's the same with this title. It's no disrespect to the managers we've had before but since day one he came in the door and he changed everything and we've done every thing he said, followed him, and believed in him."

The Reds skipper tweeted, "Wow. What a 24 hours! Being able to celebrate together as a team last night is something we'll all not forget. However I want to send a message too to all of you, our amazing fans. It is a true privilege and an honour to represent and captain your great club. We know it's been a long wait but to all of you Reds, this one is for you. When the time is right, we can't wait to celebrate with you all. Thank you for always believing in us. Now we must focus on the next seven games and finish the season as strongly as we can before we get to lift that trophy. To each and every Liverpool fan out there, You'll Never Walk Alone."

Later, he said he "cannot express" what Klopp has done for the champions and hopes the manager will stay "for a long time yet".

In a wide-ranging interview with Kelly Cates for 5 live, Henderson praised Klopp's attitude in victory or defeat and added, "We want to perform for the manager, for the football club, for the city."

The captain commented: "When you win, he's on the dance floor and partying but to be honest, when we lose, the way he handles that is incredible. I always felt he had that belief in this team that after each final we maybe did not win, we would come back stronger, or when we have won, he knows that we'll keep going. This is why it feels so good, to give something back to everyone, especially the Premier League title everyone has wanted for so long. You have to give a lot of credit to the players, who have been outstanding, but ultimately we all follow the manager. From day one since he came into Melwood, what he's done has been unbelievable, from inside the club to outside [it]. I can't express enough how much he has done for this football club since he's been here. Hopefully he's here for a long time yet and we can continue this journey together."

Henderson joined Liverpool from Sunderland in 2011 and had been captain since 2015, involved in all four of Liverpool's titles under Klopp, "We want more trophies and to stay with the same mentality and desire, which I have no question we will. I feel as though there's still more to come from this team. We've had an amazing year and that's just driven us on to want more. Hopefully that will never change and I have got no doubt about that with the type of players we have and the mentality in the dressing room."

Liverpool could still seet records for most wins in a season, most home wins, most away wins and biggest winning margin. "Now we are Premier League champions, which was the goal at the start of the season, we have seven games left and we want to win all seven," Henderson said. "That's not easy but that's our mentality. If we can do that, you're talking about records and amounts of points. We can't think too far ahead, which I don't like doing. Our next game is a huge game against City, who are an amazing side."

Andy Robertson delivered his usual no nonsense assessment: "When people thought we might drop points we have shown the world, 'No, that's not us'. Leicester away was the perfect example. So many people were talking about us being fatigued or jet-lagged. There was no chance that was going to happen and we proved a lot of people wrong that night. Time and time again we have proven people wrong, with our mentality and our resilience. Hopefully that continues to be the case, because the minute we stop we will have trouble. But we will not allow it, and the manager won't allow it. As long as it is like that we have a fine chance to win trophies every season."

Robertson pin pointed confidence and belief that got them over the line in such an impressive way. He said: "It was the Champions League final. We'd got the hurt of the Premier League, and if we had to go home after the last game of the season against Wolves that would have been really tough. But the fact is, we took the next step. Winning the Champions League made us champions, it made us winners and we got the feeling for it. That's why we came back in pre-season as if this year was going to be our year for the Premier League, that we were going to make it our year for the league and we were going to go out and do it. We just felt we were going to show everyone we can win the league, could go again and get the better of Man City this time. And we did that from the get-go. From day one we showed it against Norwich at home and we have continued that. We've probably been in a league of our own this season."

Trent Alexander-Arnold insisted breaking the points record was a further motivation for the club. "I think we have got a chance of that becoming real. The points record is one that is difficult to beat, but I think if we can surpass that, then it will hopefully stand for a really long time."

Gini Wijnaldum tweeted this message to Liverpool supporters. "Thank you for the support. You guys show me the meaning of what it is to never walk alone."

Brendan Rodgers traced Liverpool's recent glut of silverware back to the £142m sale of Philippe Coutinho. Rodgers had snapped up Coutinho for a bargain £8.5m in January 2013 from Inter Milan when he was manager. Rodgers, at Anfield from June 2012-October 2015, analysed: "The money they gained from Philippe has enabled them to buy Van Dijk, Alisson and Fabinho - three players who have transformed the team. They have been consistently the best team and to get the title after such a long wait, I am delighted for all the supporters. It is very fitting as they have been brilliant this year. They have looked like a machine. The team have so much quality with professional players who play at the highest level. I texted Jurgen Klopp last night and Jordan Henderson who I know very well. I am delighted for them all. I also pleased for the ownership who came into football new and each year they have learned about the game and are fantastic owners who deserve that success."

Former Liverpool boss Gerard Houllier said, "I feel happy and proud. Happy because I think it's a very hard-won reward for the fans and for the players and I think I feel proud because I'm a Liverpudlian. It means firstly a relief and a feeling of very indescribable happiness. When you wait so long, when it comes you're even more happy. First of all we have to stress they've achieved a fantastic performance. Jurgen Klopp has won in style, he won with his philosophy, they are very generous in their efforts and very good at not just outplaying the opponent but scoring in practically every game. This season they were simply phenomenal and it's a continuation of what went on last season."

Kop legend Ian Rush was among those leading the plaudits, saying: "He's been absolutely fantastic. What he's doing again. When you used to see him, he'd give you a big hug. He's always got a smile on his face, you go away smiling and want to give everyone else a hug! He's always laughing and joking and makes everyone feel happy. When you look at Kenny Dalglish and Bob Paisley, they would do it in a different way but everyone would come away laughing and joking. They are all one big family but you need a leader and Jurgen is that leader. He's doing that. He keeps everyone's spirits up."

John Barnes believed this success was achieved with old-fashioned values. Roberto Firmino is his favourite player - "he can do everything." But the chemistry comes from the dugout. Barnes had met Klopp on a number of occasions but they do not have a close relationship. "How happy could we have been last year? We lost one league game and won the Champions League! They could have rested on their laurels. Jurgen told them to forget it and go and do it again. I'm sure he will do the same thing this summer. Keep doing it. This team has the potential to be great. If they stay together and if Jurgen Klopp stays and they continue to do what they do... I know this team CAN do it."

Danny Murphy said, "Now he's won the two biggest trophies, can he do it again? Can he get these players motivated to do it over a space of three-four seasons because that is when he'll ultimately be considered as one of the best. It makes it even bigger that they've been waiting for 30 years, it gives Klopp even more kudos. One of his biggest qualities has been his motivational skills, it would have been understandable for them to be a bit sluggish early on, played the victim if you like, but no he hasn't allowed that. I don't see a problem with him not being able to motivate the side again - it's a young side, there's no superstars, no one is strolling about. They are relentless, they've got a relentless appetite to win games."

Mark Lawrenson added, "I had too many beers and not enough sleep last night but once every 30 years I suppose I can cope with that. I was on LFCTV for a special live show after the Chelsea versus Man City game finished and Liverpool were confirmed as champions. We didn't come off air until 12:30 in the morning and I didn't get home for a good few hours after that. We were broadcasting from Chapel Street in the centre of Liverpool rather than using our studio next to Anfield and, when I finally left and headed for bed, the streets of the city were littered with fallen bodies sleeping off what was one heck of a party. It was typical of Liverpool fans really - they always know how to celebrate, and obviously our first league title since 1990 is a pretty good excuse. When Willian scored it was a case of 'here we go, this is a done deal' but my phone had started going nuts much earlier in the night, when Christian Pulisic's goal put City behind. I've seen the scenes outside Anfield but it was great to be in the middle of town for all the celebrations - we were in a studio that is basically soundproof but you could still hear the fans outside - people were driving round and round, waving flags and beeping horns all night. The atmosphere on the show was brilliant and it was great to speak to Jurgen Klopp too - he came on the show from Formby Hall hotel, which is where he and the players were watching the game. Of course in a perfect world they would have won the Premier League title on their own pitch in front of 50,000 fans, but we aren't living in a perfect world right now because of the coronavirus pandemic. There will be more big moments to come, and some of them will be weird - the trophy lift at an empty Anfield after the final home game of the season against Chelsea on 18 July for example. But there will be a victory parade through Liverpool at some point and from my experience that is when the whole city comes together anyway, even more so than when you win it at your ground. That really will be a day to remember for everyone. Right now, the Liverpool team will be doing exactly the same as the fans - sitting back and reflecting on a brilliant achievement."

Former Liverpool defender Alan Kennedy, a four-time title winner, "I hope this team sticks together and enjoys the winning side of it. This could be the start of a great era for Liverpool. Liverpool weren't going anywhere four or five years ago, Jurgen Klopp has given them another level. He's built the team around every player, every player has been looked at and he doesn't buy players that don't fit. He's built a great team which he had to, to rival Manchester City. Now they've overtaken them. Manchester City will strengthen. I enjoyed the game last night, it was two good teams who want to play football and will be around in the years to come and I think it will be a decent campaign next season. Liverpool will have to strengthen, the pressure will be on and it's how they cope with it. I hope they can dominate. It's about Jurgen making sure he get's the right players and the board backs him. The wins they have accumulated has been incredible but it counts for nothing now, they've won the title and they must start again. Look forward to next season."

Phil Neville, winner of multiple titles with Manchester United added, "It's a phenomenal achievement. When you look at past title winners I think Liverpool are up there with the best, with the ruthlessness, the goals they score, the style in which they play and they have an unbelievable manager."

LeBron James joined in with the celebrations. The basketball star, who has shares in the Merseyside club, tweeted his delight. The LA Lakers' association with the Reds dates back to 2011 when he bought a two per cent share for around £5.28m and, thanks to the club's recent success, that value skyrocketed to £26m. "PREMIER LEAGUE CHAMPIONS! LET'S GO @LFC #YNWA" The 35-year-old shared an image on his Instagram story and retweeted several posts from the club's official Twitter account during the celebrations. Virgil van Dijk spotted James' tweet and replied: "Tell 'em" followed by a grinning face and trophy emojis. James won three NBA championships and was named as the most valuable player on four occasions. He visited Anfield in the past and posed for pictures in front of the tunnel and dressing room.

Sean Cox has congratulated the team. The Irishman suffered life-changing injuries outside Anfield two years ago when he travelled to Merseyside with his brother for the Reds' semi-final first leg against Roma in 2018. Cox, a father-of-three, was subject to an unprovoked attack by away supporters which left him in a coma with serious brain injuries. He underwent extensive rehabilitation at the Walton Centre in Liverpool before he was transferred to a Dublin hospital, able to return to his home in Dunboyne in March 2020. His family congratulated the team on his behalf. "Sean couldn't be happier for Liverpool being crowned champions and sends his love and congratulations to Jurgen Klopp and the entire club. The Cox family are so delighted that Sean got the opportunity to go to Anfield on a couple of occasions earlier this season and meet many of his LFC sporting heroes. Liverpool FC is a huge part of Sean's life and he hopes to be back in Anfield before long."

Several Premier League clubs sent messages of congratulations as indeed did the Premier League themselves plus a number of overseas clubs including LiverpoolFC1915 in Uruguay!

Manchester United boss Ole Gunnar Solskjaer commented, "Any team that wins the championship and a Premier League deserves it and they deserve credit. It's a hard league to win, so well done to Jurgen [Klopp] and his players." He warned expectant United fans that it much more difficult for the Red Devils to win title now than it was in their heyday under Sir Alex. United are without a top-flight title since Fergie retired after their triumphant 2012-13 campaign. "We've got to be honest enough to say it is more difficult now. We've always had challengers, whether it was Arsenal, Chelsea, Liverpool. But most of the time it was just one of them challenging us. Finishing third wasn't normal. Now there are at least four, maybe five teams that can win the league and the cups."

Sir Kenny Dalglish revealed Sir Alex had written to him. Dalglish shared a fierce rivalry with his fellow Scot, in his first spell Dalglish led the club to three league titles, while Ferguson won 13 in his entire time as United manager. Dalglish said of Ferguson, "you go through the older generation, Fergie, Brian Kidd, Mike Summerbee – all the old foes who went through the football at the same time as us, maybe a wee bit ahead of us – and at the end of the year you send a letter of congratulations and say well done," said Dalglish, "That continues through. It is a great compliment. You are in competition and rivals, but to have the intelligence so that you are magnanimous enough to send in a letter saying congratulations. These days it has gone more technical, you get your texts or emails off the people who you have been competing with all your life in football. They would wish it was themselves who won it, but they are proud to pay homage to other people as well. It has always happened. You just congratulate each other and at the same time hope it is you next year. It was just congratulations.

You are not at war. People shake hands before every game and after every game. You are in competition obviously, but it is manners to say congratulations and well done."

Barcelona striker Luis Suarez hailed Jordan Henderson as "one of the best captains in Liverpool's history" while expressing his delight at seeing his former club win the Premier League. "It's a pleasure for me to speak with you and the Liverpool fans. I am so excited as well because I played for a few years there and I have so many friends there," Suarez told liverpoolfc.com. Henderson is the only player remaining at Anfield since Suarez's time on Merseyside. "When I saw last year [him winning] the Champions League, I was so happy for him. Why? Because as some people know he had some problems with his dad and he had really good moments and some bad moments in Liverpool. When he lifted the trophy, the dream is done but this season I [will be happy to] see him lifting the [Premier League] trophy because he is a really good person. I speak sometimes with him and I said to him, 'you have a really good chance this season' and he is so excited. We watch some [Liverpool] games when we can and we see that Jordan, he is the captain from the midfield. He speaks a lot and for his teammates this is so important, when they have confidence with the captain. For me, Jordan is one of the best captains in Liverpool's history. I am so happy for him because when he arrived in Liverpool they had a not-really-good moment. He came in from Sunderland and it's difficult for an English player, when they come to a bigger club. I think when he had near him Steven Gerrard, he can see how Stevie is, how he is all of Liverpool. I think the best teacher he had is Steven [Gerrard]."

As for Klopp's team, he pin pointed their biggest strength. "I think the mentality of the players is so important on the pitch. We arrived in Liverpool 3-0 up, but when you play there they have the supporters and the manager [and] the players are so focused and concentrated on the pitch. It's difficult. They scored in the first 10, 15 minutes and they got the confidence to continue their play and in the second half they played fantastic. We need to accept that and if we'd have scored one goal we would have had a really good chance to continue, but I think they are really good players. When you see the atmosphere of Anfield, this is the motivation and when you come back [after his suspension in 2013] and the supporters help you, this is so important. When the players accept that you come back to help the team it's so important for your focus and your confidence. I think we need to not forget how we did it that year because we didn't have a lot of players. We had a really good chance to win the league but I think we are [still] really happy with this season."

As for the title, he concluded: "For me, this is amazing for the supporters, for the players and for the so many people working inside Liverpool. So many people work there and for the last 30 years they didn't know how it felt for Liverpool to win the Premier League. They have a really good chance to enjoy this this time and I think they are so happy and they are excited for the moment that Jordan gets the trophy. I think they needed this moment, for the Liverpool supporters, for the Liverpool club, for the people, for the Scouse people. I am so happy for them."

★

The only fly in the ointment in the days following the title win was the behaviour of some of the club's supporters. Crowds gathered in Liverpool for the second night in a row despite pleas from Jurgen Klopp, the club, and the local major. Mayor Joe Anderson said Covid-19 was "still a real risk" as celebrations got under way again, 24 hours after the club's title triumph was confirmed, the mayor tweeted a photo of a large crowd gathered next to the city's Mersey Ferry terminal. He wrote: "Clearly too many people intoxicated and causing anti-social behaviour. I urge you leave the city centre now it is not safe."

He went on to say "councils simply do not have the power to move people on or prevent them from gathering. If you know someone who is there, please message them and ask them to come home." Metro Mayor Steve Rotheram added his own message echoing Mr Anderson's. "We're not saying this to be party poopers but hundreds of people have already died in our region because of Coronavirus," he wrote. "Until it's safe for us to come together to, please celebrate at home."

Earlier, Anderson, who warned that this would happen, said it was "disappointing" so many had ignored advice. Merseyside Police's Assistant Chief Constable Rob Carden also expressed dismay at the scenes. "Unfortunately, as we have seen throughout the lockdown period, not everyone adhered to the regulations in place," he said. "Although the vast majority of celebrations were good natured, a large number of people chose to gather outside the stadium." He added that "in the days ahead", fans should only celebrate with "members of your household and in your social bubble", adding: "As we all know, Merseyside has been disproportionately affected by Covid-19 and we must all do what we can to prevent further cases and deaths." Liverpool had registered 544 coronavirus-related deaths up to 12 June and 1,677 cases up to 25 June.

Announcing that the city's civic buildings would be lit red for a week to celebrate the club's achievement, a council spokesman urged "ecstatic fans to try and maintain social distancing guidance to prevent the spread of coronavirus". Council chief executive Tony Reeves added that it was "vital we don't throw away the months of hard work for a weekend of celebration".

Anderson said he had "warned that I was concerned about the numbers that would turn up, not just outside Anfield but in other parts of the city centre. The gathering at Anfield was a little bit frustrating where people believe, wrongly, that we're over the worst of the pandemic. In the euphoria... people have decided to ignore advice, but it's gone, it's happened. We'll have to see whether there's a spike in coronavirus as a result of this." He added that it was "disappointing, in the same way it was to see the scenes on Bournemouth beach. But if Chelsea or Manchester City had won the league, we would have seen the same scenes outside Stamford Bridge or the Etihad. We are where we are."

The city's council had already begun investigating the Atletico match. The family of Reds fan Richard Mawson, who died with Covid-19 after attending the game, called for an inquiry.

Worse still, the night ended with a number of injuries and footage also showed a man aiming a firework at the Liver Building where a small fire started in a balcony area. Liverpool ECHO editor Alastair Machray criticised the behaviour of a "minority" of supporters. He said: "Once again we see the minority wrecking it for the majority. The mass gatherings need to wait until it's safe to have them. It's natural that people want to celebrate but when it crosses into violence, vandalism and a threat to public health it's hard to fathom." Mayor Anderson posted on Twitter: "More in sorrow than anger, like most LFC fans and residents, I condemn those that brought a negative focus on LFC and our city. The pics, videos showing people's behaviour is being talked about instead of the fantastic achievement of LFC. Thank you to those fans who have listened." Metro Mayor Steve Rotheram tweeted:

"Nobody is more made up than me to see LFC champions again but this is dangerous. We're not saying this to be party poopers but hundreds of people have already died in our region because of Coronavirus. Until it's safe for us to come together to, please celebrate at home."

A joint statement from Liverpool FC, Merseyside Police and Liverpool City Council read: "Throughout the last week, Liverpool Football Club, Merseyside Police, Liverpool City Council and Spirit of Shankly have worked together to consistently remind people that the region is still disproportionately affected by the COVID-19 pandemic and ask people to celebrate LFC's Premier League title win safely. Several thousand people turned up at the Pier Head on Friday June 26 and some chose to ignore the social distancing guidance and risk public safety. The potential danger of a second peak of COVID-19 still exists and we need to work together to make sure we don't undo everything that has been achieved as a region during lockdown. When it is safe to do so, we will all work together to arrange a victory parade when everyone can come together to celebrate. Until that time, the safety of our city and our people continues to be our number one priority. Our city is still in a public health crisis and this behaviour is wholly unacceptable."

FOOTBA11 LEGENDS

Normally I would start my Footba11 Legends section by congratulating Jurgen Klopp, Jordan Henderson and the entire staff of Liverpool Football Club for their amazing team effort to achieve winning the English Premier League with a record seven number of games left to play. On this occasion however, I would like to congratulate some very dear friends David and Catherine on the arrival of their son, Neo David, who weighed in at 8lb 8oz on the same day Liverpool won the English Premier League. Now to congratulate Jurgen Klopp and team!

We are hopefully all passionate about something in our lives, and if you are reading this fabulous book, Premier League Champions at Last Liverpool Football Club, will be an important part of your life and passion. The Covid pandemic has re-aligned the important things in our lives; our families, the elderly, vulnerable and neighbourhood values which may sometimes have been overlooked in our normal busy day to day lives. Thirty years ago, on 24th July 1990, my daughter Rebecca was born and it was an immensely proud moment in my life. Who would have thought we would be celebrating her landmark birthday in such surreal times.

Liverpool Football Club were perennial Champions and I, like any other football fan, could never imagine Liverpool having to wait 30 years to win the league title again.

I have had the opportunity through Footba11 Legends Ltd to meet Legends from bygone years. Sir Kenny Dalglish always makes me smile, as he did in his interview when it was confirmed Liverpool Football Club were Premier League Champions. It has been fabulous arranging signing sessions, creating some bespoke shirts and football boots for Iconic players and we have lots of memorabilia on sale at footba11legends. We are also launching a digital magazine called *FloodLight*, as every fan loves those European nights, especially Liverpool fans!

Kenny Dalglish received his Footballer of the Year Trophy in 1979 from the Blackpool Legend Sir Stanley Matthews and I'm sure Kenny did not envisage becoming Sir Kenny Dalglish some years later in 2018. AXA, one of Liverpool's current sponsors, commemorated their

Advertisement

sponsorship of The AXA FA Cup on the 10th November 1998 using Sir Stanley Matthews as The Legend of The FA CUP. The sponsorship ended when the FA decided to reduce the number of sponsors. AXA's sponsorship and vision allowed me to purchase a famous replica Blackpool Matthews AXA 53 commemorating the Famous Matthews Final of 1953. Sir Kenny Dalglish is a fabulous ambassador for Liverpool Football Club and for the beautiful game, and it was very fitting for BT Sports to interview him from his home raising a glass of bubbly to his beloved Liverpool.

Kenny also signed Jordan Henderson from Jordan's hometown team Sunderland in 2011. Jordan has shown his leadership qualities and versatility for the team under Jurgen Klopp and has managed to carry on being a great captain, as too was Steven Gerrard.

The 2018 to 2019 season was a fabulous season for Liverpool Football Club. My family and I were travelling back from holiday when the Champions League Final started. My 14-year-old son Seb and I were watching the game in the airport departure lounge and my wife Carrie and daughter Annabel were reflecting on a great family holiday and plotting surprises for my birthday the next day. Seb and I thought Liverpool would win The Champions League Final and both wanted to see Georginio Wijnaldum and Jordan Henderson lift the trophy due their time playing for Newcastle United and Sunderland and their performance in the semi-final against Barcelona.

As season ticket holders at Newcastle United, it can be a tough watch at times, but Gini always played with a smile when at Newcastle. Gini's two goals against Barcelona in the semi final still amaze me to this day. He is a tremendous guy and player.

I was telling Seb about Alan Kennedy, another player who had to move to Liverpool to win trophies scoring two winning goals in European Cup Final wins. Champions League secured Jordan Henderson (Hendo) on the 1st June 2019 and shared some fantastic scenes with his dad Brian at the end of the game.

Roll on the rest of the 2019-2020 season so much to look forward to I even had a few speculative bets on Newcastle United to win the Premier League as the odds were better than when Leicester won it at 500-1! My son Seb and I travelled up from Newcastle to Edinburgh to watch Liverpool's pre-season game against Napoli. I caught up Gini Wijnaldum before the game and congratulated him on the Champions

Peter Reid, Eugene Oei and Sir Kenny Dalglish

League victory and his two goals against Barcelona.

My mate Harry Harris had written Liverpool FC 2018-2019 The Official Story and I gave a couple of copies to Gini, just in case he did not have it. Gini's smile again was as broad as the Tyne and he smiled even more when I told him we were Toon season ticket holders and had come up to watch the game with a few nights in Edinburgh.

When the team checked into the hotel in Edinburgh the meet and greet was done by a Scottish guy who is a life-long Liverpool fan. He was so honoured to be given the opportunity by his company and colleagues to show Mr Klopp to his room. This is the positive effect which sport and football has on people. Jurgen is an effervescent character and fabulous advocate of team ethos and unity. This is not only important in sport, but in everyday life too.

Lots of CEO's throughout the world are motivating their teams to get through the difficult times the current pandemic finds us in and to and give their colleagues the encouragement to do the right things and to go the extra mile. Public transport, which many fans depend on for travel to and from matches, has been badly hit. The tradition of the Open Top Trophy Bus is a must see for fans. I went along to see the Leicester City Open Top Champions Bus tour as I was in Leicester for an event with Harry Harris the author of this book.

Liverpool Football Club's players have certainly put the extra miles

Advertisement

in. When I spoke with Jordan's father, Brian Henderson, I was inspired to hear of his emotion at seeing his son lift the Champions League given time Brian was diagnosed with cancer way back in 2013 and so must have been a far-away dream. I took Brian to see a new training method for goalkeepers and he joked with me that he had played for England too. I said "amateur" level and his laughing response was that this was for the police representative team, he had me hook, line and sinker!

The City of Liverpool is fabulous and I have friends who three family members are Liverpool fans and two are Evertonians.

My friend Stewart Taylor from Bryken Engineering is Red through and through, as too is his brother Phil and his dad. Stewart's mum Lesley, and sister Natalie are Evertonians and the banter is great. I have been trying to speak to Stewart for 24 hours but I guess he is celebrating big time! I love the history of sport and culture, Liverpool Football Club's first game at Anfield was on the 1st Sept 1892 against Rotherham Town. Liverpool won 7-1 in windy conditions and in goal for Rotherham Town was Arthur Wharton, who was the first black professional footballer in the world.

Arthur started playing football as an amateur at Darlington, he also played for Preston North End but left to concentrate on a running career. He was the first man to be officially timed running the 100 yard dash in 10 secs at Stamford Bridge. Chelsea and Stamford Bridge being the place where it proved impossible for Manchester City to catch Liverpool amazing start to the 2019-2020 season.

Champions At Last!